TIGER ACE • MICHAEL WITTMANN

THE LIFE STORY OF
PANZER COMMANDER
MICHAEL
WITTMANN

TIGER ACE

GARY L. SIMPSON

Schiffer Military History
Atglen, PA

Dedicated to the memory of my beloved mother
Anne Marie Simpson

Book Design by Robert Biondi

Copyright © 1994 by Gary L. Simpson.
Library of Congress Catalog Number: 93-84858

Printed in China
ISBN: 0-88740-526-6

We are interested in hearing from authors with book ideas on related topics.

Published by Schiffer Publishing Ltd.
4880 Lower Valley Road
Atglen, PA 19310
Phone: (610) 593-1777
FAX: (610) 593-2002
E-mail: Schifferbk@aol.com.
Please write for a free catalog.
This book may be purchased from the publisher.
Please include $3.95 postage.
Try your bookstore first.

Contents

INTRODUCTION

The story and military exploits of SS-Hauptsturmführer Michael Wittmann has interested many people around the world since the end of the Second World War, including military training schools, military museums, military historians, and the general reading public interested in military affairs. Wittmann's story has fascinated this writer and historian since the early seventies and have been actively seeking and obtaining pertinent data and information on this individual's brilliant panzer exploits ever since. Extensive research, travel, and interviewing has been conducted in regards to this book endeavor to uncover only the true facts and situations that Michael Wittmann encountered on the field of battle with his various vehicle crews on the Eastern Fronts and also on the Western Front which encompass the dates from September 1, 1939 to August 8, 1944.

There have been numerous articles dealing with Michael Wittmann which have been printed in Germany, England, Canada, France, Japan, and the United States, but none doing complete justice to the scope and understanding of this man's life and combat experiences. Wittmann's military exploits stand out from all of the rest, as through the results of his efforts, his Sturmgeschütz III and Tiger I panzer crews succeeded in utterly destroying 138 enemy tanks and 132 anti-tank guns and field artillery pieces. Thus, Michael Wittmann was the "Ace of Aces" (in the German Panzer Corps) in the true romantic sense, with his impressive combat record never being beaten at this time of writing. This man's life has generated increased interest over the years, as it is an inherent aspect of human nature to know more of those who have stood out from all of the rest.

With the story of Michael Wittmann, we are viewing a man not at the top of the military pyramid but at a lower level upon which the whole military structure depended. There have been many publications written on such famous generals as Patton, Rommel, Guderian, and many other military figures of the twentieth century. However, these high ranking officers commanded vast armies in the field through close coordination with their field commanders, and as such were usually removed from direct combat roles. Wittmann on the other hand, was placed in the heat of battle and was a true hunter (Jäger) in every respect. He had the distinction of independent thinking, and the uncanny sense of 'smelling out' the enemy's tactical intentions, and exploiting these skills with firepower, armor, and mobility. However, the true formula for a successful panzer crew is close coordination and the willingness to work together as a fighting team; highly trained, motivated, and extremely efficient.

Not only is the armor aspect of Michael Wittmann's panzer exploits to be thoroughly explored. I intend to illustrate the unique working relationship between all of Wittmann's panzer crew members, with special attention being directed to his first (and also famous) Tiger I gunner, Balthasar "Bobby" Woll. Wittmann and Woll had an understanding not only of their Tiger I tank, but also of their crew's needs. This situation resulted in achieving and maintaining a very highly coordinated and technical environment in the face of the enemy. In any armored fighting vehicle (AFV) the relationship between the panzer commander and his gunner is crucial to the survival of the vehicle and its entire crew. The gunner has to interpret what his commander desires, and ideally anticipate his orders. Strict discipline but added flexibility within Wittmann's second in command (i.e. his gunner), enabled Woll himself to exploit a tactical situation independently of his commander in the event of Wittmann being involved with the many tasks called upon as a vehicle commander, e.g. monitoring the radio, giving other commands to other crew members, directing other vehicles of his platoon or company.

Michael Wittmann had come up through the ranks of the German Wehrmacht and understood the meaning of being a private, then corporal, plus the added duties of becoming a NCO, before being commissioned an officer. This advantage was not uncommon in the Wehrmacht or the Waffen-SS as every graduating officer had to have prior NCO combat experience before being permitted to apply for officer training. Wittmann was somewhat distant from his subordinates after becoming an officer, but he cared for them deeply and never forgot where his military roots had originated. Wittmann called his panzer crews by their first names, or nick-names, which tends to illustrate that some of his prior NCO instincts were still evident in his new officer role. This action would also suggest that he regarded his crew members as individuals of an elite combat team, and not just as component parts of his armored fighting vehicle. In uncovering Wittmann's personality we can see that with his prior NCO training and combat experiences, his technical ability and leadership qualities were second to none and aided him and his crews to survive the many harsh panzer battles that they would be encountering together time and time again. Military expertise in the usage of terrain, tactical appreciation, and lastly, and most importantly, the use of master gunnery skills was instilled from the outset until these abilities were second nature to him as breathing itself! Without the desire, drive, and determination to win the battle at hand, the above prerequisites and disciplines would have been an empty void. The warrior's creed, 'Kill or be

Killed' were the only deciding factors where death or victory were the only eternal truths.

Battle tactics will be dealt with in this book, as well a key panzer battles that Wittmann and his panzer crews were involved with during the Second World War. From the offensive battles of Poland, France, the low countries, Russia, and then Normandy in 1944 we will witness the tactics that the German Panzer Corps employed until they went onto the defensive after the battle of Kursk, which was the largest panzer conflict of the entire war.

Michael Wittmann's star was raising even before the battle of Kursk, however, during this monumental panzer battle he was to become even more famous. In all fairness, he was placed into the limelight during and after the battle of Kursk where his documented history really began. However this writer has obtained additional information pertaining to his early commander exploits as an armored car commander (Sd.Kfz.222) in Poland and France, which will help to clearly illustrate the valuable combat lessons learned at an early date, with which his military experiences were based upon. A great deal of information (and some photographs) have been uncovered pertaining to his combat experiences while serving as a vehicle commander in German Sturmgeschütz III Ausf. A (assault gun based on the proven Panzer III chassis mounting a 7.5cm L/24 gun) in Greece and then in the early battles of "Operation Barbarossa", the invasion of Russia on June 22, 1941.

Michael Wittmann seemed to be in the right places at the right times and made the correct tactical decisions in exploiting his attacks upon the enemy to the fullest degree possible. Many times he attacked enemy headquarters and through these assaults disrupted his opponent considerably. A prerequisite prescribed in all training manuals at the time stated: "If the head or brain of a body (or enemy) is deactivated, then the rest of the body cannot function". Such is true with the headquarters of any military unit that is attacked in this manner, as the remainder of the unit is denied guidance from above and will be lost due to command structural inconsistency.

Michael Wittmann was raised on a farm and was very combined with nature as a direct result. As a boy living in an agricultural environment he formulated certain attitudes towards nature that helped in establishing his life long dream of owning and operating his own farm and raising a family. He and his brother hunted on their father's farm land and surrounding area, owing to the fact that this activity was an important necessity of every day life. Acquiring hunting skills at an early age that provided food for the family table was an important and rewarding aspect of his beloved farm life.

Another very important factor that must not be overlooked was that young Michael was exposed to farm machinery during his childhood and as a young man. Having worked on and operated these machines with his father and brother, Wittmann at a very early age acquired a thorough understanding of the various functions, and idiosyncrasies of powered farm machinery and gained a sense of security in dealing with farm machinery after understanding how it functioned. He also acquired a respect for these machines as a working tool, but was also fully aware that if one was not careful in their use, serious accidents could and did often occur. We can clearly understand that at this time in Wittmann's life, he had established a meaningful and working relationship with the tools of his trade. However, Wittmann was to give up his future career as a German farmer in 1934, and as with many other youths of his time, the lure of the newly formed Wehrmacht appealed to his nature. Wittmann joined the German Wehrmacht on October 30, 1934 as an ordinary private, and after his basic training, enjoyed his new duties at his first posting at Freising. His exposure to powered farm machinery I feel, is one of the most important attributes in Wittmann's character and make up, as without this knowledge and exposure to this type of equipment, his success in future armored fighting vehicles he would command would have been somewhat limited as a result.

Also necessary to the understanding of Michael Wittmann and his success on the armored battlefield is an appreciation of the functions and capabilities of the armored fighting vehicles he was placed in charge of; a sort of metamorphosis of man and machine, that was the most fundamental basis of his story. A considerable amount of research has been devoted pertaining to the vehicles that Wittmann served in and commanded (see Appendix IV and V) and are described in detail in their respective chapters. The reader has been provided with many pertinent details dealing with these vehicles, and will greatly help to illustrate to the reader the various functions, operations, and capabilities Wittmann and his panzer crews had to contend with in the heat of battle.

The most important military vehicle that we will be dealing with in regards to this story is the famous German Tiger I tank (Sd. Kfz. 181). This heavy armored fighting vehicle was feared by all who were unlucky enough to oppose it in direct fire combat. It was also feared through the combined efforts of its powerful high velocity 8.8cm KwK 36 L/56 main gun and the massive thickness of its armor plate which was almost impregnable, especially in regards to its frontal areas. Such was the reputation of the Tiger I Panzerkampfwagen. With these attributes and being handled by such combat veterans as Michael Wittmann and his highly trained crews, the Allied combat encounter equation as stated: "For every Tiger I tank, we must send in four Shermans and expect to lose three", was quite correct! This was true nine times out of ten, but the reader will find that this equation was not always justified. Wittmann's talents and experience in the field of battle proved that a well trained crew in a Tiger I could, and often did, help to stem the tide of surmounting Allied numerical superiority. However it will be pointed out that Wittmann and his Tiger I crews did have inherent disadvantages with this vehicle, that the Tiger I was not a totally invincible fighting combat machine by any means. Used in an offensive manner, in open terrain with wide fields of fire, proved very convincing for its panzer commanders and crews. Once committed to such terrain as encountered in Normandy (44) in the defensive mode, also helped to hinder the Tiger I in its basic need to be able to exploit maneuvers where open terrain was not readily available. Street fighting in built-up areas was another dangerous aspect of armored warfare and was to be avoided as much as possible depending on the mission at hand. During the Normandy (44) campaign German panzer were involved with this type of engagement, but only committed when an important or vital objective was needed to continue the advance.

The most important and most famous date that will be dealt with in this book is June 13, 1944. On this day, Wittmann and his Tiger I crew were to carry forth the most famous single-handed panzer encounter of the entire war, or for that matter, any war, in the French town of "Villers-Bocage." Wittmann with his crew and former gunner Bobby Woll (now a panzer commander, who's own Tiger I was undergoing repairs) set out on an ordered reconnaissance patrol of the area in front of his company and in the direction of a hill tactically marked height 213 on his Normandy map.

As Wittmann emerged from the cover of a small wood (on foot) with his Tiger I panzer concealed near height 213 he was very surprised to witness (after being informed by a nearby infantry squad) the arrival of a large number of British tanks, half-tracks, and infantry support carriers belonging to the 4th County of London Yeomanry (4th C.L.Y.), 'A' Squadron of the 1st Battalion, plus the Rifle Brigade, all part of the 22nd Brigade of the famed 7th Armored Division. All were headed in the direction of height 213 but were to be held up on the road in order for a reconnaissance patrol to pass them, and then to take a much needed break. As the vehicles of 'A' Squadron (4th C.L.Y.) rolled past Wittmann's hidden position he realized that this unit was about to mount a flanking maneuver against Panzer Lehr which was the Leibstandarte Adolf Hitler's sister unit and had to act accordingly to prevent certain disaster that was quickly unfolding before his eyes. Wittmann ran and returned and remounted his Tiger I and placed his crew on battle alert and moved off in the direction of the 4th C.L.Y.'s R.H.Q (Headquarters section) tanks being protected in between 'A' and 'B' Squadrons. His vehicle engaged the R.H.Q. tanks inside "Villers-Bocage" and knocked out three Cromwell tanks but did not see a fourth tank of this section as it had backed out of sight. Wittmann and his vehicle then moved down the main street of the town and bumped into 'B' Squadron which was guarding the vital road junction to Caumont and was fired upon. After firing his 8.8cm main gun and missing the leading M4A4 Sherman 17pdr Firefly at the road junction, Wittmann then decided to return to his company for additional vehicles with the intent of returning to capture the town and road intersection. As his vehicle was maneuvered 180°, the massive Tiger I headed back up the main street of "Villers-Bocage," but shortly afterwards, ran into the fourth Cromwell tank (from R.H.Q.) that had been stalking him from the rear. The British tank fired two 75mm main gun rounds at Wittmann's vehicle, but harmlessly bounced off the thick hide and causing little or no damage.

Wittmann's gunner destroyed this vehicle with one well placed shot of 8.8 cm AP through its turret, and as it started to burn, the German heavy panzer and its crew made their way back to their company area.

After regrouping with his company, Wittmann returned to battle with three Tiger Is and a Panzer IV Ausf. H, as his plan was now to attack 'A' Squadron, reenter "Villers-Bocage", capture it, and then secure the vital road link to Caumont. By this time vehicles of 'A' Squadron had been pulled off to the right side of the road and were parked nose to tail in an effort to keep close rank; so close in fact that their main gun barrels were swung to the right side of their superstructures and over the rear decks of the proceeding vehicles. Wittmann immediately detected this blunder and attacked 'A' Squadron with his three other panzers positioned to his right flank in order to knock out any enemy tanks that might try and escape to the north. Wittmann and his crew alone succeeded in knocking out the entire line of Allied vehicles as he moved past these targets of opportunity via a dirt cart track that paralleled the N175. After this violent armor engagement was completed, Wittmann regrouped, and then reentered the town of "Villers-Bocage" for the second time.

'B' Squadron had now taken up defensive positions in the town along with a detachment of 6pdr anti-tank guns belonging to the Queen's Regiment. As Wittmann moved towards the town square and road junction (the objective), one of the 6pdr anti-tank gun disabled his Tiger I by jamming his left track and suspension system. Wittmann and his crew escaped unharmed to fight another day. The remainder of his panzers were knocked out behind him by an M4A4 Sherman 17pdr Firefly, and Cromwell tank gun fire.

Even though Wittmann's four vehicles were destroyed by the enemy, the damage inflicted upon the British 22nd Armored Brigade was overwhelming with over twenty-five armored fighting vehicles being knocked out in under thirty minutes. The 22nd Armored Brigade was in such a state of shock, that it took several weeks before it could regroup, reequip, and reorganize in order for it to be combat ready once again. Wittmann's single handed panzer attack had indeed saved Panzer Lehr from certain destruction and as a direct result of this brave action against the 4th C.L.Y., this courageous and daring panzer commander was award the Swords to his Knight's Cross with Oak Leaf, and on June 22, 1944, was promoted in the field to the rank of SS-Hauptsturmführer (Captain).

On August 8, 1944, the man that had destroyed over twenty-five British armored fighting vehicles at "Villers-Bocage", plus 119 vehicles on the Russian Front was killed with his crew while engaging a superior force of M4A4 Shermans mounting 75mm main guns, and an M4A4 Sherman 17pdr Firefly belonging to the 1st Northamptonshire Yeomanry, a first line armored cavalry regiment of the 33rd Independent Armored Brigade in and around St Aignan-de-Cramesnil.

SS-Hauptsturmführer Michael Wittmann can be titled as one of the "Great Captains" of armored history, as he certainly had a combination of acute observation with uncanny intuition; the ability to create surprise tactical assaults and cause havoc which threw his opponent totally off balance; the speed and thought and the actions that allowed an opponent no chance for immediate recovery of his forces; the mixture of strategic and tactical senses that allowed him to 'feel out' a battle as it developed and carry it out to a successful conclusion; plus, the power and ability to win the devotions of his panzer crews so as to be able to work and fight together as an efficient and cohesive combat fighting team.

It seems clear that Michael Wittmann had a sense of what was possible and had the great ability to make the impossible, 'Possible'!

TIGER ACE

Chapter I

ON THE FARM

April 22, 1914 – August 1, 1934

Michael Wittmann was born on April 22, 1914 near Vogetal, Upper-Palatinate in the German agricultural community of Oberpfalz. Wittmann's father (Johann Wittmann) had been a farmer all of his life and enjoyed the daily routine and rewards of farm life. Michael's child rearing was no different than any of his other counterparts in and around Oberpfalz, and he too enjoyed all aspects of growing up on the farm. He had two sisters and a brother to share all of his childhood experiences with, and had a very normal and care free upbringing. The Wittmann family belonged to the Catholic church and were involved with the many activities that their perish offered. Each and every Sunday they all attended mass and prayed together. Catholicism was a very important ingredient in regards to the make-up of the Wittmann family, and helped to weld them together as a God fearing and respected family in their farming community.

Young Wittmann worked with his father and brother day in and day out and established early in life self-worth and a sense of working together as a team which no doubt would be used later in his adult life.

Wittmann's love for the farm life was illustrated by his eager enthusiasm to learn all he could about his chosen trade. He would awaken early in the morning ready for work only to be greeted by his father and brother who were also very eager to began the days work. After a hardy breakfast prepared by Frau Wittmann and her daughters, the Wittmann men would venture out into the workfields and perform any and all tasks as needed. Michael and his brother learned a great deal from their father and respected him greatly as a teacher, instructor, mechanic, a man of the soil, and most of all, as their friend with whom they could come to at any time of the day or night and ask questions about their environment. Michael knew early in life that any problem or obstacle could be over come with the aid of his father and brother if all pulled in together to solve a problem. Any questions that were asked by his two sons, were always answered by Herr Wittmann and explained in as few words as possible in order to be direct and expedient. It was quite clear to both Wittmann boys, if one did not ask questions or make inquires concerning a problem or setback, one would find oneself lost due to indecision and non-aggressiveness.

Michael was always open to others who had an idea, comment, or opinion in regards to topics and current affairs that related to farming and life in general. Many times he would just listen to his friends about that daily lives and make mental notes especially concerning new ideas about live-stock, plowing, and other aspects of farming, but was very keen on the situation of Germany as a whole. He would always think before he spoke and this resulted in that he could make a statement or decision without making too many mistakes or miscalculations. As time went by, he generated basic ideas about himself and the exciting world around him. If he needed to know the answer to a question or problem, he would not let anything or anyone stand in his way.

By being so open, courteous, and warm to others, and caring about others before himself, Wittmann was able to make friends very easily. There were times when the whole farming community would gather together to help a new family either build them their new farm house or barn or to help in the fields, it did not matter. Togetherness, and the feeling of being a part of something important stimulated young Wittmann which he would carry with him all through his life as an intrinsic part of his character.

As far back as Michael could remember, he had always been interested in powered farming machinery. This was established from witnessing his father using the basic farm machines that were so vital to their farm's survival. From a very young age, his father was very careful not to let him too close to any farm machine until he was confidant that his son understood how it operated, and what it was used for. Too many farming accidents had occurred to young boys on the farms and in the city factories, so safety and caution were two important terms in their daily vocabulary. As Michael grew older his father would take him over to a piece of farm machinery and first explain to his son what the machine was used for and its functions. This type of interaction with his father was something that always thrilled him as he felt very secure in that his father would take the time to show him the basic understandings of the farm devices. After Michael understood how a certain machine functioned and operated, his father would allow him to control the device and repair it if necessary. However, his father clearly stated to both of his sons that if a machine was well taken care of (preventive maintenance) any tool of any trade would last for a longer time. These lessons were highly instilled into both sons and was never to be forgotten. Oiling move parts, tighten up pulleys and fan belts, plus making sure the machines were filled with petrol and oil levels checked were just part of making sure that these important machines were up and running for the tasks at hand on the Wittmann farm.

The internal combustion engine was to revolutionize all aspects of powered machinery with regards to farm vehicles taking important steps to further improve the productivity of all German farms. After World War I there had been a great shortage of food stuffs and as a direct result many farms were constantly trying to improve upon their yield. The Wittmann farm was not to be without these types of new machines and every effort was made to obtain the best equipment possible.

Living on a successful farm and always having enough food for the table was common place for the Wittmann family, but Michael soon learned that this was not so throughout greater Germany. It was highly stressed that all productivity pertaining to each and every German farm, was vital to the depressed German economy. As farm machinery grew bigger and more powerful, so too their complexity which forced each and every farmer to become an even better and reliable mechanic. As these various types of equipment started to appear on the Wittmann farm, his father, brother, and Michael himself, were more than eager to learned about them. In order to keep pace with the fast expanding technology of the outside world, the Wittmann men read as much as possible and learned all they could through the close inspection of the equipment, application of use, and maintenance of their powered metal steeds.

Michael and his brother performed a great deal of hunting for the family table and through out their childhood developed a keen sense of stalking out their prey. In the beginning it was quite apparent that Michael's love for animals would be an inhibiting factor in shooting and killing game, but in the end, he knew that he had to kill game in order to provide fresh meat. There were many times when he and his brother did not shoot or catch any game but they never gave up and would continue the hunt regardless.

However, Michael was also very combined with nature and enjoyed just taking a long walk along a quiet stream, or a run through a nearby meadow. He felt that he could think more clearly to himself at times if he was alone and would often wonder what the future held for him and if he would be happy. All he wanted out of life was to be a farmer, marry, and raise a family.

Wittmann's love for animals would always be part of his nature and had many pets on the farm. Taking care of farm animals was not just part of the daily routine for Michael as he regarded them as his friends, and would become highly upset if any of them became sick, lost, or ill treated in any way. Even as he grew older, his love and care for animals was always of the highest degree and would never let them go hungry and would stay up all night in order to attend to a new born calf or a sick horse.

However, on January 30, 1933 everything was to change through out all of greater Germany. Adolf Hitler came to power on this day and abolished the hated Treaty of Versailles which had limited the German army to 100,00 men, plus no planes, tanks, or heavy artillery were allowed in its inventory. World War One veterans were outraged that many of them could not rejoin the German army after the armistice, and many were equally upset as to whether their sons or grandsons would be able to 'serve' the Fatherland. Hitler vowed to rebuild

Germany to its former glory and initiated a new armaments program to expand the Army, Navy, and Air force ten-fold.

Another organization that was established by Adolf Hitler was the German Reichs Arbeitdienst (German Voluntary Labor Service) who's sole purpose was to repair roads, build bridges, work in the forest, and to conduct all types of labor in order to rebuild Germany from the ground up.

As the fever of rebuilding Germany spread through out the country like a fire-storm, many young men were caught up in its vortex. One of these men was Michael Wittmann as the thought of helping his country rebuild was very close to his heart. At the age of twenty, Wittmann joined the Reichs Arbeitdienst on February 1, 1934 and belonged to this organization until August 1, 1934.

The work involved with being a member of the Reichs Arbeitdienst was very hard indeed, but having worked for so many years on his father's farm allowed Michael to excel in this new environment. He made many new friends and learned much more about the world about him. The vast majority of the work he was doing was out of doors while living in canvas tents being the norm. The close relationships with his fellow workers again made Michael feel as though he was part of a group effort and all working for the same goals; this, he enjoyed to the fullest.

Living off the land was not new to Michael but at this stage in his life he learned what it really meant when it came to living and working with a large number of people for an extended period of time. He again had the opportunity of listening to others pertaining to certain problems not only in their work-camp, but also on the international level. He was working with people that have come together from all over Germany and from all walks of life. It was all very interesting to say the very least, but there were also problems that had to be settled among themselves. If any disagreements or grievances came to be, everyone had a chance to air their opinions with feed-back. Michael soon found out that if people were to work together in total harmony it was vitally important to understand other peoples needs, worries, and background information in order to obtain a comprehensive picture of their whole being. Camp fire talks and sing-alongs were very popular activities after working hours where everyone could relax, tell stories and jokes, plus discuss their childhoods and relate an episode in their life that had lasting memories or had taught them a meaningful lesson. It was also found that being able to express ones feelings openly helped to settle nerves, fears, and other anxieties. As the days and weeks past, Wittmann was able to learn a great deal about his co-workers from these fire side talks and soon knew everyone by his or her first-name and a little about each others background.

After his tour of duty with the Reichs Arbeitdienst Michael was planning to return to his father's farm to continue on with his agricultural career. However, many of his friends felt the patriotic lure of the Army life and joined up immediately to help fill out the ranks of the rapidly expanding German military.

Michael Wittmann then decided to give up his planned career in farming and on October 30, 1934 joined the German Army as the military way of life now appealed to him for the first time in his life. Michael Wittmann was to be posted at Freising, Germany and was assigned to the 10th Company, Infantry Regiment 19.

Chapter II

ENTRY INTO THE GERMAN WEHRMACHT

October 30, 1934 – September 30, 1936

Wittmann's first and lasting memory of the German Wehrmacht was when he stepped off of the troop train at the Freising railway station and was boldly greeted by a rough looking training sergeant who was to escort him and other recruits to the nearby training camp. This rigid individual was a very strict professional and was wearing an extremely smart and tidy uniform that was second to none. After being told to climb up and into an awaiting military truck, Wittmann found himself sitting next to many quiet and equally bewildered young men. No doubt, all who were present had many thoughts swimming around in their heads, and wondered what was now in store for them in their new environment. After travelling for a number of miles their transport approached an establishment that looked very foreign to them and as the vehicle stopped at the guard post and gate all present were very nervous. After proper papers and identification were presented the truck moved slowly forward towards a barracks type building. As soon as the truck pulled up to this building and stopped, the training sergeant riding in the front of the vehicle jumped out and blew a whistle and shouted to the recruits to jump down, line up, and stand at attention in front of their new 'home'! Everyone scrambled from their transports and lined up as best as they could under the circumstances. Michael was now in the hands of the famous German Wehrmacht and promised to himself that he would make a good soldier for the Fatherland at any cost.

After the usual indoctrination and paper-work that had to be presented, processed, and signed all of the men of Wittmann's training unit started their rigorous infantry training. One of the first lessons learned was that they were a team and if they were to be a successful infantry squad they all had to pull and work together. It did not matter if they were cleaning their barracks or stripping down their weapons, they all had to learn the same organized steps together. Should a certain individual have trouble in one area of training, his fellow comrades would lend assistance until the task was accomplished to a set of standards. Day in and day out the men of Wittmann's squad went through the daily routines of being awaken very early in the morning, and then making sure that their barracks was in one hundred percent tip-top shape and everything in proper order. Uniforms and all details pertaining to their clothing was to be absolutely perfect. After their training sergeant inspected their barracks and their personnel appearance were they allowed to stand down and begin to start with their day. Before breakfast the men would perform all calisthenics and running as if they were allowed to eat first the end result would be many of the young men falling out behind or vomiting due to their morning meal being churned up in their stomachs. Only after all of their physical exercise were the men allowed to eat a hearty meal to satisfy their tremendous appetites. As time went on it was found that many individuals who were quite thin in stature put on weight and those that were heavier started to lose weight. It seemed a strange phenomenon but was a common occurrence with most training camps. Wittmann's weight did not change a great deal but he did notice that his body strength was increasing and his muscles seemed to grow firmer every day. The current and popular saying, "A strong body means a strong mind", was instilled into the being and soul of each and every young recruit that came under the influence of the German Wehrmacht.

The daily drilling and marching transformed Wittmann's infantry unit into a very spirited fighting force with all of his comrades striving to meet their training sergeant's high standards. Wittmann could sense on a daily basis the close togetherness of his unit as their training continued and knew that if they were ever deployed as a fighting unit in time of war he would be able to trust anyone of his comrades with his life. At times during the infantry training all of the recruits were given the task of being the squad leader and lead the men into various types of mock battles. Wittmann enjoyed his opportunity when it came, and made careful study of the terrain, performed accurate map reading, and positioned the men in such a manner, so as to conceal them from the probing eyes of the umpires and training staff. He always planned ahead for any contingency that might occur as he knew that in time of war one had to rely on other avenues of approach if a tactical deployment went askew. All of the young recruits were very careful in not allowing their squad to be ambushed or encircled by their 'opponents', as every available tactical trick in the book was utilized to out fox any force that tried to overwhelm their squad while on training maneuvers.

There were times, however, that nothing seemed to go right for Wittmann's infantry squad and lessons that went wrong had to be done over and over again. Even if it was in the middle of the night or during a downpour of rain his squad had to endure all until they accomplished their training mission to the established standards. It was all very hard work, but in the end, all who were involved knew that if their training was not performed in the correct fashion in peace time, many horrible causalities would result in time of war. Lessons to be learned now meant that Wittmann's squad had to be pushed and then pushed again in order to accomplish their mission by their training NCOs. No matter how difficult the task, they also wanted to prove to their training sergeant that they were eager to learn, and wanted to complete any and all training tasks as outlined by their daily schedules.

At the start of their infantry training Wittmann and his comrades were shown the various assault tactics which were not easy to learn and to carry out. Holding ground under fire was an experience that took nerves of steel and extremely strong discipline and drive. The only way that this kind of training could be carried out was under live fire exercises. As a result, Wittmann's infantry squad were to be taken out to a training range which was set up with a MG-34 machine gun and crew. They were then ordered to crawl on their backs from one side of the firing range with the bullets from the machine gun whistling by only inches above their heads. This dramatic type of training provided a 'real' sensation of what it was like to be fired upon and would never be forgotten. Needless to say, this 'Live Fire' episode welded Wittmann's infantry squad even closer as it instilled into their minds the thought that talking about being under enemy fire in a classroom was one thing, but actually being under live fire was quite another! During this training Wittmann could see and also feel the fear emitting from his fellow comrades-in-arms and he too was not all too happy in regards to crawling through the muck and mire toward their intended objective. It was all just part of their infantry training and if not given this type of training now, what would happen if they found themselves in a similar situation in the face of any future enemy. This under the wire and through the mud with live fire was performed over and over again and at times all the men felt like frighten moles burrowing a swath through the earth.

Map reading was one of the most important training courses Wittmann and his squad had to learn while continuing their infantry training. It was vitally important to know where they were at all times while out in the field. If they did not know their position, they could easily be caught in their own planned artillery barrages which could result in many deaths. Classroom training was provided initially with very strict tests taken by one and all. Wittmann performed very well in dealing with this topic and was very much at home in the out of doors with his squad. As prearranged, the training instructors would give the recruits wrong map references with the result being they would become lost, or set up for an ambush by another infantry element. Wittmann quickly learned to realize the importance of checking and then re-checking his map coordinates and other pertinent details while conducting a field mission.

Up to this point in time, Wittmann had never seen a panzer (tank) until he obtained his first chance during panzer hunting and destruction techniques training. The first panzer he was exposed to was the early model of the Panzer I Ausf. A which was just coming into service with the Wehrmacht. This was a very small machine with a crew of two men, i.e. a vehicle commander (panzer commander) who operated the two 7.92mm Dreyse MG-13 air-cooled machine guns as used for the main armament, mounted in a very small and cramped turret. The second crew-member was the driver and positioned in the hull of the vehicle to the left of the center line. This vehicle had only 13mm armor protection and was only effective against small arms fire. Wittmann and his comrades had heard rumors about light panzers being developed by the Wehrmacht and German industry but did not think they would ever see one of these machines because of the cloak of secrecy and security surrounding their manufacture. It was clear that his infantry squad were to learn more about this new panzer very shortly.

One day, Wittmann and his infantry squad were informed by their training sergeant that they were to start their new training in regards to knocking out and disabling panzers. He and his comrades were marched out to a training field and paid witness to a strange gray colored (almost black) machine with a full set of metal tracks. As they came closer, they could see that this was indeed one of the new Panzer I Ausf. As, which mounted two 7.92mm machine guns. A very robust panzer commander was standing upright in his opened turret hatch and smiled down upon the wide-eyed recruits. It was very clear that he was going to give Wittmann and his comrades a run for their money in regards to trying to knock out 'his' new panzer! After jumping down from his armored steed, he gave a comprehensive overview of his panzer and explained the various features. Special attention was given to the metal tracks, as if one was to slip or fall under them, or into these deadly devices, serious injury or death would be the only result. After a safety talk, the recruits were allowed to inspect the Panzer I Ausf. A. close up.

At first, the recruits were not sure how they were supposed to climb aboard the new panzer. Some simply grabbed the metal fenders and tried to pull themselves up and onto the machine. Others tried to climb up the front glacis plate but found that it was slippery from wet mud being splattered from vehicle movement. Still others tried to climb onto the rear engine deck and found that this area of the vehicle was still quite warm and the two exhaust mufflers quite hot! It was soon learned that the best way to climb aboard this machine was to place ones foot onto one of the road-wheels, step up and onto the track fenders and then sit down on top of the superstructure next to the one man turret.

Wittmann waited his turn to inspect this new weapon of war and thought to himself how similar this machine was to many farm tractors he had seen on the farms back home. The smells from this machine were also very familiar to him, as the oil and gasoline fumes and vapors instantaneously brought back memories of working with his father and brother on their machines before, during and after harvest time. A personal connection between man and machine was planted this day, but would not blossom until a number of years later.

Finally, it was Wittmann's turn to climb up and enter into the new Wehrmacht panzer. He then correctly climbed up and into the Panzer I Ausf. A and was very surprised how little space was available for the panzer commander. Few if any creature comforts were provided but it was appreciated that the commander and driver had a degree of protection inside the vehicle if under fire from small arms and light artillery bombardment. The mobility offered by this type of machine also allowed Wittmann to realize that this new panzer could be used to exploit rapid reconnaissance patrols and if fitted with a radio transmitter, could easily rely important tactical messages back to its awaiting strike force once the enemy was located. This machine could also cross difficult terrain and obstacles with ease and give suppressive fire at the same time.

Having stirred his mechanical curiosity, Wittmann wanted to know more about this vehicle and asked the panzer commander additional questions relating to the Panzer I Ausf. A and its component layout, armaments, and operating features. He asked if the crew felt safe and secure in this new armored fighting vehicle? What was it like to operate it with all the hatches closed (buttoned up) during training maneuvers, etc. The panzer commander answered many of his questions, but was stopped short by the training NCOs present, as they were now ready to start the day's training.

After this brief, but interesting inspection of a new weapons system, it was indeed time to return to their daily training schedule. Wittmann and his fellow recruits were told that they would be subjected to various destruction techniques in which they could destroy enemy panzers at close ranges with hand-held charges, mines, and if need be, could as a last resort throw logs in between the road-wheels and tracks there by jamming its complete suspension. They could also hide in trees and jump down upon an enemy panzer and smear mud on the optical devices (periscopes, episcopes, telescopes) or simply place their steel helmets over the vision devises and blind the panzer crews.

Another dangerous technique was the use of gasoline, where by one of the infantrymen would jump down for a tree or nearby building onto the engine deck and pour the liquid onto the vehicle. After removing oneself from the enemy vehicle, and at a safe distance, a hand grenade would be thrown onto the rear engine deck, explode, and disable or destroy the vehicle. If the infantrymen could surprise an enemy panzer with its hatches opened they were instructed to throw any type of hand grenade into the vehicle with devastating results. Another technique was to allow an enemy panzer to roll over their positions (e.g. a slit trench, etc) and then climb onto the back of the moving vehicle and place a magnetic mine or satchel charge in a vital area or under any overhang of the turret. The resulting explosion would disable the vehicle, and if they were lucky, blow off the turret.

Infantrymen were also instructed to place magnetic mines onto the belly plates of enemy panzers as they crossed over their slit trenches and would detonate a few meters away causing total destruction as the belly armor was the weakest area of any armored fighting vehicle. Special care had to be taken into account in regards to a number of these tank hunting techniques, as one had to be very careful in not exposing oneself to machine gun fire from other enemy vehicles from behind or to the left and right flanks. Usually, the infantry squad would provide suppressive fire to the other nearby enemy panzers or would attack all of the vehicles at the same time there by distracting all of the crews.

Anti-tank mines also played a very important part in regards to infantrymen destroying enemy panzers. One of the earliest combat techniques was the placing of mines on the tracks of a halted or stalled panzer. The idea behind this was as the vehicle started to move forward the mine would travel along the top of the track until it was forced over the front idler or sprocket wheel, fall to the ground, and then be detonated by the weight of the vehicle as it ran over the mine. This avenue of approach in knocking out an enemy panzer was very effective indeed, and also allow the infantrymen to seek cover. The resulting explosion usually blew a track off the vehicle's suspension, but did not kill the panzer crew. Once the vehicle came to a halt, its crew would then have two choices, stand and fight, or bail out and try and return to their rear lines. The latter was usually the case. Once the doomed panzer crew tried to escape, they were picked off one by one by the ever present infantry squad.

Fuzed mines were often thrown up and onto the enemy armored fighting vehicles in the hopes of landing close to an air-intake, vision blocks, or if possible down and along the front slope of the vehicle. Quite often the blast from such a mine was enough to blow open hatches, crack or graze vision optical devices, and generally cause panic in regards to the enemy panzer crew to abandon their vehicle. Mines tied to a small rope or wire was another quick way of assuring a kill after they had been hidden to one side of a road where enemy panzers were expected to travel. The leading length of rope was laid across the road and was sometimes buried under the surface by a small amount of dirt. Once the enemy machine was heard approaching the rope was pulled and five or six mines were immediately placed across the road in its path. This was done just before the vehicle was in position. If done so too early, the panzer commander or his driver would certainly detect movement of the mines and avoid this type of ambush. The mines were pulled across the road when the enemy panzer was about three to five meters from point of impact, the result being that the vehicle was sure to run over one or two mines instantaneously which in turn detonated the remaining mines. Causing five or six mines to detonate at the same time may have seemed wasteful, (not to mention the utter and complete destruction of the enemy panzer) but in order to make certain that the enemy was removed from the battlefield this type of expenditure was deemed justified. Magnetic mines, hollow-charged and sticky mines were also used to destroy armored fighting vehicles but it took nerves of steel to approach any enemy machine, attach the mine to it, arm it, and then run for cover in order to protect oneself from the resulting explosion.

Sometimes the mines would slip off of the vehicle being attacked, and explode harmlessly on the ground giving the crew of the vehicle a warning that tank hunting teams were ever present in the area. It was vitally important that the infantrymen placing the mine on the vehicle was quite certain that he located an area upon the machine where the mine would stay in place before arming and making his escape.

Different tactics were required if the infantry squad needed to take prisoners for questioning and interrogation. Smoking a panzer crew out of their vehicle required the use of glass smoke grenades. Since the smoke was so irritating to the crew of a buttoned up panzer the recruits were told to throw smoke grenades in and around direct vision devices and air in-take ventilators. With choking smoke soon filling the enemy vehicle the crew had no choice but to abandon it. Smoke grenades were sometimes tied in twos (one each at the end of a short piece of light rope) and thrown over the barrel of an enemy panzer with the result being that the smoke would impede the vision of the tank commander, gunner, and especially the driver. Once blinded the enemy panzer had little choice but to surrender. Smoke grenades were also used to lay down small smoke screens in order for the infantry to crawl forward on their hands and knees to positions to attack enemy vehicles at close range.

One of the first steps taken by the German Wehrmacht after the development of the new panzers was to familiarize the infantrymen to any and all weaknesses of armored fighting vehicles, and constant attempts were made to conquer the natural fear of attacking enemy panzers as seen by such an individual in his slit trench or fox hole. It was clearly illustrated in training that most men in battle would in fact be overawed by the approach of fast moving light panzers which would lead to anxiety and the hopeless feeling of being alone and isolated on the modern battlefield. Even after anti-tank techniques training it was predicted that it would still take considerable determination by an infantrymen to perform these types of assaults in the face of the enemy. However, by working and pulling together as a team, the infantry squad would overcome this fear and stabilize their respective sector of battle.

All panzers offer very limited visibility for their crews, especially when the crew is tactically employed and buttoned up. This situation is additionally hindered by the vibrations of a moving vehicle which causes the men inside the panzer a very blurred image pertaining to the outside world about them. This point was stressed many times in training and gave the lone infantrymen a needed boost of spirit when attacking an on coming enemy machine. The infantrymen knew that he could lie in wait, undetected, unobserved, with weapons ready at hand, and attack the vehicle when it was in a position to his choosing that offered the least resistance.

Mine fields were also very important and many days of training were taken up in the correct manner of performing this vital and necessary task. There were various patterns that had to be learned and of course the trainees used dummy mines in the beginning, but as time went on, they were instructed to use 'live mines' which resulted in special handling and care as if one mistake was made, horrible injuries and death were a direct result. Mines were also wired to trees which when detonated would fall across an important road or road junction, blocking such avenues of approach. Anti-personnel mines had to be set up around the perimeter of a defensive position in order to prevent enemy infantrymen infiltration especially during night-time. Elaborate systems were devised incorporating antipersonnel mines and were very effective for deterring enemy attacks. Establishing booby traps utilizing various types of mines (e.g. S-mines, box mines,and egg-shaped grenades) were also learned by Wittmann and his squad. It was also taught that one could take a standard stick grenade (potatomasher) and wrap four, five, or even six S-mines around this weapon and produce a very deadly ad hoc anti-tank hand thrown explosive device. This type of weapon was only used if there was a short supply of the standard anti-tank devices on the battlefield. "Necessity is the mother of invention" and this statement was brought out time and time again. The simple infantrymen had to make do with what he had available, and if he found himself facing the enemy he better be able to protect himself in any way he could. Whether if it was a standard weapon, a home-made one, or a captured weapon, it was to be used regardless.

Another weapon used by the infantrymen was the 27mm Leuchpistole (Walthers) and was standard issue to an infantry squad. This weapon was basically a signal pistole but could also fire HE (high explosive) grenades (H.E. Grenade 361 L.P.) and could knock out light armored vehicles at short combat ranges. The 361 L.P. consisted of a standard egg-shaped grenade attached to a projector stem fitting into the barrel of the pistole, which was provided with a special loose smooth bore liner. Special care and highly accurate aiming was stressed with this weapon as its range was very dubious at times. The 27mm signal pistole could fire some forty different signal cartridges (e.g. smoke, indicator/tracer, and single illuminating star with parachute). Another use for this weapon was for an infantrymen to climb on board an enemy panzer and fire the tracer round into the engine compartment or if extremely lucky, into the turret through an open hatch. Whether he fired a tracer or smoke round they would either cause a fire inside the vehicle or blind and smoke the crew out. This type of assault tactic was only used if a lack of a proper weapon was not readily available.

Smoke mortars were also very important in dealing with infantry training as they could be used in a number of different ways on the field of battle. These weapons could lay down a smoke screen for the infantrymen which was always needed when assaulting an objective of great importance. Smoke could also be used to mark enemy positions too difficult for the infantry to attack with the idea being that friendly air to ground attack aircraft could locate and then destroy these highly marked positions. It was shown how smoke mortars could also blind panzer crews that were approaching a certain position there by allowing infantrymen to move forward under cover to try and knock out these machines. If the enemy panzers halted due to the confusion involved they could be dealt with accordingly by the infantrymen using their hand placed mines, and other explosive devices. If the on-coming panzers did not stop, but slowed down due to low visibility, this also gave the infantrymen time to plan an attack using the best destruction techniques available to him to destroy the enemy machines.

The 8cm s.Gr.W.34 was the standard heavy mortar used by the German infantry and this weapon was very important in laying down suppressive fire to the enemy. If used during an enemy armored attack it could be used to good effect by forcing the panzer commanders to button-up there vehicles, especially if these mortar rounds were falling onto and detonating in and around their vehicles. This weapon was also very handy if enemy panzers were carrying mounted infantrymen. If a mortar round could be dropped on or near-by to a vehicle this usually had enough force to either kill everyone on the outside of the vehicle, or cause many to be blown off with serious injuries. Mortars were originally developed for indirect fire power meaning that these weapons could fire over trees, building, and rain down death on an opponent very swiftly with excellent results. Training of this type of warfare was very thorough and much attention to detail was stressed pertaining to the type of round being fired, wind and weather conditions, plus likely points on the terrain maps where the enemy was apt to place forward observation posts, weapon pits, etc. Ammunition was always at a premium during training and careful attention to map reading was absolutely necessary to conserve on training rounds. No matter what role the 8cm mortar was to be use for, it was an extremely useful weapon for the infantrymen as it was very versatile and easy to transport, maintain, and operate.

Field radios were another very important piece of equipment that Wittmann and his squad had to learn to maintain and operate. The majority of the recruits were not familiar with radios and the closest anyone of them had ever come to such a device was in their civilian homes where they simply turned them on and off. A number of these young men had never seen a radio! It took a great deal of time and effort to train people on the use of, functions of, and maintenance of German wireless equipment. The infantry sets that the training schools utilized were of the new type, and special care had to be taken so as not to damage them while in the field. As always, the training started in the classroom with the basics, and then there were the tests to be taken pertaining to usage and maintaining these communication devices as they progressed with their training programs. Only one man in the squad was to carry a radio, but if that man was injured or killed in combat, another man in the squad would have to carry and operate it as a result.

Hand to hand combat was taught to every combat infantrymen and Wittmann was soon learning how to kill a man with a knife, with the butt of his rifle, or with any available weapon at hand. It did not please him very much, but if confronted in combat with an enemy opponent with the same intentions he knew that it would be "Kill or be Killed."

The rifle range was an interesting part of Wittmann's training as he enjoyed it a great deal. He had learned a great deal about light weapons during his infantry training but also had experiences on the farm pertaining to hunting for game. The German Wehrmacht 98K rifle was a very well designed weapon and Wittmann was soon learning to take it apart and put it together again even while being blind-folded. This training was vital in the advent of his weapon having to be disassembled in the dark. Many hours were spent in the barracks cleaning, oiling, and checking and then re-checking this weapon to make sure that it would function properly in any circumstances. If his weapon jammed during a combat mission, or if a component part of the rifle was loose from wear, it could be a matter of life and death in the face of the enemy. Every day Wittmann and his squad were marched out to the firing ranges and practiced firing their 98k rifles until they had accurately zeroed in their sights.

Once this was accomplished they would start their daily tasks of trying to obtain the best shooting score of the day. Wittmann always made sure that his sights were free of any dirt or any other foreign materials that might impair his vision when aiming at any given target. He would slowly take a breathe of air, hold it, take careful aim, and then squeeze the trigger. Usually, his aim was fairly good, but one had to take into account for the type of day it was, the windage, and other factors involving physical fitness, stance, and awareness of the correct target.

Advanced infantry training included the firing and maintenance of the standard 7.92 MG-34 machine gun which was the mainstay of the infantry corps and proved time after time to be a highly reliable weapon. Three men were allocated to this weapon, e.g. one man as the gunner, and the remainder being ammunition carriers and loaders.

Other advanced infantry training covered infantry fire trenches, machine gun trenches, mortar weapon pits, field gun weapon-pits, anti-tank (PAK) gun weapon pits, semi-static and static field fortifications, field structures above the ground, semi-permanent machine gun bunkers, accommodation bunkers, anti-personnel obstacles, anti-tank obstacles and concealment techniques. All vitally important to the survival of any infantrymen on the field of battle.

As Wittmann's infantry training started to come to a close he felt that he and his squad had learned a great many new skills and they were a very viable fighting team. All the long hours of sweat and toil made them realize that it was all worth the time and effort they had endured. They all felt that they had accomplished a great deal and would be able to survive on any training or actual fighting mission handed down to them by their superiors. The majority of the men never thought that they would ever make it through all of the difficult tasks placed in front of them by their training NCOs. All of the sore feet with giant blisters that hurt so much was now behind them. Their strained backs that had to carry all of their field equipment issued to them over kilometers of extremely difficult terrain were now straight and powerful, and nobody would ever forget the sharp bark of their training sergeant to get up off the ground and move forward even more kilometers even though everyone was on the edge of total collapse. The heat, the dirt, the sweat, and the clang of equipment draped over their tired bodies would finally terminate for the time being. How soon would they be back at their new profession of being a Wehrmacht infantrymen, no one really knew, all they could think of was to return to their homes and loved ones.

At their ceremony for their infantry graduation, it was quite apparent that if Wittmann and his new comrades had not worked together as a team, they would pay a very high price on the fields of any future battles. Dressed in his best and cleanest uniform, Wittmann was very proud of all that he and his comrades-in-arms had endured through the past few months. What lay ahead of them nobody knew, but it was very clear that the rise of Adolf Hitler meant only one thing for the new and rapidly expanding German military machine! The hand-writing on the wall was only too obvious, that utter and total war was imminent!

Chapter III

ENTRY INTO THE LEIBSTANDARTE ADOLF HITLER
October 1, 1936 – August 31, 1939

Michael Wittmann served in the German Wehrmacht until the date of September 30, 1936 attaining the rank of Gefreiter (Private First Class). On October 1, 1936 he decided to become a candidate for membership in the Allgemeine-SS which interested him a great deal at this time. The Allgemeine-SS was something new, exciting, and offered a soldier more military pay, higher status, and additional retirement benefits, etc. In joining the Allgemeine-SS, there was a certain air of becoming one of the elite, the 'thing to do' for ones country. The uniforms were much smarter, and firearms, equipment, and training schools were of a much higher standard. The Treaty of Versailles which was established after the First World War by the Allies dictated that the German military would comprise only a 100,000 man army, limited weapons, no armored fighting vehicles, and only light artillery pieces. For many in post-war Germany, this action was a political slap in the face and no doubt was one of the basic fundamental building blocks for Germany to one day re-establish her fighting forces in relation to what they had once been before and during the Great War. To large numbers of German youths (and veterans of World War I who were not allowed into the post-war military), it had been instilled by their fathers and grandfathers that it was their patriotic duty to serve the Fatherland in the ranks of the German army, but many thousands of young men found an empty void due to the rules and regulations as laid down by the Treaty of Versailles. Many veterans who had served in the trenches during the Great War had a very difficult time in rejoining their old units and regiments as their ranks were quickly filled shortly after the signing of the Treaty. As a direct result, it took a great deal of effort and time to review past military records and experience which slowed the entire process even more so. With the abolishment of the Treaty of Versailles by Adolf Hitler and the establishment of the Allgemeine-SS, a German youth could serve his country as long as he passed all of the entrance requirements and exams, plus was the correct height and weight, and was physical fit for duty. Michael Wittmann passed all of the above requirements and enthusiastically entered the Allgemeine-SS.

The economic state of Germany during the 1930s was at an all time low. Thousands of people were out of work and there were long bread lines and many soup kitchens feeding thousands throughout greater Germany. It took a great amount of money just to feed a single family; wheelbarrows full of German Marks were needed just to buy meager necessities for every day life! Thousands upon thousands of German people were starving in the streets with little if any relief on the way for those that managed to stay alive. There was a substantial amount of farm products being produced, but very little of it was being correctly distributed due to bureaucratic red-tape, bickering, strikes, and riots. Even during the Great War, there were shortages, but the situation that arose during the third decade of the Twentieth Century forced many people in Germany to seek a rapid solution that would elevate their country out from the deadly clutches of total depression.

There was one man that seemed to fill this requirement, a man who had been a simple corporal in the Great War, who had fought in the living hell of the front line trenches, a man who wanted to see Germany rise again to all of its former glory; to be a strong provider for all of its people and to have once again extended economic stability. No man or woman would ever have to stand out in the middle of the streets in the dead of winter and wait for what little food was available to feed their hungry families and relatives. The German populace were also very concerned about the hated scourge of the east, communism, as the Bolsheviks were certain to try to introduce their doctrine upon the weaken German economy.

This man was Adolf Hitler who had seen what had happened to Germany after the Great War. The limitations forced down on Germany by the Treaty of Versailles meant a slow death for the German economy with no recovery in sight. He detested the extremely poor state of affairs involving the German military which in turn forced many armaments factories and other ancillary companies to close down due to the total lack of contracts stemming from German military procurement offices. Most of all he saw a nation of people slowly being bled white and it was time for a radical change to save greater Germany. Once Adolf Hitler came to power on January 30, 1933, he soon eradicated the Treaty of Versailles and immediately set forth a massive reconstruction plan to re-establish the German military machine.

The German military would once again be a mighty fighting force with no foreign powers dictating the terms of their country's defense. Jobs would be plentiful, major manufacturers would be allowed to produce the products not only for stronger defense, but also for every day necessities needed for so very long. Germany was to be a self-sufficient state that the German people could be proud of and not have to rely on any outside help from countries that surrounded her bare and exposed borders.

These major events established the background setting for Wittmann's decision to become a candidate for his membership in regards to the Allgemeine-SS (or General-SS). With the constant growth of the German military system, renewed "esprit de corps" was generated near and far. On November 1, 1936 Michael Wittmann was selected as a member of the Allgemeine-SS and was assigned to the 1st Sturm of the 92 Standarte (1st Company of the 92nd Regiment) in Ingolstadt. For the next month he was given many tests which were written and oral. Additional medical tests were extremely high and if one was physically weak one was dismissed. If an individual had even one filling in any of his teeth or had a tooth missing this was cause enough for not being accepted in the ranks of the Allgemeine-SS. It was plain to see that one had to be in one hundred percent physical and mental condition to continue on as one of Hitler's elite. Inner discipline, camaraderie, firmness in a serious crisis, the willing to learn new ideas, new military tactics for the modern battlefield were all incorporated in the training programs to ultimately turn out an all new and elite fighting force for the new German order.

Now that he was a member of the Allgemeine-SS, Wittmann felt that he had accomplished a major goal in his life. He would spend the next six months learning new skills in the art of modern warfare, plus the new German ideology that had manifested itself with the new Führer's directions. This ideology was very pertinent in his training but Wittmann did not agree on every aspect pertaining to its applications. He did however, look upon it as the rules and regulations establishing the new order, and would carry on with his desires to be a well trained soldier. One had to conform to the new order if one was to move ahead in its wave of re-establishing the country as a whole and well functioning world power. During this time many young men were caught up in the excitement of a new adventure, the start of something that would cause world attention, the act of saving ones country from the hands of foreign countries dictating their terms to be meet forthwith. It was a time for a new lease on life, a time for Germany as a nation to once again stand on its own feet and have equal parity with other nations around the world, to have country-wide self-esteem once again in the world money and investments markets. This was the goal Adolf Hitler would be striving for, but it would take every man, woman, and young adult in Germany to achieve this objective. Although he did not know it at the time. Michael Wittmann was to be a vital part of this nation-wide endeavor.

Wittmann was sent to the SS school at Lichterfelde in Berlin on April 1, 1937 and was incorporated into the military branch of the SS (SS-Verfugungstruppe or Waffen-SS) and joined the ranks of the Leibstandarte SS Adolf Hitler. The recruiting requirements for the Waffen-SS were extremely high and it was stated in many Leibstandarte recruiting pamphlets as echoed by Adolf Hitler, "I will have no one in my Leibstandarte who is not of the best Germany can offer." Any applicants who wished to join the Leibstandarte had to be between the ages of seventeen and twenty-two years of age. He also had to be at least 5 feet, 11 inches tall (later changed to 6 feet, 0.5 inches) and of the highest physical fitness attainable. Any man who was allowed to join the Waffen-SS had to be Nordic in appearance, as this statement was written down in the Waffen-SS guidelines that every Waffen-SS man must be of extremely well proportioned build; for the individual must not have disproportion between the lower leg and thigh; or between the legs and upper torso; otherwise an exceptional bodily effort is required to carry out long military marches. Appearance was to be truly Nordic in every aspect, the point being made that in his daily attitude to discipline the Waffen-SS man should not behave like an underling, that his gait, his hands, everything should correspond to the ideal with which the Waffen-SS had set as a standard for its personnel. His Aryan pedigree, too had to be proven, from the end of 1935 every Waffen-SS man had to be able to produce his record of his ancestry back to 1800, for the officer corps, back to 1750. If any trace of Jewish or other "undesirable" ancestry was detected, the man was either refused entry, or if it came to light later, was immediately ejected from the Waffen-SS. Sepp Dietrich (over-all commander of the Leibstandarte Adolf Hitler) commented in disgust that some forty good specimens at least were kept from joining the Leibstandarte every year due to doubt concerning ones ancestry. Any woman wishing to marry a Waffen-SS man had to present her ancestry for examination, as well as a photograph of herself in a bathing suit!

Membership in the Waffen-SS was totally voluntary, and even when the exigencies of total war forced it to accept a large number of conscripts, this aspect remained important. As a Waffen-SS instruction put it: "A decision to join the Führer's military force is equally nothing less than the expression of a voluntary determination to continue the present political struggle upon another level." From the year 1935, membership in the Leibstandarte and SS-VT counted towards military service, but the terms of service was extremely hard, a minimum of four years for the enlisted men, twelve years of the NCOs, and twenty-five years for officers. Before 1939, a member of the SS-VT could always obtain his release from its ranks if he were sufficiently determined to do so, but the advent of the Second World War put an end to this situation.

Although considerable restrictions were placed upon recruitment pertaining to the Waffen-SS, for example, before the war it was not allowed to place advertisements in the local press, the desire of many young Germans to become members of an ideological and military elite, coupled with Hitler's endeavors to keep his guard up to strength, ensured that the Leibstandarte, unlike any other armed Waffen-SS unit, would have few if any man-power problems. However, these standards inevitably took its toll both in quality and quantity, and by 1943 the Leibstandarte had been forced to lower its over all provisional standards.

Ethnic Germans from Hungary, Slovakia and Rumania some of whom were in their late fifties, were even to be found within the ranks of the Waffen-SS. The last draft received by Hitler's Guard, consisted of an assorted collection of personnel from the Luftwaffe, the Navy, and the factories, a proportion of whom were above the active service age.

Once in the Waffen-SS, the aim of the commanders were to create a supple, adaptable soldier, of athletic bearing, capable of more than just average endurance on the march and in close combat. The Waffen-SS man was to be as much at home on the battlefield as on the athletic field. After training in the Waffen-SS and SS-VT one was expected to cover 3km (1.88 miles) in twenty minutes while in full battle-dress (a total weight of 60 pounds). This was made possible by the great emphasis placed upon physical exercise and all out sports activities, which were made an integral and continual part of the training program and every day life of a Waffen-SS man. More time was spent performing exercises in the field, on the firing ranges, and every day duties were expected to be carried out on a rigorous training schedule. More emphasis was placed in the classroom learning the theory of tactics, than was practiced in the Wehrmacht units and attention to dress parade drill was given less consideration. This type of training lead to greater standards of battlefield movement and gunnery which was appreciably higher than the average soldier in the German Wehrmacht.

Any and all training exercise were made as realistic as possible with the result being that every soldier in the Waffen-SS was exposed to live-fire ammunition and artillery expenditures. Having first hand experience of this nature only too vividly simulated what the conditions would be like if he was under fire at any given time. It was stated and practiced in the Waffen-SS that each soldier was to be fully accustomed to his weapon and all of its functions and also to being within fifty to seventy meters of the explosion of his own artillery fire. The Wehrmacht often openly criticized the Waffen-SS for the casualties which inevitably occurred during peace-time maneuvers. The Waffen-SS openly stated that for every drop of blood in peace-time spilled; saved streams of blood on the battlefield of the future. "The end product of the training was a high standard of soldier, a man who was an "Assault Trooper" rather than just an infantryman or panzerman; someone who, when acting in concert with his fellows, would by blows of lighting rapidity split the enemy into fragments and then destroy the dislocated remnants" (Steiner).

Training in the Waffen-SS had made Michael Wittmann a very apt soldier, well disciplined, highly motivated, resourceful, able to take a difficult situation and lead it to a very successful conclusion. Wittmann was now indoctrinated into a military organization that not only would lead any and all military assaults in the face of the enemy, but would also be called upon to sort out any stoppages in the front lines time and time again.

Wittmann retained his former rank, but is now a SS-Sturmman on November 9, 1937. During this time period he is being trained in the role of an armored car crew member. The type of armored cars that were available to the troops of the Leibstandarte were the Sd.Kfz.222, and the Sd.Kfz.223 which were four wheeled machines with light weapons mounted. These vehicles were very well designed and were very fast machines and were ideal for their intended role as reconnaissance cars. The Sd.Kfz.222 carried a crew of three, e.g. vehicle commander/ gunner, loader, and vehicle driver. The Sd.Kfz.222 mounted a 2cm (20mm) KwK 30 or KwK 38L/55 cannon and a 7.92mm MG-34 machine gun for its main armaments. The Sd.Kfz.223 was very similar to the Sd.Kfz.222, but had a smaller nine-sided turret and was armed only with a single 7.92mm MG-34 machine gun plus MP-38 or MP-40 machine pistols. This vehicle was a radio car (Funkwagen) and carried long-range radio equipment and had a crew of three, e.g. commander/MG-34 gunner, radio operator, and driver.

Upon serving with these vehicles, Wittmann became a driver of a Sd.Kfz.222. His aptitude pertaining to these types of fighting vehicles was very high indeed and his love for the automobile made it very easy for him to enjoy his new assignment. He studied every aspect of these armored reconnaissance vehicles and carefully read the training manuals pertaining to their use, maintenance, and on-road and off-road capabilities. During his drivers training the first item pertaining to these vehicles to become accustomed too, was the extremely limited vision offered by this machine in regards to the driver's forward field of view. The Sd.Kfz.222, and Sd.Kfz.223 had only four vision slits, e.g. two direct front, left and right side, whereas one had to be very careful in judging distances when operating in a built up area; such as a city street or in a crowded column of military vehicles. The second feature pertaining to these armored cars was that they had an inverted steering wheel (due to the sloping of the frontal armor plate) which was very awkward to operate. Ones hands had to be placed on the steering wheel at an acute angle and over a long period of time this position would cause fatigue in regards to the driver's hands, arms, and lower back. Careful selection of vehicle speed and terrain (if operating off the road) was vitally important. If the driver hit a bump or undulation he could cause serious harm not only to himself (e.g. hit his head on the roof of the car and cause neck and head injuries) but to the rest of the crew.

Driving this type of armored car became fairly routine after learning the correct procedures, but the vehicle driver had to be alert at all times in the advent of the vehicle commander issuing additional directional guidance. The vehicles had R/T intercommunications which made it easier to hear and obey any commands as given by the vehicle commander. If the armored car was travelling at high speeds (80kph = 50mph) the commander had to shout his orders to his crew as the passing air interfered with his inter-communication devices. If travelling at a lower speed (40kph = 25mph) he still had to speak in a loud voice due to the engine and transmission noises.

The driver of the Sd. Kfz. 222 armored car was in a little world of his own, tucked away in his very cramped driver's position in the front portion of the vehicle. His only entry and exit from the vehicle was through a large flap like door located on each side of the vehicle's hull. The reason for the two flap doors was in the advent of the car being hit and rolled over on one side; in this event the driver could escape out the other side door. These two doors also helped in the loading of the armored car with ammunition, food, tools, and any other necessary items the crew felt would be needed for a combat mission. If additional ammunition was stored in the driver's compartment (which was done many times in combat) he would on instruction from the vehicle commander hand it up to the loader when needed and then be feed into the vehicle's weapons. The driver was also responsible for the maintenance of the vehicle and had to make sure that the armored car was performing properly at all times. If a fault was found, the necessary forms were to be filled out and turned into appropriate maintenance personnel. If the armored car did not function correctly during a combat mission, lives could be lost due to the failure of the driver to perform his respective crew duties. Wittmann soon learned all of the tasks expected of him in maintaining his Sd. Kfz. 222 from changing and repairing a worn out tire to pulling out the engine and transmission.

Serving in a reconnaissance unit pleased Wittmann a great deal and enjoyed the training even though he had to sit uncomfortably for hours in his driver's seat. However, having the opportunity of spear-heading an assault was very exciting to him and his comrades, and generated the feeling of living on the edge while in this mode of operation. It was stressed time and time again, that if the enemy was sighted first it was the mission of the reconnaissance units to report back their positions, number of vehicles, and troop strengths, etc. If they were to engage the enemy any and all element of surprise would be lost with the end result being that the enemy would be alerted that hostile forces were present in the immediate area. Should the enemy forces detect the reconnaissance units due to poor selection of terrain, the armored car commander would have no choice but to engage with his weapons, and then make a hasty retreat. The driver would then idler the engine while the engagement ensued and would place the transmission in reverse, to insure that the vehicle could perform evasive maneuvers on a moments notice.

As Wittmann's reconnaissance training continued he and his other comrades were taught all of the correct procedures and tactics needed to survive on the modern battlefield. As time past on they were given comprehensive classroom instructions on the theoretical uses of the armored cars and were shown that these machines were the fastest vehicles available for their mission, were considered highly armed for its tactical purpose; it also had a wide radius of action for spear-heading an attack and proved to be a great asset for any armored division using this type of vehicle for its eyes and ears. A standard German armored reconnaissance unit was capable of being deployed up to 100km (60 miles) ahead of its division at any give time with a frontage generally laid down by corps and could be extended in the case of an emergency, to as much as 75 miles. On open flanks such as those later encountered on the vast steppes of Russia in 1941-42 it was frequently expanded even further through tactical necessity. Also at times, the armored division would send out a reconnaissance unit with orders to move in various directions when air reconnaissance desired, rapid additional information so as to obtain a clear and informative understanding of the tactical situation before launching a major attack or counterattack. If aircraft were used, the enemy would no doubt assume that an attack was imminent and would alert any and all units in the area under question.

Operational reconnaissance was performed by very special assault units. The reconnaissance detachments special operations was to locate enemy troop concentrations, avenues of approach, railway transports, types of equipment being moved, aircraft landing sights (to be used for advancing air transport, fighters, and tactical bombers), any anti-tank bunkers, and other obstacles blocking their line of march, etc. The armored reconnaissance units were the modern equivalent of the cavalry and were used time and time again to seek out, locate and report back to their headquarters any and all tactical information that was pertinent to the over-all plan of attack.

During 1938 the German Wehrmacht set up special armored reconnaissance units which formed the framework of the Panzer and Panzergrenadier divisions, the Panzerdivision Aufklarungsabteilung (armored division reconnaissance unit) and the Infanteriedivision Aufklarungsabteilung (Infantry division reconnaissance unit). The standard German armored division had a reconnaissance unit containing an armored car squadron, three armored reconnaissance companies, and support weapons grouped in a heavy company. This formation was really the spear-head of the division, moving forward along all possible avenues of approach ahead of the division to weed out any resistance, brush aside weak opposition, seize bridgeheads, road junctions, and any fortified hamlets or villages. Its established task was to obtain any and all information pertaining to the enemy's strength and disposition, thus enabling the divisional commander to plan and formulate his planned attack. The standard German armored reconnaissance unit was then composed of a headquarters, a headquarters company, and an armored car squadron and three armored reconnaissance companies.

Towards the end of Wittmann's armored car and reconnaissance training, he was given the opportunity to take command of a Sd. Kfz. 222. He was very pleased at first, but soon realized that he was taking on a great deal of responsibility, plus had to oversee two crew members as well. However, it was not too long before this young soldier was busy conducting tactical exercises with his crew and performing all of his duties to the fullest:

Wittmann was now positioned in the turret of the Sd. Kfz. 222 which was also extremely cramped despite being larger than that of the Sd. Kfz. 223, and was in the shape of a shallow truncated ten-sided pyramid. A hinged wire-mesh anti-grenade screen was fitted over the top of the fighting compartment for added protection. This divided along the centerline of the vehicle and could be folded outward from the turret to facilitate firing of the main armament, which had proved very difficult with the screens closed. The screen was also used as a framework to attach camouflage netting or foliage during tactical maneuvers.

The 2cm KwK 30 or KwK 38 (the latter being an armored car version of the standard 2cm aircraft cannon) both were fully automatic weapons firing from a ten-shot magazine at a rate of 280 rpm in the case of the KwK 30 and 480 rpm in regards to the KwK 38. These weapons could fire both armor-piercing (AP) and high explosive (HE) ammunition. The co-axial 7.92mm MG-34 machine gun was also mounted in the turret of the vehicle on the left hand side. Both weapons were mounted on a central pillar incorporating the traverse and elevation gear and was attached to the floor of the fighting compartment. Sighting the main gun and MG-34 was accomplished by the use of a telescope, and a pedal operated firing mechanism was employed to fire the weapons. Traverse and elevation were controlled by a single hand-wheel, and the elevation was such that the weapons could be used against aircraft. Concentric with the gun mounting, the turret was traversed from the mounting by means of a linking arm incorporating a spring shock-absorber. Two mechanically fired smoke projectors were also fitted to some vehicles one on each side of the turret.

On later models of the Sd. Kfz. 222 and companion vehicles the thickness of the nose plate was increased from 14.5mm to 30mm and double hinged flaps were provided for the driver. Vehicles based on the Model B chassis had more powerful engines and minor improved details.

Michael Wittmann soon finished his armored car and reconnaissance training and continued to sharpen his skills as a Sd. Kfz. 222 armored car commander.

Chapter IV

THE INVASION
OF POLAND

September 1, 1939 – September 25, 1939

September 1, 1939 found Michael Wittmann as a SS-Unterscharführer (Sergeant) in command of an Sd.Kfz.222 armored car posed on the border of Germany and Poland. During the uneasy summer of 1939 the German Wehrmacht and Waffen-SS mechanized units were positioned like a giant sickle ready to sweep into Poland on a moments notice from the German High Command. Hitler's decision to enter war with this country set in motion a campaign which would utilize fifty-five divisions, which included every German armored, motorized and light division which would cross the Polish landbridge; a mostly open and rolling country-side tailored made for a fast 'Blitzkrieg' panzer assault without any natural defenses to deter the advancing German military forces. From September 1, 1939, Michael Wittmann was to be in continuous combat for the next five years with the Leibstandarte Adolf Hitler (LAH).

On August 30th, 1939 the German High Command realized that total war was inevitable with Poland and sent out the code words which set O-Tag (Day 1) as September 1st, with H-Hour being set at 04:45 hours. Long columns of artillery guns, panzers, and men went forward to their prearranged assembly areas and expertly camouflaged their vehicles and respective positions. As the last moments of peace-time slowly ticked away on their watches, every man including Michael Wittmann wondered if he would ever see his family, home, and friends again? His five years of military training was now going to be put through the acid test of real combat. How would he perform under the appalling and ruthless conditions of total war? If he made a mistake it no doubt would cost him his life as well as those of his armored car crew. Everything must be done by the book, as if performed the correct way, as it had been done in training, they would have a successful assault with little or no causalities.

Sitting in his small turret of his camouflaged Sd. Kfz. 222 armored car Wittmann could not detect other vehicles of his unit as these machines were also expertly concealed. Special care had to be taken to insure that the probing eyes and ears of the Polish Army did not locate or detect any German vehicles or concentrations of men and materials. All of the vehicles near the frontier were under strict orders to extinguish any and all head-lights, shiny surfaces on vehicles (e.g. windshields, mirrors), plus any type of smoking was highly forbidden. The various German military formations simply melted away into the thick forests which hide them from any observation being performed by the enemy.

As the advance time drew closer and closer, Wittmann made any and all final surveys of his terrain maps, rechecked all of his weapons and equipment and was then satisfied that all was in perfect order. He quietly briefed his crew on what to expect, and outlined the tasks that were expected of them and generally tried to calm his crew down by being very positive and illustrating his military professionalism and military bearing.

As H-Hour drew closer, every fighting soldier on the border grew more tense, not a word was spoken, the men involved were ready for any contingency. Everywhere along the border a mammoth mechanized fighting machine was waiting for the arrival of H-Hour! For many brave men, this would be their first and last battle, to others it would be the start of a long and drawn out and bloody war. Michael Wittmann also wondered if this would be his first and last battle, or would it only be his baptism of fire which would lead him forward to other more serious and dangerous combat engagements. His only thought at the time of H-Hour was to utilize every ounce of training that had been instilled upon him by his training instructors. Only working together as a fighting team was the only true formula for success and survival on the modern battlefield.

The Polish Army which went into the field during the time of the German invasion was both qualitatively and quantitatively inferior to the Wehrmacht and Waffen-SS units. The Polish Army was only able to deploy thirty-two divisions, which were not up to the high standards of the new and fast paced German military machine now opposing their front line troops. The German military forces enjoyed through out this campaign a superiority in infantry of 2.3:1; of 4.3:1 in artillery, and in panzers 8.2:1, for in the latter case the Poles had only nine companies of 8 ton panzers and twenty-nine companies of armored weapon carriers. Although both armies used horse-drawn transport and guns the Polish reliance was almost absolute; 92 per cent of all military wheeled transport being horse drawn.

As 04:45 hours arrived Wittmann and his Sd. Kfz. 222 armored car crew slowly moved forward in an attempt to locate any and all suspected enemy locations. It seemed a relief to be actually moving ahead still hidden in the darkness of the early morning rather than just sitting on the frontier. Every eye and ear was strained to detect or hear any movement by the Polish forces as it was the responsibility of the Aufklarungskompanie (reconnaissance company to radio back any signs of enemy action or maneuvering.

The area of operations dictated to the Leibstandarte Adolf Hitler had been determined by von Rundstedt, the Wehrmacht Group Commander, who demanded additional reconnaissance strength for his Tenth Army's left wing The Leibstandarte Adolf Hitler was placed into the line for this purpose and to act as a link between the Eighth and Tenth Armies. As being part of Army Group South, the Leibstandarte Adolf Hitler's first major objective approaching from the vicinity of Breslau was to strike forward to the fortified frontier line and to capture an important height behind the Prosna river.

As Wittmann and his reconnaissance company moved forward with the advantage of surprise and speed, plus great elan their unit was able to cover three to four miles within seventy-five minutes after departing the frontier. After the expected and initial confusion of an army on the advance over enemy territory was overcome, the movement forward was continuous even though the Leibstandarte Adolf Hitler units did come under fire from the Polish 10th Infantry Division in prepared positions equipped with 3.7cm anti-tank guns. The Prosna river was crossed by the Waffen-SS units with the majority of the frontier positions being over-run by the German military forces. Then military trucks moved forward carrying the infantry assault teams which lead a charge up the opposing heights to secure the surrounding area. With great fluency that intensive training brings to a fighting unit, the rifle companies disembarked and moved forward behind a covering artillery barrage, putting into practice those lessons of fire discipline and tactics which had been instilled into them on the barracks square at Lichterfelde and on numerous maneuvers through out Germany. The momentum of the attack was gathering breakneck speed and neither Polish fortifications nor the Polish Army itself or the varied difficulties of the Polish terrain could halt the advances of men like Wittmann and all of the other volunteer soldiers who were fighting for the Fatherland. The first planned missions went like clockwork, the assaults progressing by huge leaps and bounds, the companies as they deployed were covered by fire from their comrades. The tactics of fire and movement proved with out a single doubt to be highly irresistible and the Polish Army was swept into utter disorder from the weight of the ensuing waves of German mechanized units.

As predicted by Polish Army strategist, defensive planning would thus allow the Army to give ground and it was further accepted that this ultimate sacrifice would develop into the loss of the most highly populated and industrial western half of the country. The end result would be a huge salient into Poland with the Polish armies being committed to its defense being greatly outflanked. From north to south two large German army groups were to attack in a three-stage operation. First of all, the Polish Army in the field was to be encircled in a double envelopment east and west of Warsaw. It would then be held and destroyed in a killing ground in the bend of the Vistula. The third and final stage would be the capture of the Polish capital and of the fortress areas.

The advance continued as another three and a half miles north-westward lead to the next major objective, the town of Boleslavecz. This advance was contested so bitterly by determined elements of the 30th Infantry Division, 21st

Infantry Regiment and armored cars of the Wolwyska Cavalry Brigade that in some areas of the attack no movement forward was possible and those Waffen-SS units which had smashed their way forward into the Polish defensive lines soon found that they were under constant and accurate fire from all sides of the salient. Hand to hand fighting soon transpired when the Poles counter-attacked with rifle and bayonets.

The leading infantry units of the Polish Army came into the attack in long lines, not quite shoulder to shoulder but very close together. The men of Wittmann's unit could hear the long drawn out 'Hurra' of the Polish troops and they could also hear in the distance the officers shouting at their men to move forward no matter what the consequences. It seemed quite strange to witness this type of action as Wittmann could not understand why the officers would shout like this as they were giving their positions away by doing so. Why were they not leading the attacks with their men?

The scene of carnage was overwhelming, there were Polish soldiers in every direction that one looked, and they accepted the high losses to halt the advance but the all out assault by the German military forces were too great for the Poles and by 10:00 hours the town of Boleslavecz was in German hands. At first, only small numbers of individuals surrendered, but then it was in groups of tens and twenties, and finally at day's end hundreds of Khaki-green uniformed men, with the Eagle of Poland glistening in the brim of their army caps, walked down the roads along which the Leibstandarte Adolf Hitler had attacked earlier in the day. It was indeed a great day for the men of the Leibstandarte Adolf Hitler and Wittmann and his armored car crew felt that because he and his fellow comrades had engaged the enemy with text book precision further actions of this type would be just as successful in the future.

The next day the Leibstandarte Adolf Hitler found itself moving in the direction of Wieuroazov, about seven or eight miles away. This town was to be the next objective for the men of the Waffen-SS units and everyone was in high spirits. The men of Wittmann's reconnaissance company were once again at the lead of the attack. One of the units headed along a dirt track leading out of the eastern edge of the town. A central column advanced along the river and the third went via Opatov, fighting through dense birch forests to sever the road west of the town. The local countryside was ideal for defense, and the Polish Army had taken every advantage in this regard. Every clump of trees hid a determined sniper, every bush concealed an infantryman or machine gun nest. The extended lines of the Leibstandarte Adolf Hitler vehicles were frequently held up as determined infantry attacks were staged at any and all points of Polish Army resistance. Because of these delays, it was not until evening that the town of Wieuroazov was attacked and overcome and secured for the night. The Leibstandarte Adolf Hitler had accomplished all of its allotted tasks, all of the objectives had been taken; 10th, 17th, and 25th Polish Infantry Divisions had been identified by the Leibstandarte Adolf Hitler and prisoners were taken from these units and also from Wielpolska and Wolwyskc Cavalry brigades.

As the Waffen-SS units moved forward of the main body of the German military forces to take up the allotted role of flank guard, reconnaissance units fanned out to seek out and locate the fleeing enemy. Wittmann's reconnaissance company were at their daily tasks of radioing back pertinent information about the enemy and also reported that one of their spahwagens (scout cars) had run over a land-mine. The driver of the vehicle was killed while the rest of the crew were only shaken up a little. This action prompted the vehicle commanders to slow the pace down as their attention was now directed to the immediate terrain in front of their armored mounts. All concerned searched for tell-tale signs pertaining to these dangerous and deadly devices but none were detected and the mission continued. It was assumed that the single land-mine that was detonated was just a single nasty welcoming card left by the retreating Polish Army. As night soon fell, reorganization took place at the battalion and regimental levels, but each company nevertheless spent the night in patrolling aggressively and stemmed off minor cavalry attacks along their newly secured lines.

Dawn broke on the morning of September 2nd with the men and vehicles of the Leibstandarte Adolf Hitler moving towards the Warta river. The unusually dry weather had lowered the levels of the rivers and the Prosna river proved to be no obstacle. The main body of the Eighth Army streamed across it heading for the next objective; the Warta river, which was the primary defensive line, and was strongly fortified with major gun emplacements and machine-guns placed in pill-boxes with overlapping fire through out. As Wittmann's reconnaissance company approached this line they were able to hold onto their positions until the main body of the Leibstandarte Adolf Hitler could reach them. They scanned the area for any signs of enemy activity but were certain that any and all Polish troops were well hidden in the fortifications until needed for further actions.

The overall German strategic plan was yielding rewarding results; the Tenth Army had begun to break through north of Chestakova and on September 3rd units from two Panzer divisions exploiting a gap between the Lodz and Cracow armies, assaulted across the Pilica river and headed north-eastward towards Warsaw. The enormous jaws of the German pincers were now beginning to close around the armies west of the Polish capital. The Polish High Command then ordered a withdrawal to a deep defensive line based on Szczercov-Lenkava. This compression of the Polish western army group was, unknown to either combatant (the beginning of the end if you like) for the Poles had been drawn into a long and somewhat narrow pocket within which they were eventually to be contained, isolated and then totally destroyed by the German military forces. However, the Germans were not to achieve this goal for another fourteen days and during those two long and arduous weeks there were to be periods of acute crisis for them at all levels of command from battalion up to that of army group.

During September 4th, the first crisis came to light when Army Group South suddenly realized that between the Warta and the Bzura rivers there was a mass of seven Polish Army divisions withdrawing in front of Army Group North. Once it had become apparent of this impending threat to its flank, Army Group South changed its front to face the force which was thrusting south-eastward. A frontal attack upon Lodz was ordered for the Eighth Army which was to continue the pressure upon its northern flank while the center and right flanks would destroy the Poles as they approached Lodz.

During this time-frame, Wittmann and his comrades were now engaged in fighting their way towards a small market town called Pabianice which was a road and railway junction at the river Ner and a strongpoint in the Polish secondary defense line. The town was occupied by a heavy garrison who artillery strength had been increased by a heavy anti-tank gun section whose morale level was very high. For three long days the men of the Leibstandarte Adolf Hitler fought the Poles with every available weapon and armored fighting vehicle; they fought their way forward through the outer defense lines guarding the Lodz region but suffered heavy causalities as a direct result. All immediate Waffen-SS forces were deployed but could only advance at a very slow pace as the Poles had been reinforced by the 2nd Kaniov Rifle Regiment as well as by a number of ad hoc units. The Waffen-SS advance was contested not only by trained military personnel, but also by trained woodsmen who combined the huntsman's skills of marksmanship with knowledge of their homeland terrain. Expertly camouflaged and often hidden in the least likely hiding places, snipers waited, and selected their targets, and fired when least expected. Vehicle commanders were instructed not to stand erect in their machines so as to provide targets for the enemy. Motor-cycles and staff cars travelling without escort were favorite targets for snipers. To prevent such tactics being utilized against their forces Waffen-SS defensive tactics against these Polish sharp-shooters was to saturate suspected trees and bushes with a rain of rifle grenades and sustained automatic fire. Many men of the Waffen-SS were killed or maimed for life because of snipers, and this type of ambush was feared more than any type of combat fighting during the Polish campaign.

Under the hot and cloudless skies of the Polish summer the determined resistance put up by the Poles turned the battle into a slogging match where every field or small patch of woods was a turning point for the Waffen-SS troopers. The Germans were fighting in a section of Poland which was highly cultivated with vast areas of sunflowers and maize were to be found. Small groups of men were swallowed up in these areas where small unit actions often fought to the last man. In carefully concealed places the Poles would hold their fire until Waffen-SS men were at point blank range. A sudden burst of automatic fire, a hand grenade being thrown, and then the Poles would vanish like ghosts until the Germans adopted the same tactic of being patient and letting the enemy approach their hidden positions and beating them at their own game. It was also found by the Waffen-SS troopers that if they wore their camouflaged jackets and helmet covers, these items blended perfectly well with the green shade beneath the sunflowers in which they themselves were travelling through. Armored fighting vehicles were usually on the side lines when it came to stalking the Poles in this type of tactical situation. An armored vehicle could be easily knocked out if travelling through sunflower or maize fields and would follow up as the infantrymen cleared paths through these suspected and dangerous areas.

If not being used in the reconnaissance role, spähwagens usually took flank cover and would lay down suppressive fire with their 2cm main gun and MG-34s if they spotted any movement or suspected enemy soldiers as they were flushed out from their hiding places. This was very nerve racking and hard work for the infantry and many brave soldiers were killed in the line of duty on both opposing sides. The momentum of battle slowed down to a snails pace as if the German forces moved too fast they would either run into determined resistance or would be allowed to venture forward only to have their rear guard held up due to enemy fire and effectively separated from the main body of advance. This way, ad hoc pockets of German assault troops would be attacked with no hope of any assistance from follow-up troops. This type of battle was a cat and mouse game and could only be overcome by careful planning and highly motivated assault troops who were especially trained and adapted for this type of deadly encounter.

Late on the evening of September 6th, Wittmann and his crew were finally able to take some deserved rest and sleep. Battle orders for the following day made Pabianice the main objective and additional orders were given that Lodz to be sealed off from the south-east along the Ragov-Vola Rakova heights. Wittmann and his spähwagen crew were awaken very early in the morning after which they started checking all of their weapons and equipment for the new day ahead of them. The first assault, against the western edge of the town during the afternoon of the 7th was carried out by the 23rd Panzer Regiment, but faced by heavy and well directed fire the panzers and other vehicles could not make any great progress. The defense tactics that the Poles were utilizing was to fire a volley of two rounds into a group of German armored fighting vehicles where as the Polish guns were indeed able to penetrate the lightly armored Panzer I and Panzer IIs at quite long distances. Even at closer combat ranges the Panzer IIIs and Panzer IVs were being knocked out by the determined Polish double punch. As a direct result of these losses the divisional commander withdrew the remaining panzers and called for assistance from the Waffen-SS infantry who in turn were sent straight into the fire-storm. The 1st and 2nd Infantry companies of the Leibstandarte Adolf Hitler them moved forward across the start-line past the panzers withdrawing under heavy and sustained fire. The intensity of the Waffen-SS peace-time training coupled with battle experience had now made the men of the Leibstandarte Adolf Hitler very proficient indeed in set-piece assaults and even before they had crossed the start-line the squads under their commanders had blended into determined tactical formations. Maximum artillery support was provided for the assault on Pabianice and artillery officers were sent up with the leading assault teams so that observed fire could be brought down on the enemy immediately upon selected targets. The mortar rounds started to fall on enemy positions and the infantry attack began to roll forward. The forward pace of the Waffen-SS advance carried it through the first line of the Polish resistance towards the center of Pabianice. Every anti-tank gun, automatic weapon and field guns were used to hold the line against the advancing Germans even a Polish counter-attack was staged in the middle of the street which was smashed by the leading elements of the Leibstandarte Adolf Hitler. Even though the Leibstandarte Adolf Hitler had made successful gains the units that had been ordered to keep up with them had not made equally successful advances, with the result being that the Waffen-SS point group formed a salient which came under fire from all sides. The Leibstandarte Adolf Hitler found that it had moved into a very dangerous situation and thus called for drastic counter measures to contain the enemy. In order to hold this salient the Leibstandarte Adolf Hitler had to position small sections of men, but together with the number of casualties and a desperate situation at hand, the Waffen-SS attack started to run out of steam. The Polish Army had no such shortage of men; as units that were withdrawing from the west were ordered immediately into this battle. The western wall of the salient began to crumble under the pressure of the Poles and the Waffen-SS could not consolidate their slender hold on the town. The Polish infantry and cavalry units came into the battle in every type of assault formation; which in turn forced the Leibstandarte Adolf Hitler on to the defensive and then began to force it back once again, resulting in street fighting and house to house fighting and finally hand to hand combat until they were once again at the edge of the town. Polish troops that had been passed by would suddenly spring out of cellars and door-ways and were often close enough to inflict serious damage to the German troops sweeping through the streets by throwing hand grenades, etc. Even HQ personnel that had move up and under the impression that the area in which they were in was secure were often under fire from hidden snipers. The fighting started to build up and a Polish attack under great determination was led forward with heavy losses being inflicted but brought the Poles up to and then onto the field that the Leibstandarte Adolf Hitler had selected for their headquarters. As this situation became even more serious, the headquarters defense platoon was called into the battle and even cooks and truck drivers were put straight into the line. The Leibstandarte Adolf Hitler defense stood firm, but at times, it seemed that the Polish onslaught threatened to over run the Regimental Command Group and to cut the life-line between HQ and the troops at the front lines. Every man stayed at his position and. eventually the Poles were driven back.

Wittmann and his reconnaissance company had been travelling around the edge of the town and they had been trying to break any and all resistance put up by the Polish troops. They were very careful not to come in direct fire with any anti-tank guns or encounter any anti-tank mines. As the hours past the intensity of the battle started to died down and both sides broke off the attack in order to carry out urgent tasks of regrouping, reinforcements, and badly needed maintenance for their vehicles, etc. The Waffen-SS took little time in reorganizing their units and were ready to resume battle on a moments notice. At 14:30 hours, the Pole charged again but the Waffen-SS were ready at their respective posts and started firing as soon as the waves of Polish infantrymen ran forward towards their positions. The Poles charged in one final, despairing effort, yelling and tripping over the bodies of their fallen comrades. The Waffen-SS soldier did not stop firing, their shower of bullets and shells forced many of the Poles to the ground for any and all cover. Some of the Polish infantry time and time again jumped up and ran forward only to be hit again by German fire. Extremely brave individual soldiers continued to advance alone when all around them had been killed or were laying on the ground mortally wounded, they too were soon hit by German fire as they charged forward once more. The heroic assault by the Polish infantry soon faltered and once again the town of Pabianice was in German hands.

The failure of the Polish assault resulted in the collection of prisoners from the Pabianice garrison who came out under the flag of surrender. It began again with numbers of tens, then twenties and then hundreds. As the Polish prisoners were marched past it was quite clear that their will to fight was now totally eradicated. They had fought a battle against superior soldiers who were better trained, better equipped, and lead by a corps of officers who had a clear understanding of modern military tactics now being used for the first time on the modern battlefield. A critical situation that had looked serious for the Leibstandarte Adolf Hitler in the morning had been overcome, where as the advances and accomplishments gained were considerable. Many Waffen-SS units had lost contact with their headquarters and it was not until the following evening that all of the units were accounted for and regrouped that any further advances could be made with any hope of further successes.

Wittmann and his reconnaissance company were ordered to hold their positions until the rest of the units could be consolidated. They had with them two other spahwagens and started to dig in and camouflage their vehicles. It had been an eventful day, but many men on both sides were killed, wounded, missing, or taken prisoner, and many could only pray that they would survive the next battle.

As Army Group South applied additional pressure on the Poles they were compelled to mount another withdrawal which resulted in a gap at Petrov and through this opening German panzer columns were able to travel down the best roads towards the Polish capital. The race for Warsaw was moving forward but additional motorized infantry support was needed to further the advance. The Leibstandarte Adolf Hitler was ordered to advance and was detached from the Eighth Army and posted to Tenth Army's 4th Panzer Division, whose advanced units had reached Ochota, a suburb of Warsaw, at 17:15 hours on September 8th.

Wittmann and his reconnaissance company were in the lead during this advance but little if any opposition was encountered but every safe-guard was up held in order to prevent any further deaths or injury to the men involved. There was great excitement in the air as the capture of the capital of Poland would mean the end of hostilities and the capture of the country.

Orders were once again issued on September 9th and a battle group made up of the Leibstandarte Adolf Hitler, the 33rd Infantry Regiment, and auxiliary units were given the task of securing the Grodish Masczovoc road, south-east of Warsaw, so as to prevent the Polish Army escaping from the pocket in which they were now trapped. Breakout attempts performed by General Knoll's 14th, 17th, and 25th Polish Divisions protected by two cavalry brigades had advanced and attacked towards Lodz but was beaten back by fierce German artillery fire with additional automatic and accurate mortar fire; as a result, this movement was stopped in its tracks and the Poles forced to withdraw to these selected killing grounds. New orders were then given to the 1st Battalion of the Leibstandarte Adolf Hitler to advance towards Oltarzev, a town on the Warsaw road, while two other battalions took up defensive positions to capture and secure Blonie, east of 1st Battalion and also on the road to the Polish capital. As soon as the 1st Battalion arrived and was in position they came under attack immediately from the Poles trying to keep the road open, which was the life-line of the Pomorze Army. Severe losses were incurred by the Poles but they hurled themselves at the Waffen-SS defensive positions regardless. The Waffen-SS positions had only light weapons to defend themselves and at times it seemed that the charging Poles would overrun their positions. It was a very dangerous situation for the 1st Battalion but at the last possible moment a contingent of their artillery arrived on the scene to save the day and were soon engaged with the enemy soldiers and halted their determined attacks. The ensuing fire-storm was murderous; every Polish infantryman was forced to the ground and dared not to even raise his head as the German fire did not stop for even one second. When the artillery guns did stop for a short period of time a number of Polish truck drivers who had been halted in long columns tried to move forward but were immediately blown completely off the roads. Their columns of vehicles were inextricably entangled and soon it was impossible to maneuver anything in any direction. During the early evening troops of horse artillery stormed out of the smoke and mist and advanced into point-blank fire of the Wehrmacht and Waffen-SS troops. They too were cut down by artillery and automatic fire and as a result made matters even worse. The Germans continued to fire into the Polish troops all through the night and when morning broke it was found that not only Polish troops, but civilians, refugees, and other people who had been withdrawing under the protection of the Polish Army had fallen victim to the German artillery fire as well. Heaped into the ditches and in the clearings along side the road were hundreds of dead and dying Polish soldiers, civilians and military horse and cattle that sickened even the battle-hardened Waffen-SS assault troops. Never in their experience at war had they seen such devastation. It was a sight that many would never forget as long as they lived. As the Waffen-SS reorganized for the next day's fighting the exhausted 1st Battalion was relieved but the 2nd and 3rd Battalions were still engaged in the difficult fighting in and around the vital road and rail junction of Blonie.

During the next two days the encircled Polish armies attacked towards Lodz but they could not advance any further; they decided to change their direction of attack and with armored cars and light tanks attacked particularly heavily against the battle group comprising the Leibstandarte Adolf Hitler, the 2nd Battalion of 33rd Regiment and the 2nd Battalion of the 4th Panzer Artillery Regiment. By this time the German Army Group had contained the Polish forces in its sector, and it was decided that it was time to advance and destroy these forces once and for all. The 4th Panzer Division was ordered to advance and close up the Bzura river pushing 28th and 30th Polish Divisions towards Modlin. By this time there was a solid mass of German panzers between the Polish forces on the Bzura and in the Warsaw area; it was a bleak situation for the Polish armies as they were now isolated with little if any help on the way to save them form this predicament. Even though it seemed clear that the resistance of the Polish forces was now drained, courage and morale remained high in other units. At Glovko the Wielpolska cavalry, reduced to a mere fraction of its former self by ten days of heavy fighting, continued to attack the German forces with great determination until it too was almost completely decimated with their 30th Division still fighting bravely in the nearby Radziwill forest. During the evening of September 12th another attempt by the Poles to breakout was planned by the 4th and 16th Infantry Divisions but was only driven back with severe losses. The Germans had established and maintained an extremely strong ring around the Poles and there was no escape.

The next day, the Leibstandarte Adolf Hitler being supported by its armored fighting vehicles attacked the high ground west of Blonie. Two columns were formed by the Panzer Regiment who were supported by a complete and fully equipped battalion of Waffen-SS. The attack began with lighting attacks with Kaputy being stormed as the panzers advance continued at full speed with strict orders that there was to be absolutely no stoppages anywhere along the line of assault. Prior to nightfall the planned objective had been taken with the line between Lesno and Bislutki consolidated and the assault troops dug in for the night. During the following days of fighting bitter opposition was met by both sides and massive losses were incurred. The battle for Sochaczev proved to be particularity fierce and after the battle the last commander was a mere private; all of the officers and NCO's had been killed or seriously wounded.

During September 16th the 35th Panzer Regiment, the 12th Rifle Regiment and the Leibstandarte Adolf Hitler made a very aggressive truck borne assault across the Bzura and reduced the weaken Polish Army divisions even further. The German pioneers worked frantically trying to construct a bridge for the advancing panzers but there was little time for the forward most troops to be held up. The panzer commanders ordered their vehicles headlong down the steep western bank into the water and began to wade across the wide and shallow river at top speed in order to not to become bogged down if they should encounter sandy or muddy areas. As soon as the panzers reached the far bank they took up immediate defensive positions but were soon under highly accurate Polish artillery fire. Every patch of undergrowth was a defensive position; anti-tank guns, mortar pits, and machine gun nests were sighted along the eastern part of the river manned by the Poles. The attack started to lose some of its steam and the Germans decided to secure their defensive positions for the time being.

With the Germans replanning their next assault the weather suddenly changed for the worse; after two weeks of fine and dry weather and rapid advance the rain poured down on the battlefield and immobilized the German panzer units resulting in that all exits from Bzura were completely clogged with every type of German vehicle one could imagine! Crossing the Bzura river with out bridging equipment proved to have been a mistake as the river was now running over its banks with few if any German armored fighting vehicles being able to cross safely. The attack was now postponed until 11:00 hours by which time additional armored fighting vehicles had been brought up and concentrated for the advance. When the attack finally went in, it was initially a single armored fist striking at the Polish positions, but at Bijsmpol the column was ordered to divide and become a standard pincer movement. The northern group reached and secured the Mlodzieszyn-Russki road and brought the fleeing Polish troops under constant artillery bombardment. The southern units were not so lucky and ran into concealed anti-tank guns, skillfully camouflaged and firing into their midst at point-blank range. The commanding general (Kurzeka) was at this time using his artillery to hammer a corridor through to Warsaw. Polish and German units were fighting head on battles with the outnumbered German troops having a difficult time in holding back the determined Polish troops. The Polish artillery barrage continued to pound the German troops and waves upon waves of the Polish infantry came in behind this barrage forcing the Leibstandarte Adolf Hitler units back a substantial distance. Finally a withdrawal was ordered and the assault troops returned in the drizzle of the late afternoon until the entire 1st Panzer Battalion and the Waffen-SS were back at their divisional laeger. The 2nd Panzer Battalion found that it could not disengage itself from the enemy and spent the entire night fighting off heavy and continuous attacks by the Polish infantry.

On September 17th the Waffen-SS renewed the attack against the Polish troops but through out the next two days little if any opposition was put up by the Polish Army. On the night of the 18th reports were coming in that across the Bzura river part of the 36th Panzer Regiment and 1st SS Battalion were in serious danger of being over run and their rescue was given top priority. This unit had also intercepted a Polish breakout and the 4th Panzer Division, taken in flank, was fighting this battle without any central command with ammunition and gasoline running short of supply . The two remaining battalions of the Leibstandarte Adolf Hitler and the 35th Panzer Regiment mounted a rescue mission on September 19th and everywhere opposition was encountered it was systematically destroyed with such fine precision that within an hour of the battle the Waffen-SS troops and Panzer men had smashed through the Polish ring and successfully linked up with each other. This maneuver marked the end and a beginning; the end was directed at the Polish troops as they now had little manpower, equipment, and most of all their morale was completely broken; it was very clear that these isolated attacks carried out by brave Polish troops were the last throes of a dying army on the field of battle. The beginning pertained to a general advance along the Vistula river towards Vysgorod and the total destruction of the Polish pocket. With its Waffen-SS component, the 2nd Panzer Battalion halted at Sladov to form a front facing east.

At this point in time the Polish army was disintegrating under the relentless artillery and German Luftwaffe bombardment and the final battles in the pocket were fought for possession of the vital Vistula road connecting Modlin with the Polish capital. As the advance of the Leibstandarte Adolf Hitler moved forward the entire scene of death and destruction could not be believed as the bloated bodies of men and animals littered the countryside blackening under the hot summer sun. Burnt out vehicles and smashed carts, and wounded men and horses were, another frightful aftermath of a long and bloody battle. All of the wounded animals were given the mercy shot that finally put them out of their misery, while the wounded soldiers were given medical treatment. No matter where one looked, the scene was the same, a broken army and its equipment shattered, broken, and burning on the charred ground.

Up to this date, the most successful and destructive encirclement in military history had been finalized with the Polish Army being struck down with no chance of ever being able to fight another day. As the first and second phase of the German High Command plan was now complete, the third phase could now be implemented with the capture of the Polish capital. The majority of German troops that had fought for the Bzura river were now withdrawn to regroup and reorganize and this battle now marked the end of the Polish campaign for them. The Leibstandarte Adolf Hitler were not so lucky and were ordered to advance towards Modlin which was a fortress area guarding the approach to Warsaw to the immediate north. The remaining Polish garrison withdrew into Forts I, II, and III and massed German artillery began a systematic bombardment of these fortifications and other isolated areas which were aided by Stuka (Junkers Ju 87) dive bombers of the 4th Air Fleet. The Poles put up a good fight, but in the end, they could not overcome the determined German advance.

Adolf Hitler visited the detachment of the Leibstandarte Adolf Hitler on September 25 and inspected No. 13 Company in encampment near Guzov. With the Polish campaign now successfully completed Hitler's Guard was not ordered to the west as anticipated, but ordered to Prague, Czechoslovakia. Upon its arrival in this city the Leibstandarte Adolf Hitler was welcomed with a rapturous reception due to its well founded combat notoriety, and then given a well deserved leave. As with all units during war-time this rest and leave period soon slipped by with the Waffen-SS men now retrained and refitted and ready for the next battles to come.

Chapter V

THE INVASION OF FRANCE

May 10, 1940 – June 24, 1940

During the bitterly cold winter of 1939-40 the Leibstandarte Adolf Hitler trained continuously for the forthcoming battles that awaited them in the west. While visiting the troops of this elite unit during December Hitler advised Sepp Dietrich that his men would soon be fighting decisive battles in regions on which their father's blood had been spilled, but did not provide any accurate or pertinent information as to these locations. As training intensified, rapid seizure of strategic bridges was stressed very highly and this not only helped to give the men of the Leibstandarte a new training goal to achieve, but it also provided an indication that their unit would be leading the assault once again. Finally, in February operational orders were handed down to Sepp Dietrich with his Leibstandarte Adolf Hitler being attached to the Eighteenth Army. The intended role of the Eighteenth Army as a contingent of von Bock's Army Group B was to secure and protect the northern flank of the German Army during the forthcoming Western campaign. The major objective of the 227th Infantry Division under whose command the Leibstandarte was now placed was to storm forward through the Dutch frontier and to capture intact, the river and its highly vital wooden and stone bridges on the axis of the advance to the Ijssel river area.

Michael Wittmann was still acting as a commander of a Sd.Kfz.222 Spähwagen. He and his crew had survived the horrors of the Polish campaign and felt very lucky to be still alive. After their updated assault training they felt that they understood what was expected of them and were anxious to put their newly learned tactics to work. During May 9th, the code-word "DANZIG" was transmitted to all the awaiting units of the German Wehrmacht and Waffen-SS units. This signal from the German High Command was to set in motion the advance to the English Channel with all out aggressive actions being inflicted as the German steam-roller moved forward towards its objectives. Soon after midnight, the battalions of the Leibstandarte Adolf Hitler moved out of their Rhineland billets and quickly advanced towards the Dutch border with the final details being completed at precisely 05:30 hours, on May 10th. As dawn broke on this day, a small detachment of Waffen-SS assault troops were able to capture an important bridge at De Poppe, with the result being that this opened an avenue of advance for the awaiting columns to enter Holland. As soon as the word came through the lines of communications, commanders tried to move any and all units through this small opening as time was of the essence and did not want their columns held up for any reasons and especially so if spotted by air by enemy aircraft. The Royal Dutch Army was the main concerned for the Leibstandarte Adolf Hitler at this time but as these military forces had been at peace for so long its military prowess, training and antiquated equipment were of such low quality, they did not have a ghost of a chance against the highly trained and motivated German fighting force. The Dutch Army had only four corps, each of two divisions, forming the bulk of the available forces at hand. Added to these forces was a light division mounted on bicycles and motor-cycles, a number of inexperienced infantry brigades, frontier battalions, a regiment of Hussars and fourteen regiments of Army artillery units. The main reason for the weakness in the Dutch artillery was that it had in its inventory highly outdated equipment which were no match for the highly sophisticated German counterparts. This non-parity was particularly acute involving their anti-tank and anti-aircraft arms which again were no match against the invading German Wehrmacht and Waffen-SS units. The Royal Dutch Army had a dual problem at the time of the German invasion as not only being under gunned and under armed they also had the problem of defending a long frontier which was an almost indefensible area of terrain spread out before their inadequate military forces. The resulting tactics was to delay the enemy line of advance as much as possible, firstly along the frontier; then along the Ijssel-Maas river line and then to hold out along the so-called Valley line, extending from the Zuider Zee southward to the Maas. During the time-frame of the German attack the main defensive positions were manned by the 2nd, 4th, 7th, and 8th Divisions. Even though this part of the country was expected to fall to any invading enemy, the Dutch Army was highly surprised at the speed in which the German military machine moved into and then across its country.

As the Leibstandarte Adolf Hitler was forming the northern flank of the 227th Infantry Division, Wittmann and his reconnaissance company were making swift advances towards the De Poppe bridge on the well-maintained roads while running into almost no opposition from any of the five frontier battalions defending the area. The majority of the road blocks were totally unmanned and if any such obstacles were confronted or demolitions set off in front of their advance, they were so ineffective that they were only considered as no more than nuisance value. To Wittmann and his men, the advance seemed to be a push over for them but he did not take any chances or become lackadaisical in his assigned duties. The first serious set-back came when his company came to the canal bridge at Bornbroek which had been blown up. This obstacle was not to stop the Waffen-SS as they utilized barn doors as improvised rafts and crossed the waterway while under heavy and accurate fire and successfully established a bridgehead. As soon as the first motor-cycles were ferried across, patrols were immediately sent out to prevent any further destruction of other important bridges on the line of advance. While the Waffen-SS pioneers were trying to construct a light bridge for the assault units to charge over, the men of the anti-tank gun company who were very impatient to cross decided to dismantle their weapons and use human muscle power as a source of power to transport their equipment across the canal. Wittmann and his spähwagen had to wait for the pioneer bridges to be constructed as they did not dare to cross for fear of bogging down their vehicle was too great and did not want to be left behind. Finally, after a few tense hours the bridge was erected and the advance began to pick up its momentum once again and shortly before midday the advance guard entered and captured the town of Zwolle where the streets were full of civilians and unprepared Dutch soldiers which significantly illustrated to the Waffen-SS men that the German arrival was totally unexpected! The Leibstandarte Adolf Hitler had travelled fifty miles in six hours and it was hardly believed that Zwolle had surrender without a fight. The men of the Leibstandarte Adolf Hitler were in very high spirits as they now all felt that nothing could stop the German planned invasion.

After the surrender of Zwolle was accepted the Leibstandarte Adolf Hitler was re-deployed to the south to join up with the rest of the Division and during this advance Wittmann's reconnaissance company surprised and captured a Dutch army unit while having their lunch. It was a battle that never took place! Wittmann's spähwagen and two others pulled right up into the enemy positions and without a shot being fired the Dutch unit commander came forward with a white surrender flag. The Dutch army was outclassed by the German military forces and Wittmann could only think at the time that if all future battles were as easy as this, the war in the west would soon be over with little blood shed on both sides.

Early on the morning of May 11th, orders were given to the 227th Infantry Division and was then concentrated into three strike columns. The 1st and 2nd battalions for the Leibstandarte Adolf Hitler forming the right flank. The center position was given to the 3rd Waffen-SS Battalion supported by a battalion from the 366th Regiment, while the remainder of the 366th and 402nd Infantry Regiment took charge of the southern sector. The total destruction of the two bridges across the Ijssek delayed the initial assault but the 3rd Battalion was able to force a crossing of the river at Zutphen and captured Hoven on the north-south main railway and by 14:00 hours had captured all of the day's planned objectives. During this rapid advance many outstanding exploits were being carried out with one in particular which was led by SS-Obersturmführer Kraas who was the leader in a daring deep penetration across the Ijssek and for more than forty-five miles into enemy territory where he captured more than a hundred Dutch soldiers who give up with little if any opposition. As a result of this singular act, he was awarded the Iron Cross, First Class; the first Waffen-SS officer to obtain this decoration during the Dutch campaign.

After the capture of Hoven, the Leibstandarte Adolf Hitler was posted from the 227th to the 9th Panzer Division and advanced via Kleve and Hertgenbusch to come into line as a follow up unit to that division's northern column. Once again, Wittmann and his reconnaissance company were at the front of the fighting and brushed aside any and all Dutch opposition as the Waffen-SS columns sped up with the Panzers during the afternoon and early evening of May 13th. At 04:00 hours the next morning the Leibstandarte Adolf Hitler supported 9th Panzer Division's advance towards the three-quarter mile long Maas bridge at Moerdijk, with the orders to relieve the Fallschirmjäger (para-troopers) unit who had successfully captured this bridge from the Dutch defenders. They were to enter Rotterdam from the south-east and to seize, by a Coup de Main, the Dutch government in the Hague. The advance was making strong progress, but it came under intermittent Dutch artillery fire which knocked out a few vehicles, but was not concentrated enough to stop the German onslaught. The advance was made along the south bank of the Maas, and across the front of the Dutch Light and 5th Infantry Divisions who were holding onto their defensive positions from Rotterdam to Rossum. The Waffen-SS again, applied modern assault tactics which surrounded, cut off, and then mopped up the enemy with lighting speed.

After bitter fighting and having delayed the advance of the Eighteenth Army, the Dutch armies lay behind the main defense line by May 14th. They were now completely cut off from their allies and had no expectations of any military assistance from either France or Great Britain. It seemed that the Dutch army as a fighting unit had been eradicated but the Dutch resistance continued for many more days which was obstructing the German High Command's plan and an ultimatum was issued that unless this opposition cease immediately, Rotterdam and Utrecht would be totally destroyed by air and artillery bombardments. After this statement was received by the Dutch they accepted it and the orders for the artillery bombardments were canceled. As a direct result of a tragic misunder-standing, the Luftwaffe did in fact bomb and partial destroyed Rotterdam.

During this bombing raid Wittmann and his reconnaissance company were on the outskirts of the city and were witness to this needless act of destruction. The young spähwagen commander could not understand why such a mistake could have been made and could only view this action as a necessity of war. After the bombing had ended his company moved into the blazing city to effect a link-up with a Fallschirmjäger unit which had landed during the first day's opera-tions and subsequently had been cut off. As they moved forward the area showed the signs of severe fighting with crashed and burnt-out aircraft, many of them Junkers Ju 52s which were scattered across the fields and along the highways. Many of the pilots were dead still in their seats with equipment strewn around everywhere one looked and was a very sad sight indeed. In a number of sectors the surrender order had not been received by the Dutch army and resistance was still very strong and had to be subdued by the leading elements of the Waffen-SS. During this confusing period an incident occured involving the German Fallschirmjäger General Student, who was arranging with the local Dutch commander the surrender terms and the disarming of his forces in the area when the advancing guard of the Leibstandarte Adolf Hitler roared up in its drive northward to the Hague. As the men of the Waffen-SS entered the area all they saw was hundreds of armed enemy soldiers whom they immediately opened fire upon having no indication that they had recently surrendered to the German forces. A stray bullet struck General Student who fell bleeding from a serious head wound and this unfortunate accident marred the successful operations which the Leibstandarte Adolf Hitler had carried out with little casualties. General Student was rushed to the nearest hospital and latter recovered from this wound.

By this time the campaign in the Netherlands was nearly over with the majority of units now regrouping and reorganizing with some rest and relaxation. The Germans overall strategy, although delayed, was not completely out of register and the bulk of the Eighteenth Army, leaving only a mopping-up force, could now be re-deployed south to help support the break-through operations now set into motion in northern France. The German High Command's strategy had secured the right flank which was the first intention regarding the west and had achieved total victory for its forces. The second phase in the overall plan was to separate the British and French armies, and then introduce the third phase of the plan which was the individual destruction of those enemy forces as soon as possible.

On May 24, Wittmann and his men found themselves now under the command of the 1st Panzer Division, part of Kleist's Group, who began to arrive into their selected positions on the line at the Aa canal, which was located along the southern and eastern side of the evacuation perimeter at Dunkirk which British and French forces had been compressed into after heavy and bitter rearguard fighting. The men of the Leibstandarte Adolf Hitler could now sense the final defeat of the Allied forces in the west and carried forth the battle so as not to allow them any chance of being able to recover. Wittmann and his reconnaissance company had no rest for days upon end and the only word that had any meaning to the German High Command was "Advance"! Men and machines were at the breaking point, but the sweet smell of success did not elude even one of the German soldiers present, it was time for yet another lighting blow from the German forces and they would not take the chance of forfeiting this prize well within their grasp.

During the evening of the 24th, the 1st Panzer Division had a long and tiring night march resulting in a number of its vehicles breaking down and being pulled or pushed off the road in order to clear the way for the follow-up machines. The 3rd Battalion was then ordered to capture the 140 foot Wattenberg, a high hill which lay to the east of the Aa canal and also dominated the otherwise flat Dutch country-side. Minutes before the attack was planned to start, an unexpected order from Hitler's FHQ forbid any such movement to transpire across the canal works toward Dunkirk. In direct and open defiance of these orders, Sepp Dietrich sent his men of the Leibstandarte Adolf Hitler into battle. Under the protection of a very heavy artillery barrage No. 10 Company stormed across this waterway and fought its way with great tenacity and entered into the town of Watten. Numerous Allied counter-attacks at times threatened to drive the Waffen-SS out of the town but the mass of the 3rd Battalion was too great and swept through the point company and then smashed the Anglo-French defenses, capturing the Wattenberg and consolidated their positions and waited for further orders.

General Heinz Guderian, then ordered an attack towards the Wormhoudt-Berques road and ordered the Leibstandarte Adolf Hitler forward with all speed and daring. The Leibstandarte Adolf Hitler, now under the command of 20th (motorized) Infantry Division, had the 76th Infantry Regiment on its right flank and the now famous 'Grossdeutschland' Regiment on its left flank. On the 27th a spoiling attack was launched by the Allied infantry from a copse east of the Wattenberg, but was only carried out by Bren gun carriers and anti-tank guns of the British 144th Brigade to try and seal off the German break-out originating from Watten.

The Leibstandarte Adolf Hitler's 1st battalion finally got its attack under way by 08:20 hours but met fierce opposition from the Allies at Bollezelle. During this attack the Waffen-SS units were under constant fire from their rear, and left flank; a sector which the 'Grossdeutschland' Regiment should have already secured by this time which cost the Leibstandarte Adolf Hitler dearly. As the assault moved forward it was found that the British resistance was now weakening and sustained pressure was maintained until the objective had been taken. The following day resulted in combined panzer and infantry forces made up of the gallant Leibstandarte Adolf Hitler, 2nd Panzer Brigade, and 11th Rifle Brigade who in turn attacked Wormhoudt. The leading units of the Waffen-SS made a determined assault through a strong defensive barrage laid down by accurate British artillery and pressed home the attack with great vigor, which was still very apparent even though the men were dead on their feet from all of the earlier fighting.

While on a journey to coordinate further attacks by his battalion near the town of Esquelberg, Sepp Dietrich was separated from his men and fired upon while riding in his open staff car.

After his automobile was struck by this well aimed rifle and automatic fire and then set alight by men of the 5th Battalion the Gloucestershire Regiment, belonging to the 48th Division, Dietrich and his adjutant were forced to hide in a muddy ditch and await their rescue by friendly forces. An attack failed by the Nos. 2 and 15 companies to reach the Waffen-SS commander, and a second attack also failed using armored fighting vehicles of the Panzer Brigade's No. 6 company. At first the German troops thought that the British opposition was being put up by first class elite troops, but it was later learned that the Allied troops who were holding the Waffen-SS at bay were only Territorial soldiers. Again and again the Waffen-SS went in to recover their commander, but with repetitive elan the British Tommies forced back Dietrich's battle-hardened men with heavy and severe losses.

Finally, the Leibstandarte Adolf Hitler's 3rd Battalion had fought its way into the southwestern corner of Wormhoudt and by 15:30 hours attacked the British which eventually relieved the pressure in and around the area where Dietrich and his adjutant were still hiding from enemy fire. SS-Oberscharführer Oberschelp's patrol, belonging to the 1st Battalion finally stormed forward under heavy fire and made contact with Dietrich and safely escorted them out of danger. Dietrich and his aide were very dirty and exhausted from this dangerous ordeal,but very happy that this incidence was now behind them. Dietrich would never forget this episode and was very grateful to his men from saving him and his aide from certain death. It was learned later that many of his other units offered to form a massive battle-group to rescue their commander what ever the cost. Plans were being drawn up when news arrived that Dietrich was safe and being returned to his GHQ in order to resume his daily duties as the overall Waffen-SS commander. When he returned to his GHQ a welcoming party was awaiting him and three cheers were heard. It had been a very interesting and dangerous day for Sepp Dietrich, and planned in the future to have an armed guard with him when travelling at the front.

As the day worn on the 2nd Battalion of the Leibstandarte Adolf Hitler moved through the positions of the 3rd Battalion and by 17:00 hours had fought it way through until it had reached the town square of Wormhoudt. Bitter house to house fighting was involved during this advance and heavy losses were incurred by both sides. During this attack, three assaults were made using only rifles and bayonets. There were many sudden and violent attacks, counter-attacks, and at one point allegedly, an attack was beaten off with panzers where by prisoners and booty was taken by the leading elements of the Leibstandarte Adolf Hitler.

At 23:45 a renewed attack was launched with the intention of advancing and securing positions along the Oost Cappel-Rexpoude road. Early the next day the Leibstandarte Adolf Hitler had advanced to this objective only to find that the determined British with whom they had been battling were reduced to a rear-guard delaying force and had allowed the majority of their forces to escape to the beaches of Dunkirk. Hitler's order forbidding any movements towards Dunkirk forced the Wehrmacht and Waffen-SS units to halt in their tracks and await further orders. The Leibstandarte Adolf Hitler was then posted to the 3rd Panzer Division which was regrouping together with three other divisions, which included a combat group whose orders stated that it was to launch a spoiling attack and to thereby frustrate an anticipated Allied offensive which was expected at any time. The 3rd Panzer Division launched this very successful operation on June 8th but by this date it was obvious that the Western Allies were in no position to stop the German steam-roller. The evacuation of the British and other Allies at Dunkirk was well under way and the only opposition that the Wehrmacht and Waffen-SS units encountered was in small feint attacks given by the French army which at that time could only postpone the German victory that was now in full swing.

The next planned activity for the Leibstandarte Adolf Hitler was for it to advance towards Aisne, travelling via Soissons and Villers-Cotterests running into only limited resistance from the French 11th Division. As the 1st Battalion of the Leibstandarte Adolf Hitler moved forward it captured Chateau-Thierry and with the Weygand Line contained, the race to the Marne began. On June 12th the river was crossed near St. Avige and the advance continued, and by that evening the battalion had cut the main railway line. Later that night the Leibstandarte Adolf Hitler was taken out of the line. While settling down in their new billets at Etrepilly fantastic new was received that Paris had capitulated and in a fever of elation the Waffen-SS men rang the bells of the small village church. It seemed that as suddenly as this campaign had begun, it was over in due course. The men of the Leibstandarte Adolf Hitler were very happy that they could enjoy yet another victory after very hard and trying combat. Everyone thought that the battle of France and the low countries was now over; they did not think that they were to be called up for further action. But to their dismay another planned attack was ordered which would throw them against the French once again on June 19th.

During this time-frame the Leibstandarte Adolf Hitler was ordered to make a headlong drive south-westward as part of the 9th Panzer Division, at the Allier river, a tributary of the Oise. The Waffen-SS were able to force a bridgehead near Moulins and directed fast reconnaissance detachments ahead of the main force to capture the bridge across the Sioule at St. Pourcain. As the men of the reconnaissance unit arrived at the bridge French troops were trying to furiously erect a barricade to deny any German forces any chance of a successful crossing. The reconnaissance detachment were too few in number and the only hope of attacking this obstacle was the element of surprise with swift and decisive actions being the order of the hour. SS-Obersturmführer Knittel was ordered by his commander to storm this ad hoc defense and in a direct and sharp cycled assault, covered by accurate fire from a pair of armored cars and mortar teams, breached the barrier, but unfortunately the bridge was blown up in their faces before they had a chance to cross the wooden structure.

SS-Obersturmführer Joachim Peiper of the 3rd Battalion's point company was now involved with an effort south of Pourcain and reported that a crossing had been made and the defenders of this town were taken prisoner and the capture of Gannat at 16:00 hours preceded a drive on Vichy. As the advance continued upon this French spa town an unexpected column of French artillery was encountered, overrun and then captured, which did not allow the Waffen-SS forces to reach Vichy until dusk. Upon reaching Vichy contact was finally established with other German military units who had captured this town, and a welcomed link-up was the order of the day. Ammunition, fuel, and food were very low for these troops and was now being distributed. Had it not been for this advance and capture of Vichy, many men would have surely been killed or taken prisoner by the French pockets of resistance still milling around the area.

On June 20th, the 2nd Battalion carried forward the attack and captured the aerodrome at Clermont-Ferrand, together with a vast amount of aircraft, including fighter aircraft of a Polish squadron, plus eight tanks and thousands of prisoners who had no chance of escape or any hope of further combat.

For the next two days the Leibstandarte Adolf Hitler were taken out of the front lines for a rest and then put back into battle again for an attack involving St. Etienne. During this assault the Waffen-SS troops encountered a troop of First World War French tanks which were representing a strong defence which was totally unexpected. These tanks had armor resistant to 3.7cm Pak weapons and heavier artillery had to be called in to take these old veterans on and immobilize them from any further actions. After a number of concentrated barrages, the French tanks were finally driven off but the town was not captured and not entered until June 24th when it fell into the capable hands of the 1st Battalion. Little did the men of the Leibstandarte Adolf Hitler know, that this battle would be their last for eight months, as they would soon be back to garrison for additional re-equipping and re-training.

The collapse of France and the low countries and the signing of the Armistice ended the campaign in the west for the German Wehrmacht and Waffen-SS units as a whole. The Leibstandarte Adolf Hitler was then ordered to move out of the area which became Vichy France and into the German held sector. A proposed victory parade in Paris was canceled at the last possible moment and the Regiment was transferred to Metz where it was to be in garrison from July 1940 to February 1941.

During this time-frame of reorganization, an armored reconnaissance battalion was established and integrated into the Leibstandarte Adolf Hitler's general make-up. Combined arms exercises by all arms were practiced until the men could perform these maneuvers with split second timing and high standards of efficiency.

Newer types of military equipment and armored fighting vehicles were now being developed for the German Wehrmacht and Waffen-SS units. One of the newest of these vehicles was the Sturmgeschütze III Ausf. A which was just entering service and be offered to the Leibstandarte Adolf Hitler.

Chapter VI

STURMGESCHÜTZ III
TRAINING & COMBAT IN GREECE

July 1, 1940 – April 29, 1941

During the training and re-equipping of the Leibstandarte Adolf Hitler at Metz, Michael Wittmann was introduced for the first time to the new German Sturmgeschütz III (StuG III = assault gun) which was just now coming into service with the German Wehrmacht. Only six of these machines were delivered to the Leibstandarte Adolf Hitler and were of the Ausf. A (Model A.) type. Wittmann was extremely impressed with these new armored fighting vehicles and could see that they offered additional protection for the entire crew than any other fighting machine in their inventory. The experienced Sd.Kfz.222 Spähwagen commander thus made a very determine effort to be trained on one of these StuG IIIs. After careful consideration with his Zug (company) commander, it was decided that Wittmann would indeed be offered the opportunity to train on and select his StuG III crew. It seemed to be a miracle come true for Wittmann to be actually given command of such a new weapons system and immediately started to study and obtain any and all pertinent facts pertaining to the StuG III Ausf. A. The first and most important aspect regarding his new assignment was that he would now be responsible in regards to three crew members under his direct supervision. The next step was to select a qualified crew and this he found very difficult, due to the fact that no one in the Leibstandarte Adolf Hitler had any practical combat experience pertaining to StuG IIIs. Wittmann therefore approached this problem by reviewing each and everyone's records in his company, and based on this information, determined who was in the running for his new StuG III Ausf. A crew.

After careful study, Wittmann selected Rottenführer Klinck as his StuG III gunner. This individual was very enthusiastic about his new assignment and had gunnery experience with the earlier Panzer I and IIs. Rottenführer Koldenhöff was selected as the driver of Wittmann's StuG III Ausf. A and had a great amount of experience in driving other German military vehicles during the invasion of Poland and France. Wittmann desired an experienced driver, as his new fighting vehicle did not have a rotating turret, unlike other German panzers of the period.

The StuG III driver was actually the third crew-member involved with gunnery as it was the driver's responsibility to maneuver the vehicle into a firing position after receiving directions from his commander, where-upon the gunner, made the final lay of the 7.5cm main gun, and then fired at the designated target of opportunity. The last crew-member to be picked by Wittmann was his loader, Rottenführer Petersen, who's job it was to load the 7.5cm main gun of their vehicle and also acted as the vehicle's radio (Funker) operator. Additionally, he also acted as an aircraft spotter (air-watch) when the vehicle was not engaged in combat. An extra duty that he was to perform was to man a MG-34 machine gun while standing upright in his roof hatch and lay down suppressive fire. This weapon was very awkward to fire as the resulting heavy vibrations caused the weapon to slide upon the metal roof of the vehicle. It took a very determined effort to be accurate with the MG-34 machine gun, but proved to be an extremely important safe-guard in repelling tank hunting teams and other types of ground assaults aimed at StuG IIIs and their crews.

The gunner and the driver of the StuG III Ausf. A remained in their respective seats during all movement of the vehicle and had limited vision to the immediate front, and very limited vision to the left of their positions. The loader's position in the StuG III offered him excellent vision if he was standing up-right in his open roof hatch which helped the vehicle commander in locating targets.

The StuG III Ausf. A was a fully enclosed fighting vehicle with a short barrelled 7.5cm L/24 KwK 37 main gun housed in a very low superstructure based on the proven Panzer III chassis. This vehicle did not have a revolving turret as fitted to most other types of armored fighting vehicles and this feature resulted in the three-man gunnery techniques developed by the German military. This resulted in highly trained assault gun teams as crew harmony was not only mandatory, but extremely vital in a tense and deadly combat situation where the entire crew could be injured or killed if one mistake or miscalculation was made while facing and engaging the enemy by any given crew-member.

The driver was positioned at the extreme forward left-hand side compartment of the StuG III Ausf. A and was only able to exit the vehicle after the vehicle commander and gunner had removed themselves through the commander's roof hatch. In an extreme emergency (e.g. fire and exploding ammunition) the driver could however exit from the vehicle through the two maintenance hatches forward of his position. This was rarely done as this would expose the driver to hostile enemy fire. Only if the gunner was incapacitated and blocked the driver's escape would this avenue of escape be attempted. Due to this situation, many exit drills during training were exercised, which allowed the driver to remove himself in any of the above circumstances.

The gunner's position was directly behind the driver and also sat to the left-hand side of the superstructure, and next to the 7.5cm main gun. His only view to the outside world was through his panoramic periscope which was used as his primary gunnery optical device. The driver and gunner of a StuG III Ausf. A were placed in a very cramped area, and was also poorly lite (for night fighting) which caused these two positions to be highly unpopular with assault gun crews through out the entire war.

The StuG III Ausf. A commander was positioned directly behind the gunner and could situate himself on a bicycle type seat if the vehicle was buttoned-up for combat or could stand upon this seat with his roof hatch open during non-combat engagements. The commander was also provided with a scissors periscope for viewing the area ahead of his vehicle while closed down during a firing engagement. For the majority of the time however, the commander choose to leave his roof hatches open (unless under artillery fire) even if he was conducting fire at the enemy due to the fact that he had much better vision from the nine to the three o'clock positions whereby being able to locate and observe enemy vehicles and infantry then viewing through his scissors periscope.

The loader was positioned to the commander's right side and to the right-hand side of the main gun. His position was much better laid out as he had to have ample room to load the main gun and also additional space to operate the vehicle's radio. Loading the main gun was no simple task and great care had to be taken in not dropping the ammunition upon the floorboards or onto his feet, especially when the vehicle was in motion or backing out of a concealed position after having fired a number of main gun rounds in order to take up another firing position. The loader was also instructed to throw any and all spent shell casings out of the vehicle as if the crew was involved in any prolonged battle field engagements these items would surely clutter up the fighting compartment's floor. In this event, the loader would be highly restricted in his movements and would also be apt to slip on the spent casings as the standard operating procedure was to oil the breech for smooth operation and every expended shell casing would have a film of grease or oil on its outer surfaces. The loader had to be very fast and agile in loading the main gun as if he could not keep up with the vehicle commander's firing orders their vehicle would surely be destroyed as a direct result.

During their training at Metz Wittmann and his new StuG III Ausf. A crew were provided with the best instructions possible. He and his crew started from the ground up and first learned the basics pertaining to the StuG III Ausf. A, and then moved on to the automotive and maintenance aspects. Maintaining their new vehicle was a vital necessity in the every day life of a StuG III crew. Strict and determined efforts were made in order to train and prepare crews for field maintenance. If ones vehicle was not maintained, it was highly likely that at a very critical moment, the machine would not function with the result being that all lives would be lost in the heat of battle. Wittmann and his crew worked together on every given task in regards to servicing their StuG III and soon found that they could strip down or replace any component part that was not functioning properly. If the 7.5cm main gun had to be replaced, due to a worn out barrel, the superstructure's roof of the StuG III Ausf. A had to then be unbolted, removed, which in turn exposed the weapon for removal. This type of operation called for support vehicles in the way of a truck or half-track (Sd. Kfz. 9/1) which was fitted with a six ton crane. The maintenance crews attached to these vehicles would assist the StuG III crew, but this was not to be the case all of the time. Preventive maintenance was the key to survival on the modern battlefield, but when a major breakdown did occur on the field of battle, it was very assuring to know that the recovery and maintenance crews were not very far away.

One of the most hated aspects of serving upon a fully tracked armored fighting vehicle is to either throw a track off the suspension while in combat, or to replace a defective or worn out track link or track pin. If this did not receive immediate attention, the track was sure to separate and be thrown from the vehicle, or if entirely unlucky it would wrap itself around the sprocket wheel and other suspension components. The training guidelines stated that a least once a week a StuG III crew would break one of their tracks (that is to say, remove one track by removing the track pin from two tracks links, thus breaking the track while the vehicle is at rest) and then reverse the process. This was indeed a dirty task, time consuming, and usually the crew being distraught over the entire affair. After the track pin was removed from the two track links, the corresponding sprocket wheel was engaged (with engine running at idle, or slower) until the track was completely removed from the vehicle. The crew then had to attach a wire rope or cable to the end of the track and then connect it to the vehicle's now stationary sprocket wheel. The driver was at his position and would then reverse the direction of the sprocket after being instructed to do so by the vehicle commander and slowly pull the track back onto the sprocket wheel. The vehicle commander would continue to provide arm and hand signals to the driver while giving voice directions to his gunner and loader until the track was winched back onto the vehicle's suspension and secured according to instructions in their vehicle handbuch. After some time and practice a StuG III crew could replace a track in about twenty-five minutes; as long as none of the track links were worn or damaged. Under harsh combat conditions this time-frame was meaningless as the StuG III crew would not dismount from the vehicle under fire and would continue to fight from their immobilized machine. Any fully tracked armored fighting vehicle can still maneuver (although very slowly) if it still has one track still functioning. The driver has to fight his controls during this type of operation as the vehicle will turn violently in the direction of the missing track. He has to guide the vehicle in the direction of his functioning track and move forward or backwards depending on the tactical situation and by orders from the vehicle commander.

This procedure was highly forbidden during training but many StuG III crews (and other armored fighting vehicle crews) did just the opposite as stated in their maintenance literature during all out combat missions. Many lives were to be saved due to this type of maneuver by StuG III crews as it was soon learned and very obvious that if one exposed oneself during a combat situation one would be quickly spotted by the enemy and be eradicated outright by hostile fire.

Removing heavy sprocket drive wheels, road-wheels, return rollers and idlers were other tasks that was highly unpopular with armored fighting vehicle crews. Normally, this meant that the track had to be removed once again in order to work on the dusty or muddy suspension components. If an inside road-wheel had to be replaced the entire bogey assembly had to be lifted via a large vehicle jack and was very time consuming. If the vehicle was situated in muddy or soft ground the jack had to be supported by a thick block of wood and measures taken so it would not slip and cause injury to the men working on and around the machine. Vehicle track maintenance was stressed to the highest degree and crew-members checked and rechecked their StuG III suspensions each and every time they stopped their vehicles long enough during their field training exercises. Track and suspension maintenance was an on-going concern and all crew-members were responsible pertaining to its up-keep at all times.

Engine maintenance and removal was another task called upon by StuG III crew-members and was very involved and at times could result in a vehicle being left behind to fend for itself until follow-up maintenance units arrived on the scene to offer needed assistance. Engine failure in the heat of battle was one fear that hung over every StuG III commander and his crew and would be avoided at any and all costs. The driver of the StuG III was totally responsible for the automotive performance of his vehicle and was to report any and all problems to his commander. The driver's operators handbuch had guide-lines stating the various revolutions being developed by the vehicle's powerplant before changing gears plus other pertinent details and information. Wittmann and his crew had the opportunity to replace their vehicle's engine more than once during training as it was again stressed in the training handbuchs that a crew of any combat vehicle would remove component parts of their vehicles whether they were worn out or not for practical maintenance experience.

Anytime that an engine of any armored fighting vehicle had to be removed, a truck or semi-track vehicle with a suitable lifting crane would be called upon the scene to lend assistance. The entire rear engine deck of the StuG III had to be removed and this was accomplished by unbolting all of the rear deck bolts holding this structure in place. Once this was completed the crew would disconnect any and all wiring, air vents, piping, etc. They would then attach the lifting cables to the rear engine deck and lift this item from the vehicle. The next task was to disconnect the engine from the propeller shaft connected to the transmission and also unbolt the floor mounts which would free the engine from the vehicle. All remaining electrical connections and control rod linkages were disengaged with the power-plant now ready to be lifted out of the engine compartment. Chains with lifting hooks were then secured to the engine via eye-bolts and lifted out of the vehicle by the crane and crew. Many long hours were needed to accomplish this operation and as a result, the StuG III Ausf. A driver was very careful and thorough in regards to vehicle maintenance procedures.

After a number of harsh experiences with having to remove the power plant from their StuG III Ausf. A Wittmann and his men decided that they would never like the idea of being without automotive power and it was stressed time and time again that proper maintenance procedures be carried out in a professional manner. Attention to detail whether it was checking engine oil or fuel levels was not to be overlooked. Even small cracks and minor damage was to be reported to the vehicle commander and written up in the appropriate maintenance reports. No detail was small enough to be overlooked at any given time. All was to be in perfect working order.

Upon completing their maintenance and vehicle familiarization phase is was now time to start their tactical training with the remaining five StuG III Ausf. A vehicles. These new weapon systems were designed to be an assault vehicle in the true sense of the word, but were also tactically attached to the infantry with whom it was suppose to support during the attack. This coordination with the infantry proved not an easy task for the StuG III crews and their vehicles as they tended in the beginning of their training to advance faster than the accompanying infantry. As soon as this problem developed determined steps were taken to correct the situation. Slowing down the pace of the StuG III in training was difficult, but after special planning and repeated coordination with the infantry, this problem was solved for the time being. In battle it was vital that the infantry were not left behind as they would have no supportive fire power from the StuG IIIs and if the assault guns did not have infantry support they could be easily knocked out by the enemy infantry at extremely close ranges. Truly, this was a highly reciprocal battlefield arrangement.

Wittmann's former infantry training in the Wehrmacht indicated to him very graphically that the StuG III Ausf. A was a God's send, as without it, many infantrymen would be killed outright if left out in the open without supportive firepower from such an assault vehicle. He could readily put himself in the place of the average foot soldier and would not want to be without this type of support during an attack in any future battles. Wittmann's concern filtered down to his StuG III crew in regards to the problem of advancing well ahead of their infantry support and after a short time all six StuG III crews could run a simulated attack and provide the needed protection to the accompanying infantry to their complete satisfaction.

If a speedy attack was called for, the infantrymen were instructed to ride on the rear engine decks of the StuG IIIs, especially if a breakout was developing and drastic measures were the order of the day. This of course did not break the hearts of the infantrymen as they were always eager to ride into battle rather than walking on foot.

All in all, it was tough and thorough training that the StuG III Ausf. A crews received and all of the vehicle commanders were very careful in not damaging any of their precious machines. If just one of the vehicles went down for repairs, it could jeopardize a day's training. Daily vehicle maintenance was absolutely critical and Wittmann was the first one to see that it was performed and that no one was relieved from duty until these tasks were completed and up to the outlined standards. It was clear that Wittmann's father's lessons on the farm had been instilled in his son and had guided him through out his training with the armored fighting vehicles at hand.

Seeing that the supporting infantry and the StuG III Ausf. As obtained all of their objectives during training was one thing, but making sure that no one was injured or killed during training was another. The Waffen-SS was known for their realistic training and it was up to the StuG III commanders to insure that no infantrymen were struck by or overrun by any of their machines. This was difficult during an exercise and many times during artillery barrages which laid down smoke for cover, a number of infantrymen were hit and knocked down by an advancing StuG III. This was unfortunate and every precaution was taken to avoid this occurrence. Even with such close coordination between the StuG III commanders and the Infantry squad leaders this mishap did occur and little could be done about it. The StuG III commander and his loader were to be at all times positioned standing upright in their roof hatches (except during a fire mission) to keep a keen eye open for the infantrymen either running ahead of the vehicles or in fox holes, or just laying on the ground readying themselves for the pending simulated attack. It was thought that an infantryman would hear a machine such as the StuG III close to his position, but, in fact many did not, as the excitement of the practice battle was very overpowering to many and the last thing that they ever dreamed of, was for an assault gun to run them down. This sort of training also benefitted the infantrymen later on as they soon lost their inherent fear of armored fighting vehicles in close quarters which lead to being able to approach enemy armored vehicles later in combat. During various portions of training, the infantry actually stalked StuG IIIs in the guise of tank hunting teams which proved very beneficial to their training and also helped to save lives on any and all future battlefields they were to operate on with or without armor support.

During fire missions, the StuG III Ausf. As would pull up to a defensive position, select the targets, and open fire as soon as it possibly could under the watchful eyes of the training umpires, with the StuG III commander trying to operate within the required time-frames as outlined in the gunnery manuals. It was stressed that a vehicle could only fire two main gun rounds from the same position, otherwise it was apt to be observed and destroyed by return fire by enemy panzers, Pak weapons, or artillery bombardment. If a StuG III crew were highly trained, they could indeed fire two or three main gun rounds at a target, but if this continued they would be reprimanded by their superiors as wasting ammunition. Normally, the vehicle commander would order the driver to reverse the machine out of position as soon as the second round was fired, regardless if the target was hit or not. During training this tactical situation was very difficult at first as the gunners and vehicle commanders had to wait until the dust that had been kicked up by the blast of their main guns to settle in order for them to observe a kill or miss. This situation developed into a spotting system where by other vehicles would observe the strike of the rounds and report over the radio network if the firing vehicle obtained a kill or not. Usually, two vehicles would fire at targets, while two or three vehicles would spot for them. Using this technique, the vehicle commander and his gunner would be informed immediately if a kill was inflicted; where as waiting for the dust to settle could have been extremely deadly especially if their muzzle flash was detected by the enemy. If the driver heard over his earphones that a kill had been accomplished with the first round, he would reverse the vehicle out of its present position and select another firing position with the aid of the vehicle commander. The loader could also direct the driver if the vehicle commander was busy with his gunner from his open hatch.

As their training continued, Wittmann found that Rottenführer Klinck had trouble disengaging from his targets if he missed on the second round as he wanted to fire a third round and often opposed the tactic of moving to a secondary fire position. Fire discipline was vital as ammunition was at a premium and strict tactical control was very necessary if the StuG IIIs were to survive on the modern battlefield. Wittmann and Klick had to work as a team and eventually Wittmann was able to calm his gunner down and assured him that steady nerves and cool calculations were the only true formula for tactical success. Everyone on board Wittmann's StuG III at one time or another realized that the gunner would be the individual who could either save the crew from approaching enemy vehicles, or by his miscalculations could doom them and their vehicle if he missed his target. Every effort was made for the gunner to receive as much training as possible in order for him to carry out his job and duties successfully.

As their training with their StuG III Ausf. A started to come to a close, Wittmann could see that he and his crew had been welded into a well coordinated crew and had every confidence in their abilities and crew duties. They had some very hard times during training, but Wittmann had to be very strict at times but his crew knew that this was very necessary in order for them to complete their training. They had learned a great deal about themselves and their new home on steel tracks. All of the maintenance training and complex field training was now behind them, but even more difficult combat situations would be awaiting them as soon as they were sent to the renewed fighting against the Allies.

Everyone in Wittmann's StuG III Ausf. A company were all now wondering where their next assignment would take them, as they had been hearing rumors that they might be heading for North Africa to bolster Rommel's Afrikakorps, or was it to be northward to Norway?

No one really knew what to expect, the only thing that could be counted upon was that the Leibstandarte Adolf Hitler would be the first unit in the line to lead the attack against the enemy. Everyone was on pins and needles, with anxiety and tension running high and an eagerness to test all of their new training and tactics as soon as possible.

It was not until October 28, 1940 that the Leibstandarte Adolf Hitler was put onto the alert as the armies of Fascist Italy decided to invade the country of Greece. The Greek army had established strong defensive measures which surprised the Italians and many reverses were inflicted upon Mussolini's troops as a whole. Due to these setbacks, the Italians asked her ally for military aid and seeing a chance to interject, Hitler committed the Second and Twelfth German armies. These military units were moved into position as soon as possible with the Leibstandarte Adolf Hitler being attached to the Twelfth army and under its control during the entire Balkan campaign. The German High Command had indeed prepared a plan to invade Greece so as to deny the British an advance base of operations in regards to the Mediterranean and the surrounding navel sea lanes. Having to rescue Mussolini's inferior troops presented the opportunity to set this operation into action with the German High Command being able to kill two birds with one stone.

During the beginning of February 1941 the Waffen-SS combat units were being moved from Alsace via Campalung in Romania and then transferred to Bulgaria from which country the Twelfth Army would strike in the direction of Skoplje in southern Yugoslavia. The occupation of this country was also in the over-all plan and the German army would seize Yugoslavia so as to utilize it as a jumping off point for the invasion of Greece. Shortages of good roads and a reliable railway network was the major factor in the mountainous areas of the Balkans and military operations were somewhat slowed down due to the rugged terrain features encountered by the advancing German forces. One solution devised by the German war planners to over-come their logistical problems was to construct large wooden rafts and load them with much needed and vital supplies and float or tow them down the river Danube. By conducting this avenue of approach, vast amounts of badly needed fuel, ammunition, food stuffs, and other necessary equipment and materials were stocked piled for the divisions pertaining to the Twelfth Army. This scheme of floating supplies saved a great deal of time and effort for the units involved and many lives were saved as during the combat engagements that followed, the German front line units always had sufficient supplies and necessities during the entire advance in the face of stiff opposition. Even the Leibstandarte Adolf Hitler, who were constantly at the front leading the planned assaults, were always amply supplied and equipped for battle. It was still highly stressed that any and all supplies sent to the front should be handled with the utmost care and that none of it was to be wasted or misdirected.

On April 6, 1941, the Leibstandarte Adolf Hitler forming part of the XXXX Corps helped to open hostilities with the 9th Panzer Division in its assault on the border town of Kustendil. The attack was made in two major columns; in the northern sector was the 9th Panzer Division closely supported by the Leibstandarte

Adolf Hitler. The objective of this formidable battle group was to bridge the Kriva Pass and capture Skople some sixty miles within Yugoslavia. After token resistance this task had been accomplished by the evening of the 7th with the units spending the following day consolidating their gains and performing vehicle maintenance and after action reports. The 73rd Infantry Division which made up the southern battle group had captured the strategically important town of Prilep and then managed to send out small patrols to hopefully link up with the Italian forces operating to the western areas of the country.

The Germany military forces drive into Yugoslavia had totally shattered its army, as the speed and determination of the Wehrmacht and Waffen-SS forces completely overwhelmed them and there was little left to halt the invasion after the initial assaults went into overall attack. The vital Vardar river line was captured on the afternoon of the 7th and German engineering units constructed a line across this waterway. It seemed all to clear that the Yugoslav army was ill-trained, poorly lead, and using antiquated equipment to face the massive onslaught of German mechanized units; nor were their divisions correctly positioned to halt the German assaults. On the morning of April 9th, 1941 a sudden link-up had been made with the Italians forces and the Leibstandarte Adolf Hitler, now spearheading the Corps advance, turned south to assist in supporting the 73rd Division. This advance was to capture the Monastir Gap, a 3,000 foot high Javat Pass some twenty miles to the immediate west of Monastir and to cause another link-up with the Italians. The Javat Pass was indeed the gateway to Greece and in order to provide the maximum storm trooper effect, Witt's 1st Battalion was reinforced with two Pak gun troops comprising of 3.7cm and 5.0cm weapons, plus motorized infantry, one troop of light field howitzers, two troops of infantry guns (one light and one heavy) and a battery of 8.8cm guns and a complete company of assault engineers. The assault engineers were a welcomed addition as their presence gave a little relief to the unit commanders, as if they needed any assistance in making a waterway crossing, or came up against any substantial obstacles or fortified positions, they could be handled and done away with much easier by these highly trained individuals.

During these rapid advances, Wittmann and the six StuG IIIs of the Leibstandarte Adolf Hitler were not being deployed in the standard maneuver formations. The rugged mountain terrain features forced the vehicles to bunch up on the narrow roads and nerve racking attention by the vehicle commanders to coax their drivers to roll forward under these adverse conditions proved to be a major undertaking. There was also heavy snow in the mountains and many of the muddy roads had ice and snow which at times would cause the StuG IIIs to spin out and sometimes caused the vehicles to slide completely off the roads. Portions of the roads had been weakened by the winter weather and in certain areas the roads had collapsed and vehicles were held up for hours while the engineers brought forward large wooden beams and other engineering apparatus to shore up these troublesome and dangerous areas. It was soon realized that a lighter armored vehicle should lead the way and test the roads so it was decided that an Sd. Kfz. 253 command semi-track would at all times conduct this procedure before allowing heavier vehicles to follow. Another consideration was that in many places along the line of advance there was thick brush and trees that came right up to the edge of the roads. This was perfect ambush country and all attempts were made to secure and avoid these types of attack. Infantry riding on the rear decks of the StuG IIIs often sprayed these suspected areas with automatic fire and stick grenades. Vehicle commanders and loaders standing upright in their respective positions scanned the area ahead of their vehicles for land mines and any and all signs of freshly turned up earth that might prove to be a hidden explosive device or booby trap.

Witt's battle group had run into the positions of the mixed Australian Brigade Group in and around the Klidi Pass. During the night the Waffen-SS soldiers were exposed to the bitter cold and snow and waited for dawn to break as a German artillery barrage would rain down on the Australian positions. During the night the assault engineers had begun to clear the mind fields which would allow vehicles of the 9th Panzer Division to advance while the men of the Leibstandarte Adolf Hitler would fight hand-to-hand battles to drive the Imperial troops from their concealed positions. All day long the battle rolled back and forth and the fighting could be heard in the mountains of northern Greece. By mid-afternoon of April 12th, the pass had been taken by the Waffen-SS soldiers and eighty prisoners, the first group of some six hundred men were in the bag. These men were from the 2/4th Australian Battalion and for the majority of the Leibstandarte Adolf Hitler, this was their first encounter with Imperial troops. These soldiers from 'down under' were not like their English counterparts; they were very arrogant and a number of them in fact were mercenaries who's appearances were very fierce and extremely unpleasant. The Australians were not as well disciplined as the English soldiers and nor did they wear their uniforms as soldiers should. They were also constantly complaining about the intense cold as they had just recently arrived from Egypt and had not been provided with warm winter clothing and heavy-duty boots.

Witt's battle group had maneuvered through the hills, outflanked the Australian defense and emerged from the south-eastern exit of the Klidi Pass on April 13th. His men and all units involved were bone tired and a number of vehicles had to be left behind due to breakdowns. Suddenly, a British armored counter-attack drove into the forward elements of the Leibstandarte but a pair of 8.8 cm Pak guns quickly maneuvered into position and soon restored the situation by knocking out the vast majority of the enemy vehicles and dispersing the remaining Allied troops.

The Waffen-SS had captured the key to the Allied positions in northern Greece with the loss of only thirty-seven killed, ninety-eight wounded and two missing which was below the anticipated loss statements. The Waffen-SS now turned in the direction of the plain that lead to the Klissura Pass as a feeling of total victory was in the air and the march forward steadily continued on. The Leibstandarte Adolf Hitler now turned towards Lake Kastoria and the Pass which was guarded by the 21st Greek Infantry Division. As the advance proceeded extensive demolitions slowed the pace and bitter hand-to-hand fighting followed once again. Other minor clashes occured along the entire length of the narrow and congested road, which was the only passage through the rolling hills.

Also during this assault of the Klissura Pass Wittmann and his Stug III Ausf. A crew showed their ability to take a very dangerous situation and bring it to a successful conclusion. During a thundering downpour of rain, Wittmann brought his vehicle to within 800 meters of the 13th Greek Division and pumped many 7.5cm main gun rounds into their mists. With his and other direct fire from other vehicles of his unit, over 12,000 prisoners were taken.

It had been a very difficult battle as close coordination was breaking down as the weather conditions were proving to be a menace with all of the StuG IIIs radios. Visibility was at a premium and it was obvious that the frigid cold was a major factor in the Greeks giving up after a long and bitter fight.

A concentrated barrage of shells and bullets opened up on the Leibstandarte Adolf Hitler point units as they stormed forward up the mountain slopes and as a result were held up for a long period of time which upset their timing schedules. It was impossible for Wittmann or any of the other armored fighting vehicles to supply support and the following artillery units could not locate any level ground to provide needed fire support. The ensuing advance developed into a battle front that dictated that the Waffen-SS riflemen would be ordered to fight as mountain (Alpine) troops. Under the leadership of SS-Sturmbannführer Kurt Meyer, small combat groups from the Leibstandarte Adolf Hitler's reconnaissance battalion formed up and made their way to the summit. As they made their way up and along the narrow goat trails, each and every man was only able to carry his own personal weapons, but others managing to advance across less difficult country, were also able to bring up mortars and other vital support weapons. As carefully as possible, these parties of Waffen-SS men maneuvered around the Allied flank but the absence of any moonlight, caused them to wander and to lose complete cohesion. The attack was then delayed until all units had been located and concentrated and in the bitter cold light of an April dawn, covered by the fire of a battery of 8.8cm guns whose crews had risked going over the edge of a steep precipice after each and every round, the renewed attack then started to regain its momentum. The Leibstandarte Adolf Hitler units continued the assault with greet vigor and rushed towards the Greeks' positions. The remaining Greek defenders stood their ground and fought with savage determination but the constant pressure asserted by the German assaults, prove in the end to be too overwhelming and their resistance quickly started to dissolved and soon hundreds of prisoners, including a Brigadier and three battalion commanders were captured. Finally, by April 15th, the road was open and men and materials were moved up to reinforce and consolidate the German positions. Then patrols were ordered out in the direction of Lake Kastoria but ran into a determined Greek rearguard from the 12th Infantry Division and Greek Cavalry Divisions. Due to this unexpected obstacle, the German advance was halted in its tracks. In pouring rain, the Leibstandarte Adolf Hitler's 3rd Battalion stormed forward in an all out attack and captured a hill tactically marked Height 800, after being provided air-cover by a Stuka dive-bombing attack, which also resulted in capturing a nearby town by the late afternoon. The German forces had indeed bagged over 12,000 prisoners in the first few days of the fighting.

As the advance of the Leibstandarte Adolf Hitler continued, it was then directed to the southeast flank to attempt an outflanking maneuver along the Servia, but heavy and constant rains and numerous demolitions impeded the attack, to such an extent that the assault was canceled and new orders were issued to the commanders. These orders stated that on April 19, the Leibstandarte Adolf Hitler was to move south-westward from Gravena to Joannina to cut off and isolate the Greek units manning the line. The Mesovan Pass was soon also captured after only token resistance. This turn of events not only covered the open flank of the Twelfth army, but effectively isolated the Greek units on the western side of the Pindus mountains. As soon as the Greek commanders knew that the Leibstandarte Adolf Hitler units were blocking the line of withdrawal for the Greek army this forced the Greek political leaders to sue for an armistice on April 21st. The Greek armies of the Center, of Western Macedonia and of the Epirus were also compelled to surrender their arms and equipment. Small pockets of resistance continued to fight, but for the Greek army as a whole, the war was now over for them.

The only remaining token of organized resistance which was now being directed against the German military troops was the British and Imperial forces and up to April 24th kept a number of German units alerted for any further assaults by the Allies. The Leibstandarte Adolf Hitler then pulled out of Arta and in a ruthless attack of over 185 miles across the Pindus mountains were astonished to see after arriving at the Straits of Corinth that the British had safely eluded capture by rapid sea evacuation. Highly determined not to lose contact with the enemy Sturmbannführer Kurt Meyer, the Leibstandarte Adolf Hitler's reconnaissance Battalion commander, commandeered a number of fishing vessels and established a ferry service from Navpaktos and transferred the entire contingent of the advance guard across the water barrier. On the 27th, the Battalion rolled down along the west coast of the Peloponnese and finally reached Pirgos. Men of the 3rd Battalion managed to capture elements of the 3rd Royal Tank Regiment, prior to advancing onward further south on the peninsula. After the clearance of the southern coast of the Gulf of Corinth which was performed by a unit of the Reconnaissance Battalion, it established a link-up with paratroopers of the 2nd Fallschirmjäger Regiment who had been fighting harsh battles at the Corinth Canal. This final link-up thus ended the three week long

Balkan campaign for the Leibstandarte Adolf Hitler. Following a victory parade in Athens the Waffen-SS units were ordered to return to barracks in Czechoslovakia to refit and to prepare themselves for the next campaigns which were certain to be fought during the summer of 1941. It had been a long and hard three weeks in the Balkans and the Leibstandarte Adolf Hitler and its men welcomed a needed rest period which would prepare them for the greatest land warfare battle in the history of mankind, .i.e., the battle for Russia.

For Michael Wittmann and his StuG III Ausf. A crew, it had been an unbelievable three weeks of hardships which included, bitterly cold weather, bad roads, constant shelling, endless hold-ups, enemy snipers, mines, and vehicle breakdowns. It did not take him long to realize that the training that he and his StuG III crew had undergone would not be put to practical use in the mountainous terrain of Greece. Nowhere were there open fields and countryside to deploy their vehicles in wide formations while giving fire support and protection to their infantry comrades. Everywhere one looked during the advance would reveal men and vehicles crowded together on the muddy and icy roads trying to further the assaults. The infantry continued to ride upon the vehicles which proved very pertinent at times, but when an artillery barrage rained down and around the vehicles, many of the infantry were swept off the vehicles with many injuries and deaths as a result. Many times the armored fighting vehicles moved ahead of the infantry who could only do their best in trying to keep up. At times, Wittmann felt very sorry for the infantry as at least he and his crew had some protection from the enemy shelling. They could button down their vehicle and hope and pray that an enemy shell did not come crashing down through the thinly armored roof of their vehicle. During all of the constant rainy downpours he and his crew could stay fairly dry and warm inside their steel home on tracks. Even though somewhat cramped for all concerned, it was better than standing out in the driving rain. On a few occasions after opening his commander's hatch and turning around he was made witness to five or six infantrymen laying down over the engine deck plate with a Zeltbahn or tarpaulin over these unfortunate individuals trying to keep out of the rain and gladly excepting much needed warmth from the heat of the engine. The infantry always suffered the most on the front lines.

All of the same thoughts were going through the minds of Wittmann's StuG III Ausf. A crew as they dearly hoped that their next assignment would be a place where it was warm and sunny and did not have to worry about staying dry and warm. Little did they know that their next battles would be fought in a place that would make them wish that staying dry and warm was the only thing with which to concern themselves.

Chapter VII

OPERATION BARBAROSSA:
THE GERMAN INVASION OF RUSSIA

June 22, 1941 – May 31, 1942

On June 22, 1941, the German High Command announced to the world that her armed forces had stormed across the Russo-German frontier with the intention of waging all-out war against the Russians. It would take four long hard years of fierce and bitter fighting between Hitler's Germany and Stalin's Russia before the Red Army could claim victory and steamroll her vast armies into German territory, and ultimately into the streets of Berlin. For the German Wehrmacht, and especially for the Waffen-SS units, this conflict was seen as a battle for civilization, where-upon the European versed the Asian, which was viewed as a continuation of a historic battle between east and west since Byzantium. The invasion of Russia was seen as a modern day Crusade with the troops of the Waffen-SS assault units going into harsh battle with their spirits extremely high and determination second to none. It was also very clear that National Socialism was battling Communism; and economically, Germany desperately needed the rich Eastern oil and grain fields to feed and power her great armies. The Leibstandarte Adolf Hitler would capture these highly praised necessities for their Führer and would again be ordered to lead the opening attacks as soon as they had crossed the border into communist Russia. The German High Command had been planning the invasion of Russia as early as July 1940, as Adolf Hitler had declared his intentions to wage war against Russia at this time. Militarily, the time had now come to eradicate the red menace on the Eastern flank, and with Hitler's Directive No. 21, set into motion all preparations, planning, and build-up of military forces for this conflict, which was to be code-named "Barbarossa!"

Three German Army Groups were to be deployed for the invasion and consisted of Army Group North, Army Group Center, and Army Group South. The Leibstandarte Adolf Hitler was to be assigned to the latter and would spend three long years of active front line duty in the southern regions of Russia. The Russian steppes were a vast area where large armies could be swallowed up and never be heard from again, as it would take huge amounts of men, weapons, and supplies to tame this wild and brutal land mass. At times, the front lines covered over 2,000 miles, from the dense woods and deep snows of Finland, to the open steppe lands of Central Russia to the high and rugged mountain tops and sub-tropical climates of the Caucasus. The initial phases of the invasion against Russia was on such a vast scale, that it required on the German side the movement and maintenance of millions of soldiers, 600,000 vehicles, 750,000 horses, and over 7,000 pieces of artillery along with 3,100 panzers and other types of armored fighting vehicles.

During the month of February 1941, the first divisions to take an active part in the invasion which formed Army Group South, began to amass all along the border. By March of that year, the total number of divisions would be increased to sixteen, and by May thirty-nine divisions were then concentrated, and by June forty-six divisions which established Army Group South as a fighting force were now ready in their preplanned jumping-off positions. The Sixth, Eleventh, and Seventeenth Armies, supported by the 1st Panzer Group which made up Army Group South, were ordered to cut off and totally annihilate the Red Armies west of the Dnieper river. Situated on the left flank and ready to move on a moments notice and to break through below Kovel was 1st Panzer Group. By applying rapid movements, it was to create pincer arms around the Russian military forces from the South-West Front and contain them in an armored fist until they had been totally destroyed or captured by the German forces operating in that area of engagement.

It was quite clear that Army Group South had insufficient strength to conduct all of its allotted missions as laid down by the German High Command. Its position ran from the southern edge of the Pripet Marshes to the Black Sea. The first maneuver it had to perform was from the frontier to the Dnieper, then advance no less than 300 miles, and then onto Rostov the main objective, which was some 700 miles to the east. All of these objectives had to be made over very difficult terrain where radio communications were extremely poor and the Russian road network were only mere dirt tracks that turned into slim bogs three feet deep which was sufficient to stall or hold up an entire Panzer Division only after an hour of rainfall. General "Mud" was the worst enemy of the German Wehrmacht and Waffen-SS combat units fighting in Russia, but there was also the Red Army who in the beginning were poorly lead and equipped, but leaned their tactical defeats well, and would one day be a force to be reckoned with on the modern battlefield. In the beginning of operation "Barbarossa", the German military forces opponent was to a very large degree an unknown enigma, and appreciations of the fighting capabilities of the Red Army as well as of the vast Russian military resources in material and manpower, were extremely underestimated by the German OKH. This misinterpretation was duly based on the poor showing of Russian troops and equipment while battling the Finns in the winter war of 1939-40. The German military and its commanders had little if any understanding of the Russian people and their armies and felt that the German assault forces would ride roughshod over the weakly defended border positions as located and plotted prior to the initial invasion. Just prior to the invasion, the German High Command issued a memorandum stating that the main defects of the Red Army at command level were the following: slowness in the face of the enemy, lack of decision making and inadequate organization. The report did continue to state and paid tribute to the endurance, tenacity, and offensive spirit of the Russian army, but there in itself laid a liability, as it was made quite clear that the vast majority of the Russian officers had little if any training in performing a successful orderly retreat and in the opening battles of the Eastern (Ost) Front, many mismanaged their forces while being encircled by the superior German armies. Little or no considerations were ever given to the individual soldiers in the Red Army as the infantry were sacrificed in the relentless attacks and officers who failed to obtain given objectives often paid the price of failure with their own lives at the hands of the firing squad. Because of this grim situation, Russian officers and field commanders were extremely ruthless in obtaining results even if it meant the complete destruction of their respective units. There was always additional Russian troops to be thrown into the battle with the Red Army High Command having little feelings about losing thousands of soldiers as long as the main objective was taken and secured to their satisfaction.

Regardless of the faults of the Russian military machine, the Red Army as a whole was indeed a very powerful force. Even with only partial mobilization, it could assemble 130 rifle divisions at its beck and call. The Russian army could muster some 10,000 armored fighting vehicles to confront the Germans which gave the Red Army a three to one numerical superiority, and with the introduction of the new T34/76 main battle tank, the German military forces found that they had nothing that could stand up against this new fighting machine in the way of their currently available panzers. Only at close range did the Panzer III and IV have any chance of penetrating the T34/76's sloped frontal and side armor plate. In June 1941, it was reported there were less than one million vehicles in the whole of Russia and that the Red Army was horse mounted as was the majority of the European armies at that time. Accordingly, in the first battles of the war, the pace of the horse and the common foot soldier generally 'set' the pace, speed, and course of advance on the Eastern Front in regards to the Red Army.

From the outlook of the Russian High command, its defensive plan viewed the southern regions as the decisive battle fronts and placed the strongest concentrations of its forces in that most important area. From July 10th onwards, Marshal Budyenny (who had taken command from General Kirponos) was now in command of the South-Western Front. According to German Intelligence reports, located and identified were sixty-nine rifle, eleven cavalry and twenty-eight armored divisions. This comprehensive military force was now defending a rich agricultural area, with little wooded terrain to concern itself with, of which consisted of flat land which was ideally suited for swift panzer assaults. The Pruth, San, Bug, and Dnieper river lines were the four basic obstacles that the German military forces had to breach, with the Dnieper as the strongest defensive line to be overcome. At Kiev, the river was three-quarters of a mile wide and offered the greatest difficulties for the German pioneer units who would have to cross this wide expense with pontoon bridges, wooden rafts, and rubber boats while under murderous enemy fire day and night. Also to be contended with was the Stalin Line which had been built just prior to 1939 and formed a very formidable presence which was used time and time again by the Red Army.

Another sinister obstacle that had to be over come, was that of the enemy guerrilla fighters in the German Army's rear. At the beginning of the war in Russia, the majority of Russian people welcomed the Germans as liberators and felt that the days of intense oppression would soon be over. In many regions where the local populace had established a "modus vivendi" with the occupying forces, partisan groups brought forth open acts of terrible atrocities and sabotage against the Germans in the hope of provoking retaliations against the now passive populations and thereby recruiting new guerrilla fighters to further their ruthless cause. The brutality and bitterness that followed, and the utter contempt for human life which characterized the war on the Eastern Front will never be repeated or forgotten by those German and Russian soldiers who fought and survived to report the harsh conditions placed upon them while performing their sworn duties.

The men of the Leibstandarte Adolf Hitler were convinced that their fallen comrades who had landed into the hands of the Red Army had been victims of summary and brutal execution within days of the opening of the campaign. It became accepted practice for officers to provide the "coup de grace" to those who could not be extracted from the battlefield as it was a matter of honor to evacuate those who could be moved rather than to have them fall under the wrath of the Red Army with the possibility of their men being tortured before being put to death. Life on the Eastern Front was very harsh and every man who served there knew that if one was to be captured it was certain death which caused the German frontline soldiers to fight to the death on the field of honor rather then to surrender into the brutal hands of the Red Army.

On June 22, 1941, the order of the day was issued and the new German Crusade was set into motion at last. The red menace to Western civilization would soon be reckoned with and every German soldier on the border felt it was his duty to rid the world of all communists, commissars, and any and all disruptive elements of communism that was now threatening western civilization as a whole. Three million German Soldiers, highly trained, highly motivated, and superior in technology but inferior in outright numbers, were now to face four and a half million Russians, who were to a large extent, unprepared and not as proficient in leadership and motivation as their German counterparts. The majority of the Red Army had almost no combat experience, whereas the

German fighting forces had been in combat since September 1, 1939, with four successful military campaigns under their belts.

The Leibstandarte Adolf Hitler was now part of the III Corps which had been determined in May, but, as a result of a shortage of spare parts for its armored fighting vehicles, it was unable to complete its operations and was posted to XIV Corps of 1st Panzer Group and was positioned in and around the Lublin area. On June 21st the Leibstandarte Adolf Hitler did in fact unload and prepared itself for immediate battle. It was on alert status even though it would have great difficulty to recover and repair any tracked vehicles that might break down for one reason or the other.

The warning flashes that came from 1st Panzer Group fixing H-Hour and the invasion date had little meaning for the Leibstandarte Adolf Hitler, who remained uncommitted until June 27th. On that day it swung out of its concentration area, and rolled down the road to Ostorwiecz following the Waffen-SS 'Viking' Division. At this point in time the Leibstandarte Adolf Hitler moved from the area of Sanomiercz to a sector south-west of Zamosc, where, early on the morning of July 1st, the main assault force reached the Vistula, breached it, and finally arrived at the former frontier line. This attack marked the Leibstandarte Adolf Hitler's entry into the Russian front campaign which would entail three tours of duty with this first tour keeping it on active service up to June 1942. For the men of the Leibstandarte Adolf Hitler, this attack was only a prelude to the hostile and fierce battles which would rage on with many of its men never to return home to be with love ones and family.

Many of the men of the Leibstandarte Adolf Hitler units were very puzzled by the fact that they had not been called into the battle and used once again as the cutting edge. It did little for unit moral and many who were at their jumping-off positions could only wonder if they were in fact being held back for a very 'special' assignment. It was with these sediments that the men and vehicles of the Leibstandarte Adolf Hitler pushed forward into the wide and forbidding steppe lands of Galicia and the western Ukraine. By the time that the forward units of the Leibstandarte Adolf Hitler had entered into active combat, operations concerning the opening battles of 'Barbarossa' had already proved highly successful with the German military forces making deep and swift penetrations into enemy held territories. At first, the German High Command felt that the Russian invasion was to be yet another `Blitzkrieg', as Adolf Hitler had stated before the invasion, "One good kick at the front door and the whole rotten house will cave in!" As the 1st Panzer Group moved forward on its preplanned assault routes, the two arms of its pincer movements swept aside any and all Russian armored countermeasures until one arm had come upon Kiev, while the second at Kazatin.

As the armored vehicles and support units of the Leibstandarte Adolf Hitler careened forward during the fine summer weather towards Luck, the entire regiment soon found itself involved in bloody frontier battles in the western

Ukraine. The German panzer crews were now battling Russian tank units trying to severe the Northern road system at Dubno and also at Olyka. At Moszkove the Red Army armored formations steamrolled forward only to be cut to ribbons by the Waffen-SS gunners from various flanking positions and drove the remainder back in utter confusion. Heavy rains suddenly broke loose and poured down upon the battlefield during the early evening and curtailed any and all further movements. However, this situation did not dampen the high spirits of the young and successful Waffen-SS soldiers at the conclusion of the first day's hostilities. Further assaults were made by the elite storm troopers as the Russians were now grasping at straws and staging ad hoc measures in order to consolidate the front line. Truck mounted Russian infantry made daring attacks in their transports and many times tried to overrun the Waffen-SS positions by this mode of attack, but were completely mowed down by heavy and sustained automatic weapons fire.

SS-Unterscharführer (Sgt.) Michael Wittmann and his StuG III Ausf. A crew were now operating in the area of Moszkov and as the sun drew itself over the eastern horizon the long shadows started to disappear as it was the morning of July 12th. Another day of harsh fighting on the brutal Russian front had begun. The twenty-seven year old assault gun commander held his hands over his eyes in order to protect them from the bright glare of the morning rays from the sun and could see the first line of German infantry moving into a wooded area to the north of his position. Everything was very quiet and it seemed that this day was going to have little if any fighting on the front lines. Therefore, he ordered his StuG III crew to perform additional defensive measures such as changing the foliage that was camouflaging their position with fresh cuttings.

Daily maintenance was top priority for their StuG III and was performed before anyone ate any breakfast. The last few days of fighting had been very bitter and harsh as the Ivans had continued to attack the Corps supply lines and the northern network of roads, which caused great delays in bringing up ammunition and fuel. The Leibstandarte Adolf Hitler had captured Moszkov and then was ordered to form a defensive front on the Rovno-Luck area to contain any Russian thrusts from the Borbin sector. During the night, heavy and constant rains had turned the roadways into rivers of knee deep glutinous mud, which resulted in the non movement of any of the vehicles and were not able to complete this strenuous maneuver as a totally cohesive force. To add to the bad and inclement weather conditions and constant enemy opposition, the 17th Army was now involved in the bitter fighting concerning the defenses of the Stalin Line. These assaults were being conducting in the hope of achieving space in order for the 1st Panzer Group to be allowed once again to make additional deep penetrations into the enemy's front lines. Once this was accomplished, the armored fighting vehicles were to be ordered to roll ahead without any pauses or delays, across the huge Russian steppe lands, whereby in some cases leaving their supporting infantry units as much as fifty miles to their immediate rear.

They were to be the 'storm-wind' of the advancing German military forces.

As soon as Michael Wittmann and his StuG III crew had finished re-camouflaging their vehicle, there was a sudden bark of an enemy anti-tank gun in the nearby woods, and then all hell broke loose. 7.62cm rounds exploded and men were flung up and into the air with such force that many were dead even before hitting the ground. After this sudden and violent attack, enemy machine guns opened up with the German positions being in jeopardy of capture. The Ivans would soon be assaulting the German lines with any and all weapons at their disposal and it was the responsibility of the StuG III commanders and their crews to stem off any such assaults being conducted against their fellow infantry comrades. The sun was now burning very hot, but the wet terrain ahead of their vehicles did not offer the enemy much of a chance to steamroll over their positions regardless of the numbers involved or expected. The fields of fire pertaining to the StuG IIIs were all very well established, all weapons were loaded and all automatic weapons were close at hand should the Russian infantry manage to crawl forward on their bellies under the 7.5cm main gun firing zones.

Michael Wittmann thought about the orders he had received not more than two hours after midnight. He had stood at the battle headquarters of Hauptsturmführer (Captain) Kurt Meyer and was given the order to assure that the reconnaissance company would be protected from the enemy in this southern portion of the woods and to hold off any Russian attack in that area. The reconnaissance company of the Leibstandarte Adolf Hitler had to now fight their way through the forested areas in order to come into contact with the light infantry battalion of the 25th Infantry Division. There were few armored fighting vehicles available to this battle sector and were thinly spread along the front line of ten kilometers. Vehicle commanders would have to venture out on their own in desperate attempts to give the advancing infantry heavy fire support to suppress any aggressive moves made by the Ivans.

Suddenly, a radio message was being broadcasted to Wittmann and as he pulled himself up and into his upper cupola position, he surprisingly heard the voice of his company commander.

"Eagle calling Buzzard! Come in!"

"Buzzard to Eagle, I read you, over."

"Roll ahead to stream at point 65.5 and guard. Reconnaissance probe reports possible enemy panzer attack!"

"We are rolling towards objective at this time, over!"

"March, Köldenhoff! 12 o'clock, forward, to that hill there!" Ordered Wittmann.

The StuG III's powerplant was now running a full rpm and moving through the under growth.

Koldenhöff suddenly and unexpectedly reported to his commander that the Maybach engine was showing signs of overheating. Wittmann was very concerned that if the engine overheated and failed, it would mean either certain death or capture of his crew if they were involved with any combat with enemy panzers. He instructed his driver to keep a wary eye on his engine temperature gauges as they moved forward towards point 65.5. Koldenhöff was also very careful not to hit any large rock outcroppings or depressions in the terrain which would cause additional strain on the engine and drive train. Throwing a track or damaging the suspension of the vehicle at this time could cause undue hardships to all concerned and disrupt the mission at hand. Wittmann was constantly giving directions to his driver as the StuG III rolled and crashed through the underbrush and then moved into a slight depression in the terrain. They then passed into a deep and unseen hole that caused their vehicle to dip dangerously forward which resulted in alarm inside the StuG III as Wittmann and his crew held on securely to hand holds and could only with great discipline keep from swearing at their lack of observation from their respective crew positions. Everyone concerned was upset for not being able to detect the large hole that their machine had just fallen into with a great jarring effect. As soon as Koldenhöff felt his vehicle drop into this large depression, he just managed to gun the vehicle's powerplant and with the Maybach engine roaring at top rpm, the StuG III slammed into the bottom of this depression and bounced on its overtaxed suspension and up and onto the other side. The entire vehicle crew were badly shaken up which resulted in a number of small cuts and bruises being inflicted, but nothing serious otherwise. The StuG III rumbled forward and finally reached the reverse slope of height 65.5 and took up a defensive posture with Wittmann and his crew scanning the area ahead of them for any tell-tale signs of the reported enemy activity.

While Wittmann and his loader were observing through two sets of binoculars, they suddenly heard the familiar sounds of panzers on the move. Wittmann ordered his driver to shut off their engine in order to be able to listen better, but was concerned about such an order in the event that it did not restart when it was needed. As it had been running hot, he figured that it would have a chance to cool down. He tried desperately to judge where the enemy panzers would appear and advised his gunner so he could fire the first main gun round and score a direct hit, which always confused and dazed the Red Army panzer commanders. They would normally stop dead in their tracks to try and locate the source of incoming fire, and when this predicted action took place, Wittmann's gunner would start and pick them off as they would be easy targets once they were completely stationary.

"There they are," screamed Wittmann's gunner, as he was very eager to place a well aimed 7.5cm main gun round into one of the approaching enemy machines.

Koldenhöff restarted the Maybach engine which roared back to life which was a relief to all concerned.

"Driver! Pull up a little higher!" ordered Wittmann, and directed Koldenhöff to maneuver their vehicle to the 11 o'clock position to obtain a better defensive stance in a clump of thick bushes. Wittmann wanted to observe the oncoming Russian panzers and was trying to locate the platoon leader's vehicle. This machine would be sporting a radio antenna, and if he and his crew could destroy this vehicle, it would help to generate complete confusion and disorder in regards to the Ivan's being isolated and cut off from higher command control.

The StuG III finally reached the circle of bushes on the hill ridge where Wittmann then ordered his driver to stop in order for his loader and himself to view the immediate forward area for the enemy armored vehicles. He tried desperately to detect the Russian panzers through his field glasses but was unable to under the prevailing circumstances.

"Another 10 meters, driver!" Barked his commander.

The StuG III once again rolled forward with its commander and loader scanning the skyline for any signs of the enemy machines. As soon as his vehicle lurched forward, Wittmann suddenly spotted the Russian panzers without the aid of his binoculars! They were maneuvering forward northeast of a ravine and as he counted these vehicles his heart started to pound as their numbers grew until he had sighted twelve Russian T34/76 tanks.

What would he do in the face of such overwhelming numbers bearing down on his vehicle and crew? Could he halt such a force with only one assault gun at his disposal? It seemed impossible for his crew and himself to survive such an attack and he did not want to sacrifice his comrades in this manner. As he was calculating this serious situation, out of a nearby wood about 400 meters away, six additional Russian T34/76 tanks came crashing out of the densely wooded area and turned towards the south. They were travelling in a wolf-pack six abreast and would arrive at his position within two or three minutes if he did not take them under fire immediately.

"How many Michael?" asked Wittmann's gunner. Klinck was a very silent type until the fighting started. The sight of the approaching enemy panzers was certainly enough for him to be brought out of his reserved nature and was ready for anything.

"Eighteen enemy panzers!" yelled Wittmann. "Not any more?" replied his gunner, who was very anxious to fire at the Ivans. "That is all that I count!" continued Wittmann.

Wittmann then gave the order for his driver to back up the StuG III and to move the vehicle around to the left-hand side of the hill as fast as humanly possible. As soon as the StuG III jerked backwards, due mostly to the tension of the nervous driver, it turned about and rolled from the top edge, and then around the hill as ordered by its commander.

"Prepare for frontal attack!" shouted Wittmann. "Load main gun with armor piercing shot!"

Wittmann nodded as the answer came back to him that all was ready for the first main gun round to be fired at the oncoming enemy machines.

The StuG III rolled forward and up to the next rise pertaining to the left-hand side of the hill and now had an unobstructed view of the enemy machines. Wittmann saw one of the Russian panzers just over 400 meters away, and rolling towards them after cresting a nearby smaller hill. He had wished that he could have detected the enemy machines when they had come over this hill, as he could have placed well aimed 7.5cm main gun rounds directly into the thinner belly armor pertaining to the T34/76s. With a powerful roar of the engine, Koldenhöff brought the StuG III forward under Wittmann's direction until his gunner could see over the rise of the hill. As soon as the vehicle was halted, Klinck would only have to make quick and final adjustments to his main gun sights and destroy the Russian vehicle forthwith. The StuG III covered the last few meters of their short battle run very quickly, and as Wittmann gave out the order to his driver to halt his vehicle, his gunner was dead on target.

"Fire!!!" yelled Wittmann.

The 7.5cm main gun round rang out with a bang, the armor piercing round finding its mark in lighting seconds, and hammered its way into the enemy machine between the turret ring and the upper superstructure and then burst into flames. With in a matter of a few seconds, the on-board ammunition caught fire and the entire vehicle exploded, blowing it apart at the weld seams. As expected, the other Russian panzers halted in their tracks as they were not expecting a lone German assault gun to present itself.

Wittmann did not lose any time in taking on their next target of opportunity. Without orders, Koldenhöff rolled the StuG III forward a bit, turned to the left, hit the brakes and locked onto the enemy platoon leader's vehicle as it was sporting an antenna. In the meantime, the loader had rammed home a second main gun round into the smoking and hot breech of the 7.5cm gun. The breech clicked shut, with the gunner on his mark for the second shot. Wittmann gave his fire command very quickly, the gunner pressed the firing trigger, and the main gun let out a loud crack as the round flew towards its target, hit and penetrated. Within a few short seconds, another Russian T34/76 was engulfed in flames. As the German assault gun was still rocking on its suspension from the second shot fired, the empty shell casing was ejected out of the breech and fell into the canvas bag hung under the breech guard. Petersen had the third round already in his hands for the next engagement and as soon as the gun recoiled and returned to battery, he slammed it into the breech with great skill. As Koldenhöff and the rest of the crew were searching for their next targets, Wittmann heard panzers firing to the east of their position, where other StuG IIIs must have been engaging other Russian armored fighting vehicles. He wondered, were they in the middle of an all out enemy panzer assault? It did not matter, as his main concern was to deal with the Russian machines at hand.

As the StuG III moved forward, they were now travelling directly into the sights of another Russian T34/76 which had not been seen by Wittmann or his loader. This vehicle had halted and had fired a number of main gun rounds at his vehicle. In all of the excitement and tension of his first few main gun rounds being fire, Wittmann and his crew had not even noticed these rounds flying over their vehicle and then crashing into the earth throwing up fountains of earth and rocks behind their position. The Russian gunners aim was extremely bad and no doubt was still trying to zero in on Wittmann's vehicle when his loader spotted the enemy vehicle. It was now time for Wittmann to evade this dangerous situation post haste and ordered his driver to reverse out of their position and move into some woods that would help to hide their vehicle. With great speed, the StuG III dipped and rolled as it moved closer and closer to this highly needed protection as enemy main gun rounds still continued to whistle overhead and then crash into the trees with a large crack. With great difficulty, Wittmann and his driver maneuvered their machine into and through the woods and were at last hidden from view from the probing eyes of the Ivans.

After travelling about half a kilometer, Wittmann ordered his driver to turn their vehicle to the south and roll forward for an additional two kilometers before they once again turned towards the east. A few short minutes later, they had reached the edge of a small wood and came to a halt as Wittmann did not want to take the chance of being observed once again. As soon as he instructed his crew in regards to his next move, he climbed out of his vehicle and jumped down onto the track fender and then onto the soft ground. His intentions was to undertake a reconnaissance probe on foot of the terrain ahead of his vehicle, whereby keeping his machine hidden from any Russian observers or enemy gunners that he was quite certain would be in the surrounding area. In the concealment of some low laying bushes, he moved carefully forward to the edge of a small clearing and sat down in a shielded position and observed the immediate area with his binoculars searching for any signs of the enemy forces. As he kept searching for the Ivans, he suddenly noticed some movement in the same woods and then located the ugly snout of an armored fighting vehicle in a hull-down position. He then was able to make out the gun barrel that suddenly started traversing ever so slowly. Wittmann was quite sure that his StuG III had not been spotted and kept observing the enemy panzer and tried to ascertain its intentions. The turret of this machine stopped rotating for a few seconds and he assumed it had done so in order to make last second final lay corrections and then fired its main gun right over Wittmann's hidden position! As a result of the tremendous shock wave, he was flattened to the ground by the blast. The firing and impact occurred during the split second that it took Wittmann to hit the ground with the result being that he was not too sure what had transpired. As he looked up from his very precarious and exposed position, the Russian panzer was totally shattered by the impact of a very well placed 7.5cm main gun round which had torn through its armor plate again between the upper superstructure and the turret of the machine. The turret was completely blown off the hull and chassis and was now sticking straight up and into the air. The turret had been launched into the air with such great force that it had been flipped over and over and landed with the gun barrel embedding itself into the ground with the turret still attached to it. It was indeed a very strange sight to behold, and never had Wittmann seen such overwhelming destruction as a direct result of a first main gun round hitting and penetrating an enemy panzer.

Wittmann was still not too clear in regards to what had just happened, but later learned from his crew that his gunner had been scanning the area ahead of their vehicle and through his panoramic periscope had picked up the motion in regards to the enemy panzer's turret. The Russian machine and Wittmann's StuG III had fired simultaneously, but Wittmann's gunner had been on his mark and utterly destroyed his opponent. After collecting his thoughts, Wittmann carefully made his way back to his vehicle and crew, but had to contend with a hidden Russian machine gun, that opened up on him from nowhere. As he climbed back up and into the security of his StuG III, he could see that there was now great clouds of thick black smoke billowing out from the shattered Russian T34/76. He then decided that he must withdraw his vehicle from this sector as the burning Russian panzer and its fiery signature would surely cause attention upon itself. As Wittmann stepped back down into his commander's cupola, he reached down and padded his gunner on his head and stated to him that he had performed his duty and congratulated him in regards to his superior observation and highly accurate panzer gunnery.

Wittmann's StuG III was once again put into immediate action with the Red army panzers that were in the surrounding area. He wanted to maneuver a few hundred meters to the south and along the edge of a wood. All around him was constant firing, smoke, and the sickening smell of burning rubber, cordite fumes, and the lingering stench of burnt human flesh. In order to survive, Wittmann had to keep his vehicle on the move, or highly camouflaged if he halted his vehicle for any length of time.

As his StuG III was moving slowly along the edge of a small grove of trees, a Russian T34/76 spotted it, and fired. The main gun round flew high and severed tree branches above Wittmann which rained down upon him and his loader. A second main gun round impacted and exploded no more than ten meters from their machine and badly shook up the entire crew. After the shock wave engulfed his crew, Wittmann and his loader found themselves pulling their numbed bodies from the floor of their fighting compartment. They were both dazed and deafened for a few minutes but unhurt. Klinck turned around in this gunner's seat and was now staring down at his commander and asked if he was injured. Wittmann first checked with his loader and then informed his gunner that everything was alright and no injuries were incurred.

The StuG III rumbled forward through the wooded area at full throttle with Wittmann and his loader once again scanning the forward area for any signs of enemy panzers. The enemy machine that had fired at their vehicle had vanished, and it was assumed that it had backed off in order to not be detected or to report to higher command. Wittmann now felt that they were out of danger for the moment and told his driver to halt the vehicle and kill the engine once again. As soon as their powerplant was shut down, Wittmann could indeed still hear the familiar sounds of an armored fighting vehicle in the vicinity, but could not locate its position or identity. It seemed that the machine was somewhere nearby, but it had also been halted by its commander with its engine only idling. Wittmann desperately scanned the forward area with his binoculars and in the nick of time pinpointed some motion which was indeed the rotating turret of another T34/76. He immediately yelled to his driver to restart the vehicles engine and as soon as the Maybach powerplant came back to life, he informed his crew the whereabouts of the enemy panzer. As Wittmann was screaming to his driver to turn to the left, he could see out of the corner of his eye, that the Russian machine had turned on its axis and hesitated for a number of seconds. This was time enough for his gunner to take careful and precise aim and fired the main gun just as the driver of the StuG III came into the correct bearing which placed Klinck's sight picture dead center on target. Wittmann's gunner did not even have to make final adjustments, he just pressed the firing trigger and destroyed the enemy panzer. For the fourth time that day, flames burst out as a colorful explosion sent flames ever skyward as the Russian machine blew up and shot out pieces of white hot metal about in every direction possible for a hundred meters.

After this encounter, Wittmann ordered his driver to reverse out of their position as he was still concerned about other enemy panzers in the area. They had been too lucky so far, and did not want to stay in the same firing position for too long. After driving for a short distance he had his driver turn back towards the west and rattled across a small clearing at full speed to the cover of some large trees. As their StuG III was moving towards this cover, Wittmann suddenly made out the outlines of three Russian panzers sitting on top of a nearby hill, their silhouettes showing against a clear blue sky and apparently not worrying about being detected. As Wittmann started to announce his next battle run, his vehicle came upon a creek at the edge of the clearing.

"Look out, go slowly through this area!" yelled Wittmann at his driver.

Koldenhöff slowed the vehicle down somewhat as he saw a medium size stream come into view. He then sped up the vehicle in order to try and force a crossing and to reach the other side as quickly as possible. As the StuG III plunged into this stream and started to move across it, the bow of the vehicle disappeared as it had now entered an unseen deep hole undetected by Wittmann and his loader. Koldenhöff stopped the vehicle at once and slammed the transmission into reverse in order to prevent the machine from becoming bogged down even further by the oozing mud bottom.

"Reverse, reverse! Quickly and carefully, Herbert!" shouted Wittmann as he warned his driver that they were now in dire straights if rapid and appropriate evasive actions were not immediately taken.

Koldenhöff did not panic as he was an expert driver. After he had placed the transmission into reverse he provided the engine with full throttle which slammed Wittmann, Klinck, and Petersen forward in their seats as a result of this sudden and violent vehicle motion. Slowly and with great effort indeed the StuG III pulled itself out of this sticky and clinging mud environment with its engine screaming a full rpm. With one final gun of the Maybach engine, the assault gun finally extracted itself out of the grasp of the muddy stream bed with the thick mud making a loud slurping and sucking sound.

"We can not cross here Herbert!" said Wittmann. "Turn around and head down stream for a better crossing sight with all speed!" Wittmann continued.

Koldenhöff spun the StuG III around to the right, and moved forward down stream with mud flying off of the suspension. A few minutes later Wittmann's vehicles came to a smaller crossing with a seemingly firm base covered with flat stones. He directed his driver to cross at this point with all speed. Koldenhöff gunned the engine and raced the StuG III across the stream without any difficulty whatsoever and reached the southeast bank. After exiting this water obstacle, Wittmann ordered him to move forward in search of the three previously sighted T34/76 panzers most likely still lurking in his immediate area of concern.

Wittmann continued to scan the area with his binoculars and once again, he spotted the three Russian panzers still sitting on the hill. It was decided to attempt to approach the flank of the nearest vehicle, as the commander of this machine did not seem to detect Wittmann's vehicle approach due to the fact that all three T34/76s had their engines running. The German assault gun was able to maneuver within 500 meters of this machine and carefully trundled in behind it in order for Wittmann's gunner to be able to fire a main gun round into the thinner rear armor plate. After they managed to reach the desired firing position, Wittmann provided a quick and precise fire command. Klinck had already locked onto his target and was anticipating the command to fire. He pressed the firing trigger with the main gun round giving out a large crack. The 7.5cm main gun round bore a hole into the engine compartment of the enemy panzer and quickly burst into flames.

The next enemy panzer was to be dealt with as soon as possible. Wittmann quickly directed his driver to turn their vehicle to the left in order to fire at this machine. However, this T34/76 managed to turn itself around in time to present its frontal sloped armor towards Wittmann's machine.

"Fire, Fire Klinck!" yelled Wittmann!

His gunner fired the 7.5cm main gun at the same instant of the frantic fire command, with the entire crew being able to witness the main gun round slamming into the frontal area of the T34/76. To their dismay, the round failed to penetrate and bounced off the vehicle with a loud clanging sound.

"Damn crap!" cursed Klinck.

Petersen panted hard as he quickly loaded another round into the breech of the hungry 7.5cm main gun and as soon as the breech sprang shut, bent over and grabbed another round in order to be ready for another fire command if needed. Wittmann and his gunner fired two more times at the ensuing Russian panzer, with the third round managing to jam the turret ring and caused the enemy machine to halt in its tracks. The last T34/76 turned away from the StuG III and rolled down the slope of the hill and into the nearby woods and was not to be see again. For the moment, Wittmann and his crew felt that this battle was now over and started to check for any damage sustained to their vehicle during the encounter with the enemy panzers with Petersen trying to make contact with their headquarters on their radio network. Nobody could foresee what was to happen next! The Russian T34/76 that had its turret jammed previously suddenly came to life and fired at the German assault gun and its crew. The enemy crew had been playing dead and had managed to free their inoperative turret and were now once again a very dangerous adversary. The first main gun round from the Russian machine impacted into the ground just in front of the StuG III, deflected off of some rocks, and howling like a banshee roared straight up into the air.

As soon as the first main gun round had been fired by the Russian tank, Petersen grabbed another 7.5cm AP main gun round and threw it into the still smoking and hot breech. Wittmann and the rest of his crew threw themselves back into their respective positions and commenced to do battle with the enemy panzer. As soon as the driver was in his seat, he started the Maybach engine and revved up the powerplant and swung the vehicle into the direction of the Russian threat. As the T34/76 came into his sight picture, Klinck fired and placed the 7.5cm AP main gun round once again between the superstructure and turret of the enemy machine. This time the detonation caused the vehicle to instantly burst into flames. The closed hatches of the doomed machine all opened at the same time with the crew trying to escape the fiery inferno from within their armored fighting vehicle. As they did so, Wittmann could clearly see that all of their uniforms were on fire with the enemy panzer crew now walking around on the ground trying desperately to extinguish the flames that caused them to look like hideous human torches.

Wittmann and his loader were transfixed upon this scene of horror and merciless destruction and then gave the order to his loader to climb out of their vehicle and to try and smother the flames with their bed-rolls. The panzer commander of the T34/76 was burnt beyond recognition and was still standing upright in his turret position. He had been very badly wounded and immobilized and unable to extract himself even though his vehicle was completely consumed by fire. The other enemy crew members were now rolling on the ground trying to put out the flames when Wittmann and Petersen reached them. They had escaped their shattered machine, but were all horribly burned and were in such severe pain, their bodies were shaking and twitching uncontrollably and were going into deep shock. Wittmann and his loader gave what little medical treatment they could and pulled the three Russian tank crew members under the shade of some small trees and returned to their vehicle.

Wittmann and Petersen remounted their machine and then continued to roll down the slope of the hill and halted. Wittmann ordered Petersen to send a radio message to his company commander.

"Buzzard to Eagle! Come in!"

"Enemy attack with eighteen panzers halted. Six T34/76 panzers destroyed!"

The radio call came back and asked for a second transmission.

"Repeat message! Having communication problems with your message, over?"

"Eighteen enemy panzers attempted to take elevation 65.5. They were halted!"

"Six enemy panzers destroyed!" explained Petersen.

"Send medical unit, we have three wounded Russians at given location!" And with that statement the radio transmission was closed.

After this battle against one German StuG III assault gun, the Russians did not stage another attack and Wittmann and his crew felt that this day of fighting had gone very well for them, but felt that if it had not been for very poor gunnery techniques pertaining to the enemy panzer gunners, they all might not have survived. It was stated as a golden rule in armored combat, that the first vehicle to fire its main gun, was usually the victor, this was a bitter lesson they would never allow themselves to forget.

While Wittmann and his StuG III crew had been battling with the six enemy T34/76s, an Obersturmführer Gerhard Bremer with a reconnaissance company had pushed through the north woods and with the support of the armored units operating in the area pushed back the Ivans under similar circumstances. Hundreds of enemy soldiers surrendered and they sang out in unison so they would not be misunderstood until their numbers had come close enough to be recognized.

"Ukrainski, Ukrainski!" They cried out and hugged each other by their necks.

There were apparently Ukrainians who were now glad that the war for them was over. They marched into captivity with great broad smiles on their tired and dirty faces.

Upon returning to his company headquarters area later in the day, Wittmann was immediately ordered to report to his divisional commander.

"Please, watch yourself Michael!" remarked Klinck who was standing next to their StuG III and examining the minor battle damage caused by the day's fighting.

"The old man will take your head off if you do not watch yourself!"

With in a few short minutes, Michael Wittmann stood at attention before his divisional commander SS-Obergruppenführer Josef "Sepp" Dietrich. Dietrich who was seated, then looked up at this brave and resourceful StuG III commander and presented a wide grin on his rough and fatigued face.

"Wittmann, you have with your StuG III stopped the attack of a reconnaissance company of an enemy panzer regiment. I honor you for your outstanding efforts, with the Iron Cross Second Class!"

Michael Wittmann wearing his Reichs Arbeitdienst (Voluntary Labor Service) uniform.

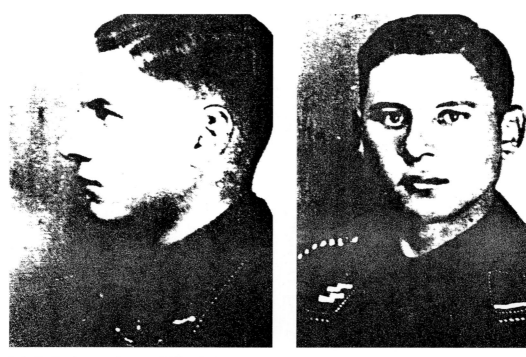

Left: Earliest known photograph of Michael Wittmann in a black service uniform, a Verfungungstruppe tunic. The single "litze" indicates rank of Staffel-Sturmmann, which he was awarded on November 9, 1937. Right: Profile of Wittmann in the same uniform. His height measured 5' 7.5" (1.76 meters).

Unterscharführer (Sgt.) Michael Wittmann (right) in Greece, 1941, as a StuG III Ausf.A commander.

Michael Wittmann and his crew aboard their StuG III Ausf.A in Greece. Note the spare track attached to bow of vehicle for added protection against antitank gunfire.

Michael Wittmann and his crew standing next to their StuG III Ausf.A, somewhere in the mountains of Greece.

Wittmann (left) after receiving his Iron Cross Second Class medal, next to his StuG III Ausf.A, on July 12, 1941, after the early battle of Operation "Barbarossa."

Wittmann with his StuG III Ausf.A in Russia, 1941. Notice the two broken front torsion bars. He nicknamed his StuG III "Buzzard."

This photo was taken by Wittmann after he and his crew washed "Buzzard" in a stream.

Wittmann and his crew pose with their heavily camouflaged StuG III Ausf.A somewhere in Russia.

Wittmann attended Officer training at the Junkerschule in Bad Tolz, where he entered June 4, 1942.

Wittmann shown wearing his infantry tunic with the black panzer collar, shortly after graduation from the Junkerschule in Bad Tolz, December 12, 1942. Note the Adolf Hitler cuff band on his left sleeve.

Wittmann and Wendorff shortly after graduation from the Junkerschule.

Wittmann poses for the camera following graduation from the Junkerschule.

Wittmann shown in profile on December 12, 1942 shortly after graduation from the Junkerschule on December 12, 1942. He is now SS-Untersturmführer Michael Wittmann.

From left to right: Wendorff, Schultz and Wittmann. LAH Tiger Company 13 officers pose in their tailor-made

"schwarz panzer jacke." Notice the *"single key"* emblem on the left front of the Tiger I.

Somewhere in Russia, 1943, Wittmann eats lunch in a captured British vehicle. He is wearing a Russian fur-lined jacket and a Russian turtle-neck sweater.

Wittmann watches with intensity on the Russian front in 1943. Tha battle scar on his chin is quite evident.

Wittmann's crew bet him a bottle of vodka that he could not "punch the tube" by himself. He won the bet and drank the bottle himself!

Michael Wittmann and Bobby Woll receive their "Knight's Cross" from Joachim Peiper (back to camera). Woll is facing Peiper on his left, and Wittmann is on his right. January 14, 1944.

Woll and Wittmann after the awards ceremony for their Knight's Cross', January 14, 1944.

An elated crew celebrates with their talented Tiger I commander.

Wittmann and crew clowning for the camera on a snowy day in Russia.

Along with his crew, Wittmann inspects the 88 "Kill Rings" on the main gun barrel of their Tiger I. It was those kills that earned the Knight's Cross for Woll and himself.

This studio photo of Wittmann was taken shortly after he was awarded the Eichenlaub (Oakleaf Cluster) to his Knight's Cross, January 30, 1944. He was also promoted to the rank of SS-Obersturmführer on this date.

With these words "Sepp" Dietrich presented the young assault gun commander with the award. Wittmann was very excited to have been awarded this medal, but felt that his assault gun crew should have also received some sort of decoration for their brave efforts as well.

After thanking "Sepp" Dietrich for this great honor, Wittmann completed a very detailed after action report (AAR) with as few unnecessary words as possible, but was very informative and outlined every pertinent detail to the best of his knowledge and memory. The battle had happened so fast that it was impossible to remember everything. His head was still swimming and he had to concentrate on every thought and sentence. Everyone who had been able to listen in on this fantastic panzer attack soon realized what it was like to come up against a very determined enemy armored attack. The true formula was to attack the enemy until the opposition was totally swept off balance and pushed aside through the combined efforts of practical experience, crew coordination, and master gunnery.

"Do you have a special wish, Wittmann?" Asked "Sepp" Dietrich.

"I would like for the three wounded enemy panzer crew members on elevation 65.5 to be given proper medical attention!" replied Wittmann.

"Sepp" Dietrich, once a Lieutenant during the First World War, and one of the very first panzer commanders in the Kaiser's Army, nodded in total agreement.

"It will be taken care of Wittmann, at once!"

After Wittmann was dismissed, he returned once again to his men who were now camped in a nearby small village for the night. As his crew saw him head towards them, they all ran to him and immediately saw that he was now wearing the Iron Cross Second Class. They were all very excited as they had been fighting together ever since the hard and bitter battles of their Greek operations in the Balkans. Indeed, they had now been welded into a very formidable fighting team. They all encircled their "Michael" for a number of minutes and all shook hands and admired this seasoned assault gun commander for his star was just now starting to shine above and beyond all of the other panzer commanders of his day. One of his crew members made a profound statement during this joyous time of celebration.

"When our "Michael" so continues, soon every youngster in Germany will know about him!"

The advance continued and as the Russian assaults lessened the Waffen-SS units were very eager to exploit and capture small towns and villages. Kiev, the Ukrainian capital was now ready for the taking, but Adolf Hitler changed his overall plan and directed his main attack upon Uman which was due south of the capital city. The mass majority of the Sixth Army then maneuvered in a southeast direction to cut off the Russians now fighting against the Eleventh and Seventeenth armies. The Leibstandarte Adolf Hitler, who were holding the northern flank, were constantly under heavy assaults from many of the nine divisions of the Fifth Red Army which were hammering repeated and heavy strikes against the Sixth Army's left flank. During this time frame, overwhelming pressure by the Ivans forced the northern wing of Army Group South to temporarily form into a defensive posture. By July 21st the offensive was resumed and the assaults towards Uman were underway once again. Also during this period of time and the resumption of the offensive by the Waffen-SS and the extraction of Red Army divisions attacking from Korosten and the surrounding Pripet Marshes, the Leibstandarte Adolf Hitler's aggressive and constant assaults were instrumental in rescuing the 16th Panzer Division from serious circumstances.

Three massive Russian tank divisions had been assaulting the 16th Panzer Division and only the arrival of the Waffen-SS units, maneuvering onto the exposed left flank, and attacking across the Sokolovka road, helped to elevate the situation at hand.

Kempf, the General commanding the corps of which the Leibstandarte Adolf Hitler was then a part, wrote: 'Since 24/7, the Leibstandarte SS Adolf Hitler has taken the most glorious part in the encirclement of the enemy around Uman. Committed at the focus of the battle for the seizure of the key enemy position at Archangelsk, the Leibstandarte with incomparable dash, took the city and the heights to the south. In the spirit of the most devoted brotherhood of arms, they intervened on their own initiative in the arduous struggle of the 16th Infantry Division (motorized) on their left flank and routed the enemy, destroying numerous tanks.

'Today at the conclusion of the battle of annihilation around Uman, I want to recognize and express my special thanks to the Leibstandarte SS Adolf Hitler for their exemplary effort and incomparable bravery.

'The battles around Archangelsk will be recorded indelibly and forever in the war history of the Leibstandarte...'

During August 3rd and operating in and around Uman, Michael Wittmann was wounded for the very first time while commanding his StuG III Ausf. A. While engaging Red Army units, Wittmann's StuG III was struck by an unknown type of artillery or anti-tank gun round. Wittmann was standing upright in his commander's hatch when the enemy round struck his machine. He was injured in the face by a shower of splinters and shell fragments which caused many cuts and abrasions. He was thrown down into the vehicle and landed bleeding very heavily from his wounds. His crew were quick to react as they thought for a few minutes that they could not stop the blood from flowing from the head, face, chin, and neck of their commander. Koldenhöff directed the StuG III to a grove of trees and halted their vehicle with the engine idling. Klinck and Petersen quickly grabbed the first aid box and started to dress Wittmann's wounds. Wittmann was conscious during this time, but was dazed and somewhat confused at to what had just happened to him. Both his gunner and loader told him that his wounds were nothing serious, but to just lie back against the engine firewall and to relax. Blood was still racing down his face and upper torso, but the brave assault gun commander laid still while his comrades patched him up as best as they could. Finally, they lifted him to his feet and checked the rest of his upper body for any additional cuts in his skin or any broken bones. Luckily for Wittmann, all of his injuries were just superficial, however, his uniform was a total mess and torn in many places. Wittmann was fortunate that he had not been standing completely upright in position, as he surely would have received additional wounds around the heart and lung areas. He was to receive on August 20th the badge for wounded soldiers in black for these wounds.

After the fall and capture of Uman the German forces stormed forwards to new objectives with full fury. Strongly defended by the 12th Cavalry Division, Bobry soon surrendered to the Waffen-SS units on August 9th with the advance continuing in the direction of Nikolaev. At Sasselje, a cross road town situated in a very picturesque setting of small lakes, was overrun from its defenders of which consisted of an cavalry and infantry division. The Leibstandarte Adolf Hitler was also situated in the Sasselje area and established a salient. Red Army troops hoping for an avenue of escape through this town were caught in a trap by the Waffen-SS which halted a major westerly move by these Russian forces. The Ivans were completely caught off guard with the vast majority of their columns utterly destroyed by German artillery fire as they ventured upon the town. Their entire mobile effort was halted and smashed, with only a very few trucks being able to turn about and flee the area. Secondary attempts were mounted by the Red Army commanders to overrun the Waffen-SS lines as coordinated attacks were staged time and time again, but with the same effect. As a last ditch effort, a major infantry attack from the east was attempted with the enemy pouring out from the sunflower and maize fields in human wave formations bent on taken the Waffen-SS lines at all costs, but in the end, these attacks were completely halted and driven back. Not to be outdone, further attacks from the west included a tank assault, supported by infantry, which was eradicated by the Leibstandarte's artillery, while its reconnaissance Spähwagens drove into the oncoming infantry and pushed them back in total confusion. After consolidating their gains, the Waffen-SS units stormed southward from Sasselje on the morning of August 17th, came upon Snigirevka during the early hours of the evening, then bypassed this heavily garrisoned town, and then rolled on towards Cherson, a somewhat large industrial city and then onto the final objective of this offensive. Harsh hand-to-hand fighting and house-to-house battles raged on as Russian Navel Marines fought man-to-man against the Leibstandarte soldiers for supremacy of the city. On the afternoon of the 20th the Waffen-SS units handed over their area of responsibility and were kept in reserve.

During August 21st the Seventeenth Army was able to cross the Dnieper and established a strong bridgehead. It was not until the first week of September that the Leibstandarte Adolf Hitler managed to cross the three-quarter mile wide river with strict orders to storm across the Nogai steppe.

It was during the drive across the Nogai steppe that Michael Wittmann was awarded the Iron Cross First Class on September 8. He was very pleased to obtain this decoration and could only praise his StuG III crew for their expert handling of their fighting vehicle. There was not much time to celebrate as the Leibstandarte Adolf Hitler was on the move through the very depressing Nogai which was an extremely dusty area with clouds of thick choking red brown dust particles hanging over the long columns of vehicles. Due to this factor the Waffen-SS units were visible for miles with the enemy being able to pinpoint their exact locations and to bring down artillery barrages with great effect. Nevertheless, the Leibstandarte and other units pushed forward towards their objectives.

A combined advance was now on which included Wehrmacht units and the elite Waffen-SS which continued from Novaya-Mayatschka which had fallen on September 9th, and then across the steppes to Kalantchak. Orders came down to carry out an all night attack on the town, but was countermanded and instead, an unexpected and immediate move towards the Crimea was announced. On September 11th, the columns of the Leibstandarte Adolf Hitler vehicles had advanced south of Nova Alexandrovka and were moving along via Admaniy entering the village of Preobrachhenko. Clouds of thick red dust had been thrown high up into the air for hundreds of feet and continued to alert Red Army units. Nothing like this had ever been encountered before by the LAH, and to many, was the first time they had endure this type of harsh fighting, as the dust choked the life out of the men and caused havoc with all of the Maybach engines powering their vehicles. Every type of protection was tried to keep out the suffocating red dust particles, as crew members who rode with their heads up and out of their armored fighting vehicles had to place scarfs sent from home over their mouths and noses and also wore the ever popular 'Rommel' goggles to keep out the blinding dust and sand. Special filters were also installed on the vehicles to stop the ingress of dust and sand, but these devices had to be constantly checked and cleaned as often as possible. It seemed very apparent that these filters had not been tested in such regions as now being encountered, with the result being that all moving parts of the vehicles were being worn out as twice the normal operating rates. It had been a two day struggle of men and machines against the elements to reach the next objective, but it was vital that the German forces secure this area as the intent was to trap another large contingent of Red Army units in this area of operations.

As the German forces advance continued into this area another ring was thrown around the Red Army units, and on September 14th, the 3rd, 9th, and 16th Panzer Divisions met at Lochivna. Sixty Red Army divisions belonging to five Russian armies were totally severed from their follow up troops, were contained, and then put into the bag. To the average German front line soldier, it seemed that the German military forces had indeed, since the opening phases of the invasion of Russia, had captured what must have seemed to be the entire Russian military might. But the Red Army High Command was constantly bringing up fresh troops, hundreds of tanks, and other related military supplies to areas outside the area of encirclement, with the Leibstandarte Adolf Hitler meeting increasing resistance as it maneuvered on the line Militopol-Nikopol heading for the Crimea. The Red Army units were now withdrawing into this peninsula which was a tactical error on their part, as they were containing themselves into an area where they could be easily captured and destroyed. Adolf Hitler ordered these forces to be dealt with and ceased the efforts of Army Group South as well as extending the length of this front by his total determination of capturing the Crimea at any cost.

In order for the German forces to enter this peninsula, it had to pass through a very narrow neck of terrain which was devoid of any appreciable cover, and was heavily fortified and strongly manned by Red Army forces. The new order for the Leibstandarte Adolf Hitler was to force open a passage through this opposing area. The first assaults stormed forward via Preobrachenko where the offensive came to a standstill in the face of a defensive position lying very secure behind a comprehensive and skillfully laid minefield and supported by a powerful Russian armored train (Panzerzug). With this type of opposition, it was very clear that the assault units of the Leibstandarte Adolf Hitler could not breach the Perekop narrows. It was painfully clear that the assault units could not take this objective as it would cost too many men's lives and vehicles lost. All of this was compounded by the fact that the armored train was sure to play havoc on the assaulting units with dire consequences. The commanders of the German forward assault units dared not to try and tackle the dense minefields obstructing their way, which would in turn reduce their forces forthwith. With the western opening of the Perekop narrows blocking the Waffen-SS, it swung its main point of attack to the eastern passage at Balykov with the hopes of catching the Russians off guard once again. The Waffen-SS units jumped off from their start positions in a thick fog with the assault detachments driving home the attack, and by 09:00 hours, they had broken through the outer defensive line and captured the Sliakov station, plus the town of Novo Alesksovka. As the assault units continued pushing their attacks eastward to Genichek, the men of the Leibstandarte Adolf Hitler stood proudly on the shores of the Sea of Azov. Located on a large plateau, the town of Genichek overlooked the surrounding countryside and the impending Russian counterattack preparations were made under the ever watchful eye of the Leibstandarte Adolf Hitler. As the attacks came in, every man and weapon visible to the Waffen-SS observers came under a lethal rain of constant and accurate fire that cut down the Ivans like a scythe through standing wheat. The Russian attacks were soon halted as a direct result of this fire. Now that the Russian attacks had been crushed, it was time for the advance to continue in and along the northern shore of the sea towards Melitopol.

During the early morning of September 18th, the three leading companies had taken defensive positions along the Isthmus of Perekop. Among them was also the reconnaissance company of the Leibstandarte Adolf Hitler under command of SS-Obersturmbannführer (Lieutenant-Colonel) Kurt Meyer "Panzermeyer" Also with this unit was the 3rd Sturmgeschütz Batterie which contained Michael Wittmann and his StuG III crew.

"Comrades, I have received the order from the headquarters of General Bieler (commander of the 73rd Infantry Division) to push on through to the Isthmus of Perekop.

Meyer paused for a moment. It seemed as if he could sense the entire company staring at him. Again, they were to lead the assault. It would be their responsibility to smash any and all of the Ivan's defenses. If they failed, it would mean that many lives would be lost due to their failure to lead the way for the follow up troops and equipment.

"We will not be alone, men! Sturmbannführer (Major) Stiefvater who was with us in Greece will be with us once again. The lead column will be lead by Untersturmführer (2nd Lieutenant) Montag!"

"Finish up!" Rang the voice of Panzermeyer through the earphones to every StuG III commander under his command. Everyone was anxious to start the new battle run as they wanted to sweep the Ivans off the face of the earth; they had the enemy on the run and did not want to let up their pursuit. The smell of tactical success was riding high in the air, as every man in the assault force was ready at his station. Every weapon was checked, and then checked again. All along the line, the vehicle commanders waited for the word: "Advance!"

Michael Wittmann looked forward and could see far to the east as the sky was growing brighter and brighter. He and his crew were waiting for the order to advance! It always seemed that the waiting was the worst part of all of it, the quiet that loomed over the battlefield was as frightening as battle itself. The Russians knew that German panzer units would be sent in first and Wittmann also knew that artillery rounds would soon be raining down into their mists and no doubt knock out many of the first line of assault vehicles. The Ivans had their backs up against a wall, and they would fight to the death as they indeed had nothing to lose by fighting aggressively. As Wittmann looked up and at his battalion commander's command vehicle he saw Panzermeyer raise his arm three times into the morning air, and then heard the static rush come in over the radio network.

"All panzers, March!"

From idle to full throttle went the engines of all the vehicles standing by, ready for anything. At the appointed rendezvous point the reconnaissance company met with Sturmbannführer Stiefvater's vehicles. After a short halt and discussion, they all continued forward in a wedge formation. The sun now colored the sky red, with the Russian prairie becoming alive with many radiant colors. This scene could have been a peaceful stroll in the countryside, only this time it would be a planned military maneuver where at any second an enemy shell could shriek out of nowhere and bring death to all who ventured forward.

Kurt Meyer's armored unit continued to travel towards the Isthmus of

Peretop at top speed when suddenly Russian soldiers on horseback made an appearance, but immediately disappeared from sight as soon as they were detected. Besides the roar of machines all around him, Wittmann could not hear a thing. Radio transmissions were kept to a minimum and with only a slight breeze blowing against his face did this help to evaporate the sweat from his brow. After maneuvering around a small hill the vehicles all slowed down a little as they were now entering into a small village where a few peasant huts were still standing.

"Take a look at that!" yelled Petersen, being very surprised, and pointed out a herd of sheep that were now trotting into the village ahead of their vehicles. Standing in his open commander's hatch, Wittmann was also aware of this very peaceful sight and could only think of his life on his father's farm which was now very far away. In a split second this completely tranquil setting was obliterated by a deafening roar of an explosion being set off just forward of his vehicle. Soon there was a series of explosions and as Wittmann raised his head back out from hiscommander's hatch, he could see and hear additional detonations along the whole length of the sheep herd. These animals had unfortunately wandered into an unexpected minefield and had set off a large number of these dangerous and deadly devices which were meant for their vehicles. As a result, these poor animals were thrown high up and into the air and when their limp bodies hit the ground they continued to detonate additional mines. The surviving animals raced even further into the minefield in panic and continued to set off even more of these ghastly devices. It was quite clear that the Ivans knew that any German vehicles approaching would be funneled into this trap as they would not expose their belly armor in regards to storming over the hill in front of the village. Thus, by coming around the hill, a minefield would be very appropriate.

"Damn, Damn!" cursed Wittmann.

"If we had driven into that minefield, we would have been blown to smithereens!"

Every soldier who had witnessed this senseless slaughter of helpless animals knew that they had been very close to being eradicated from the face of the earth and had it not been for these poor creatures, many of Kurt Meyer's men would be now lying dead inside their vehicles surrounded by Ivan's gardens of death. All felt very lucky indeed!

A few seconds after the last landmine exploded, the enemy opened fired on Meyer's men and vehicles. Main gun rounds from T34/76 tanks and Pak weapons fired into the German vehicle formations, and within a very few minutes, many of Meyer's armored vehicles were penetrated and set on fire. One StuG III was hit from the left side and blow completely off the road that lead into the village and started to burn. Then suddenly, another Russian armored train that had been operating in the area made an appearance from the railway head and quickly opened fired with its 10.0 cm main guns at the German vehicles.

"Panzerzug!" shouted Panzermeyer over the radio network.

As soon as this warning was announced, the armored train once again opened fired. Two large explosions tore up the ground quite close to the left-hand side of Wittmann's vehicle which in turn threw up large fountains of earth and rocks in all directions. He was somewhat dazed and through blurred eyes he saw a StuG III near his position shutter to a halt and then blow up. Yet another StuG III was hit by this fire and had its left track blown completely off of its suspension, with the crew baling out onto the open ground and running for cover of a nearby machine.

"Retreat, turn about!" came the voice of their commander.

All of the surviving German vehicles turned as ordered, with the roar of the next salvo of enemy rounds rushing through the air, becoming louder and louder until these projectiles smashed into their midsts sending dirt, rocks, and lethal shrapnel about the battlefield, which bounced off and rattled against the protective armor plating. The column finally made it to the other side of the hill and were safe from the firing. The appearance of the formidable Russian armored train had not been expected and there was little that Panzermeyer's men could do about it, and the firing range involved. The only tactical solution available was to call in air support to handle the matter, but there was insufficient time and few ground attack aircraft on call in the immediate area.

The reconnaissance vehicles were continuing to cover the retreating panzer columns with a watchful eye. Wittmann and a number of other StuG IIIs were also firing their main guns at some suspected anti-tank guns although not certain as to their true positions. Once the armored train had started to fire at their machines, everyone involved was very jumpy and every clump of trees and bushes large enough to hide an enemy weapon was fired upon. As the retreat continued, Wittmann ordered his gunner to pump 7.5cm HE rounds into nearby trees to prompt Ivan to exchange fire with their machines. It was also felt that the armored train was only a diversion, and as soon as the German forces reversed their direction, the Russian anti-tank gunners would open up on them from their flanks during this time of indecision. The Red Army was learning their tricks of the trade on this new modern field of battle. The Perekop narrows was to be firmly held by the Ivans for the time being.

A German artillery barrage was then called into play which helped to keep Ivan's heads down, which also forced the armored train to retreat and disappeared from sight. Wittmann and his comrades then proceeded for an additional four kilometers to the west, halted, gathered up all of their forces, regrouped and reorganized themselves.

On the evening of the 18th, the Leibstandarte Adolf Hitler was relieved by the 73rd Infantry Division. "Sepp" Dietrich moved his brigade into the middle of the Isthmus of Sjalkov, which had been forcibly taken and in the end fought their way as far as Geritschesk. Melitopol was to be their next intended objective. Preparations were taken for a direct assault into the city as it was now possible to attack at night and take the city in a single armored sweep.

This time, Wittmann's StuG III "Buzzard" was escorting the frontal assault group. Just ahead he could see the command vehicle of Kurt Meyer in the fast fading light of the day. To the right hand-side of his vehicle was a large group of motorcycle combinations mounting MG-34 machine-guns in their sidecars ready for the order to advance. To the left and about fifty meters out were two screening mobile Pak guns. All was ready for the attack, every man in every vehicle checking and then rechecking their respective weapons.

Wittmann and his company had arrived at a predetermined grove of trees that had been located via a captured Russian map. Untersturmführer Stolle led the advance forward with great skill and determination.

"We rendezvous with the first company! All vehicles follow me!" was the instructions now being aired over the radio network.

The German vehicles rolled forward the best they could as it was now growing darker. They were travelling through an open field and then headed for a wooded area where they found Stolle's forward unit halted in their tracks. Every effort was being made to break through the enemy lines of resistance, but Russian "Ratschbun" (7.62cm) anti-tank guns proved to be a hard nut to crack. Everywhere one looked, they could see these types of rounds smashing into vehicles with a loud bang. Hand-grenades were also being thrown at the German armored fighting vehicles from all around, but the vast majority of these weapons were of only nuisance value. Something had to be done very quickly as if Kurt Meyer did not regroup and stage another attack, the Ivans were sure to mount a counter-attack.

"Attack!" was the order given by Panzermeyer.

Wittmann gave his driver the same command as he stood upright in his open hatch in order to observe the dark and hostile terrain ahead and on the lookout for the enemy to present himself or the flashes of his anti-tank gun muzzle brakes. Machine gun fire whistled by either side of his vehicle as he gave constant and concise directions to his driver as he was trying to guide his machine through the forward edge of the battlefield. He was also being careful in staying clear of any hidden hollows and depressions that could throw his crew around inside the vehicle, or cause damage to the vehicle and its suspension. It was very difficult to see in the dark and Wittmann did not want to take any chances of making a tactical error or becoming lost or immobilizing his StuG III. The Ivans then started to fire their antitank guns into the forward leading German vehicles. The large majority of these projectiles missed their mark and crashed into the ground forty to fifty meters behind the advancing vehicles. As the German vehicles were not storming forward and travelling about half speed (due to the night-time conditions) it was assumed that this was the main cause for the inaccurate firing. In the continuous gun flashes to his immediate forward viewing area, Wittmann saw that their command vehicle had turned around and was heading back in his direction. He was not sure what had transpired, but figured that its commander needed protection. Suddenly he saw a flash from a gun barrel of a Russian T34/

76 tank and in an instant, guided his driver to the 1 o'clock position and waited until the next flash to appear. In the split second that the surrounding area was lit up by this fearful illumination, Klinck carefully aimed, and then fired his first main gun round. Luckily his aim was good as the 7.5cm main gun round penetrated the enemy panzer and ignited the on board ammunition. Within a few seconds of the impact, a great fireball lit up the sky, and exposed the enemy machine's semi-hidden position. After the initial explosion, Wittmann and his crew could see that the Russian panzer was no more than a heap of useless scrap iron. The flames leaping from this vehicle provided many of the other German vehicles better visibility and the assault continued!

Wittmann gave the order to move out and as his machine rolled forward his driver managed to ram into a tree trunk that his commander failed to pin point. The StuG III lunged forward and upright and threw Klinck out of his seat and into Wittmann's lap. The entire crew cursed under their breathe, but were all soon back to their stations and seeking new targets of opportunity. They were now receiving additional enemy fire when Koldenhöff managed to maneuver the vehicle to the right just as an artillery round crashed into the ground not twenty meters from where it have been travelling seconds before. Finally, Wittmann and his tired and battered StuG III crew pulled up next to their commander's control vehicle, which was being fired upon by two anti-tank guns at close range.

"Full throttle! Run them over, quickly!" yelled Wittmann.

In all of the resulting mass confusion, the Russian gunners had not seen or heard Wittmann's StuG III approaching from the left-hand side of their weapon's pits. Wittmann's machine drove right over the first anti-tank gun and crew and headed for the second. The gun crew of the next weapon jumped clear of the StuG III as its tracks crushed this menace and disappeared into the night. At the last minute, a number of the Ivans turned for a few moments and fired automatic weapons at Wittmann whereupon he ducked down inside his vehicle for protection. After rolling forward for about fifteen meters, Koldenhöff brought the vehicle to an abrupt halt via Wittmann's command with Klinck then firing a number of 7.5cm main gun rounds at the same time in order to keep the enemy's heads down. He then fired at another anti-tank gun that had been detected after firing at them, but missing the German assault gun altogether. Wittmann gave the order once again to open fire, with Klinck firing into total blackness. Nothing happened! He had missed his mark, again, another flash from the enemy anti-tank gun, and once again Klinck fired his weapon, still there was no sign of a kill. After this exchange of fire, Wittmann broke off the attack on this position. Klinck was burning mad, as he could not understand why after firing two well placed main gun rounds of 7.5cm (HE) he had not scored a hit?

"Enemy from behind!" was the message over the radio net.

This warning came from Panzermeyer who was frantically trying to make contact with the rest of his vehicles. Wittmann yelled at his driver to turn their vehicle about as fast as possible, and to head towards the enemy to their rear. The StuG III was swung around with full throttle and crashed into a small grove of young pine trees as they had little time to select an easier rearward route. They were now mowing down small trees in an effort to bear their main gun at the enemy who had by now come into close firing range. Tree branches now littered the upper superstructure of the vehicle were as Klinck's view to the outside world via his panoramic periscope was blocked as a direct result of the unwanted foliage. Wittmann immediately jumped up and out onto the roof of his vehicle and quickly kicked and pulled off the pine boughs. Once accomplished, he jumped back down into the vehicle and continued to guide his driver through the woods and also keeping his gunner informed of any new targets presenting themselves. They finally reached the edge of the woods and spotted the same command vehicle and once again pulled up alongside it to try and find out what the situation was at this time and further orders.

After conferring with Panzermeyer, there was no doubt about their present tactical situation, and indeed, they were cut off from the rest of their battle group. The rest of the vehicles were now to the west, and the northwest!

"We are sitting in a sack, Wittmann!", remarked Kurt Meyer.

"Oh, we will come through!", was the reply from Wittmann.

"We must make contact with the rest of the battle group and supply trucks, as if we do not, we will run out of ammunition and fuel!"

In the next hour both of these vehicles travelled back and forth together over large sections of the battle area. Both commanders continually searching for their comrades. The enemy was everywhere and the Ivans fired at any and all movements as made by the German vehicles. Wittmann and Panzermeyer managed to break free of the constant Russian attacks, as each was providing the other with supporting fire, e.g. Meyer and his crew would fire automatic weapons at any infantry trying to stalk Wittmann's StuG III and Wittmann's vehicle offering massive main gun fire to opposing enemy tanks.

Till the break of dawn, Wittmann and Panzermeyer searched for the remainder of their battle group through a strange and hostile land. They had been vastly outnumbered at all times, but were extremely lucky that they had the cover of darkness to conceal their whereabouts for the majority of the time. As the sun lifted itself over the eastern horizon both vehicle commanders headed in a westerly direction with the sun at their backs. Koldenhöff tore through the terrain like a test driver with Wittmann and the rest of the StuG III crew hanging on for dear life! As the two vehicles rolled forward the terrain ahead of them started to become very familiar to them all. They soon found that what was not possible, was indeed possible! They came through all of this harsh and bitter fighting only to find themselves at the very same location where they had started from in the first place!

On September 19th, the leading elements of the Leibstandarte Adolf Hitler reached Rodionovka and established defensive positions with the right flank emplaced around Lake Molochnoye. These thinly secured positions were under constant Russian assaults by troops pouring in from the Russian bridgehead on the western bank of the Molochnaya river. To many of the Waffen-SS who were fighting at this location, it was stated that the fighting had been the most ferocious ever encountered on the Eastern Front.

In order to reach Melitopol the advance took four long and arduous days with loose and highly unstable sandy soil being one of the worst difficulties encountered by the Leibstandarte Adolf Hitler which helped to bog down many of the wheeled vehicles and clogged a great number of the engines along the line of advance. On September 21st, a recall order was given to the Leibstandarte and once again, it was back to the western entrance of the Crimea. This time the task at hand for the LIV Corps and especially the Leibstandarte was to attempt again the capture of the Perekop narrows. On September 27th, the Ninth and Eighteenth Red Armies threw themselves into a massive counter-attack, thereby destroying the Roumanian troops who were opposing them and drove deep into their rearward areas. The attack was headed in a northerly direction and to cut off the Russian advances the Leibstandarte was transferred from Nish Serogosy, in the extreme southern sector, to Gavrilovka, and on to the outer left flank, so as to be positioned as the major linchpin in the overall defensive posture. The first objective was to place an assault company across the Dnieper and form a bridgehead at Kamenka. This tiny outpost would be utilized to break up any attacks thrown in by the Russian High Command and could be a staging area for any future offensive operations. The second objective concerning the Red Army offensive was to bottle up their armored units who were still rampaging around twenty-five miles behind the front battle lines and causing havoc with Wehrmacht and Waffen-SS follow up supply trains and other types of equipment.

Under the various assaults by the German forces the Red Army crumbled under the thrust by the Waffen-SS and Alpine units. The counter-offensive rolled in on September 30th, and from the town of Dnieperovka, which was located to the Leibstandarte's left flank, the advance stormed eastward, across a massive anti-tank ditch at Elisabetovka and then on to Balki. Every effort was made to keep men and vehicles moving at top speed.

As vigorous German assaults smashed into the flanks of the overstretched Russian troops, the Red Army had insufficient resources to defend themselves in regards to the continuous and relentless German attacks. As a result, the Dnieper bridgehead suddenly ruptured and von Kleist's 1st Panzer Group, now renamed the First Panzer Army, rolled towards Rostov with the intent of catching and totally eradicating the Russians in a wide and encircling maneuver.

The Russians were on the run, but in isolated positions, the Red Army infantry was well dug in, and put up a defiant stand, but in the end were mowed down by the steadily advancing German assault detachments. Thousands upon thousands of the Ivans were thrown into this battle and sacrificed. The numbers ran so high that an estimated tally ran as high as ten thousand Red Army soldiers killed. Masses of enemy soldiers and vehicles struggled to cross the Dnieper via a single wooden bridge at Terpinye. Upon the approach of the Leibstandarte's reconnaissance battalions on the western bank, the signal for the Russians to blow the bridge was given by the local Red Army commander. This order did not even take into account that this structure was completely packed with Russian troops and vehicles! As soon as the order was announced, the engineers blew up the only escape route across the Dnieper river.

During the rapid advance towards the Dnieper river and in and around Terpinye Michael Wittmann was wounded for the second time on October 8. His injuries were very much like the ones sustained on August 3rd, but was also injured in the upper right thigh. He was brought to a medical aid station behind the lines by his StuG III crew, where his wounds were cleaned and dressed. He was very anxious to return to battle, but was told that his wounds had to be observed for a few days by the attending Waffen-SS doctor on the scene. Wittmann protested the doctors decision, but in the end was out of action for two days. As the result of these further injuries and Wittmann's daring dash on the field of battle, he received additional wound badges and much praise from his comrades and higher authority. Also at this point in time, Wittmann was recommended for officer cadet school and accepts. It would not however be until June 1942 that he would start his officer training.

The next objective for the First Panzer Army was Taganrog, which laid on the far and distant eastern horizon. The Leibstandarte and the Alpine troops were ordered to assault and take Stalino, which by Eastern Front standards was only a stones throw away; only 250 miles from their jumping off positions. Prior to this assault, German intelligence reports outlined that the defense of Stalino was entrusted to fresh, and highly trained Siberian troops. It was certainly obvious from these reports that the Russians were preparing for a long and drawn out winter campaign which was very unsettling. The German High Command had not anticipated that the invasion onto Russian soil would last any longer than the warm summer months of 1941. It was felt that their 'Blitzkreig' tactics would result in a short summer campaign and the Russians would fall back once that first kick at their rotten door had been implemented. Because of this over confidence, the German military supply infrastructure did not stock pile large amounts of special cold weather engine oils and lubricants, nor did it warehouse warm winter clothing such as warm insulated parkers, snow boots, wool lined gloves, or heavy woolen underwear for the men of the German war machine. It was learned only too late that the Russian Front campaign would indeed continue until and throughout the winter of 1941/42. As a result, many German soldiers would be removed from the battlefield not from the sting of an enemy's bullet, but from the horrible cases of frost-bite which could lead to gangrene, and was feared more than anything else on the Eastern Front.

The only fighting troops not prone to frost-bite were the Panzer and StuG III crews. They at least had the warmth from their vehicle engines to help deal with the biting wind and cold. One had to be very careful not expose skin to the bare metal of their machines, as large chunks of flesh would be torn from hands and arms as a direct result. Many of the vehicles had to be started numerous times during the bitterly cold nights in order that their engine oils and fuel lines did not freeze solid. It was still to be found in the mornings that three or four inches of frost would be clinging to the interiors of the vehicles. Once this thick frost melted during normal operating, the resulting water would drip down into the bowls of the vehicles where it would cause electrical shorts and put the vehicles out of service until this problem was located by maintenance personnel and then replaced or dried out the wiring for starters, fuel pumps, and oil pumps.

At Romanovka, the pursuit battles were fought under harsh conditions and many German casualties were the result. Bad luck had fallen upon the Reconnaissance Battalion as it had missed the opportunity of capturing the Red Army commander and the port of Berdyansk. Mariupol was the next immediate objective and if the Wehrmacht and Waffen-SS units could manage to capture it, the Red Army units in the area would have their backs again to the Sea of Azov with little if any chance of escape. The trapped Russian troops made every effort to break out of this entrapment but were completely cut off from the rest of the Russian forces and supply lines. Terrible losses were suffered by the Ivans and resistance broke down so completely, that the German fire from the high river banks cut down the Ivans like raw wheat at harvest time. The encircled Russian T34/76 tanks also tried to make a determined breakout but were destroyed by the German troops by pouring gasoline over the vehicles and setting them alight with handgrenades or with tracer ammunition. Explosive charges carried by some men were thrown up and onto the approaching Russian machines and were utterly destroyed after the charge detonated. These types of tactics soon became wide spread with large numbers of Russian tanks being knocked out of action in this fashion. The infantrymen who had in the past been highly susceptible to enemy panzer attacks with their high explosive main gun rounds, deadly and raking machine gun fire, and crushing wide steel tracks had a field day ambushing the panicky T34/76 tank crews. 'Panzer Stalking' became a sort of a game for the German troops fighting in Mariupol and even some artillery and Alpine units took up this most dangerous and deadly sport. It was soon found to be quite easy to knock out the Russian machines at close quarters with explosive charges rather than using highly needed and limited main gun rounds in regards to the German armored fighting vehicles now being held back in reserve on the outer edge of the surrounded town.

The German armored units then pushed forward through Berdyansk, through a line of fortifications outside of Mariupol and headed directly towards the city proper. The forward units rolled up the straight roads taking on and successfully beating off any opposition that presented itself and crashed their way into the town. Street fighting of heavy proportions and bitter hand-to-hand combat followed but in the end, the city passed into the capable hands of the Waffen-SS attackers. The battle for the Sea of Azov was now over and the German military forces in that area were very happy to have had such high standards of combat with minor losses. The Russians never knew what had hit them, as every German assault that was sent in, resulted in the Russians reeling back to try and regroup, but as they lost complete control over their troops, massive losses were the end product. The battle for Mariupol was a classic example that once a military assault is started, it must at all costs be allowed to continue to roll ahead. Once the momentum of battle had been achieved, it must never stop until the enemy forces are outwitted, contained, and its only hope for survival is to surrender.

The battle for Taganrog began on October 11th and it was not until five days later that the 1st Battalion was able to establish a bridgehead across the Mius river at Koselkin. Once this bridgehead had been consolidated the entire unit passed through it and continued to make lighting strikes in the direction of Taganrog. The 2nd Battalion, who were holding its position in and around the bridgehead on the 1st Battalion's left flank, were engaged very heavily by Russian T34/76 tanks and suffered extreme losses before the attackers were driven off and the situation restored itself. It took three days until the Leibstandarte Adolf Hitler was able to capture Stalino with Taganrog falling on October 17th.

During the proceeding weeks of heavy action and constant rain fall, the advance first slowed and then was completely halted in regards to the assault planned against Rostov. After all attempts were made to push forward in a sea of unexpected mud, the Leibstandarte and III Corps were not able until the middle of November to reach their new objective. As the rains came down on the Waffen-SS units west of Rostov, it was quite apparent of things to come for the German forces. As the troops lay hidden in their concealed positions, the mud and slime of the Russian steppes constantly sucked vehicles, and panzers down to their axles and track fender lines, plus found its way into every piece of clothing and even into the food rations. Even the men of the Waffen-SS units who had endeared hardships for many months could not overcome their most hated enemy in this harsh and hostile land, "General Mud"! This natural foe could not be destroyed by shooting it dead, or even by trying to blowing it up with high explosives. As time wore on for the German troops, the only thing on one's mind was the ever present thick earth brown substance that made their every day life on the Russian Front even more frightening. Severe dysentery, bronchitis, and other serious crippling lung infections ran rampart through out the units and resulted in great losses to sickness, that a times, reduced rifle company and panzer crews to levels where men were on constant duty, usually exposed to inclement weather and normally without proper food supplies, warm clothing, and precious ammunition.

The critical situation that arose on the Russian Front for the German forces was solely placed on the front line soldier. There were many logistical difficulties which included the differences between the German and Russian railway tracks (in regards to gauge) which resulted in German supply trains having to unload in western railyards and then be reloaded onto Russian rolling stock. Just this one disadvantage in regards to the Russian Front was a major factor in deciding if the front line troops were to survive or not. The total lack of modern roads greatly slowed down the arrival of highly needed supplies and also set in a psychological sense of being lost, as at times, there were no visible signs to navigate by. The Russians destroyed every single available bridge in order to hold up the German advance and ever increasing interference from partisan attacks lowered the morale of the German troops and all combined greatly in helping to cut off the combat units from their supply columns and command bases. The infantry, however, were to suffer the most, as the majority of these men had marched over a thousand miles in the first four weeks of the war and were now without adequate boots and woolen socks. Sickness and constant casualties were reducing the German military forces faster than replacement could reach the forward lines. Many companies totaled less than fifty men, which was a quarter of their normal combat strength. Horses were man's 'best friend' on the Eastern Front as the majority of supplies that actually reached the front line troops were packed in by these overworked animals. On average, one thousand horses a day were dying either of starvation or from the hostile weather conditions, which severely halted the delivery of much needed ammunition, spare parts for vehicles, and food. The Red Army seemed to thrive in these adverse conditions and continued to counter-attack the open, northern flank of the 1st Panzer Army, And yet, this was only the beginning of the Russian winter! The first frosts had been witnessed during the early November days and on the opening day of the final attack upon Rostov had seen the first prolonged duration of wet and heavy snowfall. If this was a taste of things to come, it was to be a very long and bitterly cold winter for the German military forces as a whole.

During this period, massive supply requisitions were being sent back through the supply channels for any and all winter necessities, which over burdened the already strained supply system right back to the German homeland factories, which were only just beginning to realize the need for such highly needed winter clothing and equipment requirements. The German military forces would pay dearly for this oversight established by their High Command, as many front line soldier would freeze to death or develop the feared effects of gangrene. One or two small amputations due to these conditions would be the norm for the average front line infantrymen.

III Panzer Corps, with the Leibstandarte Adolf Hitler under its command opened the assault upon Rostov on November 17th. The winter conditions presented a new problem for the movement of the German troops, Snow now covered the Russian minefields with many vehicles being either destroyed or disabled as a result of accompanying infantry and engineers not being able to probe for these deadly and destructive devices. Biting cold also altered mental capabilities and many units were lost as snow blindness was ever present. The Russians had also beefed up their defensive positions and armored attacks were only halted and smashed as a result of sheer human determination and effort by the Panzer and StuG III crews. On the 20th, Rostov had finally fallen to the Germans and an important contribution to the success of the battle was the capture of the Don river railway bridge intact by units of the Waffen-SS Reconnaissance Battalion. At the end of this days fighting the Corps order of the day listed 10,000 prisoners, 159 field guns, fifty-six panzers of all types and two Russian armored trains as war booty.

On November 21, Michael Wittmann was awarded the Panzer-Kampfabzeichen (Tank Assault Badge in Silver) and was very happy with this decoration. It was presented as the result of twenty-five panzer assaults and proudly attached it to his uniform. Once again, his StuG III crew were very excited in regards to this medal and all concerned congratulated their commander and friend for a job well done. Wittmann was quite aware that he had been very lucky in his recent panzer assault exploits, as many of his comrades had been killed and seriously wounded. He knew that there was to be many more bitter encounters with the Ivans, and could only wonder if he and his crew would survive under these harsh and brutal conditions. He prayed for the safety of all of his comrades and hoped for the best.

It was not long before the Russians sent in the inevitable counter-attacks with full force. Waves upon waves of T34/76 tanks with infantry mounted on board rolled towards the German defensive lines. High explosive rounds were fired at the approaching Red Army machines so as to not only destroy the vehicles forthwith, but to also kill as many of the 'tank desant' troops as possible. Any Russian infantrymen who managed to survive and take to the open ground were soon cut to pieces by heavy and constant German automatic fire. Whether hit with HE rounds or automatic fire the Russians who were caught out in the open snow covered fields resulted in a blood bath with little or no escape.

Life on the Russian Front in the southern regions was very harsh for all concerned. There were usually no defined battle lines, no out-posts or listening posts to speak of, just small penny-packets of desperate men trying to hold off the enemy and relying on mutual support from one another. The staple diet for the German troops was a thick mixture of ground buckwheat (called Kascha) and millet porridge, and the ever present Russian black bread. If the men were lucky, a pig or cow, and even horse meat was cut up and large chunks of who knew what would end up in this hot and bubbling mass. The German army lived on this type of food for months and many loss between twenty and thirty pounds off of their frames in the first few months of the winter war. Water had to be melted down from snow at times, but this operation had its draw backs as if a fire was started, the resulting smoke would be detected by Ivan, plotted, and within a few minutes artillery rounds would come screaming in and around the suspected areas. Every effort was made to keep all weapons from freezing up and it was found that if ordinary sunflower seed oil was applied this would indeed solve this common but dangerous problem. Other ad hoc methods used to stay warm was to pile fist sized stones around a central stove (usually in a captured house or hut behind the lines) and leave them there until they were too hot to handle with bare hands. The stones were then wrapped in a rag or other similar item and passed out to the infantry or guards in their respective posts to help keep out the bitter cold. This worked well, but usually was only good for warming the hands and upper torsos. It was not possible to place these hot stones in their worn out jack-boots, so straw and newspapers were inserted into their foot-wear which resulted in a primitive form of insulation. Face protection was another very important item that was used extensively on the Russian Front with special masks being sewn together with draw strings to try and keep out the biting cold and stinging ice particles that hindered the vision of all vehicle commanders. Even igloos were sometimes constructed to keep out the cold and many were built to various measurements. Wheeled vehicles in the snow were utterly useless so large Russian sleds were impounded and utilized to haul light field howitzers and medium anti-tank guns (3.7 and 5.0cm types) being towed by large draft horses. Each side also stripped their dead simply in order to obtain additional warm clothing for the living. At times, the infantrymen were known to be wearing five to six layers of clothing and with as many pairs of socks (if available) that their foot-wear would allow. During the first Russian winter, the German troops were not as concerned about the Russian assaults thrown against them, as they were in keeping out the deadly winter cold.

Everywhere life was paralyzed by the extremely bitter cold for Army Group South, and according to captured and passive Russian prisoners, the winter of 1941 was a somewhat mild one. The troops of the southern sector could only wonder what it was like to be posted with Army Group North! Certainly, for these troops, every day life in the northern regions of Russia must have been a freezing hell!

As temperatures continued to plummet, the German panzer and heavy field guns froze up to the point where they could not be used for any operations whatsoever. Only the infantry weapons could be used to ward off the Russian assaults and at times it seemed an impossible task for the lone German infantrymen to hold their thinly defended lines. Usually, the infantry units in the forward defensive positions were never offered relief or hot food, and were constantly outnumbered and totally isolated, and subjected to unbelievable hardships. It was not uncommon for five or six men to share a single cigarette or to share one or two chocolate bars. Many of the men who did not smoke at the beginning of the Russian winter campaign, soon took up this habit in order to just have a source of heat near their half frozen faces. For the vast majority of the German soldiers operating on the Russian Front, just being able to inhale warm tobacco smoke into their lungs seemed to have a great psychological effect that help to stem the extreme cold that surrounded them every second of the day.

The Russians never seemed to give up and sent in relentless assaults upon the defensive lines of the entrenched German Wehrmacht and supporting Waffen-

SS units. Savage assaults were directed at the German lines as the Ivans were not only trying to kill every last enemy soldier in sight, but they also wanted to secure these positions in order to remove themselves from the very cold temperatures. The German defenders of course realized this, and fought with deadly determination and tenacity to drive the Ivans back. To be forced out of their prepared and covered positions (or huts in captured villages) and exposed to the naked and harsh elements of the frozen steppes, plus being subjected to the Buran (the icy wind) meant certain death within a few short hours. Being wounded during the winter months on the Eastern Front was one of the most terrifying experiences a man could endure. Once wounded, the blood leaving the body would freeze instantly and a sort of shock would set in and kill a perfectly healthy man in a short period of time. It was found that light wounds that healed very quickly in the summer, would cause death in winter.

Despite Adolf Hitler's orders to stand and fight to the very last man and round, the German military forces withdrew from Rostov. Plans were being drawn up to prepare for a renewed offensive by Army Group South to attack and race for the Don-Donetz line at Fuhrer's Headquarters while in the immediate combat zones the under strength Waffen-SS companies were stemming off assaults by Siberian rifle units spearheading the attacks in human wave tactics across the frozen waters of the Minus river. These fighters were highly trained in the art of winter warfare and donned white winter camouflage suits and usually were equipped with snow skis for rapid movement and skilled maneuvering. These Russian storm troopers were very fierce and if hit by a German bullet would keep coming on until shot three or four times. This was a very severe problem among the German front line troops who at first did not understand this unusual battle field phenomenon. It was finally realized that the intense cold was the major factor in that these troops were so excited and wild eyed in regards to being involved as the leading attackers, and with the cold numbing the senses, they in fact did not even feel the penetrating sting of the initial rifle rounds.

During the winter of 1941/42, the weather hammered the German forces with such fierce severity that it inhibited all out military activity; although limited maneuvers were carried out to some degree. During the month of February a Russian offensive and some local breakthroughs near and around Dnieperpetrovsk forced III Corps to seal off the Russian advance with the Leibstandarte Adolf Hitler holding the thin line while German operations were slowly being carried out. Shortly afterwards, the spring thaw came with warmer weather conditions with the frozen ground of a few weeks earlier now becoming a sea of sticky, knee deep mud with all movement being ground to a standstill. Only pack animals and men on foot with great determination were able to traverse the surrounding terrain with any results. Some of the pack animals were so loaded down with equipment and supplies that many died where they fell and were of course stripped of everything including their meat and fur. It was not until May that full forced military maneuvers were carried out of any size and vehicle drivers had to be very wary of areas that were not completely dried out from the spring thaw. Hitler's Instruction No. 41 illustrated that the south of Russia was to be the decisive front and the mission of Army Group South was to attack any and all Red Army units in the area of the Don and to capture the Caucasian oil-producing centers and refineries.

On May 12th, 1942, the opening offensive was delayed via a Russian spoiling attack, but within one week the German armored pincers had sealed off the Russian bridgehead south of Kharkov. After this successful battle the men of the Leibstandarte Adolf Hitler moved back to Stalino for rest, refitting, reinforcements, and for additional retaining. During this period of reorganization, the threat of another assault landing on the coast of France forced the German High Command to transfer the Leibstandarte from command of Army Group South, and brought it to the Western Front where it was stationed and gradually increased its strength in men and equipment until it was once again recalled to the Russian Front.

During the Leibstandarte's posting in France, various studies and analyses of the first year of the Russian Front battles clearly indicated that at the highest levels, Adolf Hitler had jeopardized strategic victory as opposed to tactical successes. Numerous Russian armies had been totally encircled and destroyed, but the Red Army as a whole had escaped total annihilation and had grown in strength and efficiency which had surpassed German tactical supremacy. Of the three German army groups fighting on the Eastern Front, only Army Group South could openly state that it had indeed achieved its given orders and objectives, and then only to a limited degree once the battles were accessed and evaluated by the German High Command.

Also during this time of reflection and study concerning all levels of the Waffen-SS command, but notably at the lowest level of all was that of the simple but highly trained Waffen-SS soldier. The overall conviction of these men had been the result of superior German training and organization, flexibility during a crisis, with military professionalism vastly outshining anything the Red Army could create. However, there was a steadily growing respect for the Red Army soldier as a fighting unit, plus, there was also a great awareness and appreciation for the vast resources that the Russians were capable of fielding to their armies at any given time. Another horror instilled into every German soldier who served on the Russian Front was the open callousness of the Russian political system which continuously sacrificed its troops in repeated suicidal attacks time and time again. The Waffen-SS as a whole viewed the war in Russia as a holy crusade, but by this point in time they were not holding onto this theme alone. Many men of various other European countries were now enlisting in the ranks of the Waffen-SS as its ideals and attitudes which once had been only German in nature, were now being felt in a dozen or more nations.

During the course of the fighting on the Russian Front, the Leibstandarte

Adolf Hitler had suffered incredible losses, but it had also gained for itself, as with many other Waffen-SS divisions in that theatre of war, a widespread reputation of elan in the assault, for total devotion to duty whether in the assault or defense, and a complete contempt for death which overly impressed the German High Command accordingly. The men of the Waffen-SS, once thought of as highly polished political garrison troops of Adolf Hitler, were now shining examples of what a front line German soldier should project, in accordance with his actions and bearing when facing the enemy in open battle.

Chapter VIII

OFFICER CADET TRAINING & TIGER I TRAINING

June 4, 1942 – December 12, 1942

On June 4, 1942, Michael Wittmann entered the halls of Bad Tölz in Bavaria and attended the 7th Kriegsreservefführer-Anwäerter Lehrgang (7th Reserve Officer Training School) Junkerschule until September 5, 1942. During this time period Wittmann would also be a member of the SS-Panzer Ersatz Abteilung until December 24, 1942. Michael Wittmann was very enthusiastic about his new military training but fully understood that the instruction ahead of him would be very difficult and challenging. Bad Tölz was a very austere training establishment which was situated in a valley in the middle of the very beautiful Bavarian Alps. Its massive stone walls seemed to engulf one into a sense of total security which, at times, was probably the appropriate feeling to have in such a formidable place. Michael had heard all of the horror stories concerning officer cadet school which now echoed in his mind and the gruelling training schedules that were to be subjected upon his person in the very near future. A million thoughts and ideas now ran through his overly active mind, but still wondered how he would perform under such strict discipline and constant control. Did he have what it took to complete this training and become a Waffen-SS officer? He had the required combat experiences which were a mandatory prerequisite to be allowed into this military training complex, and had proven his leadership skills and capabilities many times under direct enemy fire. He also understood that his military superiors would not have highly recommended him for this type of training if they did not believe in his abilities and his combat record. His family was very proud of the fact that he had been selected for officer training and had sent him their letters of congratulations and best wishes. It was very clear to Michael that many people had cast their eyes upon him for successful completion of this training. He was now highly determined to advance himself up through the ranks not only for his family and close friends back home, but also to return to his panzer unit with up to date military and tactical knowledge that would ultimately help to save lives on the field of battle and smash the enemy advances at every opportunity. This was to be his new goal in life.

The next few days were very uneventful for Michael Wittmann as he was involved with the processing center at Bad Tölz. He was given the usual indoctrination to the training school, records check, medical examination, and was given a room which he would share with five other cadets. New uniforms, and clothing, plus field gear were also issued with everything placed in their wall lockers according to strict regulations.

During this indoctrination at Bad Tölz, it was stressed that every new officer coming out as an SS-Untersturmführer would have to project a reputation for cool calculation under fire, and efficient leadership in a crisis. Every tactical decision would have to have an air of success, even though the situation seemed hopeless at the start, and his decisions on the field of battle would have to be based upon a sound basis of strict military discipline and tactical principles.

Training at Bad Tölz was to be very intense and those that were to be instructed had to be in tip top physical condition at all times. One of the first attractions that Michael noticed during his early exposure at Bad Tölz was that the sports facilities were second to none. The make-up and architecture provided that there was no waste or impracticalities in this section of the school. Position and composition of the numerous areas gave the entire school an artistic form and concept and also provided the cadets with a fantastic view of the Alps. A complete stadium with a full size playing field for soccer and field handball were provided along with a track and field facility for running, high jump, broad jump, and discus throwing. There were also bleachers for many spectators under which were locker rooms, dressing rooms, showers, and storage boxes for field equipment. There was also an area for basketball and tennis courts available for anyone that desired to play these sports.

Bad Tölz also had a complete indoor gymnasium with double flooring which measured 42 x 21 meters for all hand games, which included handball, basketball, volleyball, indoor soccer, and indoor hockey. For certain indoor track and field events additional special features were also available which included a 21 x 9 meter padded area for high jumping, broad jumping, pole vaulting and shot put and also heavy netting to catch indoor discus throwing events.

A modern swimming pool which measured 25 x 15 meters was one of the most popular sports areas to be taken advantage of in which water polo was also played. The swimming pool was provided with a 1 meter, 3 meter diving boards, and a 5 meter platform board.

Boxing, fencing, bicycling, and even bowling was provided for the cadets at Bad Tölz. Skiing and horse back riding was also very much indorsed as these two sports events were to be utilized during the fighting on the Eastern Fronts. At certain times, the only means of transportation on the field of battle would be the horse and snow skis, so it was highly imperative that the cadets learned to be horsemen and also to be skillful with a pair of snow skis. A fully equipped blacksmiths shop was built in order to properly shoe man's best friend on the battlefield, and all were expected to have knowledge of this ancient art.

A great deal of thought and planning had gone into the construction of Bad Tölz in 1936 and every part and detail was thoroughly examined by its planners and builders. If this Junkerschule was to turn out the best officers in the German military, it had to provide every essential piece of equipment needed for every day training. For every task outlined in the training schedules, there was pertinent equipment to carry out the training mission. Nothing was left to chance, workrooms for weapons training, with every known piece of German semi and automatic weapons were available for use and training. Pioneer equipment such as bridging and pontoon apparatus, fully equipped automobile and truck stands for inspecting and evaluating motorized equipment were available for the cadets. A fully equipped machine shop was also provided in order for the cadets to be able to repair equipment in the event of a breakdown. A photographic lab was also established in order to develop reconnaissance photographs or any photos that would be used for tactical reasons. Heavier weapons were also introduced to Wittmann and his comrades and spent many hours working in the Waffenmeisterei. They were taught how to strip down weapons such as the 3.7cm Pak gun, and 7.5cm leichtes Infanteriegeschütz. This type of training was not new to many of the men under constant supervision, but proved to increase their overall knowledge and also helped to reassure them that they were being exposed to all of the latest types of equipment and weapons.

However, the continued training that Michael Wittmann had undertaken was to be the most difficult of his life, and it was soon very apparent that entering Bad Tölz was not to be all fun and sports. Marching and field training seemed to take up the majority of the time, and full field gear was usually always carried. One could not fall behind as the pace of training did not stop or slow down for anyone. There was great comradeship among the cadets and Wittmann made many friends during his training. These friendships lasted long after his officer training at Bad Tölz, and it was these friendships that saved the day on the field of battle when the situation seemed hopeless.

The field training that Wittmann and his fellow cadets endured was second to none. Weeks and weeks of this type of training molded the men into a very close knit group and Michael felt very comfortable. Whether it was on the training ranges firing their 98K rifles, or assaulting prepared positions, he could see that as every day passed, his ability and knowledge grew to such a degree, that he excelled with every aspect and challenge of his officer training.

There was training with 10.5cm field howitzers, flame-throwers, and weapons firing with the MG-34 standard machine gun. All types of assault training was given with these weapons, with no details or techniques being overlooked in order to obtain the objectives as outlined. Squad, platoon, and company level assaults were performed over and over again, which gave the cadets ample time to adjust to the changing conditions on the training fields. If an attack or assault was performed in an unsatisfactory manner, it would be restaged until it was conducted in the correct manner as prescribed by the training manuals.

Light and heavy mortar and antitank training was given a great deal of attention, as the majority of the cadets would be placed in the infantry divisions at the front. The 8cm mortar was the mainstay of the front line infantrymen, so detailed training was performed under the careful and experienced training instructors. Training with anti-tank guns was given high priority which resulted in many hours studying and maintaining these types of weapons. Ammunition was at a premium, so every round fired at a target was expected to be a direct hit, or at least to have hit a vital part of a simulated enemy armored fighting vehicle.

During the winter months of training at Bad Tölz, field marches were conducted in the surrounding mountains under adverse conditions. Skiing proved to give the men a new type of mobility and a great deal of instruction was given in the art of snow skiing. Still, the training was harsh under winter conditions, but the vast majority of the men under training knew that if they were posted to the Eastern front, this type of training would most likely save them their lives more than once, especially if they were fighting as infantrymen. Careful handling of weapons was the order of the day during winter operations, as the intense cold would often stick or not allow the bolt actions of their weapons to operate efficiently. Every precaution was taken to avoid these types of stoppages, especially if being timed by an instructor with a stop-watch.

The class-room training was very comprehensive, but the men preferred to be out of doors and in the field. The training instructors who were giving these classes knew that being cooped up for any length of time seemed to have an adverse reaction upon the cadets. So, long walks were taken in order for the men to clear their heads and stretch their legs.

As Wittmann's training continued at Bad Tölz he was always trying to perfect his skills as he wanted to be the best cadet in his class. There were times when new problems were placed in front of the cadets and they had to group together and solve the tasks at hand. Wittmann was always on hand to provide advice to his comrades but again still listened very intently to any other suggestions put out by the group. There was always a great deal to learn and digest while being trained at Bad Tölz, and even after hours, many of the cadets would stay or study together in their rooms or go to the sitting rooms or library. A real sense of togetherness was the general feeling among all of the men.

Upon returning from field maneuvers, Wittmann still could not believe that he had a shared room with five cadets and thought of these accommodations as sort of a luxury. For the past two years he had seen harsh and constant combat and was not accustom to having a heated room with a bed with clean sheets. It all seemed very foreign to him, but it would not last for long, as he would soon be back at the front to take on the Ivans. He better enjoy his comfortable surroundings while he could, as the cruel Russian Front would return him to a savage environment where smaller battles would be fought for ownership of wooden and mud huts in order to escape from the frigid and icy weather of the Ost Front.

Wittmann was very pleased with his training and was very happy to have the opportunity to train at Bad Tölz, and was now understanding what was expected of a Waffen-SS officer and the many new responsibilities that would be placed upon his shoulders once he was commissioned. Day in and day out Wittmann and his comrades were receiving the best possible military instructions by the most prestigious military training school through-out greater Germany. On numerous occasions the cadets were asked to share and explain their experiences on the Eastern Front and other campaigns they had fought in and would try and outline their battle and assault tactics and how they were executed. All and all, these classroom talks were very beneficial for all concerned and a great deal of additional knowledge was gained.

No doubt, the cadets at Bad Tölz were extremely determined young men who not only wanted to become officers of the Waffen-SS, but also wanted to return to their former units with any and all new knowledge that would help to put the Ivans on the run. Too many German lives had been lost especially on the Russian Front, and with their new training and combat skills under their belts in the art of modern warfare, they would return to their respective areas of operations with courage, determination, superior leadership capabilities that would turn the tide in favor of the German Waffen-SS units and the Wehrmacht units which they would help to support in the field of combat. Upon completion of his officer cadet training and passing out as a SS-Untersturmführer on December 12, 1942 from Bad Tölz, Michael Wittmann was then posted to the Heavy Panzer Replacement and Training Battalion 500 (PzErs-und Ausb.Abt.500) in Paderborn. Shortly afterwards he was sent to northern France and trained on the new Tiger I Panzerkampfwagen (Sd.Kfz.181) at the Ploermel troop training grounds. The officer training program at Bad Tölz had been extremely thorough and comprehensive and had provided Wittmann with a great deal of new knowledge and training that would prove vital on any battlefield of the future.

Shortly after being commissioned an officer in the Waffen-SS, Michael Wittmann was to meet for the first time, his future wife to be, Hildegard Burmester. Wittmann and his fellow officers were having a small party at a nearby restaurant not far from Bad Tölz. Fräulein Burmester was a waitress at this establishment and was attracted to this very young officer. After their first meeting, they both started seeing each other and to write letters once Wittmann was posted to Paderborn and Ploermel.

Prior to graduating from officers cadet school at Bad Tölz, Wittmann and his fellow comrades had heard rumors pertaining to a new and formidable heavy panzer just coming into service with the German panzer forces. It was stated that this new wonder weapon would crush the Allies and bring them to their knees with its powerful main gun and heavy armor plate. No one had seen this new panzer, and it would not be until Wittmann entered the panzer training grounds at Ploermel, would he pay witness to this new and powerful German armored fighting vehicle.

Upon his arrival at Ploermel, Wittmann understood that there was indeed a great amount of additional learning and studying to be performed. He was also very excited about being posted to the new panzer training school, and looked forward in receiving detailed instruction and operations of the new panzer in question. After the usual in-processing procedures and typical paperwork signed and stamped, plus new black panzer uniforms, all was ready for the new training to begin.

It was not until two days later that Wittmann and his fellow comrades were able to actually see and inspect one of their future armored mounts. After eating a hardy breakfast, all of the men in his training group were lead to a large maintenance building and approached a large sliding door where they could hear the sounds of men working on vehicles. All of a sudden, the giant sliding door began to open very slowly, and as it continued to do so, all present could hear the whirl of a starter motor and then the familiar sound of a Maybach engine roaring to life. Everyone was a little taken back as they were not quite sure what to expect next! With an extremely loud gunning of the vehicle's powerplant, and the clanking of metal tracks, a huge panzer lurched its way out of the maintenance shop. All of the men and including Wittmann stepped back a few feet as they were now somewhat concerned that they would be run down by this steel monster if not given proper distance. As Wittmann was forced to step backwards, he almost tripped on the man standing behind him, but kept his eyes constantly focused on the enormous gray colored panzer emerging from its hiding place. As the machine started to come out of the maintenance building, the first section of the vehicle that was present for all to view was the huge and menacing muzzle brake of the main gun. As soon as it had poked its way out of the darkness of the work-shop, the men were overwhelmed by its sheer size! The gun barrel then began to slide out from the shadows and continued to present the longest gun barrel the men had ever seen on a modern German panzer! The majority of the panzer commanders were overawed as they had never seen such a wonderful sight! They had all served in armored fighting vehicles that had very short 3.7cm, 5.0cm, or 7.5cm main guns and could not believe what they were witnessing! Finally, two large driving sprockets made their appearance and exposed extremely wide battle tracks, which were two and a half times wider than anything produced previously. As the rest of this machine made its way out into the light of the day, the men were utterly speechless! Never had they seen such a total mass of superior armored weaponry! For Michael Wittmann, he could clearly understand that he and his comrades were to be given a truly revolutionary panzer which for him, would offer him and his future panzer crews added protection from anything that the Allies could present on the armored battlefield. Gone were the days of thinner plated armored fighting vehicles in which he had been wounded many times. As soon as Wittmann paid witness to this new panzer, he immediately felt a new sense of security filtering through out his entire being. He would now have a machine that would be highly instrumental in winning future panzer battles for him and his men, and most importantly, would provide the German military ground forces a cutting edge in defeating the Allied panzer units which at this time, did not have anything equal to this new and heavy panzer: The Tiger I Ausf. H (Sd.Kfz.181) Panzerkampfwagen.

The Tiger I roared and rolled around the maintenance yard for about five minutes and performed a number of short feats. It first of all completed a figure eight in order to show its tight turning radius, and then continued to clank pass the men with dust and dirt flying into the faces of the stunned men watching without speaking a word, with the ground trembling under its fifty-six tons of weight and then pulled up to where the men were standing and then shut down its engine. A very dashing and highly experienced panzer training instructor by the name of SS-Obersturmführer Georg Schonberger pulled himself up and out of the now opened panzer commander's cupola and jumped down to the ground where his new students stared up at him with mouths wide open! He let out a loud laugh as he stepped towards Wittmann and his comrades and padded one of the men on the back. He knew of course that his grand entrance and performance had instilled a sense of fear and awe into these men, but was totally aware that the vast majority of the men wanted to climb up on his Tiger I and inspect it and study this weapons system from front to rear, and inside and out! Before he allowed anyone to clamber aboard, he gave everyone a safety briefing and told them that they were to touch nothing and to ask questions first. Look but do not touch, was the order of the day.

After this important briefing, the men were allowed to climb aboard the Tiger I and inspected the vehicle first hand. Wittmann was one of the first to stand in the panzer commander's cupola, which pleased him a great deal. Again, a sense of security was firmly established from within his person and felt that nothing could possibly stop this combat machine from completing any and all missions on the field of battle. Flashbacks came rushing back to this young officer pertaining to the number of times that he and his crew in their StuG III had taken enemy main gun round hits and the serious wounds and deaths that occurred as a direct result. The armor plating of the Tiger I was at least two or three times thicker, and it would take a most powerful enemy panzer weapon or anti-tank gun to successfully penetrate this massive steel box on tracks. The Tiger I had as its main gun the 8.8cm KwK 36 L/56 which was the most powerful main gun mounted in a German panzer at that time. Wittmann knew with this kind of firepower he could destroy enemy panzers at gunnery ranges far superior than any other panzers in the Allied inventory. As he continued to study this huge machine, he also had many questions to ask Obersturmführer Schonberger about this new panzer. He inquired if he could drive the Tiger I and was told that he and his fellow students would all in turn have a chance at a later date to operate the vehicle in every crew position in order for them to familiarize themselves with this new and potent armored fighting vehicle.

The Tiger I training was very thorough and comprehensive. All of the students who had been selected for this course were experienced panzer commanders or gunners who had served in the Panzer Corps and had combat experience. Ploermel had indeed received some of the first Tiger I Panzerkampfwagens from the Henschel factory and every preventive measure was taken in order to keep these new machines in top operational order so as to allow the training instructors to pass out as many Tiger I panzer commanders as possible for the bitter fighting that was now raging on at the Russian front, and in North Africa. If a machine broke down, or if a sudden mechanical problem arose during the training sessions, factory maintenance personnel would be on hand and called in to inspect the vehicle in question with a very comprehensive technical report being produced on the spot and appropriate actions taken not only at the panzer school, but also incorporated into design details at the factory.

During Wittmann's Tiger I training at Ploermel, the Leibstandarte Adolf Hitler was serving as occupational troops in France. During their brief posting to France, the Leibstandarte Adolf Hitler were practicing and refining their combat tactics, plus strengthening their depleted unit levels for anticipated future battles. This unit was made ready on the demarcation line on November 6, 1942, and on the 21st, were transferred to southern France, as their next phase of occupational duties.

Michael Wittmann was very eager to start his training with the new Tiger I Panzerkampfwagen and was presented with all pertinent training and technical manuals (handbuchs). The students were also given a handbuch entitled 'Tigerfibel' (D656/27) , which was a 91-page publication illustrating the every day up-keep and maintenance of a Tiger I while using cartoon type characters and lovely well-built blonde females expressing various mottos pertaining to vehicle care. Wittmann and his comrades were very impressed with these vehicle guides and studied them from cover to cover.

Finally, after a short period of time, Tiger I training was to begin. The first vehicle position that Wittmann was to be instructed upon was the panzer commander's station. Other fellow panzer commanders were given instruction in regards to other crew positions, but in time, all would obtain instructional blocks in all pertinent stations. The panzer commander's station in the Tiger I was located at the 8 o'clock position in the turret of the vehicle and was provided with an armored cupola. This was the first attempt to move the panzer commander's location from the central position (behind the main gun) to the left side of the turret. The panzer commander's cupola was fixed and was welded to the turret roof and offered him all round vision via five vision slits (7" x 5/8") backed by 94mm laminated vision blocks, however, no armored shutters were fitted for added protection. A small sighting vane was incorporated into the front vision block (12 o'clock position) which enabled the panzer commander to roughly guide his gunner onto selected targets. Brow pads were provided on these vision devices which greatly helped the panzer commander in positioning his face for a clear view and to prevent any eye or facial injuries. Positioned between each vision block was a protective rubber cushion (five in all) which also helped in protecting the panzer commander's head during rough movement and travel. In the earlier panzers (notably the Panzer III and IV) the commander's vision was excellent, particularly in that he could see nearly all round his vehicle. The distance between the vision devices and the edge of the turret; the slope of the turret roof and the height of the vision devices above the general level of the turret roof, were all main factors in determining whether or not the terrain could be seen near the vehicle in any given direction. These various factors were all present in the Panzer III and IV owing to the fact that the commander's cupola was located at the rear of the turret. Forward vision had not been as outstanding because the whole length of the turret was in front of the cupola, but this was overcome to some extent by sloping the roof downwards from the cupola and further by raising the cupola above the turret roof line. Compared with vision in other directions, the panzer commander's near vision forward was not as important, as vision in this direction was also covered by the turret gunner, driver, and hull MG-34/radio operator. In contemporary Allied tanks that had been captured and studied, the commander's vision devices were placed to one side of a square flat-topped turret. This meant that on the whole, vision was good in only one direction (over the nearest turret edge) and liable to be bad in other directions, because of the distance between vision devices and turret edge. On the Churchill tank, the vehicle commander had a blind spot which extended out to 120 feet on the right-hand side of the turret which could prove fatal in a combat engagement against enemy infantry. Also, because of the lowness of the periscopes on the roof, visual fields were badly obstructed by fixtures such as ventilating domes, plus hatch covers that projected above the general line of the roof level.

As Wittmann was to discover, in the Tiger I, it appeared that the designers did not consider near vision to be so important for the panzer commander. With his cupola placed to the left rear position, vision to the left and rear of the turret was excellent, but it was extremely poor to the right and right rear. It was immediately pointed out that part of this blind area to the right of the panzer commander's field of vision could be seen through the loader's vision device. By using rapid head movement the panzer commander was able to obtain maximum fields of vision from each of the constituent blocks, by being provided with a continuous view of the terrain around the vehicle with a slight overlap between the peripheral fields of each vision block. If the vehicle commander looked through the center of any given vision block without head movement, there would be a blind zone of 15 degrees to 20 degrees between it and the next vision block. The fact that the panzer commander viewed the outside world through a narrow fixed aperture in front of each vision block did not mean that the vertical field was reduced. The entire available field of vision could not be seen at once, with vertical head movement being needed to cover it all.

The generally cramped position of the panzer commander made it very difficult to turn around and view the outside world to the immediate rear. Again, vision to the right rear was limited, and also due to the position of the rear mounted turret stowage bin. This limitation could have been reduced by sloping its top surface more steeply as was done on the earlier Panzer III and IV. This right rear blind spot was ideal for tank hunting teams and if close to the ground they would be totally invisible within 100-120 feet from the vehicle.

The panzer commander's armored cupola was 50mm thick at the top and 80mm at its base at 90 degrees to the vertical. The internal diameter of the cupola hatch was a mere 18" and proved to be very cramped and uncomfortable. The cupola mounted a single piece hatch that was hinged between the 2 o'clock and 3 o'clock positions, and was spring loaded for easy escape in the event of an emergency. This hatch had three locking handles which secured the hatch while buttoned down for battle field engagements and artillery bombardment, with the interior of the hatch being padded to offer some protection for the commander's head to reduce injury over rough terrain. For the protection of the commander's head while observing from an open hatch, a special locking device was incorporated into this hatch. This locking device consisted of a thick metal lip that was spot welded to the 2 o'clock position on the cupola. Welded to the 2 o'clock position on the top of the hatch was a spring loaded metal clip that mated with the metal lip on the cupola once the hatch was fully opened. This was a very important safe guard for the panzer commander not only for observing the enemy opposing him, but additionally saved him from having the hatch coming down on top of him or having his head or fingers injured during a firing engagement. Also mounted at the 12 o'clock and 6 o'clock positions were two small tubular mounts for the vehicle's hand operated rangefinder. This device was not used to any great extend on the Tiger I as exposure was a critical factor while engaging the enemy, and additionally, this devise was very awkward to handle and operate successfully especially while the vehicle was in motion.

Fitted directly above the panzer commander's head (inside diameter of cupola) was a simple device called the target indicator ring. This device was graduated from the 1 o'clock to 12 o'clock hours and contained 360 gear teeth. The panzer commander was able to have instantaneous bearing information by viewing this rotating instrument. The target indicator ring was linked to the turret race via a connecting shaft fitted with universal joints and driven off the turret gear rack. The connecting shaft was situated to the panzer commander's immediate left. As the turret was being traversed, the target indicator ring would also rotate thus providing the panzer commander with correct degrees of bearing. The vehicle gunner was provided with a single dial target position indicator, similar to ones fitted to the Panzer IIIs and IVs. It too was graduated from 1 o'clock to 12 o'clock and carried a pointer off the turret rack also by means of a pinion gear and universal jointed shafts. The panzer commander's target indicator ring and gunner's single dial target indicator were thus synchronized and assured that both individuals were locked on the same enemy target. These devices were in reality an early azimuth indicating system and proved to be very beneficial in regards to modern panzer gunnery. The target indicator ring also helped the commander and gunner in closed up areas (e.g. wooded areas, fighting near buildings, street fighting) especially with all turret hatches closed in regards to orientating the main gun barrel out of the way of any oncoming or dangerous obstructions.

Between the 1 o'clock and 2 o'clock positions in the panzer commander's cupola, a swivel mount was to be found for the vehicle's S.F. 14/Z scissors periscope (battery commander's periscope) This optical device was originally a 10-powered binocular instrument used for observation and measuring azimuth and angles of sight in conjunction with artillery units. This optical device was also used through out the 8.8cm Pak 18 and 36 weapons for the same purposes. The scissors periscope provided the Tiger I panzer commander with additional observation capabilities and greatly increased his vision from the 10 o'clock through 2 o'clock positions. However, the scissors periscope's tubular arms could not be swung down to a horizontal position (being located inside the commander's cupola) to increase the stereoscopic effect of the instrument and was seldom used as a direct result. Two disadvantages of this mounted optical device was that in an extreme emergency, the panzer commander had to remove it from its mount in order to exit from his position. If the vehicle was hit and set on fire the gunner had to anxiously wait until his commander cleared his hatch aperture, which was very unnerving considering this was the only avenue of escape for the vehicle gunner. The second disadvantage with the scissors periscope in position was that the commander's hatch had to be left opened and in the locked position. If the hatch was left unlocked, the motion of the vehicle would cause the heavy hatch to crash down and damage the optical device and cause injury to the commander's head and upper torso. Additionally, artillery airbursts would rain down lethal metal fragments and thus cause further injuries. If the Tiger I was over run during a battle field engagement with enemy infantry, the commander would find himself in a very dangerous situation. He would not have sufficient time to secure the scissors periscope, after which, he would have to expose himself in order to release the locking device on his hatch. As a result of these many disadvantages, the scissors periscopes were rarely used a great deal of the time as it proved more of a liability than an asset.

Instruction was then given to Michael Wittmann in regards to the various controls and operations of the turret. Directly in front of the panzer commander's position and fitted to the turret's interior roof were the following items and controls. In the 12 o'clock position a festoon lamp could be found and used for illumination during night maneuvers and also while buttoned up. In the 11 o'clock position and 1 o'clock position were two metal handholds welded to the turret roof for the panzer commander to grasp during rough movement of the vehicle. These same handholds were also used by the gunner to help to lift himself up and out of his seat during rapid exit from a damaged or burning vehicle.

Located at the 10 o'clock and 2 o'clock positions in the turret roof were switches for the vehicle's smoke generators (Nebelkerzenabfeuerung). The smoke generators sets were located one each side of the turret directly in front of the gunner's and loader's vision devices.

Each switch contained three buttons and once depressed by the panzer commander or gunner would activate one of the six smoke generators. The top smoke generator (or smoke candle) of each set had an elevation of 30 degrees and was on a parallel axis with the keel of the vehicle. The center generator had an elevation of 35 degrees and was inclined outward with their axis at 15 degrees to the keel line. The bottom generators also had an elevation of 35 degrees, but were inclined further outboard with their axis at 30 degrees. The smoke generators were of the Nb.K 39 90mm type, six of which were carried, one in each discharger. No spare generators, primers or generator spares were carried, however. Although smoke was an effective cover method for panzers, the Tiger I smoke generators were of somewhat limited value as it was very difficult to conceal such a huge vehicle of this type. Once smoke was present on the battlefield, it was apt to draw immediate attention upon itself, and also gave away the vehicle's tactical position.

On the left interior wall of the Tiger I turret were the following fittings, straps, and containers. A metal coaming was formed at the base of the turret wall and was used as a receptacle for maps and any other items the vehicle commander needed at an easy reach. Placed to the right side of this coaming was a metal box for the commander's field glasses. A plug for the commander's revolver port was located slightly behind and to the upper left side of the connecting shaft for the target indicator ring. This item was to be used while the vehicle was undergoing submersion operations. The vehicle's signal pistol was stowed on the left-hand turret wall in line with the commander's traverse handwheel position. This weapon was the standard Walthers 27mm (1.032) signal pistol (Kampfpistole) which was rifled and carried a small dial sight for use with H.E. grenades. Another metal box was fitted just below and forward of the signal pistol's position and contained instructions for sealing the turret for underwater operations. After the omission of the special submersion equipment, this box was used for other items that the panzer commander and gunner needed for their respective vehicle positions.

Forward of this metal box was an electrical panel containing an emergency battery for the firing circuit in the event that the primary circuit failed. Also mounted to this panel was a change-over switch and the panzer commander's and gunner's radio sockets for their headphones and throat microphones. Fitted beneath the electrical panel was a container for the gun mounting book, describing procedures for correct main gun and machine gun settings. All of the fittings inside the Tiger I were not welded directly to the turret wall, but instead, were attached to metal straps that were spaced welded. This arrangement proved very beneficial especially when hit (but not penetrated) by an enemy main gun round. The force of the impact and resulting shock wave usually would cause items welded directly to a turret wall to fly loose and injure the crew in the vehicle. The Tiger I method of securing its interior fittings would not result in such a situation as outlined in the above; as the metal straps spaced the items a quarter of an inch away from the turret wall. Thus, the resulting shock wave was somewhat defused and less injuries occurring.

The panzer commander was provided with an ingenious three position seat which allowed him various modes in which to command his vehicle during a combat mission. The seat was bolted to the turret ring (via four large bolts) with cushioned seat and back pads provided for his added comfort. The commander had the following alternative seat positions: Sitting on the back rest which could be folded up to a horizontal position via a release handle on the top of his seat. In this position, the commander's head would be positioned outside of his cupola for unobstructive observations. The second position was for the commander to be sitting on his normal seat pad with his back rest folded down in its normal position, being that the vehicle would normally be buttoned up in this mode of operation. The third position would entail that the commander's normal seat pad would be swung down to a vertical position with the commander now standing on the turntable (turret basket floor). This position would also be used while being buttoned up and gave the commander a little more room to move about in, plus he could fire his hand-held weapons better through his pistol port.

The panzer commander was provided with an auxiliary hand operated traversing hand-wheel that was bolted to the turret ring to his left-hand side. There was no hydraulic power at his position, as it was only provided for the gunner in the Tiger I. If the gunner's hydraulic power failed the commander could assist the gunner by using his hand operated turret traverse hand-wheel in order to rotate the heavy turret which weighed fifteen metric tons. Bolted to the turret traversing hand-wheel casing and running vertical to it, was the power drive casing from the hydraulic power traverse pump and motor, which in turn traversed the turret via the gunner's foot control pedal. Mounted to the power drive casing was a folding footrest for the commander and thus offered him a normal seating arrangement. Nevertheless, the commander's position was still very cramped and very uncomfortable.

The panzer commander's pistol port at the 8 o'clock position helped him in suppressing any attempts by enemy infantry from attacking his vehicle from that direction. The commander could fire any number of weapons through this firing port, but usually used the vehicle's MP-40 machine pistol in conjunction with this aperture. This port was closed by means of a rotating armored shutter operated by a hand lever. The shutter contained an eccentrically positioned aperture, which could be moved into and out of register with the similar sized aperture in the turret wall. Above and to the rear of this pistol port was a strap for the panzer commander's gasmask, and was readily available in the event of enemy gas attack. Directly behind the commander's seat was a strap that held his water bottle, which was also highly needed due to the extreme heat experienced in the vehicle especially during main gun engagements. At the rear of the turret interior wall were a number of metal boxes that contained spare vision blocks for the commander's cupola. In the 6 o'clock position were two larger boxes that held the commander's and gunner's headphones and throat microphones when not in use. Below these boxes were two additional boxes that stored the cartridges for the vehicle's signal pistol. Twelve red and green cartridges were in the left box and twelve white cartridges in the right box. Between the cartridge boxes was the location for the hatch keys. To the right of the commander's seat (6 o'clock position on the turret race) was a metal clip and socket for the co-axial machine gun when the vehicle was operating totally submersed while making river crossings. A wire basket was welded to two metal straps that were welded to the turret basket floor beneath the commander's seat. This basket was used for flags, and any other items that the vehicle commander desired at his immediate disposal.

A metal plate was bolted to the turret roof between the panzer commander and the 8.8cm main gun which further cramped the commander in his fighting position. However, this plate helped to protect the commander from the gun breech which could injure his right elbow and lower body during full recoil once a main gun round had been fired. It also cut down on the backflash which could blind the commander for a few vital seconds and cause him to have difficulty in spotting and tracking enemy vehicles during early and late operating hours of the day. The biggest disadvantage of this protective device was that it isolated the commander from his loader. The loader in the Tiger I was not provided with any type of communications device whatsoever in his position and was expected to hear all of the commander's fire commands with the naked ear. The metal plate muffled the commander's voice and needless to say, the vast majority of these plates were later removed in the field. The commander could also assist or help the loader to remove jammed spent shell casings and defective main gun rounds from the main gun breech once this plate was done away with.

One curious feature of the panzer commander's position in the Tiger I was that the commander was not provided with any means to fire the main gun of the vehicle. In theory, the gunner was viewing the target of opportunity from the same plane as the main gun and was able to accurately determine whether or not if he could score a direct hit on an enemy vehicle. The Tiger I commander was only able to help guide his gunner onto target and once identified by the gunner, would he allow his gunner to perform final main gun laying procedures and firing of the 8.8cm weapon. If the gunner became incapacitated during a firing engagement the commander and the rest of his crew were in dire straights as they would have to remove the gunner from his position in order for the commander to operate the gunner's controls. There was no room for the commander to reach down or slip pass the gunner to fire the main gun! This type of situation was very dangerous and Wittmann and many of his fellow officers could not fully understand why provisions were not incorporated into the commander's position such as a secondary firing switch or emergency trigger located in or near the commander's left hand?

Upon completing his training in the panzer commander's position, Wittmann fully understood all of the operations and functions as outlined to him by his instructor. A great deal of knowledge was learned and it had come to him much easier than expected. This of course was due to the fact that his early exposure to farm machinery and his experiences in operating and maintaining Sd. Kfz. 222 armored cars and StuG III Ausf. A's allowed him to pass his final examinations with flying colors.

The next crew position that Wittmann was to be instructed upon was the gunner's position. The gunner was seated directly in front of the panzer commander in the left forward side of the turret. The gunner's seat was mounted lower than the commander's seat so as to be parallel with the 8.8cm main gun. This seat was non-adjustable and was mounted 21 3/4" above the turret basket floor on an extension arm welded to the hollow casing of the elevation handwheel shaft. The gunner was provided with a manual elevation handwheel to his right and was the only device for elevating the main gun. The firing handle for the 8.8cm main gun was located on this handwheel being mounted on its back face. In this position, it proved very handy for the gunner, as he had a mere few inches to reach in order to fire the 8.8cm weapon. To the left of the gunner's position was a manual traversing handwheel mounted to the turret race. Located at the base of this handwheel housing was the gunner's single dial target position indicator which allowed the gunner to know the exact position of the turret in relation to the hull of the vehicle. Located at the extreme left-hand side of the manual traverse handwheel housing were the locations for the connecting shafts for the target indicator ring and the commander's manual handwheel. In the event of a hydraulic failure, the commander could again assist the gunner in traversing the turret while engaging an enemy target. They were interconnected by means of universally jointed shafts, but the commander's handwheel could not be operated without first disengaging a plunger type locking device on the gunner's handwheel. The radius of the gunner's handwheel was 5 1/5" which involved 720 (1/2 degree/turn) revolutions for full 360 degree traverse. The radius of the commander's handwheel was 4" and involved 595 (.6 degree/turn) revolutions for the same travel. Both handwheels were geared with considerable reduction into the turret rack via the gearbox above the gunner's handwheel, and resulted in the turret traverse via hand power being critically slow.

For power traverse the turret was powered via the main engine through a hydraulic unit consisting of a variable delivery pump and motor with two speeds available. The drive to a power take off at the rear of the gearbox, through an auxiliary gearbox situated centrally below the revolving turret floor and vertical shaft passing through this floor. The unit itself was bolted to the turret basket floor. The drive from this unit was taken to the turret rack through bevel gears and various shafting. The auxiliary gearbox was provided with a gear lever situated to the left rear of the bow machine gun / radio operator's position and to the right of the main gearbox.

The gunner's main traverse control consisted of a rocking footplate under his right foot. To traverse the turret to the right, it was rocked forward, to traverse left, backwards. Variable speeds to the left and right were obtained, within the limits of the two-speed control, according to the angle in which the footplate was positioned. This footplate was in a comfortable position, but the arc of movement (24 degrees) was too extreme for smooth operations especially by the heel of the foot. Fitted to the right front of the rocking footplate was the gunner's foot pedal to activate the co-axially mounted MG-34, this being of rod and lever type. It was placed for use by the gunner's right foot, thus the MG-34 could not be fired when the turret was being traversed by hydraulic power, unless the left foot was used! Powered traverse was usually set on 'low' as this setting proved to be the best for ease of tracking enemy vehicles at all speeds, but had a very wide neutral zone. On 'high' setting tracking vehicles was much more difficult and corrections by hand traverse were usually necessary.

Sighting the 8.8cm main gun was through the use of an articulated binocular telescope, type T.Z.F. 9 (b), mounted on the left side of the main gun. It was a binocular development of the T.Z.F. 5 series with very similar optical characteristics. The telescope was of a stationary type, the eyepieces being slung from the roof on a strengthened support, and locked in by a metal pin, with the lens being bloomed. Graticules in both eyepieces were illuminated from the same light source by means of a divided prism inserted in the center of the graticle box. The interiors of the telescope bodies were smoked in order to prevent any reflection that would impair the gunner's accuracy while engaging an enemy target.

A standard type range scale for the 8.8cm main gun and MG-34 was provided in the right-hand telescope. It was adjustable to give ranges from O - 4000 meters (in hundreds) for the main gun and from O - 1200 meters (also in hundreds) for the MG-34. Range was put on by means of a standard type lever vertically mounted under the telescopes. The range scale and aiming mark glasses were not bloomed. There was a graticle with horizontal and vertical adjustments for the gunner in each telescope, however, these adjustment controls were most inaccessible, and adjustment was difficult when the telescope was mounted in the turret. An adjustable rubber brow-pad was provided for the gunner's comfort and safety which helped to cut down on injuries while in action from the jarring and rocking of the vehicle while firing the main gun, and also helped the gunner to keep his face positioned so he could sense the strike of the round (if not too much dust was kicked up into the air) and for tracking his next targets. There was also no open sight incorporated into the T.Z.F. 9 (b) being contrary to earlier German panzer gunnery practice.

A clinometer on the left-hand side of the gun cradle was mounted for the gunner's use held in position at the top by means of a stud and at the bottom by a spring-loaded plunger. The stud was on an adjustable eccentric, to which was welded a knurled disc with seven drillings. When the disc was turned, alteration of 1 mil was caused in the relative elevation of clinometer and main gun. Thus, a total adjustment of 9 mils was possible in the clinometer mounting by using a combination of both sets of drillings.

The clinometer arc was graduated on the left-hand side from O -400 mils (25 degrees) of elevation, in black figures, and from O - 100 mils (5.6 degrees) depression, in red figures. On the right of the arc was a range scale (for use with H.E. rounds) graduated from 0-80 (in hundreds of meters). The range of 8000 meters corresponded approximately to 151 mils (8.5 degrees) on the left-hand scale. Provision was made for illumination of a leveling bubble with a plea bulb being used for its light source.

An alternative position for the clinometer was provided outside the left cradle side plate, to the rear of the first position. In order to mount it in that position, the securing pins had to be reversed.

The gunner fired the 8.8cm main gun via a standard German electric primer type firing system found on most period German panzers. It was operated by means of a segment shaped trigger handle (bar) mounted on the same axis behind the elevating handwheel and parallel with the handwheel rim. It was a 12 volt system supplied from one of the vehicle's two batteries. Standard German electrical safety devices were also provided, which prevented firing of the main gun if the breech was not completely closed. A mechanical safety switch, of the type fitted in the Panzer III and IV was mounted near the top right-hand side of the breech ring. This switch broke the firing circuit each time the gun was fired; the gun could not then be fired until the loader had reset this switch.

The breech mechanism of the 8.8cm main gun was a scaled up version of the standard German panzer gun type, as fitted on the 5.0cm KwK 39, and 7.5cm KwK 40, as mounted on the Panzer III and IV respectively. It incorporated the usual falling wedge breech block, (which had two drillings in the lower portions for lightness), and S.A. operation by means of separate clock springs for opening and closing. The electric firing pencil was of a very robust construction, and had external insulating bushes. The main gun had a detachable breech ring provided with two gun lugs, the right-hand one being of open type to facilitate removal of the buffer cylinders without having to remove the gun. The recoil gear was of standard German panzer gun pattern, it consisted of a hydraulic buffer on the right side of the main gun, and a hydro-pneumatic recuperator on the left. A spring-loaded hydraulic reservoir with the usual hydraulic safety switch being mounted transversely beneath the gun was also provided. The reservoir was much larger than that mounted in previous types of panzers.

The cradle for the 8.8cm main gun was again of standard welded construction and was generally similar to that on the 7.5cm KwK 40 (long), but on a larger scale. The left-hand gun lug was provided with bronze shoes and ran in an anti-rotation guide inside the left side plate of the cradle. A deflector guard was bolted to the cradle, and was not hinged and effectively divided the fighting compartment into two separate unequal sections. The deflector guard also carried a small capacity (approximately 10 cases) empty cartridge bag on three brackets. This bag helped the loader in that he was not apt to slip and fall on spent cases that would otherwise impair foot movement during the loading procedures and prevent cartridges jamming the turret basket. A recoil indicator was also bolted inside the left side plate of the main gun cradle for the gunner's usage. The gun port water seal was operated by a knob on the top of the cradle above the 8.8cm main gun.

Mounting for the 8.8cm main gun was of external mantelet type. The mantelet was cast in one piece and consisted of a large rectangular external shield of approximately the same size as the front of the turret, behind which was a cylindrical portion, roughly hollowed out at the back, working inside the turret. There were two designs of the mantelet, apparently in parallel production, one was with flush finish on the front face, the other had a raised portion round the telescope openings for added protection. Each turret side wall formed a cheek, carrying a fixed spherical trunnion; these trunnions were fitted into split spherical bushes in the sides of a cylindrical inner mantelet. The trunnions were continued outward through the cheeks of the turret walls to form two of the three lifting points for the turret. The front of each cheek was chamfered away above and below the trunnion axis to allow the elevation and depression of the gun mantelet. The 8.8cm main gun was off set four inches to the left which thus allowed the loader ample room for loading the main gun, but somewhat cramped the panzer commander's and gunner's positions.

The 8.8cm main gun was mounted very far forward, with the mounting being considerably muzzle heavy. This was counteracted by means of a large cylinder, containing a strong compression spring (with adjustable compression), horizontally mounted above the right-hand side of the turret ring to the right of the loader's position. The spring was compressed by a piston, the piston rod being connected through a system of levers to a small subsidiary compression cylinder and to the right-hand side of the cylindrical inner mantelet. Without this balancing device, the performance of the 8.8cm main gun would have been reduced considerably. Upon halting the vehicle to engage an enemy target, the gunner would have to wait for the main gun to settle as it would nose down for a few vital seconds; these few seconds could be critical if a first round hit was necessary for survival. With this type of balancing device incorporated into the firing system, the gunner was assured fast, and accurate firing of the 8.8cm main gun as fitted to the Tiger I.

The accuracy of the 8.8cm KwK 36 L/56 main gun was remarkably consistent. Normal patterns of firing (five AP main gun rounds) presented all hits in an area of 16" x 18" at 1200-1400 meter ranges. The normal rate of fire was shown to be five to eight main gun rounds per minute. However, with harsh and continued combat experiences ahead, this rate of fire could be improved upon.

The co-axial machine gun (MG-34) to be used by the gunner of the Tiger I was located to the right side of the main gun and was activated by the foot pedal mounted to the front of the gunner's hydraulic traverse rocking foot control plate. This machine gun had the new type feed block (used on the Infantry MG-34 for taking 50-round belted drums). This weapon offered feed from the left-hand side only and proved to be very awkward in rearming the weapon with a new belt of ammunition; especially while the vehicle was moving over rough terrain. The cradle for this machine gun was very similar to that on the Panzer IV, incorporating a spring buffer and carrying two belt bags (one full and the other one for empty cases). It supported the firing linkage and also the belt guide, with check pawl, to prevent the belt from running backwards. Vertical and lateral zeroing adjustments were incorporated and provisions were made for swinging the machine gun body clear for changing hot and worn out barrels. There was a total of 5700 rounds of 7.92 ammunition for the co-axial and bow MG-34 machine guns altogether, but in every day combat missions of the future, additional ammunition was to be carried. Twenty-two belted bags carrying 150 rounds each were stowed in the fighting compartment for the co-axial machine gun. Sixteen belted bags were stowed in the forward compartment for use with the bow machine gun. The two MG-34s could also be dismounted from the vehicle and be used in the infantry role if the vehicle was knocked out or immobilized by enemy gun fire or land mines.

The loader's position was located to the right side of the 8.8cm main gun at the 3 o'clock location and allowed ample room for this crew-member to load the main gun. The loader had to make sure that the main gun was working properly at all times and checked and then rechecked all oil and hydraulic levels before and after firing engagements. He was provided with a padded seat that was mounted parallel with the main gun and was bolted to the turret traverse housing. Thus, when the vehicle was moving, and not under enemy fire, the loader sat facing towards the rear of the turret. This seemed an awkward position for the loader, but proved pertinent while loading his weapon, as if this seat was mounted anywhere else in his area of operations, this seat would have obstructed his performance in regards to his respective duties. Directly forward and above the loader's seat was the co-axial MG-34 machine gun and was responsible for loading and maintaining this weapon at all times, and would clear any and all stoppages incurred during firing of this secondary weapon. To the left of the MG-34 co-axial machine gun was the safety switch for the main gun as the loader had to insure that this device was reset before the main gun could be fired by the gunner.

The loader had the same type of episcope as the gunner (10 o'clock position) at the 2 o'clock position in the turret wall. This device helped to cover part of the panzer commander's blind spot in this area of the turret. However, the loader was restricted in obtaining a comprehensive view rearward due to the location of a kit bin to the left of his episcope which in turn prevented complete movement of his head. During combat engagements, the loader would have little time to view through this small viewing aperture, as he was generally too busy loading the main gun or servicing the co-axial MG-34 machine gun. The panzer commander usually had his head out of his armored cupola before firing, and was able to view this area from his position. Directly below the loader's episcope was the black cylinder that contained the balancing equipment for the 8.8cm main gun. As this compressed spring counter weight device was very important in regards to accuracy and proper balancing of the main gun, very strict attention was given to its maintenance and up keep. Above the balancing cylinder in the 3 o'clock position and mounted on the turret wall, were four belted bags of 7.92 ammunition for the co-axial MG-34 machine gun. On each side of these ammunition bags was mounted two water bottles which were a vital necessity during any sustained fighting with the enemy. Above the rear most water bottle was the loader's gas mask which would be used in the advent of the enemy using poison gas or thick smoke screens that could penetrate the turret through an open hatch. Mounted underneath the water bottle was a device called the projectile ejector which was used to remove any defective 8.8cm main gun rounds that became jammed in the breech of the weapon during a fire mission. To the right of the projectile ejector was the main escape hatch of the vehicle located at the 5 o'clock position on the right turret wall. This was the only avenue of escape for the Tiger I crew should the vehicle be blown over or tipped over upon itself in the field. Due to the torsion bar suspension of these vehicles, escape hatches located in the hull bottoms was an impossibility. In an emergency, the entire crew of a Tiger I could escape from the turret escape hatch. The driver of the vehicle had to be somewhat ambidextrous to crawl from his position to this aperture, but in an extreme emergency, anything was possible. This escape hatch was always closed during combat, and only opened for escape. It could also not be closed from inside of the vehicle.

To the right-hand side of the turret escape hatch was the main fuse box for the vehicle and bolted to the turret wall. If a fuse blew out for one reason or another, the loader could easily replace the worn out or broken element. Next to the fuse box was the position for the commander's MP-40 machine pistol with three magazines available, which the loader could load and charge and then hand to the vehicle commander if their machine was being boarded by enemy infantry or Panzer assault teams.

The vehicle loader was the busiest crewmember of the Tiger I and had to be extremely proficient in his crew duties. He too, had to be very ambidextrous as the vast majority of the 8.8cm main gun rounds were stowed in very inaccessible areas of the fighting compartment and turret basket. A large number of these main gun rounds were stowed in the track panniers (two sets on each side of the vehicle)which contained 32 rounds each. The loader had to be very cautious while reaching for these rounds as if the gunner was traversing the gun turret, it was quite easy for the loader to lose fingers, a hand, or an entire arm! Directly below the track pannier ammunition bins were two smaller ammunition containers (two, each side of the vehicle) that held four rounds of main gun ammunition (usually armored piercing = AP). The loader again had to be very careful in reaching for these rounds as he could cause injury to himself if the turret was rotated without proper warning. Directly beneath the loader's position and under the turret basket floor was an ammunition bin that contained six rounds of AP ammunition. The loader had to lift a hinged section of the turret basket floor in order to reach these rounds, and could only obtain these projectiles when the turret of the vehicle was positioned at the 12 o'clock location. Six additional AP or HE rounds were stored next to the driver on his left side pannier. This brought the total number of 8.8cm main gun rounds to ninety-two, thus offering the Tiger I crew with a large supply of ammunition for sustained engagements in order to carry out their missions.

There were no ready-racks supplied for the loader's use in the turret basket of the Tiger I and this was indeed a problem which needed attention. The only alternative was for the loader to stack as many main gun rounds as he could onto the turret basket floor prior to an anticipated engagement. Thus, he was supplied with at least six to eight ready rounds available for main gun engagements. This solution was not entirely practical as they tended to roll around on the turret basket floor due to the movement of the vehicle, which caused the loaders to slip and fall and reduced their performance. This trade off, was however, in itself, a clear matter whether the loader wanted to be thrown off balance at times, or have a plentiful supply of ready ammunition on hand. The latter was usually the case, as in combat, as it was pointed out by the Tiger I instructors, whom ever fired off the first main gun round would usually be the survivor.

The loader had his main vehicle hatch above his position which was rectangular in shape and was usually left opened during a firing engagement. Normally, it was closed only during an artillery bombardment, sustaining artillery air-bursts, or with enemy infantry in the nearby vicinity. As the number of spent shell casings began to pile up in the canvas breech bag, the loader would have to throw these hot casings out of his open hatch in order for them not to jam the recoil of the main gun, and also to prevent any ejected spent casings from flying around inside the turret after being forced out from the breech.

The biggest disadvantage the loader had in the Tiger I was that he was not provided with any type of internal communications device in which to communicate with the panzer commander or the rest of the crew. During fighting engagements, the commander had to shout out in a loud voice in order for the loader to hear his fire commands. As a result, the rest of the crew had their eardrums sent ringing from the commander's boisterous speaking, and proved to be a problem throughout the service life of the Tiger I. One partial remedy was the removal of the commander's backflash plate which not only allowed better verbal communication with the loader, but both men were in visual contact with each other as well.

After completing his training in the turret of the Tiger I, Wittmann was then given comprehensive training in the driver's position which was located in the forward left-hand side of the lower hull. The driver was provided with a padded seat which had various controls to either side. Starting at the 12 o'clock position the driver was provided with an armored vision block which had bullet proof glass and was his main source for forward vision. This vision port could be closed down as much as required by a balanced pair of rising and falling shutters, operated by a handwheel on the right side frame. This was backed by a laminated glass block (70mm x 240mm x 94mm thick) and gave good to adequate vision and protection.

Above the forward vision block were bored two apertures for the normal driver's episcope, consisting of a pair of K.F.F.2 cranked telescopes, but it was found that the vast majority of Tiger Is had these holes plugged or welded shut and the episcope carrier frame and fittings removed. In the 2 o'clock position there was a stowage box for spare vision blocks in case there was need for replacement. Directly below and in the 3 o'clock position was the driver's main control panel which contained all pertinent temperature gauges and switches for starting and operation of the vehicle. The control panel was mounted on the top of the vehicle's transmission which divided the driver's and bow machine gun/radio operator's positions. Below the driver's control panel was the selector control which allowed the driver to select appropriate gear settings while driving the vehicle over all types of terrain. Just below the selector control was the drive change lever (direction control) which allowed the driver to engage first gear or reverse gear. On either side of the driver's seat were located one each, emergency track steering levers. Normally, the driver steered the vehicle via a steering wheel (located just below the driver's main vision block). If this steering device failed due to damage by enemy fire, the driver could utilize these steering levers accordingly. To the left of the left-hand side emergency steering lever was the hand-brake which could hold the vehicle from rolling forward if parked on undulating terrain. The driver was provided with a standard arrangement of clutch, foot-brake, and accelerator pedals. At the 10 o'clock position, the driver was also provided with a gyroscopic direction indicator which was used to keep the vehicle on a steady course either during night time movement, movement during a large smoke screen, or for movement during inclement weather. This device could also be used if the vehicle was conducting underwater operations pertaining to rivers and lakes.

The driver of a Tiger I was a thoroughly trained and skilled mechanic and was carefully selected for his crew positioning. He was responsible for locating correct terrain features while driving his vehicle and was also to avoid any and all obstacles that would either break or damage component parts of the vehicle, or cause injury to the vehicle crew. This individual was to report any malfunctioning components of the vehicle to the panzer commander and to write a report in order for maintenance personnel to know immediately what the problem consisted of so as to repair it as soon as possible.

The bow machine gunner/radio operator was located in the right forward section of the hull of the Tiger I and was also provided with a padded seat, with his backrest being attached to a swivel type mount bolted to the inside right wall of the hull. In an emergency, this backrest could be swung up and out of the way if the bow machine gunner/radio operator needed to exit the vehicle through the turret escape hatch. Starting at the 12 o'clock position, this crewmember was provided with an MG-34 machine gun in a ball mount with a K.Z.F.2 telescope which offered 18 degrees of vision when the weapon was being fired. Elevation of the mount was 20 degrees, depression 10 degrees, traverse 15 degrees left, and 15 degrees right. This weapon was also fitted with a headpad for firing which helped to stabilize the weapon. To the right of the MG-34 machine gun and stowed in the right pannier of the vehicle, were sixteen belted bags of ammunition for this weapon. They were carried in the usual machine gun sacks (Gürtsackes) and readily available for use for the bow-machine gun during combat. Metal ammunition boxes were also carried at times if the canvas sacks were not available. Mounted in the 3 o'clock position directly below the machine gun sacks was the gasmask for this crewmember. Mounted behind the gas mask were spare prisms for the periscope for this individual's circular hatch in the roof of the superstructure. To the bow machine gunner's 7 o'clock position was the handle for the power take-off device for turret traverse and the bilge pump. This man was responsible for operation of this device and to make sure that it was always engaged while the vehicle was in a combat situation. He would also make spot checks to insure that this device did not disengage itself during an encounter with the enemy which could ultimately cause utter disaster for the entire crew.

The bow machine gunner/radio operator of the Tiger I was also responsible for all radio communications within the vehicle and also for platoon and company level radio transmissions. In the 9 o'clock position and mounted on top of the vehicle's gearbox were the radio sets for the vehicle. The Fu 5 and Fu 7 radio sets were the standard equipment carried on board a Tiger I with Fu 5 being the standard panzer radio, with the Fu 7 being the standard ground to air co-operation equipment. The bow machine gunner/radio operator was an extremely vital crewmember in the Tiger I as he kept the panzer commander and crew aware of what was developing tactically during an engagement with the enemy and also could provide necessary suppressive fire via his hull mounted MG-34 machine gun if enemy infantry or soft skinned vehicles were located in the forward area of the vehicle and within his fire zone.

After Michael Wittmann completed his training and successfully passed all of his written and operational tests pertaining to the Tiger I, it was time for him and his fellow officers to start their training with their respective Tiger I crewmembers.

Wittmann was soon to meet his Tiger I panzer gunner who was SS-Rottenführer Balthasar "Bobby" Woll, who was extremely eager to learn his new trade as a Richtschutze. Woll had been an electrician during peace time and also had worked as a common laborer. He had entered the Waffen-SS on August 15, 1941, and had been a member of the Hitler Youth from September 1933 until September 1939. Woll was a very serious individual who was very keen on making sure that everything was in an orderly fashion. He was very cool and calculating and was a person who did not take chances when lives were to be at stake, especially during gunnery training pertaining to the Tiger I. Woll's manual dexterity was second to none after he was to master the gunnery controls in regards to the 8.8cm main gun of the Tiger I.

Wittmann's Ladeschütze (loader) was to be SS-Rottenführer Kurt Berges who was a very quiet young men and was to prove to everyone that he was to be an excellent loader. During training maneuvers he would become quite excited during gunnery sessions, as this type of training seemed to bring more life out of this individual. He enthusiastically loaded the 8.8cm main gun rounds into the breech, and was able to continue to load as many rounds as he could under the commands of his new panzer commander. Berges it seemed, would never let Wittmann's crew down during a fire mission. He was always prepared and ready for the next fire command.

SS-Rottenführer Gustl Kirschmer was Wittmann's Fahrer (driver) who had been a panzer driver for many years while serving in the Wehrmacht and the Waffen-SS, and had operated a large number of military vehicles during this time period. He was to prove himself a superb driver and mechanic and pampered his vehicles with loving care. He was constantly checking all oil and fuel lines and water levels, and was on the alert for any knocks or pings that would indicate trouble inside or outside the vehicle. It was also imperative that he gave special and close attention to the vehicle's track and suspension system, as these component parts of the vehicle were the most vulnerable to enemy fire and day to day wear and tear from the terrain features the vehicle had to contend with during operations. Kirschmer was a very safe driver and would make sure that rough terrain features were to be avoided at all times, and if he did encounter rugged terrain in regards to tactical reasons, he would not charge over it and bounce and knock the crew around as a result. The one major habit that Wittmann liked about Kirschmer's driving was that he learned very quickly not to slam on the vehicle's brakes in a violent manner. The vast majority of the drivers that Wittmann had seen training, would slam on the vehicle brakes when ordered to halt for a firing mission, which would throw the other crewmembers forward in their respective seated positions, and knock the loader off of his feet. It was to prove imperative that drivers be somewhat soft on the brakes of a Tiger I, as the gunner would lose the majority of his sight picture through his optics and lose track of the enemy targets until the vehicle had time to settle on its suspension system. Thus, the driver was very instrumental in allowing the gunner to keep his forward view of the enemy even while halting the vehicle and taking up a defensive posture. The gunner could also injure his eyes if the driver smashed down on the brakes, which would cause immediate danger to the vehicle and crew. It was very important that the vehicle commander be given a competent driver, who not only needed a mechanical background, but also comprising a common sense mentality of how a vehicle should be operated and a 'sixth' sense allowing the driver to locate and fix problem areas just by the feel of the vehicle and its equipment.

The last man to be incorporated into Wittmann's Tiger I crew was his Funker (radio and bow-machine gun operator), SS-Rottenführer Herbert Pollmann. Pollmann was a very likable fellow and had served in the Panzer Corps during the opening phases of the war. He had been a radio operator in various armored fighting vehicles and knew his job very well indeed. He was also an expert in regards to the operations and maintenance of the MG-34 machine gun and was very skillful with this weapon.

All in all, Michael Wittmann felt that he had been presented with a highly talented and motivated Tiger I panzer crew, which would be vitally important in regards to the upcoming panzer battles that they would surely be involved with as the Fire Brigades of all out panzer assaults against the Allies. Their new and impressive rolling armored fortress and home would be used time and time again to smash through the enemy defenses and to lead the German ground forces to total victory. Still, it would be his responsibility to train his new Tiger I crew and to mould them into an extremely cohesive and highly trained fighting combat team. Their panzer training together would be very fast paced, but Wittmann knew from his StuG III training and fighting encounters with the Ivans that every day of intensive training he and his crew could now obtain on the ranges and maneuver fields, would help to insure their survivability on the modern field of battle against the Allies.

Wittmann and his new Tiger I crew were sent to the Henschel Tiger I factory in Kassel with other numbers of their comrades to obtain their own individual vehicles. It was believed, that each individual panzer crew would function and maintain their own vehicle more enthusiastically if they were to operate the same vehicle in combat. Upon arriving at the Henschel Tiger I factory, Wittmann and his crew were eager to take over a vehicle and to start their training together. After proper paperwork was signed and everything checked in regards to their factory fresh Tiger I Panzerkampfwagen, all vehicles were loaded onto special rail-road flat-cars. All vehicles were fitted with their narrow transportation tracks, with their wider combat tracks laid under the hulls of the vehicles.

Upon their arrival back at Ploermel, the vehicles were off-loaded via a special ramp and driven to the maintenance areas. The wider combat tracks had been pulled off the flat-cars via heavy chains attached to them and their parent vehicle. At this point in time, the heavy combat tracks were fitted to the vehicles by maintenance personnel.

Wittmann's Tiger I training with his new panzer crew started on the day after they arrived back from the Tiger I factory at Kassel. Each crew-member had already been given some instruction in regards to their new vehicles, while the panzer commanders had provided detailed information to their respective crews while in transit to and from the Henschel panzer works. Before the panzer crews could mount their new vehicles, each panzer commander was to go through a comprehensive safety briefing as injuries at this early stage of training were to be avoid at all costs, as they would only slow down the much needed training time.

As their Tiger I training finally began, Wittmann was still very excited about being offered the opportunity to train on these powerful and massive machines. He could also sense that an air of infectious enthusiasm had set in with all of his crew members, and was eager to answer any and all questions asked. If he could not answer a question he would make a mental note of it and consult the training and maintenance personnel stationed at Ploermel, and return with an answer for his crew. Attention to detail was the order of the day during and after their training, which was a major factor in saving lives on the field of combat.

The first few days of Wittmann's training on the Tiger I was indeed very fanciful for him and his new crew. The majority of the training was devoted to driver training which took some getting use to. Even though Kirschmer was an expert driver and mechanic, he had some troubles driving the 56 ton panzer. The Tiger I was the heaviest armored fighting vehicle he had ever encountered in his military vehicle driving career and was not comfortable at the beginning of his training in regards to the acceleration features of this huge panzer. He logically assumed that this vehicle would need heavy handling and initially would crash down on the gas pedal. This action caused the vehicle to jerk forward and then nose down accordingly, where as he would then try to over compensate on the brakes with dire results for the entire panzer crew. The Tiger I was also very sensitive in regards to its steering capabilities as Kirschmer soon discovered. In fact, the driver of any Tiger I could turn the vehicle to the left or right with only two fingers while operating the vehicle's steering wheel. This also lead to another problem for Wittmann's driver, as while trying to maneuver the Tiger I on the driving course, Kirschmer continued to slam down on the accelerator pedal and then would hit the vehicle's brakes in a non-soft manner, to compensate once again. This action caused his entire upper body to lose control as he (along with the rest of the crew) would be thrown forward by this action. This in turn caused him to pull the steering wheel to one side or the other, which caused the vehicle to careen from one side of the road to the other. Wittmann and his crew were very patient with Kirschmer but they could still feel the pain and sores around their waists and legs from being banged around in their crew positions. Wittmann fared the worse of all, as he was being constantly slammed into his armored cupola aperture and had at times bruises completely around his waist which proved to be very uncomfortable and extremely painful. If he choose to sit down in his three position seat, his legs were always banging into Bobby Woll's lower back, with his knees crashing into Woll's neck and head!

After the first few days of driver training, Kirschmer finally started to settle down in his driving techniques, with Wittmann and the rest of his crew somewhat relieved at the thought of not being thrown and bounced around in their respective positions within their new steel box on tracks. On occasion, Kirschmer would hit a bump or hidden depression obscured by dust or smoke, but at least he was in control of the new heavy panzer which lead the rest of the crew feeling a little more safe and secure.

As the driver training continued, Kirschmer found that the fifty-six ton giant panzer was very responsive and he improved his driving skills even more so. He was able to obtained constant vehicle speeds up to 40 kph, and across country the Tiger I could still maintain speeds of up to 20 kph.

Wittmann at times still had to remind his driver.

"You have to drive with your head and not with your ass! Think about what you are doing Gustl!"

It was quite clear to all of the men, that for successful fighting on the front, they would be very dependent upon the vehicle driver to bring them out of many difficult situations or tactical engagements with the enemy.

The next phase of training for Wittmann and his Tiger I crew was panzer gunnery. At the beginning of this training, Wittmann, Woll, and Berges were instructed to report to the firing ranges where they were to train on emplaced Tiger I turrets (Panzerstellungs) which were mounted on large concrete blocks. These turrets were situated so as to train the panzer commander and his turret crew in the art of accurate gunnery techniques. The only movements that were possible in regards to the training turrets was traverse left and right, and elevation and depression of the 8.8cm main gun. Rolling and pitching movements were eradicated for the time being and thus offered the turret crew a very stable firing platform in order to properly conduct their gunnery training. The 'revolving stage' was the nick-name given to the Tiger I turret and turret basket by its panzer crews and was a term used throughout the Waffen-SS panzer units. Utilizing an entire Tiger I for this type of training was thought at the time very unproductive, as the vast majority of panzer gunnery was performed in a stationary fashion, which would leave the driver and bow machine gunner/radio operator little to do and wasted valuable training time. With the panzer commander, gunner, and loader being trained in an emplaced firing mode also helped the turret crew to always remember to bring their vehicle to a complete halt prior to firing the main gun. This type of training also helped the gunner to obtain a 'feel' for his main gun controls without having to contend with other idiosyncrasies of the vehicle. It was quite obvious that the gunners would have to deal with other functions, noises, and movement of the vehicle in combat, but it was highly essential that he concentrated on the main function of the vehicle which was to place steel on target before the enemy had a chance to do the same.

In the beginning of the gunnery training it was not easy to engage and hit targets even while in a stationary position, as the fired main gun rounds fell short or over the targets. Bobby Woll was no different in regards to early gunnery practice but soon learned the correct settings and adjustments pertaining to the 8.8cm KwK 36 L/56 main gun. Wittmann's fire commands were always accurate and correct and would lay Woll unto target and then provide him with final adjustments before ordering him to open fire. Berges was very much at home in his loaders position and was soon ramming main gun rounds into the smoking and overheating breech of the 8.8cm weapon. The loader was the busiest crew-member of all, as he still had to load the 8.8cm main gun and also replenish the co-axial MG-34 machine gun. Only when Wittmann and his turret crew passed all of their required gunnery tests, would they be reunited with the rest of their crew for additional comprehensive training. Long hours were spent on the firing ranges and a gunnery instructor was present at all times to help and guide the panzer commander and his turret crew through the motions.

After Wittmann and his turret crew completed their initial gunnery training in the emplaced Tiger I turrets, they were once again back with Kirschmer and Pollmann. These two panzer crew-members had not been wasting time for they had been both going through an extensive vehicle maintenance program and both had cross-trained pertaining to each other's vehicle positions. If the driver was ever incapacitated during combat, the bow-machine gunner would have to replace this individual, so it was imperative that the bow machine gunner/radio operator was thoroughly trained for the driving and up-keep of their vehicle in the field.

Finally, Wittmann had his entire crew back and they started their last phase of panzer training. Wittmann was now trying to mould his panzer crew into an extremely close knit fighting team and used every ounce of energy and knowledge he had to create a cohesive fighting unit. Everyone on board his Tiger I felt that there was something special about their panzer commander and it all boiled down that he had a great amount of combat experience that no doubt would save their lives in the heat of battle. And secondly, they knew that "Michael" cared a great deal about his panzer crew and would help them with any personal matters that arose concerning their families, etc. They all felt very comfortable with Wittmann as their commander and would follow him anywhere and do anything that he asked of them.

As their training continued, Wittmann was still not sure how well Bobby Woll would turn out as his gunner. It would be Woll who in the future would be responsible if they were to survive during a panzer dual with the enemy as their lives would be placed in his hands. In all fairness, it would be a team effort to survive any combat engagement presented to any panzer crew as this theme had been instilled into the crew at the start. Still, it was only the gunner who could destroy an enemy vehicle and thus received as much thorough training as humanly possible. Wittmann carefully guided Woll onto targets of opportunity and made doubly sure that his gunner was firing at the correct range panels, etc. During these firing courses Wittmann was to stand upright in his turret cupola and was constantly straining his eyes in order to make sure that he himself picked out the appropriate targets. As expected, Woll had a problem viewing through his sighting telescope while the vehicle was in motion. The vehicle movement greatly distorted his vision and the interior harmonic vibrations made it almost impossible to view through this sighting device. In the beginning he would place his head directly into the eyepiece of his telescope, and try to keep track of and locate target panels outlined to him by Wittmann on the ranges. This was a very sound practice, as long as Kirschmer did not slam on the brakes for one reason or the other at the last seconds before firing, otherwise Woll could receive injuries to his eyes and face. It only took one bad experience in having one's face smashed into the sights to be highly wary of this happening once again. It was quite obvious that Woll had to depend on his commander's directions a great deal as Woll (and other gunners) had great difficulty in locating targets, especially if the vehicle was moving at high speed.

It would still take a great deal of effort on Wittmann's part to turn out an efficient Tiger I panzer crew before they would be transferred to the fighting now raging on the many fronts and especially the Russian campaign. Wittmann was highly determined to produce a well trained crew, but it would take a very steady hand and close co-operation with his men to totally achieve this goal.

Wittmann and Bobby Woll developed a very close working relationship between them and it was very apparent that this bond would help to weld their crew together even further. These two individuals work very hard together and solved any problems whether they related to the mission at hand, panzer gunnery, or maintenance on their vehicle. Wittmann also called his new crewmembers by their nicknames which tended to indicate that he did not consider his men as just part of the vehicle's make-up, plus, he did not forget his NCO roots.

The Tiger I panzer training proceeded along with Wittmann and his crew aggressively storming through the various practice maneuver areas and firing ranges and increasing their skills accordingly. Bobby Woll was developing into an excellent panzer gunner and did not often miss targets of opportunity that presented themselves. Wittmann's crew was finally settling down and he felt they would perform well on the field of battle and not let him down in the face of the enemy. After only a few weeks of training with his new panzer crew, he found himself relaxing somewhat and enjoyed his training and gunnery sessions with his men. All through the training it was stressed time and time again, that any armored fighting vehicle was only as good as the men operating it. This statement was enforced on all aspects of the training pertaining to the Tiger I, and was to never be forgotten.

During one of the live fire engagements Bobby Woll was to say excitedly, "If we only had this powerful panzer earlier in the war, we could have destroyed even more Allied panzers!" "It's a damn good thing that we have it now, Bobby!", replied Wittmann.

Wittmann and his crew learned very quickly that the Tiger I used 535 liters of fuel for only 80 kilometers during normal maneuver operations with the 12 cylinder Maybach HL 210 P 45 gasoline engine. With vehicle accessories, their heavy panzer also used up 82 liters of oil very quickly and hourly maintenance checks were extremely vital. Engine and transmission oils were constantly monitored by the driver from his instrument panel with any major problems or major leaks being reported to their panzer commander.

Indeed, one of the biggest disadvantages in dealing with the Tiger I was the slow rate of turret traverse. If any targets on the firing ranges were located before or past the 10 o'clock or 2 o'clock turret positions, the gunner had a very difficult time in traversing the fifteen ton turret to the desired firing angle as dictated by the panzer commander. This was a disadvantage for only a very short period of time before it was realized that if the driver of the vehicle turned the vehicle's hull towards the intended target, this action would help to compensate this problem area. Wittmann was still quite aware of his days when fighting the Ivans in his StuG III and had to instruct his driver to swing their machine into the direction of the enemy before his gunner could fire their 7.5cm main gun

Now, while Woll was traversing the turret, Kirschmer would bring the hull of the vehicle to the left or right depending on the selected target and directions from Wittmann. This gunnery technique would bring Woll onto target much easier and quicker, and saved precious seconds during tense firing missions. On the field of battle, these few seconds would no doubt make the difference in regards to who would fire off the first main gun round in a fire fight. This movement normally placed the heaviest armor plated areas of the vehicle towards the enemy and if the opposing panzer did manage to fire off a main gun round, its impact on the Tiger I would be minimal, especially at acute directions in regards to angles of attack.

Wittmann and his panzer crew were now finishing their Tiger I training and had worked extremely hard all through this preparation for combat. Bobby Woll was now a crack shot in regards to the 8.8cm main gun and was receiving very high marks on the various firing ranges. Kirschmer mastered the art of driving the 56 ton Tiger I and the early cuts, bumps, and bruises sustained by the rest of the crew were now just a bad memory. When a range target came into view, Kirschmer would carefully ease his vehicle into a good firing position and slowly bring the heavy vehicle to a gentle halt. Meanwhile, Bobby Woll would be given quick and accurate directions from Wittmann, the sight picture would come into view just as the vehicle came to a stop, whereupon Woll would have an excellent view of the target and fire the main gun round onto target!

Before their training ended, a number of other exercises where performed by the Tiger I crews. One of which was the act of loading the vehicles onto dummy railway flatcars. The vast majority of Tiger Is would be transported by rail to their final destinations prior to entering all combat zones. As a result, this type of training was critically important for all respective Tiger I personnel. At the start of this training, all vehicles were fitted with their normal combat tracks as this was necessary as the vehicle drivers would be more apt to stay on the loading ramps leading up and onto the dummy flatcars. After this was mastered, they would replace their combat tracks with narrow transportation tracks. This was very heavy and strenuous work and it took the entire crew to change these sets of tracks.

Before the narrow transportation tracks could be fitted, the combat tracks were removed by removing one track pin (one pin connected two track links), thereby breaking the tracks. The driver engaged the driving sprockets and effectively pulled the tracks off of the suspension to the front of the vehicle. Once these tracks were removed and positioned out of the way, the narrow transportation tracks were to be fitted.

A strong metal cable that was stowed on the left hand outside vertical wall of the superstructure was removed and then attached to the front drive sprocket, travelled over the road wheels and idler wheel, and then secured to the tracks behind the vehicle. The driver would start the vehicle engine, engage the transmission and clutch and slowly drag the tracks (one set at a time) up and over the rear idler wheel, over the road wheels, and then onto the drive sprocket itself. As soon as the tracks engaged the drive sprocket, the driver would disengage the transmission from the engine on signal from the panzer commander. Once the sprocket came to a halt, the panzer commander would have the driver inch the track forward until it reached the top of the sprocket and started to lower itself to the ground. At this point the metal cable was removed. On signal, the driver would stop the track and then have the vehicle crew force the track down and line it up with the vehicle road-wheels until it travelled the full length of the suspension. After this was accomplished, the crew would connect the track together in and around the rear idler wheel by inserting a track pin between two track links. The opposite set of tracks was mounted in the same manner. The crew could then loosen or tighten the tracks via a track tensioning device located in the lower rear plate of the vehicle.

Wittmann and his crew practiced these operations for many hours and disliked this portion of their Tiger I training. Changing tracks for practice and loading their vehicles onto dummy flatcars on a smooth and solid surface in a training yard was one thing, but having to change tracks in the field or throwing a track while in combat only helped to illustrate fully the fact that the vehicle tracks were the most venerable component parts on their new panzer. Special attention had to be given to the vehicle tracks which usually entailed the driver and bow-machine gunner/radio operator to dismount every time the vehicle came to a halt in a secured area and visually check the tracks and suspension for any foreign materials such as rocks, logs, and barbed wire that could foul or dislodge the tracks from the vehicle. It was also extremely vital to check the metal track pins for ware and tear and report any signs of damage to the vehicle commander for repair or replacement.

The last and most dangerous portion of training with the Tiger I consisted of underwater submersion which was also highly disliked by all the men under instruction. The Tiger I had been designed for complete submersion to a depth of approximately fifteen feet of water which necessitated very special arrangements for ventilation for the supply of air to the engine under these conditions. The crews of the vehicles were provided with breathing apparatus while underwater and received comprehensive training in regards to this type of equipment. The majority of bridges in Europe could not support the weight of the Tiger I and this was the reasoning behind the submersion equipment fitted to these vehicles.

To prepare the vehicle for underwater running, all butterfly valves in the engine compartment were closed by remote control, as controls were mounted on each side of the rear engine bulkhead of the fighting compartment activated by the turret crew-members. A sliding valve in the induction trunk of the air circulating fan was moved to the rear and thus air was taken entirely from the front of the vehicle through the gearbox cowling, and delivered as before through the exhaust jackets to the air chambers at the rear. After the butterfly valves were closed, air could not pass into the radiator compartment as beforehand. The two chambers were interconnected by a trunk fitted with a pipe incorporating a butterfly valve, when open, and thus air was discharged into the top of the engine compartment. Air replacement for the crew and engine was effected through a stack pipe (snorkel) which was erected on the rear engine deck of the vehicle. The stack pipe was incorporated into telescopic sections, and when not in use, the three upper sections were stowed in the lower section which was permanently fixed to the inside of the engine decking. Spigotted loosely into the lower section was a pipe connecting to a rectangular section of trunking on the hull floor of the vehicle. This trunking was an open end terminating beneath the turret floor to deliver air to the panzer crew. All doors, hatches, and venting had rubber seals with the turret ring being sealed by an inflatable rubber ring. The vehicle's bilge pump was driven via the engine through the power traverse auxiliary gearbox. Engine exhausts remained the same with exhaust emitted directly into the water through non-return pop valves on top of the exhaust silencers.

After learning all aspects of submersion operations with their Tiger I, Wittmann and his crew felt very confidant with their new panzer. They had run the course of training together and had been fine tuned into a very cohesive fighting team that Wittmann had dearly hoped for at the beginning of their training at Ploermel. He could now appreciate the fact that he now had a panzer crew in which he could depend on, and was very eager to prove to his superiors that they could achieve any mission or objective given to them in the future. It would not be long before Wittmann and his crew would be put through the acid test of brutal combat on the vast steppes of the Russian front.

It was now Christmas 1942. Once again Michael Wittmann returned home to his family for holiday cheer and fellowship. He knew only too well, that very soon a new and dangerous assignment would be forthcoming. He and his former comrades were already very familiar with the Russian front and the extremely harsh fighting and living conditions that took every ounce of energy and raw courage to survive its hot summers and bitterly cold winters. For the moment, Wittmann tried to put all of the horrors of the Eastern front out of his mind, as it was an unforgettable time for rest and holiday celebrations with his family and friends; a short time to live and feel the breath of every day living, that could only be felt with total peace and complete tranquility.

Chapter IX

RETURN TO RUSSIA

January 9, 1943 – March 18, 1943

The second campaign in which Michael Wittmann and the Leibstandarte Adolf Hitler fought on the Russian front covered the months from January 1943 to March 1943, and was to include a large number of climactic panzer battles, with the loss and recapture of Kharkov becoming one of the largest battles encountered during this time period. Tremendous losses of men and equipment were incurred by both the German and Russian military forces where men and machines clashed day in and day out in regards to assigned objectives and cities. Wittmann and his Tiger I crew were to be tested to the lengths of their endurance time and time again, as Tiger I units were always used as the 'Fire Brigades' for the vast majority of the panzer assaults against the Ivans. All of the Tiger I crews' training was to be put to the acid test as the German war planners had extremely high hopes paced upon these highly motivated and trained men to help stem the tide of mounting Russian battlefield numerical supremacy.

As the combat fighting continued up to the winter of 1942/43, a set pattern of constant war on the Eastern front had taken on the swinging-motion of a massive pendulum, first arching ever eastward with the German summer assaults, and returning westward, as the Russian army battled its brutal and harsh winter campaigns to regain German held territories. Only during the rainy seasons of the spring and fall was the momentum of both forces halted with each opponent reorganizing and reequipping. Static defense was the order of the day, except in isolated areas, with only minor tactical operations being carried out, which included the taking of enemy prisoners for ruthless and prolonged interrogations, by both sides.

A gap of some 200 miles was the net result of the Russian winter offensive of 1942/43 that had overpowered Army Group South, destroyed the German Sixth Army at Stalingrad and through this wide gap, between Voronezh and Voroshiovgrad, the Red armies spearheaded westward towards the Dnieper river. In the southern sector, the Third Red Tank Army was ordered to drive forward a line covering Poltava-Dnieperpetrovsk-Saporzhe to isolate the German forces there against the Black Sea,and then to annihilate them accordingly. As the Red armies advanced on this particular battle area, they were to by-pass Kharkov from the north and the south, although they had severe difficulties with support trains and manpower replacements; this advance however, was still able to maintain its momentum up to the end of January 1943. The Russian armored assaults started to fan out as they advanced, giving a great deal of opportunity for well placed counter blows by German units directed to their open and unprotected flanks. By this time, the German forces on the Russian front were too weak to cause any decisive effect upon the Red army steamroller and would need not only massive reinforcements, but truly needed an outright miracle in order for the entire southern wing to keep from falling into Russian hands.

As a direct result of the constant deterioration of the Eastern front as whole, the SS Panzer Corps, comprising the Leibstandarte Adolf Hitler, Das Reich, and Totenkopf Divisions, were ordered on January 9, 1943, to the Russian front with all speed. These three SS Panzer units were given total rail and road priority with the Leibstandarte Adolf Hitler and the majority of Das Reich soon concentrated in the Kharkov area and then moved directly up to the front lines. The Leibstandarte Adolf Hitler was given the task of taking up defensive positions along the Donetz and Das Reich was to establish and hold advanced outposts east of the river line. As was common on the Russian front, divisional sectors covered vast areas; for example, the Leibstandarte Adolf Hitler's bridgehead at Chegevayev encompassed some seventy miles with the extremely thin line held by the Grenadiers further reduced when Witt's Panzer Grenadier Regiment was ordered to Kubyansk so as to be ready and available for a proposed assault southeast of Alkatavka, only made matters worse for the German forces in this area.

This was the background of events that had developed just prior to Micheal Wittmann's return to the Russian front. The Red army was now a fully equipped and experienced force that was not to be underestimated as their tactics had changed dramatically since Wittmann had done battle against them in his thinly armored StuG III Ausf. A assault gun. The Russians no longer sent in their armored fighting vehicles in piece meal fashion as they had done in the past. The Red army was now operating in massive waves of gargantuan aggression with a central command overseeing their every move. It was quite apparent to all panzer commanders fighting in this theater of operations, that every main gun round would have to find its mark in order for their vehicles and crews to successfully survive the Russian hordes.

The remaining Leibstandarte Adolf Hitler units held the line, standing solidly against the rolling tide of the Russian armored attacks, while a number of confused and retreating units, (German,Italian, and Hungarian), flowed westward towards the safety of the bridgehead. The first week of February 1943, proved very costly for the Russians, as highly determined attacks were staged on the outer outposts pertaining to the Leibstandarte Adolf Hitler's defensive perimeters which resulted in these positions being withdrawn to regroup and to stage a more comprehensive and cohesive defense. Later, in blinding snowstorms, which were constantly slowing down the Red army's advances which aided the Germans in smashing their opponents assaults, especially against the key bridgehead position at Pechenege, where the Ivans were thrown back with heavy losses of men and vital equipment, were taken on by men of the Leibstandarte Adolf Hitler who were prepared to die rather than to break under the pressure, or to be captured. Byelgorod, north of Kharkov, was then evacuated and Das Reich withdraw to the protection of the Donetz, fighting desperately every foot of the way. Other German units on either flank of this activity were less fortunate as Russian probing patrols found, particularly at Shiyev, a forty-five mile gap between the right flank of the Leibstandarte Adolf Hitler and the left flank of the 320th Infantry Division. An immediate attempt to close this gap was thus avoided by the Corps concentrating an attack force which in turn avoided the encirclement of the German forces in this area. The number one priority was to smash the Russian attacks in their tracks, and to set up defensive positions where ever terrain dictated such a stand.

In order to proceed with these operations, a strong and comprehensive German Battle Group was established, under Sepp Dietrich's command, which would be sent directly into battle. In bitterly cold temperatures that constantly dipped 20 degrees below zero, often heavily outnumbered and obstructed by deep and blowing snowdrifts, a three pronged, armored attack moved forward. During periods of clear weather, Stuka dive-bombers had successfully soften up the avenues of approach with high explosives, which helped to clear the way, and also created craters for the infantry to hide in and fight from, when receiving return fire from the Ivans. The Leibstandarte Adolf Hitler reconnaissance battalion was on the right flank of this maneuver with the 'Der Führer' Regiment of Das Reich, along with the Leibstandarte's Panzer Regiment, forming the center attack column, with Witt's 1st SS Panzer Grenadier constituting their left flank. Great demands were placed on these Waffen-SS units as the assaults went in for the overall attack.

Untersturmführer Michael Wittmann and his Tiger I crew were now under the leadership of Hauptsturmführer Heinz Kling who was a very resourceful panzer leader and highly respected by his men. Prior to their next battle run to try and throw the Ivans off balance, Kling's vehicles had taken up defensive positions, with his panzer commanders and himself now studying the situational maps of the area ahead of them in great detail. It was found, that the capture of a small village named Merefa, which was on the Red army's main supply road, would be highly instrumental in ambushing the Russians as they approached, if it could be captured by Kling's panzer company. The second objective would be to attack straight across the Red army salient and make contact with the main body of Army Group South, and to reestablish a continuous front line and hold it until additional German forces could be rushed into this defensive line.

"That small village there is Merefa, behind us is Kharkov. The Ivans will most likely attack here and then surround Kharkov," stated Kling.

All of Kling's men were now trying to locate Merefa on their maps and to follow the course of advance that their commander had laid out for them. They all wanted to make certain that nobody became lost or were left behind in the assault which could lead to being encircled by the ever present enemy.

Serving along with the younger panzer commanders was a very rough and austere older man by the name of SS-Oberscharführer (Technical sergeant) Georg Lötzsch, who was called by everyone present, the "Panzer General" due to the fact that he had thorough and detailed knowledge of every operation and function in regards to the massive and powerful Tiger I Panzerkampfwagen. Georg Lötzsch had come out of the General SS and then became a member of the Waffen-SS in 1933. He was a highly skilled auto mechanic and was quite pleased with himself when he received his first Tiger I to command while on active duty on the Russian front. This individual had been involved with the entire development program dealing with the Tiger I, and had vast knowledge and practical experience in the Tiger I production workshops and was also present during the initial trial runs of this vehicle. Lötzsch was a very important person to have nearby in the event of a major breakdown in the field of combat regarding the Tiger I. He was considered a panzer wizard in being able to locate or detect the source of trouble before follow up maintenance personnel could arrive on the scene. It was clearly understood that his vehicle was to be highly protected at all times by the other Tiger Is in the unit as his comrades-in-arms did not want anything to happen to this highly talented individual. At thirty years of age, he was also looked upon as one of the old boys of the unit!

Wittmann returned to his Tiger I after his map reading session with Kling, climbed up on top of his turret and slid into his commander's cupola. He put on his earphones but pushed them a little ways towards the back of his head so he could also hear his comrades around his vehicle in order to make sure that he heard any verbal commands to move out, plus any commands coming in over the panzer radio.

"What's up, Michael?," asked Kirschmer.

"We roll to the ready point and hold until Kurt Meyer has returned from the Donetz with the reconnaissance unit."

All of a sudden, the radio cracked out the expected order!

"Attention! Chief to everyone: March!!!!"

Upon the command to move out, all of the Tiger Is rolled forward through the now falling snow with full speed. The half strength platoon of Höflinger was ordered to position itself to the right flank of Wittmann's Tiger I which in turn provided added protection and fire power. Wittmann could see the individual panzers of his platoon moving through a deeply cut gully directly in front of his vehicle. Suddenly, the lead panzer sunk out of sight into this large depression whereas he tried to raise its panzer commander over the radio network. Wittmann's first thought was that this vehicle had run into an expertly camouflaged anti-tank ditch now covered with thick snow, but before he received a returned radio transmission from the vehicle in question, he saw that it was pulling itself out of this depression and moved forward towards the objective.

"Damn! I can not see anything more to my front!," yelled Wittmann's driver.

"Keep rolling forward!," was Wittmann's replied.

Wittmann knew that the driving snow was building up against his driver's forward vision devices and would have a very difficult time observing the way ahead. He would have to concentrate on the lay of the terrain, and try to keep his driver on course the best he could under the circumstances. Meter after meter, his Tiger I crawled through the high snowdrifts trying to keep pace with the other vehicles of his unit, who had now fanned out, but staying within sight of each other. The rest of his crew simply stayed at the ready in case the enemy presented themselves from hidden anti-tank gun positions or dug-in T34s. Wittmann's loader had already chambered a main gun round in the breech in order for Woll to have ammunition at his beckon call. Berges was standing upright in his loader's hatch and was observing for the enemy to the right and right rear of the vehicle. Wittmann was scanning the terrain to his left and left rear, while Woll, was trying to observe the forward area of the moving vehicle, but had difficulty in establishing a good sight picture in his binocular telescope. Wittmann finally spotted a small nearby road and had his driver maneuver their machine towards it in the hopes of finding solid footing in which to travel upon. They quickly reached this road which went through a grove of standing birch trees that swayed back and forth as the heavy vehicle roared through and past them. As Wittmann and his crew entered the edge of this wooded area, a radio message came in over the company frequency.

"Everyone halt! Position yourselves so you can immediately witness the arrival of the enemy when they come out of the village!," was the order given by Kling.

After this sudden order, all of the Tiger Is halted into new defensive positions with their crews ready for combat with the Ivans. Wittmann had his driver position their machine at the edge of the birch trees, and waited for further orders. After every Tiger I had taken up a defensive position, all of their engines were shut down in order for each and every panzer commander to listen for the oncoming Russian panzers. As soon as all of the vehicles were silent, the men could hear the distant sounds of some fighting in the direction of a nearby river.

"I am going ahead on foot to see what is developing!," stated Wittmann. "Berges, you come with me!"

Wittmann grabbed his MP-40 machine pistol. Berges also took another weapon and they both climbed out of the security of their Tiger I and made their way forward to try and locate the enemy. Woll instinctively took the place of his vehicle commander and put on Wittmann's headphones and throat-micro-phones to monitor the radio and to keep the rest of the crew informed as to any new orders or developments.

As Wittmann and his loader carefully crawled along the edge of a small creek near the edge of a village, they could still hear gun fire and movement of vehicles, but could not locate the enemy. They then moved forward and came upon the entrance of the village without being detected. Suddenly, Berges gave a warning signal to his commander! As if rooted where they stood, they then quickly fell to their knees and hid themselves behind a small stone wall.

"There Untersturmführer!", whispered Berges.

Wittmann soon made out the lines of two Russian 7.62cm anti-tank guns hidden in two houses with only the muzzle brakes of these weapons protruding through the blown out windows. It was a lucky chance happening that Wittmann and Berges had located these two very dangerous weapons, as if they had tried to storm and attack this small village with their vehicles, they would have been surely fired upon by these highly concealed Pak guns and no doubt would have suffered the consequences.

Wittmann stated in a low voice, "Paks are deadly to us, we will have to do away with them"!

The two panzermen crawled forward a bit further until they had reached one of the nearby huts and then moved into a farmyard until they soon came across a forward enemy observation post. This was enough for Berges, and tugged at his panzer commander's arm.

"Lets return to our panzer, Berges!" said Wittmann

His loader did not need to hear another word from his commander. Unseen by the Russians, they both returned to their Tiger I and quickly radioed the company commander. As soon as Wittmann had reported the situation, he explained to the rest of his crew the positions of the Pak guns and the forward enemy observation post. Suddenly, there was activity over the company radio network. It was indeed, the company commander once again!

"Wittmann, you roll with your platoon into the village and travel as far as the other side. Wendroff's platoon will cover the right flank and attack the village from the southeast if that should be necessary!"

Wittmann again instructed his men in regards to their respective duties. All was ready, Unterscharführer Kurt Kleber was to attack the Russian observation post, as soon as the assault began. The "Panzer General" Georg Lötzsch was to take out the hidden anti-tank gun at the left side of the village while Wittmann was to go to the right side of the main street of the village and attack the other concealed enemy Pak weapon.

Höflinger and Rottenführer Karlheinz Warmbrunn (a former gunner now acting as a panzer commander) were to travel to the right and to the left flank and fire at any opposition in sight. They were to be travelling at full speed which was felt would help to surprise the enemy gunners and throw them off their aim.

Everything was now set, the company commander stood up in his turret cupola and gave the signal to attack! The Tiger Is all made a formidable noise as they rolled forward with all main guns trained in the direction of the village called Merefa. The panzer commanders all knew that the snow would help to muffle the sounds of their metal battle tracks, but also were highly aware that their engine noise would be a dead give away to the Ivans manning the Pak guns.

Michael Wittmann was very excited to be back in action once again, but was to keep a cool head. He gave directions to his drivers and tried his best to keep them on a steady course at all times, Kirschmer changed gears as quickly as he could and with full speed they rolled towards their objective. To the left and to the right, and behind him, Wittmann could hear the roar of all of the power plants of his sister vehicles as he pulled forward his earphones in order to make sure that all was ready for the opening phases of his first combat engagement against the enemy with his Tiger I Panzerkampfwagen.

"Prepare for attack!" shouted Wittmann to his tense crew.

As Wittmann closed his commander's hatch, the street in front of his vehicle suddenly was ablaze with fire from every direction possible. The first rounds of the anti-tank gun whistled over the top of his Tiger I turret with a great rush of air. Wittmann then ordered his driver to halt, Woll had already aimed the 8.8cm main gun and all he needed to do was to make a last second adjustment to his sight picture. Wittmann gave out hius first fire command, and with a powerful crack, and the rocking back of the vehicle, the main gun round flew out and into the direction of the enemy Pak weapon. Two brief seconds after the firing, there was a bright flash of red and orange as the sound of the explosion echoed through out the village. The H.E. round had found its mark as the anti-tank gun had been totally smashed along with its crew. There was now a cascade of fire and smoke, as the surrounding ready ammunition for this weapon had also been hit and detonated. The house that had hidden the anti-tank gun was now a pile of burning timbers and lit up the overcast sky with its sheets of flame licking the heavens.

"Hit!" cried Woll as Berges was already loading the next main gun round.

All five panzers were firing by this time, as the quiet and sleepy village now came to life as Russian infantry tried to take cover and hold off the Tiger Is' assault. Wittmann ordered his driver to advance into the village. Pollmann was now firing his bow mounted MG-34 at anything that dared to move which helped in keeping the Russian infantrymen at bay. The Tiger Is continued to roll further into the village with all speed, and pushed the Ivans back as they advanced. Wittmann could see through his vision blocks as Russian infantry were running across the streets and tried to direct MG-34 fire at them via Pollmann's and Woll's respective weapons. He could also see the tongues of fire leaping out of the blown out windows of the destroyed buildings. He then could hear the pings of small projectiles striking against the front 110mm armor plate of his vehicle as the Russians in total desperation were now firing light caliber anti-tank rifles at his vehicle which were merely bouncing off the thick hide of his machine. Their only chance was for them to fire a well placed round into the driver's vision block or gunner's frontal telescopic apertures, or perhaps damage the tracks. With the Tiger Is moving at top speed, there was little hope for the Ivans in regards to stopping these massive vehicles.

"Panzer traps!," cried Woll.

His commander immediately instructed his driver to slow down in order to avoid these dangerous obstacles. If they smashed into these barriers they would surely crush the first one or two concrete obstructions but would no doubt cause damage to their battle tracks if they tried to crash through the remainder. Wittmann was also very concerned about hanging up his vehicle on these obstacles and becoming immobilized, and thus becoming easy prey for any nearby enemy anti-tank gunners. Kirschmer slammed on the brakes and veered to the right in order to avoid the barriers with everyone inside the Tiger I being thrown to the left of their respective positions causing minor cuts and bruises. Soon they had reached the opposite side of the village and as Wittmann opened his cupola hatch he paid witness to the smashed anti-tank gun that the "Panzer General" had minutes before knocked out with dead and dying Russians laying face down in the snow. The Ivans had all stayed at their posts, but had been eradicated by Lötzsch's marauding Tiger I.

As Hauptsturmführer Kling's Tiger I was moving through the village his right track caught the edge of a low stone wall and mowed it down as a direct result. His driver then over compensated his steering actions and crashed into the side of a nearby house. Plaster, timber, and roofing materials poured down upon his vehicle with a great crack. Kling ordered his driver to bring his vehicle to an abrupt halt. Half of the roof of the shattered building was now dangling on top of his turret! The driver also succeeded in stalling the engine of the vehicle and then tried desperately to restart his stationary machine. Finally, after several attempts the Maybach came back to life, with Kling now ordering his driver to back up and bring his vehicle back into action. As the vehicle was reversing from the damaged house, it was readily apparent that the roof of this structure was firmly emplaced on his main gun and turret, and effectively blocked his gunner's view to the outside world. Kling was also blind from his turret position and ordered his gunner to rotate the turret to try and free itself from the clutches of the wooden structure. After a few minutes, it started to fall apart, as Kling also had his driver move forward and then slam on the brakes in order to try and slide it off. For a few brief moments, this desperate scene seemed quite comical, but indeed was a very dangerous situation for Kling's panzer crew. In utter desperation, Kling then ordered his gunner to fire off a number of main gun rounds in the hopes of blasting this mass of broken timbers and shingles off of the turret. The idea being that the blast and resulting shockwave would blow the vast majority of these materials free of his turret. This last ditch attempt along with the other ad hoc measures finally removed the wooden roof, with Kling relieved as they moved forward to rejoin the rest of his company. Had they not been able to free themselves, no doubt, the nearby Russian infantry would have surely tried to either board this vehicle or would have knocked it out with other conventional means, such as mines, TNT, placed charges, or by a hastily placed anti-tank gun round.

During this period of time, Wittmann had ordered Kirschmer to slow down their Tiger I and was prepared to provide Kling with supportive fire over his rear deck, if the Ivans had tried to destroy Kling's machine. It was now seen that all of the Russians were retreating with great speed from Merefa, as the village was firmly in German hands. However, all crews were ordered to remain in their vehicles, as Kling was not too sure about remaining Russian snipers who would be hidden in the surrounding rubble and destroyed buildings. The German panzer crews scanned the area ahead and in all directions via their optical devices, and also fired volleys of main gun rounds and machine gun fire into the buildings in order to try and draw fire from any hidden Russian weapons and crews that might still be lurking in the shadows. No return fire came forth, so it was assumed that the area was safe for the panzer crews to exit their vehicles for the time being. However, the Tiger I gunners stayed at their positions and at the ready in order to suppress any firing that might commence once the panzer crews removed themselves from the security of their machines. By this time, Kling, his loader, driver, and radio operator were outside of their vehicle and were throwing, kicking, and pulling off what remained of the wooden roof that had dropped down onto their vehicle turret. Every little bit of debris was removed as even a small piece of brick or metal pipe could jam their turret and this was utmost in their minds as they were clambering over and around their turret and main gun clearing away any and all materials that had not been shaken or blown off previously.

Wittmann suddenly gave a loud shout to all concerned, as he saw a column of Russian armored fighting vehicles moving back towards the village! Behind these machines was a command vehicle with additional infantry on foot trying to keep up.

"Attack! Attack!," was the order given.

The Russian machines were now at full throttle as they approached the village. They rolled in single formation upon the main road as they continued to try and take over the German held positions. Suddenly the leading T34/76 made a mad dash towards the main street, stopped, and started to rotate its turret towards Warmbrunn's Tiger I. Woll observed this action and traversed his turret and fired his main gun as soon as the enemy machine came into his sight picture. The high velocity AP main gun round tore into the turret of the Russian tank and blew it completely off its superstructure. This was called by the German panzer crews 'Tipping ones hat', especially in regards to Tiger Is and their deadly and accurate 8.8cm main guns. None of the crew were seen to escape from the doomed enemy machine, as the on-broad ammunition ignited and blew pieces of white hot metal in all directions. The other Tiger Is were now firing at the large number of Russian vehicles, as they tried to storm forward. Enemy tanks were exploding in and around the supporting infantry as they were now forced to dive for cover. Ammunition trucks that had ventured too far forward were hit and exploding one after the other in rapid succession. Russian infantry were now running into the streets as the flimsy buildings they were hiding in gave little protection against the powerful blasts of the Tiger I's 8.8cm main guns, which were now firing at almost point blank range. The main gun rounds past right through the structures, but the concussion of these projectiles were the deadly factor which killed or flattened the Ivans as they tried to flee from the firing zones. As soon as the Tiger I crews saw the Russian infantry running out into the bare and unprotected streets, the vehicle gunners were ordered to open up with both MG-34 machine guns, on instructions from the panzer commanders in order to conserve on main gun ammunition.

Upon dealing with the enemy infantry in the streets of Merefa, main gun rounds were then once again directed at the remaining Russian tanks and supply trucks. The enemy column could come no further without being totally destroyed by the German heavy panzers. Several of the surviving T34/76s tried to turn about and make a run for it, but were forced to turn off the main road and into the nearby snow covered fields. As soon as they slipped off the road, they became stuck fast in the mud and snow as even their broad metal tracks could not support their weight and were picked off one by one by the Tiger Is. As this fierce and harsh battle started to wind down, Wittmann heard some firing that was coming from the right flank of the Russian column.

"There's the company commander!" yelled Woll with great excitement.

Wittmann ordered his Tiger I forward toward the exit of the village and was now directing Woll while he fired at the fleeing enemy after positioning his vehicle into a hasty defensive position with the other vehicles of his company. The Tiger I of the company commander had been firing at the enemy from the right flank, and Kling had now pulled his vehicle up next to Wittmann's.

"Well done, Wittmann!," praised Hauptsturmführer Kling, "That was quick and clean!"

Wittmann nodded without saying a word while standing in his open commander's hatch, and now waited once again for the start of the next engagement. It seemed to Wittmann that the battle was over as soon as it had started, but then looked down as his watch and noticed that seventeen minutes had elapsed since they had assaulted the village.

An hour past by without incident. The men smoked a few cigarettes and tried to eat some of their rations. Wittmann's Tiger I crew were very silent, as the hard fought battle had taken a great amount of their energy, and were all drained. Wittmann made sure that his crew drank enough water to replace the body liquids that has been lost during the battle with the Ivans. Wittmann also thought very deeply about the battle for the village of Merefa, and went over every detail to check if he had covered any and all avenues of approach while engaging the enemy panzers and infantry. While pondering over his actions the radio in his vehicle came to life with his company commander ordering all Panzer commanders to come to his new defensive position for a briefing. Wittmann yelled to Pollmann to accompany him and they both headed in the direction of Kling's Tiger I. As Wittmann and Pollmann were heading towards Kling's location, they ran into an enemy infantry squad trying to infiltrate their lines. Pollmann spotted the Russian infantry and grabbed Wittmann's jacket at the last second and pulled him to the ground. They hid in the snow covered bushes and waited until the danger had past. As soon as it was safe, they both ran back to Wittmann's vehicle and alerted Kling about their dangerous encounter. The warning went out, and every vehicle commander was on the look out for any signs of the enemy infantry trying to pass through their hasty defensive positions.

After about twenty minutes, there was no sign of any Russian infantry or any attacks upon the vehicles. Perhaps the enemy patrol had seen Wittmann and Pollmann, and each other had frighten each other off in the confusion? What ever the case may have been, the panzer commanders posted a guard either on or near each vehicle, just in case the enemy tried to assault the Tiger Is after dark. As the sun soon began to set, the panzer crews heard the sounds of firing in the direction of the returning reconnaissance patrols and were happy to learn that they had not received any casualties. By this time, it was pitch black and biting cold, but Wittmann knew that Obersturmbannfüher Kurt "Panzer" Meyer would have pertinent information on the enemy positions for the Leibstandarte Adolf Hitler's next attack again the Ivans.

The men of the Leibstandarte Adolf Hitler and especially the personnel of Wittmann's platoon had fought extremely hard during the month of February. By midnight, on February 11th, the village of Merefa was now secured by the Waffen-SS but only after bitter panzer assaults and house-to-house fighting. This then was the first panzer battle for Michael Wittmann and his Tiger I crew, and highly illustrated to them of the great potential of their new heavy panzer if used in a daring and lightning manner. The long arm of the 8.8cm main gun, allowed the panzer crews to destroy enemy panzers even before they came within their standard firing ranges. The 110mm armor plate of the vehicle's gun mantelet offered great protection if hit by T34/76 main gun rounds and other types of projectiles fired by Russian armored fighting vehicles of this class. Indeed, the crew members of Michael Wittmann's Tiger I felt that nothing could stop or destroy their armored mount which created a sense of security and the willingness to face the overwhelming numbers of Ivan's panzers even when the German Tiger I crews were out numbered five to one.

On the morning of February 12th, Vodologa Starekovka had been captured and 'Der Führer' Regiment had successfully taken Borki. The Waffen-SS columns thundered forward for more than thirty miles and rolled across the Russian spearhead severing it completely and isolated VII Guard Cavalry Corps;

however, during this period of time, Sepp Dietrich's command was cut off and isolated from the main body of the advancing Waffen-SS units. As the battle roared on both sides fought with great elan, but in a confused state for supremacy of the battlefield both German and Russian forces suffered extremely heavy losses as a direct result.

In order to hold the Donetz, an ad hoc battle group was established as many German front line units were being decimated by the Russian hordes. These units were combined with other SS regiments as desperate measures were introduced to help stem the tide of the Red Army's relentless attacks and advances. Hamlet after hamlet was assaulted and taken under control of Russian forces with the Waffen-SS units now losing control of many of the forward sectors along the front lines. Smiyev was now torn away from Waffen-SS control by heavy and very fierce Russian attacks, whereas Ternovaya was about to fall to Red Army pressure even though every attempt was being made to counter the Russian steamroller tactics. At the village of Rogan, the Waffen-SS were stemming off repeated and heavy assaults, but man power and much needed ammunition were at a premium and many German casualties being the end result. By the 13th and 14th of February the battle suddenly reached its climax, whereas the last Waffen-SS reserves were ordered into the battle. The Russian attacks had been so overwhelming that the Corps front had been greatly expanded that the line became a series of strong points and every able-bodied man was ordered to the front lines, which included cooks, truck drivers, and other non-combat personnel. Even some of the walking wounded were sent back to man their posts in order to help hold off the massive Russian assaults. Valiant efforts were made to consolidate the Russian attacks, but in the end, they were to prove too powerful and too many.

Completely isolated and fighting a typical soldier's battle, Dietrich's battle group was on an assault southward to hopefully link up with Fourth Panzer Army. Savage fighting was the result and all to typically, Dietrich and his men fought many trying battles, where there seemed too little hope for tactical success. Also during this period of isolation, the leading elements of the Reconnaissance Battalion were cut off in and around Bereka and also cut off from their armored support, and were desperately short of ammunition and fuel supplies. SS-Sturmbannführer. Max Wünsche commander of the 1st Detachment of the SS-Panzer Regiment, personally set out with his charge and broke through the Russian encirclement, and for this heroic action as well as for his action in knocking out and destroying fifty-four Russian anti-tank guns, and other enemy pieces of equipment received the coveted Knight's Cross on February 28, 1943.

What was to follow was another series of bitter fighting that lead to counterattack after counter-attack, and severe fighting that was to continue around the villages and small towns for days on end! Many small hamlets and villages were taken, lost and then retaken, and then loss to the Russians once again. The towns of Alexayevka and Bereka changed hands so frequently during this time period that hundreds upon hundreds of burnt out and wrecked vehicles, smashed artillery positions, plus scores of dead German and Russians mixed in together on the fields of battle would never be forgotten by those who had witnessed such mass destruction. The Russian armies had in fact taken a terrible beating but were in no way defeated by the German military forces. They continued to storm forward as nothing had happened to their fellow comrades as the never ending Russian supply system, continued to pump more men, tanks, and artillery pieces into the fray at an alarming rate which had a profound effect upon German morale. The German field commanders could see that these two towns could not be held for much longer, and tried to establish a plan to make their escape in order to avoid being trapped and destroyed. Before this plan could be set into motion, an order came from Hitler's FHQ that dictated that the German forces were to hold these towns at all costs. The situation was now even worst than before and with this order placed upon the already overburden troops, the Waffen-SS commanders were thrown into disarray. Would they dare to disobey their Fuhrer, to whom they had sworn an unconditional obedience to, or were they to save their men and what little fighting equipment that was left to salvage. SS-Oberstgruppenführer und Generaloberst der Waffen-SS Paul Hausser (the overall Waffen-SS Corps commander) totally ignored Hitler's direct orders and decided to evacuate his troops as soon as possible. There was very little time to react, for the only possible escape route to the west was no more than a mile in width and constant Russian patrols had already taken Ossnova, an eastern suburb on the line of escape. SS-Sturmbannführer Joachim Peiper commander of the 3rd Bn, 2nd SS-Panzer Grenadier Regiment of the Leibstandarte Adolf Hitler was ordered to recapture this town and used every trick in the book known to be applied by this very skilled tactician. However, the Russian defiance was too strong and Peiper's armored assault group was pushed back with heavy losses in men and especially in regards to armored fighting vehicles. On the morning of February 15th, the first leading Red Army assault troops captured the south eastern parts of Kharkov and by that evening, they were in the north western sections of the city. The Waffen-SS units were forced by sheer numbers to evacuate the city and withdrew behind the protection of the Uda river.

Vicious fighting continued all along the south sector and on February 16th, a battalion of 'Der Fuhrer' went in to breach the encirclement around the Leibstandarte Adolf Hitler's armored reconnaissance battalion and two days later, 'Der Führer's' 3rd Battalion reinforced an assault spearheaded by Witt's regiment, which by now had been whittled down to no more than battalion strength.

Tanarovka was finally reached, and while the main fighting force of the Leibstandarte Adolf Hitler fought defensive battles north of Krasnograd, 'Das Reich' was to cover sixty miles against totally fanatical Russian resistance from the Sixth Red Army, but was able to make contact with the Fourth Panzer Army now at Novo Moskovsk. As a result of the Russian army's advances, the German front line areas were doomed to destruction. Every attempt was made to ward off the Russian steamroller, but these determined last ditch stands were to no avail.

The Leibstandarte Adolf Hitler reached Bereka and Alexayevka after bitter rear guard fighting. Wittmann and his Tiger I crew were very tired, hungry, and cold, but did not have time to waste as they and the other vehicles of their unit formed up in Alexayevka, and then established a defensive perimeter to protect themselves from any further Russian attacks launched against they forces. During this time frame, SS-Obersturmführer von Ribbentrop (son of the foreign minister) was seriously wounded by a Russian rifle bullet which punctured one of his lungs. He should have been taken out of danger and sent to a rear area field hospital, but refused on the grounds that he did not want to leave his men and his command during the fierce fighting that was constantly raging in his combat unit's area of defense.

Ribbentrop's statement to his men was the following!

"First when the last soldier is flown out, will my turn come!"

The Russian attacks continued with full force and fury, and it seemed that their numbers would never run out. If two or three hundred Russian soldiers were mowed down by sustained automatic machine gun fire, another two or three hundred Ivans would take their place. They fought their way into the area of Kharkov and finally managed to surround the entire city.

During the night of February 16th, a strong Russian force attacked the small village where Wittmann's platoon was positioned. The guard was only able to recognize the enemy panzers in the nick of time, and gave a warning shot via a red flare to alert the Tiger I crews of the impending danger.

Wittmann had been sleeping in his full uniform and sprang to his feet as soon as he had been awakened by this warning signal. He did not even have time to put on his black shoes, as he ran with full force to his Tiger I in his socks! His crew was kicking at his heels as they followed him from a pleasant hut to their fighting vehicle. They all jumped up and onto the superstructure of their machine and threw themselves into their respective positions. Wittmann's driver cranked up the engine and gunned the power-plant in anxious tension to let his commander know that all was ready in regards to movement of the vehicle. As soon as his crew was ready, Wittmann gave the order to roll forward to engage the enemy threat. Wittmann could well remember, the many times that the panzer instructors at Ploermel had drilled into them the proper way of clambering up and into their vehicles. They had practiced this drill over and over again, in order to instill into them that the enemy would not wait for them to ready themselves, and that the first side to fire a main gun round, would usually be the victor.

As all of the Tiger Is were rolling out to meet the challenge, Wittmann and his crew were now leading the way towards the approaching T34/76s and were soon selecting targets of opportunity. The few infantrymen available who had been sent out on patrol to the nearby houses in order to keep them free of Russian infantry waved on the heavy panzers as they roared by. Half an hour later, the danger was over, as the Russian panzers did not venture any further than 2000 meters from the edge of the village. Once they came under fire from Wittmann's Tiger I, they did not dare to move forward and it was quite clear that the Ivans did not want to become involved with an unknown force without proper reconnaissance. Wittmann ordered his crew to stand-down and returned to their prior defensive position. As soon as he secured his vehicle in this defensive mode, he leaped out of his armored cupola, and reported the incident to his company commander, and then returned to his vehicle and was soon fast asleep on a mattress of straw that his crew had laid out for him.

The battle for Kharkov was now entering into its last stages. Poltava, the main supply station for the German Wehrmacht had been taken over by the Red army. On the afternoon of February 14th the Russians entered the northwest section of Kharkov and pressed forward with great speed. The German forces had received on that same day Hitler's new order that they were to hold the city "At any costs!" But General Hausser gave the order on February 15th at 12:50 hours to retreat into the Udy section.

The 13th Heavy Panzer Company was now travelling in a rear guard action while holding off stubborn Russian counter-attacks, in order that the Russians did not overtake the long columns of the Leibstandarte's vehicles. It was up to the Tiger Is to stem the tide of Russian panzers that were trying to catch up with the retreating German forces. Once again, "Bobby" Woll proved his outstanding ability to score direct hits on the advancing Russian panzers, which no doubt saved Wittmann and his crew many a time from being either knocked out or captured by the Ivans. It was not until the following day, February, 16th, that the German forces were able to shake off the enemy panzers and then resumed their daily tasks of establishing strong defensive positions and resupply their ammunition shortages.

On February 17th, General Hausser visited the panzer battle groups and brought with him some very good news, which was highly needed at this time in regards to extremely low morale. A massive German counter-attack was to be launched to drive back the advancing Russian forces. A concentration behind the Mscha river by the Corps was planned and the 'jumping off' positions would be in and around the town of Krasnograd where the Waffen-SS units would be ready to take part in Manstein's counter-offensive with the main objective being the recapturing of Kharkov. During the next few days of bitter fighting the capture of Jerememkevka and Nichni Orel were stated as only local or minor engagements, and conducted during a spell of mild weather which helped to regain the momentum of the determined German advance.

In some areas, small scale encirclement operations to eliminate troublesome sectors were conducted and additional attacks purposely switched from flank to flank to further confuse the Russian commanders were common during this period of time. On February 20th, Pavlograd fell due to highly determined assaults with the conditions for successful counter-attacks being firmly established, which resulted in the Russians taking up once again strong defensive positions in this area.

Manstein's plan to decimate the Russians was plain and quite simple, first he would let the Russians advance and then trap them in a pocket consisting of anti-tank weapons and panzers skillfully concealed which was accomplished on February 21st, with both First and Fourth Panzer Armies positioned in the advent of any further counter-attacks. The SS Panzer Corps, was allocated to the Fourth Panzer Army's left flank, which began its assaults on the 22nd and within three days of harsh and bitter fighting, was to be found fighting in a north easterly direction, and had managed to capture Losowaya where it linked up with Wehrmacht panzer units battling Russian resistance from a westerly direction. Due to these German counter maneuvers, the majority of Popov's Armored Corps was thereby encircled and subsequently destroyed as a fighting unit. The Russian armored units in this area were brought under Corps artillery fire at ranges of 15,000 yards and were utterly destroyed. A small number of Red Army units succeeded in breaking out of the German encirclement by illustrating a complete disregard for losses, but the vast majority of the First Guards Army and Popov's armored units were smashed with little or no chance for recovery at that time.

It did not take long before the Russians reacted to this costly rebuff and a counter-offensive by the Third Guards Tank Army was anticipated at any time. A constant alert for enemy activity was the number one priority for all front line German troopers, with many men having little or no sleep for days on end. On February 28th, the Leibstandarte Adolf Hitler launched a new spoiling attack to keep the Russians off their guard and sent out assault units to capture a set of commanding heights east of the Bereka-Yefomevka road. As the attack opened up, the direction of the assault was suddenly altered to suit the fluid situation, with the spearheading panzers ordered to head for Valki, nearly one hundred miles to the north! During this assault, the Totenkopf Division was brought into the fighting to help close the flanks. At the end of this three day battle, the XV Guards Armored Crops had been encircled and with this, the preliminary stage of the German plan was over and the counter-offensive could commence as planned. The counter-offensive opened well and ran its course, with front line German losses being light. The Russian losses were staggering, with over 600 panzers and over 1,000 guns and artillery pieces of all calibers lost or damaged.

An armored assault spearheaded by the Leibstandarte Adolf Hitler smashed its way forward from Staroverovka on March 4th, which included Panzer IV Ausf. H point panzers, with Tiger Is giving supportive heavy fire power. Following these vehicles, the Sd.Kfz.251 personnel carriers with their cargos of experienced infantry, and then the Sd.Kfz.222s, 223s, and 232 armored cars as follow ups. With lighting speed, the Russian forces were firstly isolated by the panzer attacks, then surrounded, and then thoroughly wiped out by the German forces.

A considerable number of Russian units had been cut off and were forced to surrender to the German forces on March 6th. The German advance upon Valki had ripped open a giant salient in the Russian defensive lines with the leading German assault units making the best out of this tactical situation. Into these gaps poured men and equipment of the Leibstandarte, with the first ordered objective to firmly establish a bridgehead across the Mscha river and then to expand it in and around Brdok. The ever knee deep and clinging mud produced over night by a sudden thaw threatened to slow down the assault, but through determined efforts by the No. 2 Motorcycle Company of the SS Reconnaissance Battalion, managed to push forward and Valki finally fell to the German forces. Kharkov was the next major objective and careful and skillful planning was employed for this attack. The advance guard of the Leibstandarte Adolf Hitler had rolled up to Peretdinaga and Polevaya pushing the Red Army forces back across the Donetz on March 9th. Once this had been accomplished, the German fighting forces could now plan an all out attack upon the city of Kharkov.

General Hausser was very anxious to reconquer this city that had been evacuated by his command and launched two surprise assaults, one from the north and the second one from the west. Supported by Ju 87 Stuka dive-bomber attacks and Nebelwerfer batteries, the SS Grenadiers went into the attack on March 10th, with the Leibstandarte Adolf Hitler driving down from the north and northwest. A double-pronged assault by Witt's regiment was also involved with this maneuver and Hansen's 3rd SS Battalion along for good measure was to severe the Kharkov-Byelgorod road with Sandig's 2nd Battalion probing forward until it was able to locate weak spots in the Russian defenses. The Leibstandarte Adolf Hitler was ordered to capture the Red Square and raced forward to eradicate any and all Russian forces in the immediate area as soon as possible. On the eastern edge of the city, Kurt Meyer's battalion cut the Staryi road, but the Russian counter-attacks aimed at Witt's regiment on the Red Square sector forced the tired SS Grenadiers into house-to-house, and not to often room-to-room battles which continued for the next three days. The last resistance was finally dealt with at the famous tractor factory in Kharkov on March 15th with the German forces illustrating to the Red Army that they too had over come the horrible Russian winter and was beating them at their own game!

Now that Kharkov was firmly in German hands once again, Joachim Peiper was ordered northwards to battle through and reach the Donetz, at Byelgorod, by March 18th. This very efficient combat leader forced his way through various Red Army assaults and used every available vehicle and means of transport that could operate and finally linked up with the "Grossdeutschland" Division, and with this operation successfully accomplished, so ended the four week counter-offensive; as all of the major objectives to consolidate the front lines had been achieved and the German military forces, once again, regained the same terrain areas which they had captured during 1942.

It was only too clear, as the hand writing on the wall analyzing the Russian winter offensive illustrated that despite the numerical superiority of 8:1 in infantry, 5:1 in panzers, as well as the Russians being more adapt in winter conditions, had been halted, encircled, and either destroyed or thrown back to their initial jumping off positions by the German combat forces. It was also pointed out that the severity of the Russian defeat was due directly in part by its inflexibility and total inability at all levels of command to alter from a victorious advance to the hardships of a total retreat. This indecisiveness was very apparent in every battle fought on the Eastern front and the German forces made use of it in every situation in order to make advances where only psychological means were warranted.

After the battle for retaking Kharkov the front lines then went into a period of relative calm and the men of the Leibstandarte resorted to the mundane duties of security patrols in and around the area of Kharkov proper. From the period of January 1st to March 18th, the Waffen-SS units on the Russian front had lost a total of 365 officers and 11,154 other ranks either dead, wounded, or missing. It was time for rest and re-equipping with much time spent on training new replacements who would otherwise not last a week on the brutal and hostile Russian steppes fighting the enemy. The battle for the Russian front was far from over and both sides took the opportunity during this period of non-action to replan, rethink, and study any and all after action reports, so as to make certain that the same tactical mistakes were not repeated in any forth-coming battles with the enemy.

During the winter offensive of 1942-43 the German Wehrmacht as a whole had been stopped and pushed back which resulted in a huge and serious shortages of manpower for which Germany would have extreme difficulties in providing. By the end of 1942 German losses had amounted to 922,000 casualties (a proportion of 14.2 percent) and by the end of 1943 to 2,033.000 (a proportion of 30.6 percent). The German Wehrmacht had declined to some three million men, which resulted in the German High Command to demand an additional three-quarters of a million men, which only a quarter of that number available to help flesh out the ranks. This situation clearly illustrated that any losses incurred on the field of battle would never be replaced with the German Wehrmacht steadily being bled white!

In regards to fully tracked armored fighting vehicles, it was shown that the German panzer manufacturing capabilities could not keep pace with the large number of panzer losses occurring during this period of time on the Russian front, where as Russian tank production had risen to 1,000 machines per month. With this vast number of armored fighting vehicles available to the ever expanding tank armies it was very obvious that the Red army would be able to throw large numbers of tanks into difficult areas where German resistance was trying to press home determined armored assaults. The Wehrmacht at this time was in dire straights but a number of heavier panzers were now being rushed through the design stages and quickly put into full production, which resorted back to the German way of thinking that quality was better than quantity, in order to rectify the tactical situation on the Eastern front.

During the middle of 1943, the question was put forward to the German High Command whether or not to further military operations in Russian or to totally turn to a defensive mode, or to maintain the military initiative by launching local assaults to try and drain the resources of the Red Army until Germany could produce enough quality weapons to replace the previous losses. At the same time, as this decision making was taking place, a more immediate and dangerous problem arose in regards to the Russian front. A massive and powerful Russian salient, over 400 miles long and 150 miles in depth was now threatening the right flank of Army Group Center and Army Group South's left wing tactical positions. A German offensive assault was now being planned to cut into this salient which would in turn be the battle of Kursk and had to be launched as soon as possible in order to help stem the tide of the Russian war machine.

The troop and vehicle build-ups were soon started for operation "Citadel", as it was to be entitled, as the overall plan was to amass and then springboard two armored forces; Army Group Center, which would be utilized for the northern arm, would then consolidate and meet the southern arm of Army Group South and within their probing pincer movements, thus trap the Red Army units and destroy them outright! Fourth Panzer Army was given the main burden of the attacks as they were massed west of Byelgorod and were given the task of assaulting at and through the Russian positions on both sides of Konarovka. They would then drive onwards via Oboyan, to try and obtain the major objective as laid down by Higher Command: The Kursk Salient.

The major plans and undertakings for the battle of Kursk, were not taken lightly by the entire German war planning staff! Officers within the Supreme Command voiced strong opposition at the extremely high stakes involved and boldly pointed out that it was sheer madness to place the military future of the German Wehrmacht as a whole on one strategically unimportant operation, which could spell the death toll for the entire German army. Hitler confessed that the thought of this operation turned his stomach and by his own decision, postponed D-Day (O-Tag) from May 1st to a succession of other dates as proposed by High Command before it was finally agreed upon to be July 5, 1943.

However, during this time of overwhelming indecision, the Russian army was given a break in the bitter fighting on the Eastern front, and was able to replenish its forces with huge numbers of men, tanks, and ammunition; plus had ample time to construct a deep, well armed system of dense fortifications which were protected by an elaborate series of minefields, and anti-tank guns. By the end of June, 6,000 armored fighting vehicles had been delivered which left the Russians very confidant of total victory over their German counterparts. The Russian High Command made it very clear that the German Wehrmacht was to be destroyed at any and all costs, and had selected the Kursk salient to be the decisive battle field upon which it would obtain military dominance once and for all. The battle of Kursk would be the new Verdun of the Second World War for the German Wehrmacht.

Chapter X

KURSK

July 5, 1943 – August 3, 1943

All through the early months of the hot summer of 1943, the German Wehrmacht and Waffen-SS assault divisions practiced and then repracticed their combat battle drill and tactics. The two most favored armored assault techniques were now the Panzer wedge (Panzerkeil) and the Panzer bell (Panzerglocke) that had been utilized over and over again against the Red Army. The Panzer wedge penetrated the enemy held line and then smashed open the breach using the new heavy Tiger I panzers with its frontal and side armor plate being proofed against medium sized Russian anti-tank guns, whereas their powerful 8.8cm main gun firepower was used as the apex of the wedge. The Panzer bell tactic was that of a massive armored penetration which consisted of two major points on the map with the destruction of the enemy within these two points. The ever present clapper of the bell was the Division Command Group, which could easily monitor both flanks across the bell and maintain proper command and guidance as needed during the planned attack. During the previous battles concerning the German military forces as a whole, it was found that the swiftly changing patterns of armored battles dictated that senior commanders be well forward with their troops for constant over-watch and control. Operation "Citadel" was to be the deciding battle for the future of the German Army, so it was quite obvious that tight, cohesive and immediate control was highly desired in order for this vital operation to be a tactical success.

The Red Army had learned a great deal since the early opening battles in June of 1941, and were not to be underestimated. Their defensive tactics against the German panzers was a direct adaptation of the German Pak fronts, with continuous rows of anti-tank guns whose awesome destructive knockout capabilities could be concentrated upon individual panzers or groups of vehicles with utterly devastating results. Minefields were cleverly situated in order to channel formations of panzers into anti-tank gun teams, who would then destroy any enemy machines that came into their over-lapping fields of fire. The Russian plan of a defensive battlefield was not entirely of non-movement.

Russian tank patrols ventured out into selected areas of the battle sectors and would on occasion, locate and encircle German panzer units and destroy them piecemeal. At the time of the Kursk battle front, there were 115 divisions of the Red army massed in the salient and was posed very confidently and secured behind the extensive belts of concrete and wooden fortifications which totaled eight miles in depth. The German army was fully aware of these fortified strongholds and made every attempt to locate them prior to their planned assaults. Aerial photographs were being taken almost daily in order to produce comprehensive maps and routes of advance which seemed to offer the least resistance.

The area of the forth-coming battlefield was a vast plain, a totally agricultural region covered either with rows upon rows of standing corn, or belts of tall steppe grass, which were cut by valleys, small hills, and many waterways of which the Donetz, Pena, Psel, and Seyn were the most tactically important to both sides. Sand roads would turn into tracks of clinging mud during heavy rains and would prove to be more of a hinderance than an aid. The terrain generally favored the Russian defensive plan as the surrounding plain rose gently towards Kursk giving the Red army defenders complete and unobstructed observation to the west.

The stronger of the two German panzer armies, the Fourth Panzer Army, with ten divisions under its overall command was allocated for Operation "Citadel." Its total strength just prior to being deployed for this battle was 1,137 fully tracked armored fighting vehicles and self-propelled guns, of which 200 panzers being the new Panther (Sd.Kfz.171) and 81 Tiger Is (Sd.Kfz.181), with the remainder being the older Panzer IIIs (Sd.Kfz.141) and Panzer IVs (Sd.Kfz.161).

The first task of the SS Panzer Corps, part of the Fourth Panzer Army, was to attack via Beresov and Sadeynoye, thus penetrating the first defensive belts of the Russian defenders. The second line of fortifications were between Lutchki and Jakovlevo and when these were broken through, the advance would follow in a generally northeastern direction. As added insurance to this operation, the 167th Infantry Division would form part of the SS Corps and would be given the task of guarding and maintaining the left flank. As the time for O-Tag grew nearer, the SS Panzer Crops, now having the combined strength of 343 panzers and 195 self-propelled guns, would roll forward into its pre-battle observation and jump-off positions. All along the front line positions, Panzer crews, Panzer Grenadiers, and infantry units were all very confidant; everything had been prepared, vehicles and weapons doubled checked, maps and all avenues of approach had been tripled checked! For reasons of strict security, all movement during the day was highly forbidden. Everyone now waited for the order to advance!

Dawn broke on the morning of July 5, 1943, which marked the first day of "Operation Citadel." To follow was a six hour long battle that would involve every known type of weapon and fighting vehicle which in turn would smash open the Russian army's first bunker lines with demoralizing effect. 03:45 hours had marked the arrival of German Ju 87 dive-bombers which supplemented the massive artillery barrage which was bombarding Byelgorod, with Tiger Is of the assaulting armored wedge rolling forward to obliterate the Red army defenses fifteen minutes later. The famous battle of Kursk had commenced, the so-called `Death Ride of the Fourth Panzer Army', was finally underway. Great hopes were riding with the 56 ton Tiger Is with their massive armor plate protection and highly accurate and powerful 8.8cm main guns. Tiger I commanders had been instructed to be very careful in regards to maneuvering their precious machines into the Russian minefields, as mine-lifting teams would mark the positions of these deadly devices by laying down alongside them; whereas they would use their own bodies to mark the gaps to allow the heavy panzers to venture forward.

The Leibstandarte Adolf Hitler battle tactics were performed with great determination as the advance continued against the Russian defenses. When a group of Russians were located, the Leibstandarte's panzers would provide supportive fire and the following Grenadiers would wipe out the remaining resistance. The rhythm of the first assaults were extremely exhilarating to the German assault troops as the first defensive positions were easily overrun with many enemy soldiers either killed or captured in the process. When the advance assault units were faced with massed heavy Russian artillery and extensive minefields, the momentum of the attack slowed down and then halted between the first and second defensive lines. The German forces did not want to lose any of its heavy panzers and again, every precaution was taken to clear away any types of mines or other explosive charges that had been planted by Ivan in the surrounding countryside.

It was now time for the technical quality of the Waffen-SS to be shown on the battlefield. Many brave soldiers and vehicle commanders were to prove themselves on the field of battle time and time again. Many were to die trying and a few would live to tell their grandchildren of their noble deeds. As the battle of Kursk intensified, there were to be many feats of heroism by the Panzer crews, Panzer Grenadiers, and Infantrymen whose survival on this savage and brutal battlefield depended on their combat skills and efficiency in which they operated and conducted their tools of their trade against the strongly entrenched Russian army. The total determination for victory in the face of the enemy against overwhelming odds, forced many front line commanders to push their men to the brink of physical and mental breakdowns!

Michael Wittmann and his Tiger I crew had waited until 02:30 hours on the morning of July 5th.

"How much longer, Untersturmführer?", asked the anxious Bobby Woll.

Wittmann looked down as his watch and saw that the fluorescent hands read 03:00!

"Still another forty-five minutes!", was his response.

Wittmann was mentally reviewing the plan of attack as laid out by his company commander. Had he considered everything, or would the Russians surprise them with an even more powerful defense in depth? Would they come through the forth-coming battle without any injury to themselves? Wittmann thought not, as the battle for the Kursk salient would be an extremely bloody battle and many of his comrades would die this day. It would take strict command over his crew to bring them out of this onslaught without loss of life or damage to their Tiger I. Wittmann continued to study his maps laid out in front of him in the early morning darkness and cast his flashlight onto them while sitting in his armored cupola. All vehicle commanders were instructed not to use their interior festoon lamps as light could be reflected up and out vision devices in their cupolas. The resourceful panzer commander was trying to determine where likely Russian anti-tank guns positions would be situated in the areas he and his comrades would be attacking within the next few hours. Anti-tank guns (Paks) were the main concern in any major assault as they would be expertly camouflaged and it took an experienced panzer commander to locate them and guide his gunner onto target. Anti-tank guns was the code-word for danger! The fangs of his Tiger I (main gun rounds) and especially H.E. rounds would spell sudden destruction to any Pak weapons that they encountered.

Finally, at 03:45, the order was given to advance! Wittmann and his panzer crew along with the rest of the heavy panzer element, were under constant and extreme pressure to storm forward and destroy the Russian defenders as soon as possible and create a breakthrough for the follow up infantry assaults. The 343 German panzers and 195 self-propelled guns rolled in broad formation through the open fields under tight control from their respective commanders. Suddenly, without warning, a large number of Russian anti-tank guns let out their sharp barks and started to pepper the area in and around Wittmann's platoon of Tiger Is.

"Attack! Attack!" yelled Wittmann through his vehicle intercommunication set. Wittmann's driver drove their massive machine forward with all speed and passed another Tiger I that had had its right track blown completely off! The crew of this vehicle did not bale out as the panzer commanders were under orders to continue fighting from their mounts even if they were immobilized for one reason or the other. As long as their vehicles could fight, they would provide support and covering fire as long as they could in regards to advancing vehicles and as long as levels of 8.8cm ammunition on board their vehicles lasted. This type of heroic fighting spurred on the advancing infantry, as it seemed that nothing or no one could prevent the German advance from failing.

Suddenly, not more than 100 meters in front of Wittmann's Tiger I, there was a gigantic flash of a large explosion, and then the deafening shock wave hit Wittmann square in his face. It was so over-powering, that he at first thought that his person had been blown completely out of his armored mount. He then found himself hanging over the edge of his cupola and struggling desperately to right himself. The Russian artillery shell had been a large caliber type and had thrown

Michael Wittmann and Hildegard Burmester were married on March 1, 1944 in Vogetal.

Michael and Hildegard relax in the German countryside after their wedding.

Wittmann (right) relaxes with friends outside a party, circa March 1944.

Wittmann is reunited with friends on a Sunday afternoon in March 1944

Wittmann used his time in March and April 1944 to visit many old friends.

Wittmann stands beside his "official" SS vehicle. His status as a Tiger I commander allowed him to use the vehicle, a rarity at that time.

Wittmann is shown here with executives of the Henschel Tiger Factory in Kassel. He is about to address the factory workers.

A Tiger I forms an appropriate podium for Wittmann to stand on at the Henschel Tiger factory. This photo was taken just before he climbed the wooden stairs to give his speech.

A large crowd of workers from the Henschel Tiger I factory look on as Wittmann speaks to them.

Atop a new Tiger I, Wittmann gives his speech to factory workers at the Henschel Tiger I factory in April 1944.

Wittmann takes a smoke break with Oscar and Robert Henschel on the floor of the Tiger I factory in Kassel, just before starting his tour of the factory.

Wittmann was presented with this 1.20th scale wooden model of a Tiger I tank by executives of the Henschel Tiger I Factory in Kassel, April 1944.

Wittmann's second company enroute to the Normandy front, June 12, 1944.

This Tiger I is being used as a tow vehicle. Notice that Wittmann's 2nd company placed the crossed keys insignia on the right side of the vehicle front. Other companies used the left side.

Hauptsturmführer Mobiüs stands in the new Panther type armored cupola of his Tiger I Ausf.E (mid-late production model) on their way to Normandy. The crew (except driver) rode on the outside of the vehicle on "Jabo" watch.

On the way to the Normandy front along the "Carpet Bombers Alleyway." Disbaled Tigers were too valuable to leave along the roadside, so they were towed behind sister vehicles.

Another of Mobiüs' 1st Company Tiger I's on the way to the Normandy front, June 12, 1944.

When stopping for vehicle maintenance, tactical measures dictated heavy camouflage be used to hide the Tiger Is from Allied eyes.

Obergruppenführer "Sepp" Dietrich (second from left) with Wittmann and other officers. Wittmann proposed taking his lone Tiger I into Villers-Bocage on reconnaissance of suspected British positions that threatened PanzerLehr.

Looking east along highway D71 from Caumont at the edge of Villers-Bocage. Notice the shell marks on the sign.

Looking north at the Villers-Bocage town square. Highway D71 enters from the left of photo. The house behind the truck is where Sergeant Lockwood's M4A4 Sherman 17-pounder "Firefly" was located during the battle.

One of the four RHQ vehicles Wittmann knocked out during the battle of Villers-Bocage.

Another RHQ casualty at the hands of Michael Wittmann in Villers-Bocage.

"A" Squadron casualties. M3 half-tracks line the road after Wittmann's second trip through Villers-Bocage.

More M3 half-tracks line the road northeast of Villers-Bocage.

This is all that remains of "A" Squadron's Lloyd carriers that were towing six-pounder antitank guns, after Wittmann decimated their ranks.

A German soldier walks by a knocked out British 75 mm Cromwell outside Villers-Bocage. The name "Shufti Cush" painted on the side of the turret, translated from the Arabic, means "let me see your p###y."

up huge amounts of dirt, rocks, and other materials and had showered down on his moving vehicle. He was now covered in dust, dirt, and had a number of small cuts and bruises. Nevertheless, he quickly regained his composure, and continued the attack. As soon as he had informed his crew that he was alright a number of enemy anti-tank guns opened fired upon his vehicle. Two rounds went flying past his Tiger I with such force that he felt the shock waves as they crashed into the ground behind his machine. As soon as Wittmann located their positions, he yelled his fire command to his gunner. Woll was extremely busy at his post trying to detect the exact positions while his commander guided him onto target the best he could as the whole area was now in a blaze of flames and exploding vehicles. Many comrades were dying on his left and right, but he could not stop his Tiger I in order to give them any aid as the advance was continuing on with no let up in sight.

Finally, Bobby Woll located the Russian anti-tank guns hidden in a bunker line and quickly traversed the turret of their machine towards these deadly weapons. Wittmann kept yelling at Woll to hurry as at any second the Russian Paks would certainly bark out at them and that would be the end of them all! Woll then fired off a 8.8cm H.E. main gun round at his first target with the high velocity round careening towards its mark. The main gun round crashed into the position at a low angle, bounced off the ground and hit the metal gun shield of the anti-tank gun. The force of the impact spun the weapon around and then flipped it over onto its ammunition boxes. There was a large explosion which was witnessed by Wittmann from the corner of his eye, but at last, he and his gunner were seeking out their next target. Another anti-tank gun was spotted firing at the Tiger I to the right side of their vehicle, so Wittmann then directed Woll onto this target. The moment that Woll fired the same type of main gun round, the anti-tank gun fired as well, and again, a large amount of dirt and rocks were thrown up at Wittmann as the enemy round hit the ground just in front of his stationary vehicle. Woll had been right on his mark, as the anti-tank gun was now just a pile of burning and twisted metal. Wittmann then ordered Kirschmer to move the Tiger I forward as the momentum of this battle run was continually moving ever forward. The German panzers were only halting in order to fire at the enemy positions and then resumed their movement onwards.

Wittmann and the other Tiger Is of his platoon then reached the first and highly shattered bunker line where the two anti-tank guns had been destroyed only a few minutes beforehand. The destruction was overwhelming as Wittmann looked down on the smashed enemy guns, the dead gun crews, and all other sorts of military paraphernalia of war blown to bits into the ground in very direction. All of the supporting Russian infantry were dead and their bodies were either flattened by the blast of the powerful German artillery or Stuka munitions as delivered earlier in the battle. There was no sign of life in and around this bunker line, but Wittmann could see many enemy panzers milling around in the distance forming up to attack the on-coming German armored armada. Obersturmführer Kling's voice came rushing over the radio network and ordered the attack to continue. As prearranged, Wendorff turned to the northeast and rolled very quickly in that direction. Wittmann and his Tiger I roared forward under heavy enemy gun fire and ordered Woll to fire a number of H.E. rounds in the directions of the enemy to keep their heads down. All of a sudden, one of the advancing Tiger Is to Wittmann's rear stopped dead in its tracks and started to burn without cause. It was soon realized that an enemy anti-tank gun had been missed and then by passed and was now trying to disable as many German panzers as possible from the rear. The anti-tank gun round had penetrated the thinner rear armor plate of the Tiger I in question and continued to burn with bright orange flames shooting high into the sky. The crew was forced to bale out and crawled back on hands and knees to the advancing infantry for safety and protection. There was not enough time for Wittmann to traverse his heavy turret to the seven o'clock position in order to take out this unexpected menace. The approaching Russian T34/76s would soon be in firing range and Wittmann could not allow himself to have his main armament aimed away from this danger. His only hope was that follow up infantry would deal with this overlooked P ak gun, as it was impossible for the spearheading panzers to locate and destroy every single anti-tank gun in the wake of their advance. There were a number of other high velocity rounds being fired by this anti-tank gun, but Wittmann's platoon of Tiger Is were now out of range and had rolled into a slight depression in the terrain which saved them from being fire upon from the rear.

As soon as Wittmann's Tiger Is came to the crest of this wide depression, they all slowed down and finally halted in order to view the terrain ahead. There was a lot of smoke and dust still hanging in the hot air and it was very difficult observing through this brown and black curtain of haze. All of the panzer commanders were not too certain about the area ahead of them, so it was decided to fire a volley into the forward ground to try to raise a response from the Ivans. The panzer commanders then ordered gunners to fire their MG-34s in order to observe metal strikes in regards to camouflaged enemy panzers and anti-tank guns that might be hiding until the German panzers could be fired once again from the rear. At this point in time, there was no signs of any enemy anti-tank guns or panzers, but the German panzer commanders knew that the enemy would not be far away. The forward lay of the land did not resemble the plotted areas on the German maps that all had studied with careful attention to detail. The Stuka dive-bombers and massive artillery barrages had turned the terrain into a desolate lunar landscape which was very difficult to maneuver in let alone locate terrain features which no longer existed!

The radio set crackled in Wittmann's ears.

"Do not stop, keep going, keep going!", was the constant order from Kling.

There was no need to repeat the order to the vehicle drivers, as all of the Tiger Is once again lurched forward to meet the ensuing enemy panzers. Setting a quicken pace, all of the German machines headed for the second bunker line but saw to their horror even more enemy armored fighting vehicles lining up for the advance against their numbers. One of the T34/76s in the first wave of vehicles fired a main gun round at Wittmann's vehicle and struck with such force into the frontal mantelet that resulted in an ear splitting crack that temporarily deafened Wittmann. His crew who were protected by the massive framework of their vehicle were not affected. The 7.6cm main gun round, however, did not penetrate the Tiger I's frontal armor plate and deflected off and shot up into the air.

Woll immediately locked onto his target and fired an 8.8cm AP main gun round at the Russian machine and scored a direct hit, which blew the turret completely off of the hull and crashed into the ground with a tremendous thud! The remainder of the vehicle was engulfed in flames with diesel fuel spurting all over the doomed tank. None of the crew were seen escaping from this fiery hell on tracks. After this encounter, Wittmann ordered his driver to advance and then suddenly witnessed two T34/76s rolling up a small depression directly in front of his vehicle. He then ordered his driver to halt their machine and to make ready for the next firing engagement. Bobby Woll was already one step ahead of his commander and was making a final lay of his main gun to take on the Ivans. As soon as he heard the main gun breech slam shut, he carefully aimed the 8.8cm weapon at the first T34/76 as it poked its way over the crest of the small depression. As soon as the under belly of the enemy panzer was in his sight picture, Woll activated the firing handle and rammed home a direct hit into the approaching enemy vehicle. The AP main gun round penetrated the thinner belly armor with great ease and then must have ignited the on-board ammunition, as the enemy machine disintegrated in Wittmann's forward vision block. The second T34/76 made no notice to this awesome destruction and continued to roll forward in the same manner. After a quick fire command from Wittmann, Woll again placed another AP round into this machine and destroyed it within a few short seconds.

The heat inside Wittmann's Tiger I was becoming quite unbearable and he knew that his crew would soon be very fatigued at their respective positions. There was however, no time for any of them to take a drink of water or to relieve themselves. This was an all out panzer assault, and no time but to concentrate on the battle itself. Wittmann could now see that the enemy panzers were even larger in numbers and would take sheer courage and total and stubborn determination to stop them before they could over run their tentative battlefield locations. He knew that it was up to him to bring his crew and machine out of the thick of battle, and for him to keep a clear head about his tactical movements in the face of the overwhelming numbers of Russian panzers bent on eradicating him and his crew from the battlefield. Another T34/76 came out of the gloom and managed to fire a 7.6cm main gun round at Wittmann's Tiger I which slammed into the left side of his turret from extreme range, but once again it deflected off at an acute angle. The shock wave of this projectile caused only minor damage but sent a few nuts and bolts flying around inside the turret. Nobody was seriously harmed, but this incident could have been quite deadly if anyone of the crew-members had been hit in the face or upper body areas. Bobby Woll wasted no time in seeking out this target as Wittmann was constantly providing him with accurate and concise fire commands. Wittmann's loader was now a mass of nerves and sweating from head to toe, as he was being overworked trying to keep up with his commander's fire commands, plus the rocking movement of the vehicle between firings. Round after round was thrown into the smoking and oily breech as Wittmann's turret crew continued to pump 8.8cm rounds into the mists of the charging enemy panzers. Woll was traversing the turret with great agility from left to right, but caused the loader to be constantly thrown off balance while trying to load the main gun and replenish the co-axial MG-34 machine gun. It was a daring feat of fast foot work and arm and hand coordination on the part of Berges that allowed such a fast and constant rate of fire in the face of the enemy.

The same T34/76 that had just managed to hit Wittmann's vehicle was now coming straight towards his machine with great speed. It was also firing on the move as fast as its loader could ram main gun rounds into the breech. The vast majority of the main gun rounds fired went astray as the undulating terrain caused the gun barrel of this vehicle to bob up and down and out of any control. As soon as Wittmann saw that this vehicle was on a wild rampage, he ordered his driver to slow down their vehicle to almost a crawl and then commanded Woll to take careful aim at this on-coming machine. Woll was quite aware of his commander's intentions and carefully swung the huge turret to the 12 o'clock position and locked onto this dangerous target. Wittmann announced his frantic fire command and Woll pressed the firing handle. The 8.8cm main gun round let out a great crack with the projectile rocketing towards its target. Even before the dust had time to obscure Woll's sight picture, he paid witness to a tremendous flash in front of him which was the end of the Russian machine. After Woll cried "Hit", Wittmann was horrified to see that the burning machine was still moving forward even though the panzer commander, and loader had baled out of their doomed vehicle. The driver and bow machine gunner were still inside the vehicle and no doubt were dead. Why the damaged and smoking machine kept coming towards them was only a guess. It was assumed that the driver of this panzer was dead or dying at his controls with his foot still on the accelerator pedal. Wittmann could see that as the vehicle moved forward it veered to the left and then to the right, which indicated that the suspension of the vehicle was being directed by the contours of the terrain and not by the steering action of the driver. Woll yelled out that he was going to fire another AP main gun round into this machine, but Wittmann ordered him not to do so, as it was a waste of precious ammunition. Wittmann could only watch this vehicle as it bounced around on the battlefield and finally saw the burning and smoking machine crash into the bunker line behind them and embedding its gun barrel into a mound of dirt. The engine stalled, and the T34/76 continued to billow out flames and oily smoke.

The Tiger Is of Wittmann's platoon were now heading towards a small village which was in total ruin and with little sign of any life. The radio transmission that was received by all panzer commanders from Kling was one of utmost caution as the Ivans were known to conceal anti-tank guns in bombed-out buildings, so as a result, the shattered village was suspect in regards to harboring the enemy. Wittmann scanned the area with his binoculars for any indication of enemy Paks or panzers, but could not observe any tell tail signs. However, while he was still searching the area ahead of his vehicle, anti-tank gun fire started to fall in and around his machine.

"Attention!" commander to everyone, Pak fire ahead!"

The Ivans had concentrated their defense very heavily in this area, which forced the Tiger I commanders to impose a frontal attack post haste. Before ordering the vehicles forward, Kling radioed to his vehicles to try and locate the positions of the enemy anti-tank guns from the flashes of their gun barrels. This was very hard to accomplish with the fog of battle still dangling in the air, so it was decided that the panzer commanders would once again order their gunners to fire a volley into the direction of the suspected enemy positions and thus draw return fire. As soon as the Ivans opened fired at the German vehicles, their locations were quickly pin pointed by Tiger I panzer commanders and locked their gunners onto target. A large number of anti-tank guns were destroyed in this manner which helped to speed up the advance. Some of the anti-tank guns were hit twice as a number of Tiger Is fired at the same time as the same enemy weapons. In the mad seconds that followed, there was little time to select targets and then report back to the other vehicles of the platoon; rather it was a time for quick and deadly action.

The order was given to advance once again! The Tiger Is all moved out under the control of Kling who was now in a state of great excitement which could be only appreciated by the fact that his unit was highly out numbered five to one by the enemy. He had to keep his area of responsibility in a fluid state of movement and could ill afford any delays that would surely endanger the time-tables established by his superiors. As the Tiger Is advanced forward towards the next line of bunkers, additional anti-tank guns opened fired on the German machines. These weapons had also been expertly camouflaged in the surrounding country-side, but had limited arcs of fire which enabled the German panzers to out flank them as had been done in the past in certain battles.

Before turning into a flanking posture, Wittmann's Tiger I was hit several times by these anti-tank weapons. The impacts on his vehicle were on the gun mantelet which presented the heaviest armor plate of his vehicle, and fortunately for Wittmann and his crew, deflected up and into the air causing little damage or harm to his men. His crew could hear the large thud that the enemy Pak rounds made upon striking their machine, and was very unnerving to say the very least. It was a very terrifying noise, as at any moment one of these projectiles might penetrate their armor envelope, and that would be the end of them all. Wittmann knew quite clearly that he must continue to lay down a shower of fast and accurate main gun fire in order to survive the maelstrom raging all around him and his vehicle.

As the advance continued forward Wittmann and Wendorff's Tiger Is were now operating quite close to each other and were giving supportive fire to one another. Suddenly, Wendorff's vehicle was hit and had its left track blown completely off of its suspension with a loud bang! He quickly radioed to Wittmann that they would not abandon their machine and would of course continue to provide him suppressive fire from his stationary position. This would help to keep Ivans' head down as Wittmann and the other vehicles rolled forward in the assault. It was always very difficult to spot the enemy while moving over rough terrain in their vehicles, so in the end, Wendorff's predicament actually helped to locate and then knockout the enemy anti-tank guns even though his stationary vehicle would draw fire upon to itself. It was hoped that the next bunker line could be captured and neutralized before Wendorff and his crew were again located and fired upon.

The Tiger Is clanked forward as the attack seemed to be in favor of the German forces as there was still wild excitement in the air. All of a sudden, Wittmann's driver hit a large rock with their machine bouncing off to the right side and threw everyone out of their seats. There was a loud cry from inside the turret, but Wittmann was not sure what had happened. Woll spoke via his throat microphone and informed his commander that his loader had smashed his hand as an 8.8cm main gun round had slipped out of his hands. His hand was injured as the result of the heavy projectile landing on top of his hand on the turret basket floor. Wittmann immediately bent down in his cupola and looked over at his loader as he was wrapping a dirty rag around his swollen and bleeding left hand. He yelled to his loader to keep feeding main gun rounds into the hungry main gun breech, no matter how much pain he was enduring at the time. Blood oozed out of the unclean and oily rag and over his fingers as sweat continued to run down his face and neck. Wittmann's panzer crew were in a very desperate situation and a minor injury such as an injured hand could be attended to after the battle was over, or during a short break in the action. It was not possible to stop his vehicle and render first aid, as this action would surely bring enemy fire down upon themselves.

Wittmann and Woll kept searching for any enemy anti-tank gun positions and were very keyed up as if they were not careful, they could make a mistake in judgement and feel the full wrath of the enemy. Wittmann decided to change his tactics somewhat and ordered Woll to fire off a main gun round as soon as he ordered his driver to stop their vehicle. The idea behind this tactic was to try and flush out the hidden enemy as the Ivans would no doubt fire back once they thought that they had been detected. Usually, they would be startled and would fire wildly which was put to good use by the German panzer crews. The enemy's fire discipline was nonexistent as their ample supplies of ammunition gave them a false sense of security as a direct result. As soon as Wittmann's driver halted their vehicle, Woll fired off an 8.8cm H.E. main gun round. Even though a great deal of dust was thrown up into the air, Woll was ready and waiting for the enemy to fire back as Wittmann then ordered his driver to pull forward and out of the hanging dust, and then for Woll to fire once again if a target of opportunity presented itself. Many enemy positions and weapons were destroyed using this firing technique and it was felt that in certain circumstances the two rounds that were utilized to locate and then destroy the enemy was justified for this type of engagement.

After a little more than an hour, the German forces had taken the third line of defenses which had been very costly for both sides. Wrecked and burning vehicles littered the area for hundreds of meters, with smoke and thick clouds of dust obscuring the terrain which caused another problem. The German panzer crews were now very concerned about their supporting infantry as they had out run these units and were not too sure if nearby infantry troops were friend or foe. No doubt, the Ivans would be using stealth and cunning in order to infiltrate the newly established front lines and dig themselves into the landscape and pop up and try to destroy the German panzers with hand placed magnetic mines, or other types of explosive charges. The German infantry units were moving up as fast as humanly possible and it was not until Wittmann and the other panzer commanders actually saw them positioned in and around their vehicles, did they feel secure and protected. The infantry dug themselves into the countryside and prevented any and all harm to the heavy panzers from any attempts by the Russians to storm forward and knockout the highly praised and valuable Tiger Is.

After a short breather, the Tiger Is were again ordered to lead the attack. Wittmann and his crew were once again ready for action. His loader had received first aid in regards to his injured hand but was still over concerned if he would be able to continue loading the heavy 8.8cm main gun rounds. It was then decided that it would be better for Berges to stack as many AP and H.E. main gun rounds as possible onto the turret basket floor. After he removed the many spent main gun casings from inside the turret basket, he removed enough main gun rounds from the ammunition bins that they were piled up to his knees, and a few standing up right so as to be readily available for rapid fire commands. His turret roof hatch was to be opened as there was no place for the up-coming spent shell casings, and would have to be thrown out this hatch after each firing.

Soon enough, all of the Tiger Is were again rolling towards their next objective with everyone trying to give the other vehicles enough space so as not to crowd or bunch each other up in the process. If they bunched up, they would present enemy gunners easy targets and would knock them out with minimum effort. If they were separated too far apart, the German vehicles could not provide each other with supportive covering fire. The platoon leaders had their hands full as they tried to direct their vehicles, monitor the radios, give directions to their drivers, detect enemy positions, and also give accurate and controlled fire commands to their vehicle gunners.

As the armored vehicles crashed forward, Wittmann was on the lookout for any signs of the enemy as he was now concerned that they might have again by-passed a number of hidden anti-tank guns as done beforehand. Suddenly there was a message over the radio network and he could just make out the voice of his friend Wendorff.

"Wittmann, our panzer is back into the fight!", yelled Wendorff as he and his crew received help from a follow-up maintenance unit and had managed to replace his blown track back onto its suspension.

"Thats what we hoped for!", replied Wittmann."Now move forward quickly and stay out of the line of fire, so you will not be attacked again!"

The crack of Ivan's anti-tank guns alerted Wittmann once again and set into motion aggressive actions by the German Tiger I crews to locate and eradicate the enemy weapons. Rounds were falling in and around all of the vehicles, but none of these projectiles hit any of the Tiger Is now rolling forward at full speed. Wittmann's platoon was in the lead, and once again he met the enemy with full fury. Enemy rounds impacted and exploded to the left and right of his vehicles with the gunners trying to locate the positions as fast as humanly possible while under extreme stress and agitation. A few anti-tank rounds found their mark and smashed into a number of the approaching Tiger Is, but the massive frontal armor protection, plus traversing the turrets to the 10 o'clock and 2 o'clock positions presented acute angles to the line of fire which helped to withstand the high velocity projectiles. Finally, the order was given to halt the vehicles in order for them to take on the Pak weapons. Woll fired a main gun round as soon as the heavy vehicle halted on its tracks so as to try and force the Ivans to keep their heads down, and also to hopefully draw fire. Wittmann by this time had located one of these weapons which fired out of sheer panic, but was not sure of the range as the smoke and dust that surrounded his vehicle and the battlefield altered his depth perception a great deal. He gave Woll the fire command post haste, but in the end the H.E. main gun round missed the target and impacted into a small incline beyond the selected target. Woll was to be heard swearing in his gunner's seat in disgust. As soon as the next 8.8cm main gun round was thrown into the breech he fired this projectile at the same target location. This time the round crashed into the enemy gun emplacement and shattered everyone and every-thing within its confines. The interesting part of this engagement was that Woll did not change the elevation or traverse of the 8.8cm main gun, but had just destroyed this position. He had sensed that the first main gun round was quite close to the target, but had seen it embed itself past the weapon. Now that the second round had found its mark without applying any sight corrections in regards to the main gun, it was assumed that the first round had been defective, and went wild and erratic upon firing.

As soon as Woll had silenced this anti-tank gun position, Wittmann was now observing a horde of Russian infantry rallying to his left-hand side of his vehicle. He ordered his driver to swing their vehicle in the direction of the enemy infantry in order that his Tiger I would be able to deliver suppressive fire at this very dangerous and new threat with both MG-34s. The Russian infantry had now moved out into open ground and were seen to be using close battle drill. An order to Woll and Pollmann was given and to stand ready for a machine gun engagement. As Wittmann was to complete his fire command, automatic and rifle fire whistled by and also struck his armored cupola, which caused him to quickly fall back into the safety of his vehicle and slammed his heavy hatch shut with rapid and determined body motions. He also gave the order for his two MG-34s to open up and take on the approaching infantry. Two of his sister vehicles also started to fire at the enemy infantry which resulted in an overlapping and deadly cross-fire which was devastating. As soon as this firing started, Wittmann and his crew could hear the screams of the fallen and dying Russian infantry as they were utterly slaughtered in great numbers. The first wave of these brave men who have been hit by Wittmann's fire were laying not three hundred meters from his vehicle and the ones that were only wounded, were crying out for medical attention. Wittmann clenched his teeth, as he knew that most likely, these men would die where they laid, unless they were removed from the battlefield by their own people. Then, without any warning, he could taste blood in his mouth, and was not too sure why or where he was bleeding from internally! At first, he thought that perhaps an enemy bullet had hit him in the face and during all of the excitement and pressure of battle had not felt this injury. Or perhaps, a sliver of metal from an enemy bullet had struck him in the mouth while giving orders to his crew after breaking up against the frontal area of his armored cupola. It turned out that he had simply bitten his tongue during the heat of battle and felt very relieved that this sudden panic from within himself, was only due to an involuntary self inflicted wound!

Once Wittmann brought himself back to reality, he felt quite stupid in biting his own tongue without realizing it! He then turned all of his energy and attentions back to the tactical situation at hand.

Suddenly, Wittmann could hear the cries for help coming in over the radio network from his comrade Wendorff, who was once again in trouble and needed assistance. The order went out! Warmbrünn and Kleber were to stay at their present locations and Lötzsch and Höflinger were to assist Wittmann in his attempt to help Wendörff. They rolled and turned towards a small grove of trees in order to hide themselves from the ever present eyes of the enemy. Underneath their heavy tracks they could hear the breaking of limbs from the trees which were being mowed down by their advance and pushed into the soft earth as they headed towards Wendörff's position. At the edge of this small wood, they came upon two enemy anti-tank guns that were firing at the German panzer forces, but had not noticed Wittmann's three Tiger Is as they moved forward. In a small depression, Wittmann located two T34/76s that had taken up hull down positions and no doubt had fired and disabled Wendorff's machine which was now on fire. The two Russian panzers were now traversing their turrets and were no doubt taking aim at the three approaching German vehicles.

"Lötzsch and Höflinger, take out the two Pak guns!", ordered Wittmann over the radio net.

"I will deal with the enemy panzers!"

Wittmann's Tiger I rolled forward at full throttle out of the small grove of trees, and as a result, was in full view of the anti-tank guns. This was a very dangerous situation, but it was vital that he maneuver his vehicle to Wendörff's aid before anything else happened to this brave panzer commander and his crew. Wittmann brought his vehicle forward until his machine was in between Wendörff's Tiger I and the Russian panzers. As soon as Wittmann's vehicle came to a halt, his driver threw its transmission into neutral and revved up the engine, so as to provide Woll with full hydraulic power in order to traverse the fifteen ton turret to the right side of the hull and superstructure.

Woll was traversing the turret as fast as it would rotate as Wittmann announced his firing data so he would be on target as soon as his sight picture revealed the Russian panzers to him. His loader had already thrown an AP main gun round into the breech as soon as he felt the turret starting to rotate and had a second main gun round between his legs in order to be ready for the second engagement. Before Woll could traverse the turret onto the enemy targets one of the T34/76s fired a main gun round. The main gun round flew towards and then past Wittmann's vehicle just above the gun, and over the top of the turret with the resulting shock wave shaking Wittmann's upper body torso. Had this main gun round hit the gun barrel, his vehicle would have been put out of action, as the projectile would have either cracked the main gun or have damaged it beyond repair.

Bobby Woll finally came onto target and fired the 8.8cm AP main gun round without a second thought to his actions. The main gun round crashed into the T34/76 and blew the vehicle apart with such great force that Wittmann could also feel the shock wave as it echoed back and engulfed his upright position in his vehicle. The second T34/76 avoided the same fate by quickly moving backwards into a nearby low depression in the terrain, thus causing Woll's second shot to impact harmlessly in front of the now disappearing enemy panzer. Shortly afterwards, the Russian machine turned quickly and was out of Woll's sight picture altogether. Wittmann and Woll scanned the forward area from their vehicle in order to locate this enemy vehicle, but at last, to no avail. It was now a game of hide and seek and Wittmann did not like the situation that was developing. Wendorff and his crew had now baled out of their machine and were hiding on the left-hand side of Wittmann's vehicle which was not good. Wittmann could not take any of them on board his vehicle as there was no room inside their cramped machine, nor could they be expected to ride on board his engine deck, as they would surely be machine gunned down by the Ivans, or worst yet, blown to bits by an enemy main gun round. If he moved off he would be forced to leave Wendörff and his crew fully exposed to enemy fire. As a result, he had to make a serious judgement call in order to save his comrades. He and his crew would make a stand and try and knocked out the enemy panzer that was now stalking them to their immediate front.

The Russian T34/76 was maneuvering to knockout Wittmann's vehicle and had been moving up and down the depression to give a false impression as to its true location. Wittmann and Woll could see the diesel exhaust fumes of this vehicle, but the smoke from the nearby burning vehicles only helped to obscure their vision and added additional confusion to this already dangerous and tense scene. The panzer commander of the enemy machine was no fool, and was using every trick in the book to try and out think his opponent. He knew that he had to surprise the stationary Tiger I in order to deliver his knockout punch. As Wittmann and Woll continued to scan the area for the enemy machine, the T34/76 suddenly popped up to their left and fired a main gun round as soon as its gunner was able to align the Tiger I in his sight picture. Wittmann saw the flash of the gun barrel and had only seconds to throw himself into the interior of his turret.

Bang! The main gun round of the enemy vehicle smashed into the left track of his vehicle which separated two track links. Wittmann's driver gave out a loud scream as the resulting shock wave overcame him in the forward area of the vehicle. There was no time to waste, as Wittmann was not sure what condition his left track and suspension was in after being hit. He ordered Woll to fire at the Russian panzer now at full battle speed heading towards their precarious position. The Russian panzer commander must have been very confident as his actions indicated that he thought that the German machine was knocked out and would try and capture or kill the surviving crew-members. Woll quickly brought the enemy panzer into his sights and fired an AP main gun round at the approaching T34/76. Once again, Woll had found his mark very well indeed! His accurately placed 8.8cm AP main gun round hit the enemy vehicle between the front of the superstructure and turret, but for a few long seconds nothing seemed to happen as the Russian machine continued to roll towards their position. All at once, the turret hatch of the enemy machine blew open with huge sheets of flames shooting skyward. The turret crew were seen trying to exit the vehicle but were all on fire as they baled out! They fell to the ground and rolled around until they were all burned to death! As Wittmann and his gunner continued to watch this horrible sight, the driver's hatch of the enemy machine started to open and they witnessed the burning driver of this doomed machine trying to escape from his vehicle which was now engulfed in smoke and flames. It was quite obvious that he was not going to be able to remove himself from his vehicle, as he was only able to pull himself halfway out of the machine. Just as the driver seemed to be giving up his struggle, the entire T34/76 blew up and threw large pieces of white hot metal all over the surrounding area. Wittmann and the other men nearby, threw themselves into any protection that was available to them as pieces of the enemy panzer was also thrown towards their whereabouts. After all had settle everyone stood up and looked at where the Russian machine had once been. All that was left of this vehicle was a large pile of twisted metal, burning rubber road-wheels, and the ever present smell of burnt human flesh!

The two anti-tank guns at the edge of the woods were soon attacked by Lötzsch and Höflinger, but the battle had not been an easy one for them. The Pak guns were well hidden and had fired a number of rounds at them with alarming accuracy. In the end, the German panzers succeeded in knocking them out and then headed back to where Wittmann's and Wendorff's machines lay immobilized. They soon rallied back to their comrades' locations and gave them supportive fire and to lend a hand in any way they could be useful. The main battle line had by now moved forward, but it was vital that Wittmann's and Wendorff's machines be given protection in the event that the Russian infantry or other enemy armored fighting vehicles made a sudden or unexpected appearance. By the time that Lötzsch and Höflinger had taken up their new defensive positions, Wittmann and his crew were now trying to remove their injured driver from the vehicle. It seemed that the main gun round fired by the enemy tank had impacted just between the inside of the left drive sprocket and the hull of the vehicle. The main gun round did not penetrate, but the concussion and shock wave had ripped away nuts, bolts, and other fixtures off from their mountings in and around the driver's compartment and had hit Kirschmer in a number of different places on his body. The torn track had to be repaired as soon as possible, but immediate attention for the driver was equally important. Together with his radio operator Wittmann pulled the injured Kirschmer out of the vehicle, and laid him on the ground where Woll had spread a blanket out.

"Its all over for me, Untersturmführer!", mumbled Kirschmer.

Wittmann stared down at his driver's bleeding wounds that were now being attended to until the medical team could reach them. Wittmann shook his head and smiled.

"Your still going to make it, Kirschmer!", stated Wittmann.

"Pollmann, please pray with me!", cried Kirschmer.

Pollmann kneeled down next to his comrade and bowed his head.

Afterwards, Wittmann stated, "Quick, get that track repaired!"

During the time that his crew were repairing their broken track, Wendorff was extinguishing the fire inside his Tiger I, as an electrical short had caused this dangerous situation. Finally, the fire was out and all was safe for the time being. The battle of Kursk was raging all around them, and it was imperative to return to the front lines as soon as possible in order to continue the assault. Wittmann had already radioed for an armored half-track ambulance (Sd.Kfz.251/8)to come to their location, and when it arrived, all hands helped to place Kirschmer into this vehicle. They were all sorry to see Kirschmer's departure, but knew that he would be placed in good hands and returned to them at a later date.

"Rottenführer Möller reporting!", was the statement made by Wittmann's replacement driver. Möller had been a driver of one of the Tiger Is that were now burning behind the front lines and was rushed up to Wittmann's vehicle as soon as Kirschmer had been wounded.

"I am here to replace your wounded driver!"

"Very good, we would like to welcome you to our crew, Möller, please help the others in repairing our damaged track!", was Wittmann's reply.

As the first day of battle came to a close, Wittmann and his crew had destroyed eight enemy panzers along with seven anti-tank guns. It was quite obvious that Michael Wittmann had shown for the first time that he had indeed matured into an experienced panzer commander of which he could be very proud. He had also shown that he not only had the courage and tactical knowledge to command, but also two vital characteristics that were essential for a successful panzer commander; instinct and intuition!

During the evening of the first day of the great battle of Kursk, the 1st SS Panzer Division had successfully broken its way through the artillery positions of the 52nd Russian artillery division. The Leibstandarte Adolf Hitler had good field positions and knocked out many Russian tanks and anti-tank guns to their credit. The German panzers were now 8km deep inside the enemy lines, but heavy and bitter fighting was to continue before the enemy could be considered beaten.

During this time-period, Wittmann and his panzer crew learned the name of the man who had led the aerial attacks that had helped to destroy the Russian bunker lines. This brave Ju 87 Stuka pilot was none other than Major Hans-Ulrich Rudel, who would one day win Germany's top military award for his exploits over the battle fields of the Russian front.

On the morning of July 6th, the sunny summer weather had worsened for the men of the Leibstandarte Adolf Hitler and their planned assault was postponed until the afternoon. Once the order was given for the attacking units to roll forward, the troops of the Waffen-SS encountered dug-in tanks of Vatutin's First Red Tank Army. Flame throwers were also emplaced to help stem the tide of the advancing German panzers and grenadiers but it took constant counter-attacks to help break up the massive wall of heavy German panzers leading the assaults.

Every local man and woman in the Kursk area had been drafted by the Russian High Command and mobilized to halt the German assaults in its tracks. Partisan activity was also escalated in order to harass any follow up German forces in the rear areas and supply routes. A large number of Red Army battalions consisted of civilians, many without boots or proper uniforms, and a great many without any type of weapons to defend themselves. It was also reported that these human waves of aggression were usually penal battalions and sent directly out in front of the regular Red Army units to detonate any and all landmines or booby traps that had been sowed in and around the line of advance. Additional reports were received that all-women battalions were fighting as savagely as their male counterparts in the Russian regular army units. It was quite obvious that the Red Army was relying on massive troop strengths to smother and disperse the thinly held German front lines.

During July 6, a twelve kilometer advance was finally achieved, but the element of surprise had not been granted to the German forces. Losses to the Leibstandarte Adolf Hitler had been heavy, 84 killed and 384 wounded. During July 7th, no decisive breakthrough was to occur. The flanks of the SS Corps were now open to repeated Russian counter-blows, for the XXXXVIII Panzer Corps on the left flank had failed to keep abreast of the Waffen-SS assaults while the right flank units progressed very little at all during the two days of constant and bloody battle. On July 8th, it was claimed that the destruction of 400 Russian panzers had taken place and indeed losses on both opposing sides had been very high. At the end of O-Tag plus 3, the German panzer units had only forty Panthers still functional for service out of the two hundred which were available at the start of the battle. Many of the crews had to bale out of their Panthers as they did not trust these new and untested machines and stated that a main gun round penetration often caused fires which resulted in their vehicles to burst into flames with little or no hope for recovering their machines at a later date. For many young crews, it was their first (and for many their last) time in face to face combat with the enemy and only experienced crews had any chance of coming through this wild inferno unscathed. Even the super heavyweights, the Porsche Ferdinands (Sd.Kfz.184) with their powerful and high velocity 8.8cm main guns and tremendous thicknesses of armor plate, suffered from weaknesses in the suspension and were frequently knocked out by tenacious and highly determined Russian tank hunting teams. In total desperation, some of the Ferdinand crewmembers fired their MP-40 machine pistols through the open breech of the main guns to try and ward off such stubborn assaults against their machines. The Ferdinands were not provided with any type of secondary armament and these vehicles suffered a great deal because of this oversight in regards to their designers. Even the German remote controlled, unmanned, demolition panzers, called "Goliath" were used against the Red Army fortifications but proved impotent in destroying these emplacements altogether, as they were picked off either by light enemy anti-tank guns, or detonated by the sniper's bullet. The Russian massive defensive positions soon halted the German attacks in its tracks. The Leibstandarte Adolf Hitler, although trying to maintain a steady forward assault, had by this time no more rhythm to so continue. The overall strain of battle was too much and everywhere on the battlefield laid exhausted men and their machines that could go no further. The German infantry slept where they had dropped, and the panzer crews, half dead from the earlier fighting while manning their precious machines, were stretched out by their vehicles smothered in a deep sleep from which not even the constant noise of maintenance and servicing crews could awake them!

On July 7th, Wittmann and his Tiger I crew destroyed a further seven T34/76s tanks plus nineteen guns of the Red Army 29th anti-tank gun brigade in and around Oboyan and Teterevino. A Leibstandarte motorcycle company was also able to race forward and through a gap in the front lines established by Wittmann's efforts and was able to capture intact a Russian Brigade headquarters. With this type of determination and pressure, the Waffen-SS panzers and their supporting Grenadiers stormed forward and in the direction of Psyolknee.

Wittmann and his Tiger I platoon were then ordered to also advance towards Psyolknee as there were Russian artillery pieces firing into the German lines. As the attack started to develop Kling ordered Wittmann to attack these weapons as soon as possible in order to silence them.

"Wittmann, turn out and destroy Ivan's artillery!" yelled Kling.

As soon as Wittmann was given his instructions, he maneuvered his heavy vehicle out of his battle position and headed towards the flashes of the heavy enemy artillery guns. He again used the cover of a small grove of trees and carefully inched his vehicle forward in order to view the area ahead. The heavy Tiger I move through the underbrush and plowed its way forward until it had reached the edge of the small wood, and ordered his driver to halt his vehicle. Wittmann climbed down from his machine and ran forward to scan the area ahead of him with his binoculars. He could now see the enemy guns firing their deadly rounds at the rearward German positions and knew that he must act very quickly in order to save the day for his comrades. He then sprang to his feet and ran back to the safety of his machine. He swiftly entered back into his vehicle and threw on his earphones and throat microphones. After catching his breath, he ordered his crew into battle action, and then ordered Möller to move out of their hiding place. As his Tiger I came out of the woods at full speed, Wittmann was now starting to provide Woll with his fire commands. The Russian artillery were still firing as the lone German Tiger I moved up to locate a firing position. The Ivans manning the artillery field pieces were thrown into sudden panic as the first 8.8cm H.E. main gun round smashed into their positions. There was a loud explosion as the first high explosive round detonated and blew up the first Russian weapon killing the entire gun crew. Wittmann had Woll locked onto the next target and with precise traverse and elevation movements, the second artillery piece was destroyed. Flames were now raging about in the immediate area of the first field piece that had been destroyed, with the fire now spreading to a nearby ammunition dump, which soon ignited with a large number of bagged explosive charges exploding with a tremendous crack which killed some of the surviving Russian artillery men. The remainder of the Ivans continued to run at full gate in order to escape from the accurate and deadly 8.8cm main gun rounds.

Wittmann and Woll were very puzzled concerning the whole affair? Why didn't the Russian artillery crews simply lower their gun barrels and take on their Tiger I in a duel? Their machine had been in range ever since the firing started.

Lucky for Wittmann and his crew that the Ivans had not fired at their armored mount, as one direct hit would have utterly destroyed their heavy vehicle. It was now very clear to Wittmann and his crew, that the Ivans had no minds of their own and no doubt had continued to fire at the rear area German targets as this is what had been ordered and if they failed to obey their given orders, they would have been arrested, placed into work battalions, or shot! Even so, it was hard to believe that they did not even take the time to fire on a single German Tiger I.

Later in the day, Wittmann and his men were operating in the area of Lutchki, where they were fired upon by enemy anti-tank guns. Kleber's Tiger I received a direct hit which caused his driver to halt his vehicle and to check for damage. Wittmann and Warmbrunn positioned their vehicles to the right of Kleber to try and draw away the incoming enemy fire. Quick and accurate German panzer gunnery techniques soon destroyed the enemy anti-tank guns. In the meantime, Kleber and his crew were able to determine that damage to their vehicle was not too serious, only that the driver was shaken up, and had stopped their vehicle in a panic. It took Kleber about five minutes to settle his driver down, and then reported to Wittmann that everything was alright.

The platoon of Tiger Is were now moving towards a small village where they planned to establish a defensive posture for the night and cautiously rolled forward. The enemy was not to be seen as they entered into the village. Wittmann and Warmbrunn did not like the situation at hand, as the capture of this village seemed too easy, much too easy! As the vehicles started to slow down in the main street, Russian infantry started to run out into the deserted street and lobed hand grenades attached to bottles of gasoline at the German panzers. As soon as the first grenade was set off, all of the panzer commanders slammed down their cupola hatches and started to back their vehicles out of the village. Main gun ammunition and MG-34 machine gun fire opened up to repel and keep the Ivans at bay which was deafening in the village street and side alleys. The order was then given out to fire continuously with both MG-34 machine guns which was hoped to give covering fire between main gun rounds. Even with all of this massive firepower being thrown against the Russians, a number of the dangerous and lethal fire bombs hit and exploded against Wittmann's vehicle. Flames were pouring off of his vehicle which was very alarming to him and his crew, but they knew if they tried to bale out of their machine they would be shot down like dogs with no mercy. It was a terrifying situation for Wittmann's crews, as if just one fire bomb was thrown up and onto the rear deck of their panzer, the ignited gasoline would drip down into the engine compartment and set the rear of the vehicle on fire. It seemed that he and his crew were living in a hot and burning hell, as everywhere Wittmann looked through his vision slits, there was bright orange flames and black acrid smoke. Their only hope for survival was to roll rearward with full force out of the village as fast as their vehicle could move in reverse. The driver crashed the panzer into reverse gear as Wittmann continued to give him instructions and moved in a rearward direction with Woll and the bow machine-gunner firing at anything that moved in their respective sight pictures.

The German vehicles finally moved backwards out of the village and were able to halt their machines and climb out to inspect the damage. The gunners and loaders were to stay at their positions and keep a wary eye for any signs of the enemy. The Ivans did not venture out of the village and it was assumed that this force had been an isolated infantry unit with no anti-tank or armor support and had thrown up an ad hoc defense to ward off the German heavy panzers. A number of the Tiger Is were still burning, but fortunately the fire bombs had done little or no damage. A small number of these primitive weapons had been thrown up and onto the sides of the vehicle superstructures with little or no ignited gasoline being able to find its way down and into the engine compartments. The panzer commanders were smothering the remaining flames with their jackets and blankets and found that some of the paint on the sides of their panzers was burnt off and any tools with wooden handles were burnt to a cinder. They were all very lucky indeed that this was the only damage to their vehicles, as this type of situation usually ended up far worse for panzer crews fighting in such close quarters.

All at once, one of the Tiger I gunners reported that he was observing a large number of retreating Russian infantry making their escape in trucks! There was no doubt, that the Russians had more infantry in the village as was first thought. They must have been in the surrounding houses during the previous fire fight, but had not revealed all their numbers for one reason or the other. There was no time for the Tiger Is to be moved forward in order to over run the fleeing Russians. Some of the Russian infantrymen were even riding horse in order to escape.

"Load high explosives and prepare to fire!" was the fire command presented by Wittmann.

The next five minutes was hell on earth for the retreating Russians. Horses that were hit by the German fire screamed in agony. The Russian trucks were blown to pieces within seconds and columns of thick black smoke filled the air and drifted over the now deserted village. It was a highly grotesque scene as men, animals and twisted and burning machines laid scattered together over and off to the sides of the dirt road leading away from the village. It was a scene straight out of a nightmare as Wittmann viewed this picture of complete desolation. It would have been better for the Russians if they had stood their ground and at least tried to fight against the German panzers, instead of just running out into the open and being cut to pieces!

After the small village had been secured by follow up units of the Leibstandarte, Wittmann's platoon was ordered to continue the battle and to move up. The Russians for the moment were on the run, and Wittmann's superiors did not want the momentum of the German advance to falter or be compromised in any way. The leading German heavy panzers had given the Ivans a bloody nose, as they could not hope to stop these powerful machines unless they had supportive anti-tank guns or armored fighting vehicles of their own. The Tiger Is of the Leibstandarte were soon operating on the eastern edge of Lutchki when they again ran into a group of Russian anti-tank guns. The leading Tiger I was hit from 600 meters away and then started to burn. The crew bailed out on fire and were instantly machine gunned down by the supporting enemy infantry. Wittmann observed this scene of quick death and ordered his crew into battle actions. The inferno was just starting, as if one T34/76 or anti-tank gun opened fired, the remaining enemy weapons would join in to be included in this orchestration of death. Shots rang out, explosions were erupting around the German Tiger Is, with sheets of flame raging up in all directions. Wittmann's vehicle received a hit by an in-coming round but again luckily deflected upwards with a loud crack! He was not sure if it had penetrated but was soon relieved to hear Woll asking him for fire directions over the radio intercom. It was hard to observe anything in the fog of battle that had been thrown up in the last few minutes, so Wittmann ordered Möller to move his vehicle forward so they would not be a stationary target any longer. As soon as they rolled ahead about fifty meters, Wittmann saw a number of large Russian panzers trying to maneuver into firing positions only 900 meters to their right.

"Fire on those KV-Is!", ordered Wittmann.

Woll was already traversing the Tiger I turret to the right even before the fire command was given, as he had also spotted the enemy panzers. Woll heard the clang of an 8.8cm AP main gun round as it was being thrown into the breech by Berges, and knew that all was ready for the next fire engagement. Wittmann guided him onto target, and as soon as Woll was sure that he could see his target, he fired the projectile at the enemy panzer as it made its approach. The shot rang out and hit the heavy Russian panzer square on but seemed to cause it no harm? Wittmann could not tell if in fact the main gun round had penetrated or had missed the target altogether. Woll quickly fired off another 8.8cm AP round as soon as he heard the closing of the breech. This time, Wittmann sensed that the main gun round had hit the enemy machine, but could not tell if the projectile had penetrated. Woll then became very nervous and traversed the turret onto the next KV I. A third AP main gun round flew towards its target and smashed against the heavier armor plate of this Russian armored fighting vehicle. There was no sign of life and Wittmann and Woll thought that perhaps the crew had baled out on seeing one of their sister vehicles being fired upon. While they were trying to decide what to do next, the two KV Is opened fired on Wittmann's stationary vehicle. The two enemy machines were now firing their weapons without proper observation or any fire discipline with their main gun rounds hitting forward, sideways, and over Wittmann's Tiger I. Even though the enemy rounds were being fired in all directions, a number of these projectiles whistled dangerously close and directly over Wittmann's open cupola hatch as he could feel the great rush of air as they flew past only mere inches from his head.

Wittmann gave his gunner another quick and accurate fire command. At a distance of only 1800 meters Woll once again fired upon the closest KV I after making a small correction in regards to his sight picture. In less than a second the KV I disappeared within a huge explosion which no doubt had been the direct result of the main gun round penetrating and igniting the on-board ammunition. The heavy Russian panzer was blown apart at the seams, and none of the crew was seen to escape. The second KV I was rotating its turret to take Wittmann on, but Woll was too close to the enemy to miss his target. Wittmann did not even have to present a second fire command as Woll pressed the firing handle as soon as the second Russian machine had come into his sight picture. Both Russian machines were utterly destroyed in less than twelve seconds.

After the battle with the KV Is the Russians had once again run out of steam. It was now time for the Tiger Is of Wittmann's unit to head north east and help to break up enemy activity that was slowing down the German advance in that area. The tired panzer crews forced themselves to conduct an ordered march towards the enemy, but it was painfully clear that the men needed a rest as they had been fighting the Ivans for days without proper sleep. On the evening of July 8th, Wittmann and his crews found themselves situated on a hill tactically marked 260.8 located between Werchnopenje and Gresnoje. Gresnoje was the objective of the Totenkopf division and Das Reich her sister unit would head northeast to encounter the enemy forces in and around Teterevino. It was decided late in the evening of the fourth day of battle, that the German forces deserved a rest in order to continue on their assaults. As soon as the order from higher command went out to the fighting units, everyone halted where ever they were positioned and fell exhausted in their tracks and collapsed into a much needed sleep.

Wittmann walked along the panzers that were now shut down for the night, but could hear the Maybach engines of the vehicles cooling down from the day's harsh fighting. Hissing and snapping as the hot metal parts returned to normal temperatures, he could also smell the burnt rubber from the fan belts and charred wood from the tools that had been set on fire earlier. The heat generated by the huge battle tracks of the vehicles could be felt six to eight inches away and wondered how much more strain their Tiger Is could take if they had pushed them much further on the battlefield without proper maintenance and repairs. His platoon still had four vehicles operational, with the fifth vehicle undergoing an engine change. This machine belonged to Lötzsch who was very busy giving guidance and instructions to the maintenance people that had finally arrived on the scene. Lötzsch did not care about sleep, as keeping his vehicle properly maintained and running was his number one priority. Wittmann had to order Lötzsch to obtain some sleep as he would be unable to continue to command his vehicle unless he had received some worthwhile rest. Lotzsch finally in disgust walked over to his panzer crew who were sound asleep, threw out his blanket and was too, soon unconscious. Wittmann now knew that he had to order someone to stand watch, something that must be done in order to bring and establish safety for their panzer company. The tired panzer commander came upon Rottenführer Klosch from Warmbrunn's panzer crew, and asked why he had not gone to sleep yet.

"Are you not tired Klosch?", asked Wittmann.

"No sir!", replied Klosch.

"You must be after all of this hard fighting!", questioned Wittmann.

"The excitement in the air has not allowed me to become tired or sleepy, Sir!", was the reply.

"Good, then you have to stand watch for the entire company!", was Wittmann's order.

"I will take the third watch, awaken Pollmann for the second watch and then have him wake me up after three hours", instructed Wittmann.

"Yes sir!", stated Klosch with a proper salute.

Wittmann finally was able to throw off his shoes and take his bed roll from his vehicle and was also soon fast asleep on the ground alongside with the rest of his bone tired panzer crew. He slept for about two and a half hours and suddenly woke up out of a deep sleep. He was not quite sure why he woke up but could hear the thud of enemy artillery far off in the distance, but paid little attention to it. It was too far away to cause them any harm. He then decided to take a short walk around the vehicles and think to himself. As soon as he had his shoes on and buttoned up his shirt, he started to walk around the immediate area of his platoon's vehicles. He continued his walk around this area and soon came upon Klosch fast asleep at his post. As Wittmann shook this man back into consciousness, the young man looked up at Wittmann in a glazed horror!

"Please, Untersturmführer, do not report me. I desire to enter officers training!", pleaded the young man who had also volunteered for a position at the front line.

"If you continue to fall asleep at your post Klosch, you will be dead long before you are ever assigned to the Junkers school. I could have been Ivan with a knife to slit your throat! Not only would it be your life in the bag, but you also placed the entire company in jeopardy!", was Wittmann's angry reply.

Klosch was as white as a sheet. He knew how strict Wittmann could be and had now put the fear of God into his tired and shaking body. Slowly the seconds ticked away while Wittmann was thinking what he would do in the case of this young and inexperienced soldier. His future laid directly in his hands.

"Go lay down Klosch and get some sleep!", ordered Wittmann.

"But I can not...sir, I did not perform my duty..."

"I will take over your watch!", stated Wittmann.

"Thank you, sir, and thank you for your kindness!"

The youth disappeared into the darkness forthwith. Wittmann now had to complete nearly two watches and knew that he would be totally exhausted in the morning after staying awake half of the night. The following hours passed ever so slowly and he had to force himself to stay awake. After about three hours he did not feel sleepy any longer as his senses were still very highly attuned from the earlier panzer battles. He and his crew had all come through a living hell the past few days and could only wonder how long it would be before the enemy would catch them off guard and kill them all with one well placed anti-tank or panzer main gun round. He retraced in his mind all of the engagements they had fought together and tried to remember every little detail and technique that was applied to survive against the Ivans. He felt that he and his men had been very lucky in certain situations, but the majority of the fire fights they had fought were under his direct command and control. He had to keep up his standards of leadership if they were to survive in this extremely hostile and harsh environment. It would take every ounce of mental stability and control to come out of this bitter fighting alive!

It was now early morning and Wittmann was now in a state of utter exhaustion and becoming somewhat ill. He could not allow himself to fall asleep as he had to set an example to the other men in his platoon and company. Wittmann suddenly heard footsteps coming towards him but could not make out who or what was approaching him in the darkness. He held up his MP-40 machine pistol at the ready and was about to challenge the intruder when he finally recognized Bobby Woll! Woll had awaken also and found his panzer commander missing and was fearful that the Ivans had killed or captured him. He immediately started looking for him and was extremely relieved when he found him safe and unharmed. Woll took over the watch for his commander as the now highly fatigued Wittmann made his way back to his bed roll, where he utterly collapsed and was soon sound asleep.

A few hours later, Wittmann was awaken by Bobby Woll.

"Commander to Michael!", stated Woll now holding a steaming hot cup of coffee under his commander's nose.

Wittmann's eyes jerked wide open and sat up as he was startled by Woll's joke. It was ascertain that Wittmann thought that he was back in battle and being called up by his company commander and had somehow falling asleep in his armored turret cupola. He took the cup of coffee from Woll's hand and slowly came out of his deep sleep. He finally put on his shoes that he did not remember taking off and hurried to speak with Kling. On his way, Wendorff and Warmbrunn joined him. Upon reaching Kling's location, they were all ordered to Regimental Headquarters.

At the Regimental Headquarters the company and divisional commanders were already gathered.

Obersturmbannführer Max Wünsche, commander of the 1st Detachment, 1st SS-Panzer Regiment, and Obersturmführer Martin Gross, commander of the 2nd Detachment, 2nd SS-Panzer Regiment waved to their comrades to hurry to their location. Wittmann, Wendorff, Warmbrunn, and Kling join the open circle as SS-Obersturmführer Georg Schönberger began to speak.

"Comrades, today the final thrust is to begin. The division "Grossdeutschland" has taken Dubrowa. The defeat of Oboyan is within our reach. We have just decoded a Russian radio transmission. It is from an army general by the name of Vatutin and he tells his officers the following: "The Germans are under no circumstances to take Oboyan!"

"That is the area of our left neighbor the Fourth Panzer Army!" remarked Max Wünsche.

"That's correct!" continued Schönberger, "But we will be pulling parallel with the division "Grossdeutschland" and also the 11th Panzer Division. We will have to maneuver very quickly in order that the Russians do not have time to fill in any of the gaps we have opened in the front lines. According to our spy planes, the enemy is waiting there with a very strong panzer element."

So it was, on July 8th/9th, the Leibstandarte Adolf Hitler was ordered to assault Oboyan and Teterevino once again as their primary objectives. The men of the panzer companies mounted their vehicles and roared off into the direction of these two areas under the supporting bombardment of Luftwaffe bombers which helped to soften up the way ahead with heavy saturation bombing.

Wittmann was once again in the cupola of his Tiger I and made ready for immediate action. Surprised and trying to concentrate on everything that was happening around him, he stood in his open hatch and looked up at the overhead fighter planes and bombers that were flying towards the enemy positions.

As he continued to observe these aircraft as they pressed ahead, Wittmann told his panzer crew that the new types of fighters were the Henschel Hs 129, the flying panzer which mounted three 3.7cm anti-tank weapons on board. These aircraft were being used for the first time in battle, and high hopes were placed upon these machines and their brave pilots. Flying low they roared forward reaching the enemy panzers in board formations. They then attacked and fired upon the enemy and left many of the Russian panzers destroyed and burning. Their attack techniques were to fire their weapons at the enemy panzers and penetrate through the thinner rear engine decks which was quite easily down with their high velocity 3.7cm weapons.

"Panzers march!", was given to all panzer commanders over the radio network.

The attack towards Oboyan and Teterevino was on at last! The German heavy panzers were leading the attack once again until they encountered the first line of anti-tank guns which were expertly camouflaged and dug into the country-side. Concrete dragon's teeth were also embedded into the expected approach zones which made maneuvering extremely difficult and hazardous. It was plain to see that the Ivans had positioned these pointed obstacles in order to funnel the forward panzers into killing zones for the anti-tank guns. Everything was at stake in regards to this battle, and once the battle started, it raged on as the German panzers tried desperately to force open an opening in the Russian defensive lines. All of the leading Tiger Is fired at the flashes of the hidden anti-tank guns, but were not able to knockout these weapons very easily. A number of vehicles were hit by these deadly weapons and many were disabled but continued to fight from their immobilized positions. The undamaged vehicles kept moving forward in order to try and steamroll over the enemy. The maintenance and recovery teams worked under brutal and dangerous conditions trying to repair some of the damaged Tiger Is, with many brave feats being accomplished under direct fire from a determined foe.

Once again, Michael Wittmann and his Tiger I crew were in the middle of the fire fight. With heroic dash he ordered his driver to roll forward at full speed to overtake some of the Russian dug-in positions. Möller had quickly acquainted himself with the fighting style of his new panzer commander, and was maneuvering the heavy Tiger I expertly about the battlefield. Wittmann guided him along and was sure to make certain that his new driver did not take on a straight line of advance for more than a few meters at a time. Otherwise this would give Ivan ample time to fix a bead on his vehicle with his weapons and thus destroy them as a result. Considering the rough and jerky motions of their vehicle, Woll was still able to locate his next target with uncanny accuracy. At this point in time, Bobby Woll was stated as being the best shot in the company, and nobody could doubt his well founded reputation as he continued to destroy Ivan's panzers and hated Pak guns in ever increasing numbers.

After the first line of anti-tank guns had been breached, the Tiger Is pulled up into tight hull-down positions in order for the follow up infantry and support vehicles to catch up. As soon as their new forward lines were consolidated, the Tiger Is were soon rolling and firing to take on the next line of Ivan's defenses. As always, the Russians had many lines of defense and if the first or second lines were breached, the surviving troops would fall back to the next line and bolster its defenses. This would be repeated until perhaps the Russians had been forced back to their fifth or sixth lines of defense which had the effect of establishing even more comprehensive resistance for the leading German assault units. It was a very frightening prospect for the German panzer crews, as they would receive the very brunt of the harsh fighting conditions and it would then be up to these brave men to push on forward regardless of the numbers encountered.

Also at this time, a number of Panzer IV Ausf. H type vehicles were fighting alongside Wittmann and his vehicles. The German panzer force was utilizing various forms of the Panzer wedge and bell tactics. The long arm of the 7.5cm main gun barrel of the Panzer IV Ausf. H was very powerful, but could not reach out as far as the Tiger I's 8.8cm main gun in regards to destroying enemy panzers and anti-tank guns. The Panzer IV Ausf. H were somewhat faster then their bigger brother, so these vehicles were soon out ahead in the open attack. As soon as they started to draw fire from the Ivans, the Tiger Is would come into play by halting to provide supportive fire in order to destroy any targets of opportunity. The Panzer IV Ausf Hs were thus being used as somewhat of an armored shield for the precious Tiger Is, with these vehicles being utilized as the spear behind this shield.

As expected, the Russians suddenly began to throw in their T34/76s in ever increasing numbers and stormed forward to assault the German panzers in an armored encirclement. They came crashing out of their dug in positions with camouflage netting still dangling from their turrets and hulls. Wittmann and his crew were ready to engage the Russian machines as there were now rows upon rows of T34/76s coming straight at them.

The ensuing panzer battles raged on for the next hour with many of the vehicles charging into each other's ranks, which resulted in a wild mix up of German and Russian machines. The panzer crews were very careful not to fire at too close a range for two very important reasons: one being that if they fired and missed their intended targets, they were more than likely to hit and destroy one of their own; secondly, if they fired point blank at the enemy vehicle there was a good chance that the resulting explosions and fragments, could damage their own vehicles. At times, this closed in fighting took on a similar resemblance of a Keys-Stone Cops movie, whereas the story-line being a great more serious and deadly.

Wittmann and his Tiger I crew were destroying their share of enemy machines during this time period, but they were also taking a great deal of fire onto themselves while fighting this extremely fierce battle. The Ivans came on with their vehicles buttoned up and seemed to be rolling forward in blind obedience and oblivious to any central control. The German panzer commanders at least had their heads out of their armored cupolas in order to obtain better observation of the confused, smokey, and dusty battlefield. If they started to receive heavy concentrated fire from the Ivans, they could easily close down their vehicles and hope for the best. The Russians on the other hand, fired on the move, which could only be labeled as nuisance value. Even if the Ivans halted their vehicles to take careful aim, their first main gun rounds were either over the target or fell short of its mark. This was not the case when German panzers were fighting in close quarters. Every AP main gun round fired was normally an outright death sentence. In desperate efforts to survive this type of vicious fighting, the Russian panzers closed in on the German machines even closer, and at times were fender to fender, which thus prevented both sides from rotating their turrets and main guns to fire upon each other. Once this type of fighting developed, there was wild and inaccurate firing going on as the Ivans in their T34/76s fired round after round trying to knock out the German machines lumbering in and around their mists. The battle evolved into a fierce and nightmareish battle for all concerned. As the Tiger I gunners also could not rotate their longer main guns towards their nearby opponents the German panzer commanders finally ordered their respective gunners to start firing at Russian machines which were not alongside them. This was an extremely deadly and vicious game to be played, as at this very close range, the 8.8cm main gun rounds would rip apart any vehicle that it penetrated which was also very dangerous for nearby friendly vehicles and panzer commanders who were still operating with their heads up. Constant and rapid chatter over the radio network was the name of the game for the German panzer commanders as they were advising each other in the hopes of not endangering their comrades when they were ready to fire at a nearby enemy machine. The radio traffic was truly intense, as at times, there were three or four panzer commanders on the radio network screaming out orders and directions while trying desperately to provide warning of their next firing engagements!

Michael Wittmann and his men were fighting for all they were worth against the Russian tankmen. This type of battle had not been taught in their panzer training schools and ad hoc measures had to be taken to survive this onslaught. The enemy was normally to be eradicated within standard gunnery ranges from between 1200-1800 meters as the Tiger I at that time could out range any known Allied armored fighting vehicle in existence. The German panzer training schools did not take into account that the enemy would have such numerical supremacy on the modern battlefield, so it was now left up to the tenacity of the panzer crews to make up their own rules of battle when faced with this type of volatile situation.

Wittmann was now buttoned up in his cupola as the smoke, flames, and white hot metal that was flying through the air forced him to take complete cover in his vehicle. He and his crew were sweating very heavily in their black uniforms until sweat dripped down and into their trousers and boots. Salty sweat in the eyes was a constant problem. Never had the situation been so trying and overwhelming for them. Wittmann's loader was working like a madman as he kept up with his fire commands which were constant and accurate within a few seconds of each other. The driver of their vehicle continued to keep up the engine rpm to ensure that Woll would have adequate hydraulic power to traverse the heavy turret and main gun of their machine. The bow machine gunner kept a wary eye to the right side of the vehicle through his periscope and informed his commander of any movement made by Ivan that would be life threatening.

During this brutal panzer battle, Wittmann continued to strain his eyes as he viewed the hellish confrontation buzzing all around his vehicle. The fog of battle once again was the worst enemy of all as it was next to impossible for him to clearly observe through his vision slits. The whole area was indeed an enormous explosive powderkeg! His fire commands had to be absolutely correct as if he made a mistake or miscalculation, they could fire upon one of their own vehicles and kill five of his comrades. The gunners of all of the panzers involved were extremely trigger happy during this battle sequence and if they hesitated for even a few mere seconds Ivan could destroy them for their apprehension. Due to this type of battle and the nervous tension that was present the panzer commanders were thrown into a very high state of despair. Every little movement that was viewed through their vision slits had to be detected, analyzed extremely quickly, and then announce their fire commands. The German panzer commanders could not and would not fire off main gun round after main gun round to keep from being fire upon by the Ivans. No, this type of encounter took cool and calculated control as they would easily destroy their own vehicles and comrades if not extremely careful and highly selective before giving a fire command. Wittmann and his crew had now blown apart five of the T34/76s, which had taken uncanny skill on the part of Bobby Woll. A T34/76 that they had rammed earlier, which had not been knocked out as of yet, was now trying to escape the strangle hold with Wittmann's vehicle. While he and his crew were firing at other targets, this enemy machine had backed up and was trying to fire at Wittmann's machine from the rear at point blank range! Luckily, one of the other Tiger I panzer commanders had witnessed this sudden maneuver by this particular enemy vehicle and placed a well aimed main gun round into the rear flank of this machine and destroyed it with a loud bang! The resulting smoke was fortunately now covering Wittmann's Tiger I from observed fire, but had also obscured his vision while still buttoned up in his machine. The thick and choking smoke had been a double-edged sword for him and his crew, but in the end, it had most likely saved them all from being detected and fired upon by other enemy panzers.

The battle continued to rage on as some of the German machines now started to move about the area at various speeds. It was quite certain that some of the Ivan's T34/76s were playing dead, and would open up on the German forces as soon as they thought that they were out of immediate danger. As expected, as soon as Wendorff and Kling started to maneuver their machines, the Ivans started firing their 7.6 cm main guns at these two very brave panzer commanders now riding with their turret cupola hatches open and standing up with their heads out. As soon as this firing occurred, the other Tiger Is opened up on the so-called dead enemy panzers and finished them off with little or no problems. Wittmann and his crew destroyed two additional panzers, which brought up their total for this day to seven enemy panzer knocked out.

As the battle started to wind down, there were many Russian machines burning with dead and dying crewmembers laying next to their shattered vehicles. It was a scene of total devastation as Wittmann and the surviving Tiger I crews made ready their departure to the next hot spot in which they were needed. The follow up infantry were now making their way forward and they would deal with mopping up the Russian panzer crews who had now given up in total despair. As their vehicles made their way off, Wittmann looked back at the unbelievable carnage and knew very well that they could have been the victims and not Ivan. Once again, they had been extremely lucky to come out of this firefight with only minor damage to their machines, as some of the other Tiger I panzer crew had not been so lucky. A number of their machines had indeed been hit in vital areas and were immobilized until recovery and maintenance crews could reach their entangled positions and were able to put them back into serviceable condition.

The 8th and 9th of July had been two totally exhausting days for the entire front line German troops. A stand down was finally given for the evening of the 9th which meant a well deserved rest for the wary Waffen-SS panzer crews. Wittmann had gone to a briefing for the next days fighting and when he had returned from his O-meeting (officers meeting) he collapsed fully exhausted onto a canvas tarp laid down by his crew next to their highly battered vehicle. He tried to sleep, but he was not able too, so by the light of a small flashlight, he pulled out a captured Russian map and studied the terrain features very thoroughly. He wanted to make sure that he knew every square meter of the planned assault route that he and his comrades would be covering in the next twenty-four hours. He did not want to give the Ivans any chance of ambushing his vehicles while advancing. As a sentry came by his vehicle making his rounds, he found Wittmann fast asleep and turned off his flashlight, and quietly covered him with a warm blanket.

The next few days of July passed very quickly for the men of the Leibstandarte Adolf Hitler. For Michael Wittmann and his panzer crew, everything seemed to happen at once. Never before had he been so tested. The Russians were holding onto their defensive positions with great tenacity. Hidden anti-tank guns had taken a great toll of German panzers and other supporting vehicles. The Ivans seemed to have more anti-tank guns than panzers! If ten were destroyed or knocked out, another twenty took their place. The German panzers had especially suffered from Russian artillery and dive-bombers raining death down from the skies. There was never a moment of silence on the ever expanding battle line. As soon as one line of bunkers and anti-tank guns were eradicated by the German advance, another hot spot had to be dealt with without any let up. Supply units had to keep very close to the fluid battlefields as if the forward panzers ran out of precious ammunition or fuel, they were doomed to be over run and destroyed.

On the evening of July 10th, Wittmann's platoon was fighting on the edge of Psyolknee once again. During July 11th, the Leibstandarte Adolf Hitler were fighting with the 1st SS Panzer Corps and had reached the area southeast of Bogorodiskojus. "Totenkopf" had driven forward on the left flank with grenadier support to assault the area in and around Psyol at Krassnyi-Oktjabr and "Das Reich" turned on the left flank to take the defensive south of Prokhorovka.

Early, during the morning of July 12, the Leibstandarte Adolf Hitler was able to cross the railway tracks and turned north towards Prokhorovka. Approaching very cautiously, the armored fighting vehicles moved up in order to engaged the 18th and 29th Russian tank corps. A panzer battle, one of the worst of the Eastern front campaign, had now begun.

The German panzer armada rolled towards the two Tank Corps of the Russian 5th Guards Tank Army who were being overrun by the German offensive. General Rotmistrov led the two Tank Corps who were now pushing against the onslaught of the heavy German panzers which were knocking out his T34/76s and KV Is with great ease after applying strict fire discipline. The battle raged on and all manner of fighting developed against the German panzers as they stormed forward under constant and demanding pressure to crack open the defensive lines of the dug in Ivans. During the initial stages of this ensuing battle, the 2nd Battalion, 1st SS Panzer Regiment, under SS-Obersturmbannführer Martin Gross's command, lead the way forward in an area of some 900 meters wide and by 1 km deep, the German panzers clashed with the Russians in a bloody panzer battle. It was Martin Gross who along with his company in three hours of closed-in battle, destroyed 90 Russian T34/76s. The immediate battlefield which consisted of a quarter square mile had been turned into a smoldering panzer cemetery. Shattered and blasted Red Army tanks littered this area. It was a wonder how Gross and his surviving panzer crews ever escaped from this dangerous and fiery inferno. For his efforts, Martin Gross was awarded on July 22nd, the coveted Knight's Cross for his heroic leadership under appalling and constant enemy fire!

On the left flank of Martin Gross were the Tiger Is of Kling's 13th Company of the Leibstandarte who were now steadily attacking the Russian defensive positions. They rolled through a grove of fir trees until suddenly, out of a nearby woods appeared a large number of Russia T34/76s in broad formation moving at top speed! This massive wave of enemy tanks broke through the German forward reconnaissance patrols and was now bearing down on the Tiger Is of Wittmann's platoon. The enemy vehicles charged forward within three hundred, two hundred, and then one hundred meters still firing their main guns wildly out of control. The German panzer crews fought like wild men to counter this awesome assault as round after round of AP shot was fired into these formations of Russian armor. The gunners of the Tiger Is at times kept their firing handles depressed so as to fire off main gun rounds as soon as the breech clang shut, so as to be able to fire as quickly as possible.

Wittmann's Tiger I crew were fighting from their vehicle with amazing speed and skill. The Russian panzers were now bunching up into individual wolf packs which made it extremely easy to obtain a kill with very little effort. If Woll did happen to miss an intended target, the main gun round would still be apt to impact into another enemy machine due to the close proximity of the enemy to each other. Wittmann's crew had now destroyed five enemy panzers, but their vehicle had taken a number of impacts from T34/76s that were firing from their left front. The massive frontal armor plate of the Tiger I again proved superior and could receive very hard punishment from the enemy.

Yet another main gun round crashed into the forward section of the hull and superstructure of Wittmann's vehicle with a loud bang! Pollmann let out a cry from below and stated that he had been wounded in the upper arm. The enemy round had not penetrated, but the resulting shock wave had cracked and thrown lethal bits of metal, bolts, and other small projectiles that had entered Wittmann's bow machine gunner/radio operator's arm. Wittmann could not halt his vehicle to give aid to Pollmann, and told him to place a medical bandage around the wound for the time being and carry on with his duties the best he could under the prevailing circumstances. Pollmann stayed very calm and applied a bandage and pulled out a white piece of cloth from his MG-34 tool kit and placed this material over the bandage so as to keep the blood flow under control. The injury was not too serious, but a lot of blood had dripped from his arm and onto the floor of his fighting compartment and looked far worse than it really could have been.

The panzer assault continued on with both sides trying to destroy the other in any way possible. Ammunition flew through the air from every conceivable angle. Panzer commanders of each side buttoned up their vehicles as they were fearful that they would be killed outright by all of the lethal pieces of steel flying through the air in all directions. Vehicles were penetrated through their engine decks, fuel tanks erupting, men on fire bailing out of their doomed and burning vehicles, only then to be caught up in the fighting using their hand held weapons taken from their vehicles while dismounting.

"Three o'clock", yelled Wittmann as he recognized the hidden T34/76 behind a large clump of bushes.

The Russian panzer was stationary, but as it started to rotate its turret, Wittmann had detected this movement and ordered Woll to engage the target. Woll reacted very swiftly and skillfully and fired his 8.8cm main gun before the enemy gunner had a chance to lock onto the mammoth German panzer. A direct hit was the result, and penetrated just under the turret of the T34/76, blowing off the turret from the chassis and ignited the on-board ammunition with total vehicle disintegration. Wittmann then ordered his driver to move the vehicle forward as soon as he was sure Woll had destroyed his target. The Tiger I lurched forward, rolled for a few meters and then halted as Wittmann saw that one of his sister vehicles was taking fire from the Ivans from three sides. This fire-fight had turned into yet another vicious panzer vs. panzer battle, and was one that seemed to take every ounce of strength from each panzer crewmember. Anti-tank guns were not present in this area, or at least they were not firing as of yet. Wittmann felt that at any moment, he and his men would hear the fierce bark of these dreaded panzer killers, and kept a wary eye open for any signs of these dangerous weapons.

Wittmann directed Woll onto his next target and with lightening speed Woll traversed the Tiger I's turret towards the enemy and fired as soon as the target came into his sight picture. The T34/76 was hit square on the driver's hatch with an AP main gun round which entered the vehicle and detonated the on-board ammunition inside the enemy machine. The resulting explosion lifted the vehicle completely off the ground and flung the remaining component parts of the machine off to one side and after which slid into a small ditch. The crew of this vehicle were not seen at all and it was presumed that they were instantly killed as the AP round had caused total fragmentation from within! Wittmann's third target was much harder to engage as its commander had quickly maneuvered his machine into a little depression and was hull down and constantly firing at the German machines milling about. The enemy panzer had fired four or five main gun rounds, which had proved to be his undoing as he should have moved his machine after firing two main gun rounds, which would have made it difficult for the German panzer crews to locate his whereabouts. After his sixth round had been fired, Wittmann guided Woll onto target and placed a well aimed AP round right through the opening of the T34/76's telescopic gun sight. Within seconds, the enemy machine was engulfed in flames and destroyed.

Inside Wittmann's Tiger I, the temperature was reaching over 100 degrees and it was not long before he and his crew was starting to suffer from partial heat exhaustion. Within the confines of his vehicle, there was the ever present smells of cordite fumes, stale air, body odor and sweat, and blood. There was very high tension in all of the crew-members voices as all five men in Wittmann's vehicle knew only too well that at any second one of Ivan's steel welcoming cards would mean their certain deaths. One wrong move in the inappropriate direction could lead them into an ambush or land-mine. Wittmann was providing quick and accurate fire commands and also guided his driver into firing positions in order for Woll to take full advantage of the terrain for his gunnery, and to bring his comrades out of what seemed to be a hopeless situation. Wittmann and his crew were practically everywhere on the blazing battlefield, and stopping just in time to destroy a threatening enemy panzer before it could caused any harm to anyone advancing with him in the assault. Fighting this type of battle took extremely brave panzer commanders, as they had to keep the enemy in sight at all times without failing to give their crewmembers correct and prompt information for the final act of blasting the enemy off the face of the earth. This fast paced battle drill was old hat to the experienced Tiger I panzer commanders of the Leibstandarte Adolf Hitler, as these men pushed their crews with constant vigor and strict control. It was very apparent that the Tiger I could be used in its proper role as a break out vehicle and storm across open terrain and take the enemy under constant fire. These machines charged forward post haste, and continued only to halt in order to fire upon the enemy vehicles pin-pointed by their panzer commanders. The rhythm of battle could not be slowed down as if Ivan was given time to regroup and defend, then the battle would transpire into a slogging match from defensive positions with heavy casualties as a direct result. Constant movement and deadly accuracy of the 8.8cm main gun was the key to success, and under no circumstances was the rhythm of battle to be broken or interrupted. One simply had to fight until the bitter end which could only mean success or death on the vast steppes of the Russian front.

The Russian tank crews were fully aware that their 7.6 cm main guns were not able to penetrate the heavily armored plated Tiger Is and in order to knockout these massive machines, they had to come into close proximity of their enemy.

The majority of times this type of maneuver was carried out by the brave Russian tankmen, they were utterly destroyed before they could close in within their killing range. One after the other, the Russian T34/76s were blown to pieces as their tank turrets were flung completely off from their superstructures as if they were some sort of child's toy. Over and over again, there were flames, smoke, twisted metal, and the horrifying screams of burning and dying tankmen laying on the armored battle field. Here the war was celebrating one of its greatest blood baths. For the men of both sides fighting on the Russian front, there were only two alternatives: kill or be killed.

As Wittmann's Tiger I roared forward attacking the Russian tanks, German aircraft appeared from nowhere and set about destroying as many Russian tanks as possible with their bombs and cannon fire. These aircraft were lead by none other then Major Hans Rudel! One after the other the Russian vehicles were attacked from the air with deadly form, and were destroyed by the skill of Rudel and his pilots with their fearsome Stukas. Russian aircraft also suddenly swooped out of the sky and a mad dog fight began overhead. The battlefield had now developed into a two dimensional death trap for Germans and Russians alike. The German Stukas were not designed as an aerial attack aircraft, so Messerschmitt Bf 109 fighters were soon called up and into the area to ward off the Russian Sturmoviks. The battle of Kursk had now reached its climax where men fought to survive and victory was now only secondary to the final outcome. Death came in many forms, and soon the entire battlefield was covered in a thick impenetrable cloud of choking dust, black smoke, and bright red and orange flames razing the countryside, which not only concealed the horrors of the modern battlefield, but also caused many men to be hidden from medical teams who were busily trying to save as many of the wounded as possible.

"We will attack along the banks of the river!" droaned the voice of Schönberger via the radio net.

"Ahead full speed!"

"Wittmann, you cover with your vehicle the right forward flank and attack anything that tries to attack us from the Northeast!"

Wittmann confirmed the order and called to his panzer commanders over his platoon net to form up. Three of his Tiger Is were soon behind him moving forward while under a light artillery barrage. His fifth vehicle finally appeared and after a few minutes all of the Tiger Is of his platoon were grouped together, but in staggered formation with their gun turrets at the 10 o'clock and 2 o'clock positions. Wittmann and his Tiger I continued ahead at the same speed, but well forward of the pack, as he wanted to make deadly sure that they were heading in the right direction to make contact with the enemy. In a short time they rolled through cornfields with hidden tank traps. All of Wittmann's vehicles managed to avoid these obstacles by swinging to their left flank and broke through this line of man made defenses without any loss to their strength. Upon reaching a rise in the terrain, Wittmann was able to make out a silver ribbon which was a small river through his vision blocks. For a few short seconds, this scene brought back his boyhood days on the farm, and the many times he and his brother swam in the nearby river for fun. He was brought back to reality when Woll spoke to his commander through the inter-con system and asked him if the enemy was in sight.

The German panzer units were now operating in and around Prokhorovka and were hoping to catch Ivan off guard and throw his time tables out of balance in order for the Germans to smash any resistance before being attacked by the massive Russian forces which never seemed to run low on manpower or tanks. If the enemy could be out-flanked and attacked from the rear it would mean the loss of many vehicles and men which would help to upset the Ivan's planning even further.

Then the unexpected happened, a radio message was broadcasted over the company radio network from the company commander. The familiar voice of SS-Hauptsturmführer Kling came over the radio network quite clearly.

"Attention! Ahead there are many enemy panzers approaching!"

One minute later, Wittmann was able to detect a large brown dust storm making its way towards his forward position. It was like a giant sand-storm that was about to smother the entire area with its light brown shroud. Wittmann gave a quick signal to his crew to stand-by for battle actions. There were over one hundred enemy vehicles of all different types now bearing down upon the small German panzer force. They were rolling at top speed and it seemed that nothing on earth could stop them short of a miracle! Wittmann immediately gave out the order to attack the enemy panzers over his radio network, and then went into his familiar combat mode in order to take on the Ivans. Every main gun round had to be a kill, or at least immobilize the enemy so as to slow down their assault.

Wittmann soon started his battlefield commands.

"Driver halt, gunner AP, fire at 1800 meters!"

All of the Tiger Is were now in a stationary position and it was quite clear that all of the panzer commanders were picking out the leading vehicles of the massed Russian steam-roller assault coming ever closer. Every gunner of each and every panzer took careful aim at one of the Red army machines and was waiting until they had entered into their 1800 mil lines in their telescopic sights. It was not long before the Ivans were within range but all were surprised when the enemy vehicles disappeared into a hidden depression in the forward terrain and sank out of sight. Wittmann was not sure when the enemy would appear again, but instructed Woll to fire at the Ivans as soon as their panzers started to climb out of their temporary cover. It was quite obvious that the hidden enemy machines would expose their thinner belly armor plate for a few short seconds and it would be up to the skill of the Tiger I gunners to take this opportunity to full measure. Woll fully understood the situation and was anxiously awaiting for Ivan's panzers to roll up from the depression. Due to the tactical situation at hand, Wittmann knew very well that the Ivans would not halt their vehicles and make a stand at the depression. No, the enemy would continue with their mission as it was now an all out battle of offensive maneuver for their forces, and the only way to be halted was to be knocked out by the German panzers awaiting their numbers.

Woll scanned the area where he thought that the enemy panzers would make an appearance. Suddenly, he saw a number of gun barrels rising out of the depression, and instantly traversed his gun turret towards them. Wittmann too, saw the Russian machines slowly coming out from cover but let Woll select his first target. Wittmann announced his fire command, Woll took careful aim, and fired his first AP main gun round at the T34/76 that was just coming into sight. The round impacted dead on, and penetrated the machine just to the righthand side of the driver's position. The enemy panzer burst into flames, stopped, and then rolled back down into the depression it had just crawled out of and blew up. Flames leaped into the air and then a second explosion filled the surrounding countryside. As all of the German heavy panzers started firing at the Russian vehicles, the sheer numbers of ensuing machines was very frightening, as the German panzer crews' fears were that they would run out of main gun ammunition before their supply units could reach their new firing locations.

The Ivans once again, had to close in for any possible kills against the heavy German panzers and could only hope for a penetration within range of 800 meters and from the flank. They pressed forward as if on a wild boar hunt and did not have time to stop for any of their comrades who were unlucky enough to be immobilized by the German panzers. To halt their vehicles to aid a comrade only meant certain death, as the German panzer gunners would instantly detect and locate any and all stationary vehicles over moving ones and destroy them without any hesitation. The Ivans came forward with determined courage that astonished the German panzer crews, and also established a certain amount of respect for the courage of these brave Russian tank crews.

Wittmann, Lötzsch, and Höflinger fired main gun round after main gun round at the solid wall of Russian T34/76s, as the enemy was now within a thousand meters. The Tiger I gunners were able to select which side of the front slope of the enemy panzer to shoot at as their excellent telescopic sights allowed this kind of deadly accuracy at this range. As soon as the surviving Russian panzers came into ranges of between 900 to 800 meters, they opened fired with their 7.6 cm main guns, but still did not stop or halt to take careful aim. They came nearer and nearer shooting while still crashing forward over rough terrain which did not seem to slow them down. It was a German panzer commander's dream as massed vehicles roared towards the intended objective, stopping to fire at the enemy, letting nothing to chance, and keeping up the pressure on the enemy. The German heavy panzers and their crews stood their ground and retaliated with the constant and sharp bark of their powerful 8.8cm main guns, even though they were extremely out numbered.

As the large contingent of Russian panzers continued to close the range towards Wittmann's platoon, he gave out additional firing instructions to Woll!

"Take the leading panzer, Bobby!" yelled Wittmann.

Woll aimed and fired.

"A direct hit!" yelled Möller, as he witnessed the destruction of yet another enemy panzer through his armored driver's vision block.

They all saw the main gun round enter the left front side of the T34/76 with a loud crack! However, the enemy machine continued to roll forward a short distance, stopped, and then blew up with a deafening bang! Wittmann had his driver move their vehicle forward a little in order to take up a better firing position. As soon as his vehicle halted, Woll fired once again and destroyed another Russian panzer before it had a chance to fire at their machine. The crew of Wittmann's vehicle now saw a panzer commander of a destroyed Russian T34/76 try and pull his wounded loader out of his burning panzer that Woll had just knocked out. He managed to extract his comrade out of his burning machine and both fell to the ground as another T34/76 near them blew up after receiving a direct hit from another Tiger I. After these two Russian tankmen landed on the ground they both sprang to their feet and ran to a nearby armored vehicle that was rolling pass them at great speed. Both of these brave men were run down by one of their own T34/76s in all of the smoke, firing, and confusion.

"Attention, it's coming your way!", warned Wittmann over the platoon radio network. The "Panzer General" whose Tiger I was to Wittmann's left-hand side was now being readily approached by a burning T34/76. Wittmann was aghast at the thought that the driver of this machine was going to commit suicide and ram Lötzsch's Tiger I as at any moment, the Russian vehicle was sure to blow sky high and take Lötzsch and his crew with it.

"Damn, damn!", yelled Lötzsch, "Driver! Move forward or they will ram us and set us alight!"

The driver of Lözsch's Tiger I rattled his machine forward to try and avoid the blazing enemy vehicle. Lötzsch ordered his driver to halt the vehicle, while his gunner took careful aim and fired at the moving target at a distance of only 80 meters. The main gun round smashed into the rounded turret and was deflected and went howling like a banshee skyward! The rolling ball of flames kept moving ever forward with Lötzsch's Tiger I crew expecting the Russian machine to blow apart at the weld seams at any second. There was not enough time to fire another main gun round at this rolling steel coffin as it was moving too fast for Lötzsch's gunner to obtain a clear sight picture. The T34/76 came closer and closer and then rammed into his vehicle before Lötzsch could instruct his driver to move the heavy panzer out of harms way. There was a loud crunching noise as the two steel machines embraced each other in this sudden death strangle hold. The flames from the burning Russian vehicle very quickly engulfed Lötzsch's Tiger I, and it was not certain if this brave and knowledgeable panzer commander would order his crew to bale out of their vehicle. Apparently, half of Lötzsch's panzer crew had lost their nerve and were now trying to escape from this most dangerous situation. He then ordered all of his crew to stay in their respective crew positions, as it was certain death for all of them if they abandoned their vehicle, as Ivan's machine guns would no doubt pick them off once they left the security of their Tiger I.

"Lötzsch, back up, my God, back up!" screamed Wittmann to his comrade over the radio.

Lötzsch did not need any further coaxing from his platoon leader, as he ordered his driver to slam the gearbox into reverse and tried to free itself from the deadly clutches of the doomed and very volatile Russian panzer. Slowly the heavy panzer inched itself rearward to free itself from the T34/76 and finally pulled itself away from its burning opponent. Five meters, ten meters, fifteen meters, and within a few more seconds, the T34/76 blew up as the on board ammunition supply detonated with an ear shattering bang! The machine disintegrated into a thousand lethal fragments and littered the surrounding area with white hot pieces of metal, glass, and human remains. Lötzsch and his crew were safe, but their panzer commander was badly shaken up with their Tiger I sustaining minor damages to the suspension and vision block devices. They indeed felt that they had been extremely lucky and had removed themselves to a safe distance in the nick of time, as if they had been any closer to the Russian machine, the ensuing shock wave and debris of the explosion would have resulted in much more serious damage to their Tiger I. No doubt, they would have had both tracks either blown off or damaged beyond repair, and serious injury to the crew. The Russian tank assaults had finally been brought to an abrupt halt after sustained and fierce fighting on both sides of the battle line. Once again, the area was littered with burning and disabled vehicles, with a number of T34/76s still putting up a gallant stand and continuing to fire at the German panzers. It had been a very long and difficult afternoon for the Tiger I panzer crews, but once again they had proved that their superior panzer training, excellent tactics and constant communications between their vehicles had halted yet another major Russian panzer thrust. Even though the Waffen-SS panzer and grenadier units had stopped the Ivans in this area of battle, the Red Army was gaining the overall advantage. Still defiant, the Tiger Is of Wittmann's platoon clung onto their current positions and waited for the Russians to regain their momentum for the next assault that was surely to come.

Wittmann and his Tiger I crew had now taken up a hull-down position and were busily taking care of their daily maintenance on their vehicle during the lull of battle. Their machine had taken a number of hits on the frontal areas, but none of these strikes had penetrated the 110mm armor plate of the gun mantelet. Wittmann took his set of Zeiss 10x50 binoculars and carefully studied the area directly in front of their position and was amazed at the horrible carnage that lay before him. There was an overwhelming number of burnt out and completely shattered Russian vehicles with a number of German panzers intermingled with them. Smoldering turrets, hulls, vehicle chassis and suspension units were strewn all over the surrounding area, plus dead crewmembers who looked like discarded rag dolls. It was a sight which defied description, which Wittmann knew would be repeated time and time again! Surely it would take nerves of steel and cunning talent to stand up to this brutal type of continuing warfare.

Suddenly, a radio message came in that "Das Reich" was being attacked on its right flank by panzers of the 2nd Red Army Tank Corps. The enemy had been able to slip through a number of openings along the front lines between the Waffen-SS Panzer Corps and the 3rd Panzer Corps under the leadership of General Breith whose Panther units were not able to break through, and were being held up by constant and aggressive Red Army opposition. The Leibstandarte Adolf Hitler and all of its heavy panzer elements would remain where they were and would ward off any additional assaults that the Ivans no doubt would throw at them. "Das Reich" would have to do the best they could under the circumstances, as it was too dangerous to pull out other Waffen-SS panzer units from the forward fighting lines.

Oberst Hermann von Oppeln-Bronikowski, commanding Panzer Regiment II (6. Panzer Division), sent Knight's Cross bearer Major Frans Bake with his panzer company and panzer grenadiers mounted in Sd.Kfz.251 armored personnel carriers (SPWs) to attack any and all isolated pockets where the Russians were holding up the German advance. Bake also had with his panzer unit a number of Beutepanzers (captured tanks) in the form of T34/76s, leading his assault force. The defending Ivans of course thought that these vehicles were part of their forces returning to their line and waved them on as these machines came into firing range. Bake's panzer crews had also painted small German Balkan crosses on these vehicle, so as to tell each other apart in the event of close in fighting. This German unit passed by a group of twenty-two Russian panzers, but were able to continue ahead as the dug-in enemy troops did not recognize the Germans in their sheep's clothing. Bake was moving in his command panzer which was a modified Panzer III (Befehlswagen) with a dummy wooden gun in place of the normal main gun armament. After his beutepanzers passed the forward Russian defensive line, his vehicle came into plain sight in front of the Red army soldiers, but they still did not fire? At any second Bake felt that the Russians would open fire after letting his vehicles entrap themselves within their respective fire zones. Still, the Ivans did not fire for some unknown reason. Their commanders apparently did not know what to do in this type of situation, or thought that perhaps friendly forces were returning with captured German equipment to be brought to the rear for study and evaluation purposes. The Ivans had certainly felt that something was fishy, but hesitated for a short time which allowed Bake and his panzer crews to make their move against the Russians with sudden and full force of their equipment.

In this moment of indecision, Major Bake made his move and sprung out from his command vehicle with a Lieutenant Zumpal following closely behind him. Each was carrying a handgrenade in each hand! They ran to the nearest two

T34/76s and jumped up and onto their rear decks and threw these explosive devices into the open turret hatches. The vehicle commanders of the Russian panzers tried in vain to close the heavy vehicle hatches, but as they were taken by total surprise, so suddenly, Bake and his fellow officer were able to knock out these two vehicles within seconds of climbing aboard these stationary machines. While continuing to run as fast as he could, Bake was able to hand another one of his handgrenades from an emptied sandbag with rope around his neck to a second officer from his unit who had just then joined the mad dash upon the Russian panzers. Grenades were thrown onto and into the nearby Russian machines, as Bake and his men made their way through the Russian positions. Soon there were a number of enemy vehicles on fire with their crews bailing out of blazing and wrecked machines. Bake and his two officers used their MP-40 machine pistols to finish off these crews as they flung themselves to the ground in and around their doomed machines. A number of the Russians in the immediate area were now firing small arms at the German panzermen, but Bake and his courageous men were able to slip away, without being harmed by this hostile fire. After this brief and deadly encounter, Bake and his two-man panzer destruction team, returned to their vehicles and were soon engaged in savage fighting from still another group of Russian armored fighting vehicles.

Suddenly, all hell broke loose. Fire continued to flash all through the early evening hours with the German panzer forces attempting to take a nearby bridge in order to push additional armored fighting vehicles into the area. Before they could storm over this vital crossing point the bridge was blown up in their faces. Shortly afterwards, came the panzer-grenadiers along side them, who began to rebuild the damaged bridge in order for the assault to continue. The next morning, Bake and his men had successfully crossed the Donetz and were standing on the north shore as the sun started to raise itself from the east. For his heroic actions under extreme and constant fire from the enemy, Major Bake would receive the 262nd Medal of Honor.

The commander of the Russian Voronezh Front with a massive force of ten corps under his command, went over to the counter-offensive and spearheaded his armored fighting vehicles against those of Army Group South on July 12, 1943. On a large plain south of Kursk, two mighty panzer armies would engage each other for the decisive battle of the entire Russian front campaign. As the Red Army tank armies converged on the German Wehrmacht as a whole, the massive blows which would be struck most violently would be against the Waffen-SS and III Corps, who would put up a bitter resistance to counter the assaults placed upon them at this time. Before the evening was able to fall on this awesome scene of brutal fighting, hundreds upon hundreds of knocked out armored fighting vehicles of both nations would foul the steppe lands where smoke from burning machines would darken the bright summer sky above. It was as though a great rain and thunderstorm was developing in this area if viewed from afar.

During this day, the German High Command reported that the Russians had lost a total of 663 tanks, and although the Russian losses far outweighed the German, the Red Army could replace their losses at an alarming rate. The German Wehrmacht on the other hand could not and did not expect their panzer production facilities to readily replace their losses; at least not in the foreseeable future. The German southern pincer began to slow down as the Ivans sent in wave after wave of T34/76 tanks which seemed to be a never ending flood. The northern arm had been stationary for days and it seemed that only by rallying the German troops to push further ahead would help to save the day. The Fourth Panzer Army had indeed established a bridgehead across the Donetz and slight gains were still being made to hold the intended objectives. Even with these small advances it was quite apparent, that "Citadel" would never attain the objectives which had been laid down by the German High Command, and by July 19th their planned attacks would be canceled. Tactical withdrawals would be handed down to field commanders to shorten the lines and to consolidate their forces.

Also during July 12th, Wittmann and his Tiger I crews encountered a large mass of Russian tanks in and around the area of Prokorovka and Teterevino which was under the control of the 181st Red Tank Brigade. There was to be no rest or sleep for the men of the Leibstandarte Adolf Hitler on this day, as their Tiger Is were ordered to advance into the wake of overwhelming waves of Russian T34/76s. The battle that developed was one that pitted well seasoned German panzer crews who on average had over two years of combat experience, against inexperienced Russian tank crews who were thrown into battle with little or no training whatsoever. Some of the T34/76 tank drivers had only eight to ten hours of instruction on the operations and functions of their vehicles. A small number of T34/76 tank crews (if they were lucky) had an experienced tank commander, but this was indeed a rarity as the vast majority of experienced armor leaders in the Russian army had been killed early on, in regards to "Operation Barbarossa." This battle was purely a conflict of numerical superiority over that of technical and tactical skill.

For Wittmann and his men, the fighting was taking its toll on their combat efficiency as they were now fighting a losing battle even if their particular area of operations was successful. Whenever the front lines were penetrated by the Tiger Is, the resulting vacuum that it created was quickly sealed by hundreds of enemy T34/76s or KV Is, which would roll in to plug the aperture that the Germans desperately needed in order to bring forward follow up troops, vehicles, and supplies. Many times these needed materials and men were ambushed by Russian tank units that appeared out of nowhere, and caused havoc on these forces trying to keep up with the heavy panzer sweeps that spearheaded the attack.

Earlier on this day, Wittmann and his platoon of Tiger Is had driven off an attack of sixty enemy panzers which had suddenly appeared on the battlefield. It was not until the panzer commanders witnessed a great cloud of thick brown dust did they have any idea that the Russians were once again throwing a massive armored armada in their direction which would call for fast thinking and very strict fire discipline. The Russians had their tanks in very close formation and it was a wonder how the following enemy tank drivers could see where they were going through this dense curtain of dust? Wittmann viewed this menacing scene with sudden fear in the pit of his stomach. If the Ivans over ran their positions there was a good chance they would be isolated from their follow-up troops and supplies. Something had to be done very quickly as if the Russians came into their prescribed firing ranges, it was quite obvious that his vehicles would not be able to withstand this kind of massive firepower at such close ranges.

Wittmann was still observing the Russian armored fighting vehicles as they charged forward with uncanny zeal. Their tank commanders were standing upright in their open turret hatches as though they had already won the war and were not too concerned about being fired on by the enemy. It had been normal practice in the past for the Ivans to button up all of their vehicle hatches when going into battle, but it was obvious that they had learned that the vehicle commander should keep his head up and out for better all around observation. It seemed clear to Wittmann that the Ivans were quite sure that the overall strength of the German forces on the Russian front had been dwindling and would now take chances like this current encounter to expose their upper body and head in order to detect the enemy more quickly. Their drivers, however, had their hatches closed, but this was normal practice, as the dust, rocks, and clumps of dirt could be easily thrown up and into their faces, which would cause them to veer off to one side or the other which would result in loss of battle formation, control, and tank gunnery.

The Ivans were now coming into range as Wittmann and his crew were in a state of high anxiety as they wanted to take on the enemy as soon as possible. Wittmann took one last look from his open turret cupola hatch and quickly closed it down for the coming battle. The loader of the Tiger I was already at his station and had thrown a main gun round into the breech and was holding a second projectile in his hands in order to keep up with Wittmann's constant fire commands. Woll was traversing the turret of the machine and was tracking the leading T34/76s and waited for his commander to provide the order to fire at the Russians. The vehicle radio system was crackling as the various panzer commanders were talking with each other and laying out numerous firing zones between the vehicles. They had also set up over-lapping fields of fire which would in fact catch a large number of Russian vehicles off guard and shatter as many as they could with their first main gun rounds.

The Ivans pressed on with their numbers and seemingly growing larger as the dark green vehicles made their way closer and closer to the German positions. The gunners of the German heavy panzers could not wait much longer as a need to depress their firing handles was ever present. The order to fire came as the tension in the German vehicles was intense with everyone posed for action!

Wittmann ordered Woll to fire at anything that was within 1800-2000 meters and was instructed to continue firing as soon as his sight picture was clear and he was sure that his shooting was steady and accurate. There was to be no margin of error as every main gun round had to rip through the armor plate of the Russian panzers and stop them dead in their tracks. As usual, Woll was very skillful in his panzer gunnery and had soon knocked out a small number of enemy machines. The leading T34/76s slowed down somewhat in order to try and locate the German positions, but could not stop for fear of being rear ended by the massive number of vehicles coming in from behind them. The Ivans were also firing their main guns on the move but this was only of limited concern to the German panzer crews.

The other Tiger Is fighting alongside Wittmann's vehicle were also making a very good account of themselves, and for a time, it seemed that the Ivans would be stopped once and for all. As the leading enemy panzers were knocked out, the surviving crews baled out and then disappeared into the rolling depressions that seemed to be everywhere in this area. The most saddening thing about this situation was that many of the Russian tank crews had nowhere to go, and were flattened to the ground by the constant firing of their own tank guns and were highly exposed to lethal pieces of white hot metal careening about the battlefield. Some of the disabled T34/76s continued to fire from their immobilized positions, but many of these doomed vehicles were rammed from behind as the second and third waves could not avoid these stationary machines, and as a result, they smashed into each other at an alarming rate. Many of these vehicles stalled out their engines and went into a frenzy trying to regain their forward momentum as outlined by their superiors. Some of the Russian machines rolled off each other as follow up vehicles continued to slam into knocked out or destroyed vehicles, whereas they would then start to climb up and over the rear decks of these vehicles and then slide off to one side or the other. The Ivans were not very successful in assaulting the German positions in this particular battle run, and after about an hour, their attack petered out until the German panzer crews could see many smoldering tank hulks laying out before their hull-down positions in some kind of gigantic panzer graveyard. Over sixty Russian T34/76s could be counted as confirmed kills.

The Tiger I crew of Michael Wittmann were all dead tired after this harsh engagement, but knew that the day was young and that Ivan would not stand idly around waiting for the German heavy panzers to counter-attack. It would be only a matter of time before Ivan would mount yet another assault on the over taxed German lines. Little time was lost as the German panzer crews checked and then rechecked their vehicles for any signs of damage that could cause a failure at a very critical moment during the next Russian attack upon their defensive positions. The panzer commanders were once again talking to each other over their platoon radios and were now discussing likely places of approach that the enemy might take in regards to their next attack. A number of the Tiger Is were repositioned into new locations in order to surprise their foe, as it was very likely that a number of their vehicle positions had been spotted and plotted, and no doubt, would result in concentrated artillery bombardment upon their positions which should be avoided at all costs.

As the German forces prepared their new and altered defensive positions, Wittmann ordered his driver to move their vehicle forward a few hundred meters and used a number of the knocked out enemy T34/76s as a sort of armored apron. His new position was an attempt to try and funnel any and all further attacks directed upon them to their left flank; thus his other Tiger I gunners could obtain flank shots while the enemy maneuvered upon Wittmann's vehicle. Time was growing short in order to position themselves properly, as the Ivans suddenly made another appearance on the battlefield and rushed forward with all of the main guns of their vehicles firing as fast as their loaders could ram home main gun rounds. All of the German Tiger Is were now returning fire at the ensuing T34/76s and a new and dangerous battle situation once again called for highly skilled and tenacious German panzer crews to stem off yet another steamroller attack by the Red army.

The circumstances were extremely tense as Wittmann held his fire as long as possible as he did not want to compromise his hidden position. A number of T34/76s rolled by his location, but it seemed that the enemy was not expecting an attack from their undefended left flank and continued to storm forward in order to take on the German heavy panzers. The fog of battle also helped to conceal Wittmann's Tiger I as he and Woll were making final adjustments in order to open up on the Russian panzers. As soon as Wittmann was sure that Woll understood his instructions, he started his fire commands which were very quick and precise. Woll had to be very careful in regards to swinging his turret to the left, as he could accidently fire into friendly forces. Wittmann was very firm in that all targets to be engaged would be fired from the 11 o'clock to the 2 o'clock position. Finally, Wittmann gave Woll the order to open fire, which resulted in his gunner knocking out a number of surprised Russian panzers with devastating effect. In mere seconds, powerful enemy panzers were turned into blazing and twisted wrecks as the Ivans had been caught in the German panzer trap. At this close range, one of Wittmann's AP main gun rounds penetrated the left-hand side of one T34/76 and then exited out the right side, and then smashed into another vehicle of the same type that was running alongside the first one. The second vehicle that was hit by this projectile came to a sudden halt with the round penetrating the engine compartment.

As soon as Wittmann had started to fire at the enemy, many T34/76s immediately turned to their left to fire at him. Once these machines had performed this tragic maneuver, the remainder of Wittmann's Tiger Is had perfect flank shots whereupon all of these machines were utterly destroyed within a minute and a half. This trap was also two-fold as once the Ivans turned their vehicles to the left, this caused a disruption in their flow of fire and movement which caused them to bunch up even further and then petered their attack out once again. Total mayhem followed, as the Russian tank commanders tried to salvage the situation, but in the end, their machines were all torched by well placed 8.8cm AP main gun rounds and set ablaze. The surviving Russian tankmen abandoned their vehicles and slipped back to their own lines while evading MG-34 machine gun fire from all available German vehicles.

The area in front of the German defensive positions was now another wasteland of dead and burning enemy panzers, with over fifty vehicles on fire which were billowing out huge black clouds of thick and choking smoke. The enemy attack had been smashed once again by the fierce determination of the German panzermen and all could be proud of their battlefield tactics and cunning. A small number of surviving T34/76s were still charging around within a circle of knocked out vehicles, but were hopelessly trapped within these confines. In utter desperation these vehicles smashed into dead tanks trying to push them aside, but it was obvious that they were not going to succeed. A few main gun rounds were fired at Wittmann's platoon by these vehicles which started a new game of hide and seek among the dead tanks. However, they were soon picked off by the expert Tiger I gunners who were leading the Russian machines through their telescopic sights and would ambush these vehicles as soon as they presented themselves in between dead panzers that they were also using as added protection.

This day had been very victorious for Wittmann and his panzer crews and could be very proud of their efforts in the face of overwhelming numbers of Russian panzers being thrown at their small but powerful panzer group.

For the next two days and nights, the German forces did not conduct any further assaults, but simply held the line against any further attacks by the Red army.

The German Wehrmacht and the Waffen-SS as a whole had lost the battle for the Russian front. Army Group South had lost a total of some 20,700 men (3,300 of whom were killed in actual combat). Army Group Center's 9th Army losses were over 10,000 men in only two days of fighting. German infantry divisions had been reduced to levels of regimental size and Panzer divisions to that of only armored battalions. (According to German sources: 30 German divisions, including 7 armored divisions were routed, with the Germans losing some 500,000 men; 1500 panzers, and 3000 guns, and over 3700 aircraft). The recorded strength of the SS Panzer Corps on July 16th was thirty badly battered Panzer VIs (Tiger Is) sixty-nine Panzer IVs, eighty Panzer IIIs, and four Panzer IIs. There were only twenty command vehicles left and in addition to this, the Germans had at their disposal, eleven captured T34/76s and sixty-four self-propelled guns. The Russians had run rampart over the German wind-storm and had now gained complete control over the handling of military affairs on the Russian front and would never lose it. The Russians had paid a high price indeed for these gains over the German Wehrmacht and Waffen-SS, as it lost 2918 tanks, 190 guns, and 33,000 prisoners. It will never be known how many Russian soldiers were killed on their home soil during this time period.

The Red Army lost no time in renewing the attack on July 20th, as they threw in attacks against the Bryansk-Orel railway. The Leibstandarte Adolf Hitler, who were reorganizing and refitting in the nearby area of Isyum, were soon back to the front line fighting along the Mius river line. The Leibstandarte was not to fight much longer on the Russian front for they were ordered on August 3rd to Italy where the Fascist regime of Benito Mussolini had collapsed completely as the result of the Allied invasion of Sicily occurring during this time-frame. The German High Command felt that it would take an experienced, tough, elite and politically reliable German division to be sent to Italy to prevent the entire peninsula from falling into the hands of the western Allies. Upon orders from Hitler himself, he decided that his Leibstandarte would be the selected German division that contained the required potential and combat experience to halt the Allies before they could obtain a foot-hold on Italian territory. During the next three months, the men of the Leibstandarte Adolf Hitler, however, spent the majority of their active duty time, as occupational forces engaged, from time to time, in hard and bitter anti-partisan operations in Northern Italy and Slovenia.

Chapter XI

FINAL PANZER BATTLES ON THE EASTERN FRONT

November 7, 1943 – March 1, 1944

With the failure of Operation "Citadel", the German Wehrmacht and Waffen-SS units as a whole on the Russian front were now the receiving end of relentless and brutal Red Army assaults, and indeed had now become the anvil instead of the proverbial hammer in regards to the bitter fighting that was now threatening to drive the German forces ever westward. The German military forces were now on the defensive mode with every town, village, and hamlet that had been captured in previous battles, now being fought for with tooth and nail in order to just hold and consolidate the thinning defensive lines. Time and time again the Ivans threw in massive tank assaults which in the end were too overpowering and once again the German forces had to retreat to the West and prepare additional defensive positions. Towns and major roadways that were once great milestones on the advance of the German earlier victories, were now only symbols of defeat for the retreating Germans.

On paper, the strength of forty-two German divisions under Army Group South did not in any way reflect the true situation when viewed at the tactical levels. If one was to study the T O & E's (Table of Organization & Equipment or German Wehrmacht K.St.N./K.A.N.) with a critical eye, one would have found that the infantry components of most units was less than one sixth of the standard establishment, and for some of them the divisional strengths in rifle companies, there was only a mere thousand weapons available. In regards to armored fighting vehicles, the Army Groups were grossly understrength for they had a total of only 83 panzers, and 98 self-propelled guns under their commands at any one time during this period. The Red Army on the other hand could field sufficient infantry, tank, and motorized and cavalry corps to give a staggering majority of 7:1 overall, and in selected sectors of the front, a 40:1 superiority. Under these conditions, the German military forces were in a very dangerous state of affairs and would need every available fighting machine to help to force back the ever surmounting Red Army Juggernaut.

Totally confidant in their vast and prevailing superiority, the Red Army was now repeating summer type offensive moves during the strategic plan of winter 1943 with tremendous results. The Russians continued to pour men and materials into battle sectors and if a temporary set back occurred and held up the advance, Russian Higher Command would then order and put in another battle group to bolster the initial assaulting forces. These tactics worked very well for the Red Army as if the first line of attack was slowed down or weakened by a determined German defensive perimeter, the second attacking line would merge with the first and so on. As a result, there would be established a solid wall of Russian aggression which at times would cover three or four kilometers in depth, and one or two kilometers in width. Against these numerical odds, the defending German forces could never hope to counter this raising tide of Russian men and weapons.

Rapid Red Army advances crushed the German defenses in and around Kharkov and captured the city, and only after a short halt, due to logistical difficulties, the Russian steamroller continued to advance until the last three months of 1943. As a result of these advances Melitopol, Saporzhe, and Kiev were to fall back into the hands of the Red Army once and for all. The Red Army advances swept on and it seemed that the total destruction of Army Group South was all but over at this moment in time. The Russian tactics were applied in every form, whether if it was to out-flank, by-pass, or totally ignore the German military forces it did not matter! The Red Army's plan was to eradicate everything in its path and if some isolated German troops were bypassed. They would soon be caught up in the follow-up waves of enemy troops ever pressing forward. The situation at hand was a very simple equation: if one did manage to survive the hordes of advancing Russian panzers, infantry assaults, Katiusza and artillery bombardments, any German soldier who was drawn into these Russian tactical vacuums, had little or no chance of any type of escape to the west.

It was against this dreary background of events that the Leibstandarte Adolf Hitler, together with other experienced Waffen-SS divisions, were recalled back to the Russian front on November 7, 1943. Immediate preparations were made to transfer these elite units back to the Eastern front where order, counter-order, and then constant disorder plagued the Waffen-SS Panzer Divisions as desperate measures had to be introduced in order to rush these badly needed and highly trained units to the front lines as fast as humanly possible. Drastic disarray and confusion had the Waffen-SS Panzer Divisions struggling to regroup and assemble themselves and once en route, units which had been detrained in the First Army Sector, were then quickly transferred to XXXXVIII Corps of the Fourth Panzer Army. This battle group was positioned in an arch south of Kiev and the Leibstandarte Adolf Hitler, one of the seven divisions of the XXXXVIII Corps, took up a defensive posture between the right and center Corps. The arrival of the Leibstandarte brought with it a gleam of new hope and many front line infantrymen as well as Wehrmacht panzer crews felt that they could instill a ray of new life under the harsh conditions they have been subjected to for so many months.

With the Leibstandarte Adolf Hitler fully reequipped, and operating with a great deal of tactical experience under their belts, entered combat for the third time on the Eastern front, the Wehrmacht units which had been holding the forward defensive lines for weeks without any signs of relief, openly threw up a loud cheer as the Leibstandarte and other Waffen-SS units arrived and took up their new attack positions.

The Fourth Panzer Army's first and most important task was to strengthen the Army Group's northern sector and then seal the opening in the line and attack the flank of the Thirty Eighth Red Army by assaulting with all speed towards Zhitomir. Its final objective was to attack and completely smash the Russian's bridgehead on the west bank of the Dnieper and quickly consolidate its forces whereupon it would force a river crossing with all speed.

From Fastov, the XXXXVIII Corps was to roll north-westward and capture Zhitomir and then severe the Russian supply route and rail connections between Kiev and Zhitomir. These operations were vital, as if the Russians could not replace their losses at a steady pace, it did not matter how many men and tanks they had in reserve as this time, as it was up to the XXXXVIII Corps to stop the flow of Russian supplies and materials from safely reaching the front lines. The men of the Leibstandarte Adolf Hitler were very eager to fight the Ivans at their own game once again, as the Leibstandarte was to be the leading assault division and was to roll northwards with the Army's 1st Panzer Division on its left flank.

On November 13th, the German attack opened upon the Red Army, but not all the German divisions had yet to arrive on the battlefield. The attack was not canceled and the missing elements were put straight into combat as soon as they had reached their pre-planned jumping-off positions. The Leibstandarte was ordered to form two battle groups. The left arm was to maneuver via Rogosna, cross over the Kamenka and Unova rivers, and slice its way through the surrounding area and cut-off the Fastov-Brodel railway line due south of Mochnachka. The right-hand battle group was to spearhead north-eastward, pass Pistachki, assault and capture Trylissi, then establish bridgeheads across the Kamenka river, roll forward and capture Fastov. After these accomplishments, both battle groups then halted in order to drive back the Ivan's counterattacks in the Mochnachka area while the other units guarded the flank northeast of Komuty as the 1st, 7th, and 8th Panzer Divisions fought an extremely bloody battle at Zhitomir, which finally fell to their numbers on November 19th. The Leibstandarte then directed itself east towards Brusilov, a town north-east of Fastov. It was in this area of operations that the first major offensive panzer battles were to be fought. Michael Wittmann and his panzer crews would be operating in this area of combat and would continue to lead many panzer assaults to successful conclusions in the face of overwhelming odds against the Red Army.

The German panzer crews of the Leibstandarte Adolf Hitler were now fighting the Russians with every ounce of strength that they had left in their now tired bodies. The panzer crews had been fighting constantly for a week in and around Fastov, and had smashed many Russian armored assaults that had been thrown against them which had reduced their numbers somewhat but the tenacity of the Waffen-SS continued to hold the line. Sheer courage and determination in the shadow of death seemed to spur on the men of Wittmann's unit, but they all knew that they could not hold the front lines unless they continued to receive fresh supplies and highly needed ammunition and fuel, which was truly their life blood. Food was the last thing on the minds of the men at the front, as survival was the most important aspect concerning all who found themselves fighting on the Eastern front.

On the morning of November 21, 1943, Michael Wittmann and his panzer crews of the 13th Company were involved in a heated and swift fire-fight near Brusilov, which was north-east of Fastov. Their Tiger I company ran into a large force of T34/76s which had sparked off an instant panzer charge which took the Ivans by total surprise. Wittmann and Bobby Woll were being very careful during this battle in regards to not using up too much ammunition as they were now low on 8.8cm main gun rounds and fuel. As soon as the fighting commenced, Wittmann ordered his gunner not to fire the main gun until he was absolutely sure that he could score and obtain a kill. Woll as always, was very eager to take on the Ivans and was ready for action! Wittmann knew that he would have to restrain his gunner, as if they ran out of main gun ammunition in the middle of an engagement, it would surely mean their deaths. The Ivans were trying to take the advantage of their superior numbers once again and continued to release large numbers of T34/76s into the sight pictures of every German armored fighting vehicle on the forward lines.

The order was given out over the radio net for the Tiger I commanders to commence firing at the Ivans. As soon as the command to fire was announced, all vehicles started to disembowel any enemy panzers that came into their respective kill zones. Even before Wittmann selected his first target, there was already many T34/76s burning in the fields that lay before him. The other Tiger I panzer commanders had not wasted any time in taking out the enemy machines which did not surprise this very experienced panzer leader in the least. Some of Wittmann's other vehicles were not as low on ammunition and fuel as he, so opened fired as soon as they could witness the Russian panzers through their optical sighting equipment.

At last, Wittmann felt that the time was appropriate to allow Woll to open fire on the approaching T34/76s. He gave his first fire command to his gunner who was already traversing the turret of their vehicle in order to scan the immediate area for targets of opportunity. As Wittmann was completing this order Woll was making final adjustments and pressed the firing handle on his elevating handwheel. Nothing happened? The 8.8cm main gun round was defective!

Wittmann yelled to his loader to eject the faulty projectile, but found that Berges was already busy pulling the breech handle back in order to clear the main gun. After a few seconds, which seemed like an hour, Wittmann heard the 8.8cm gun breech clang shut, as a second AP round had been rammed home and ready to fire. Instead of issuing another fire command, Wittmann announced "Fire" to his tense and anxious gunner. Woll had already locked onto the first target Wittmann had selected and continued to track the enemy while the loader was placing the new main gun round into the breech. With a great crack, the main gun round flew out and slammed into the frontal slope of the rampaging enemy machine with a loud bang! The explosion that resulted from the projectile passing into and through the vehicle's hull was deafening. Bits of white hot metal were flying about the air as this Russian vehicle continued to roll forward until blowing itself apart at the weld seams after its on-board ammunition ignited! The battle was now becoming extremely dangerous for the German defensive lines as the Russian tankmen were trying to close in on the Tiger Is. The German panzer commanders knew that if they allowed the Ivans to intermingle with their limited forces they would lose complete control of the engagement. Round after round of main gun ammunition was fired at the Russian panzers, but ever forward they came with full fury!

By this time Wittmann was very low on ammunition and it was imperative that his vehicle be returned to a rear area supply point. The battle was developing into a fierce struggle for control of the area which prevented him from disengaging from the fire fight. A number of deadly anti-tank guns suddenly opened up on the German forces as they had been hidden and highly camouflaged and had not been used until the Ivans saw that the German machines were being moved forward. Indeed, a small number of the Tiger Is had pulled forward in a show of force that was hoped to ward off the advancing waves of Russian armor. As soon as this was accomplished, the sharp bark of the Ivan's anti-tank guns could be heard. One of these dreaded weapons was now firing at Wittmann's vehicle from his right flank. There was no time to lose as this anti-tank weapon had to be eliminated as soon as possible.

Wittmann and his supply of ammunition was now down to eight main gun rounds of AP and it was quite clear that Woll would have to obtain first round hits in order to survive. His commander provided him with a fire command to take out the anti-tank gun that had by this time fired two rounds at their vehicle. Woll fired his weapon and destroyed this gun within seconds. After this firing engagement, a number of additional anti-tank guns were located about five hundred meters to their left with Wittmann ordering his gunner to take them under his fire. Woll was given his instructions and after making his final lay to target, fired off a main gun round and destroyed the second anti-tank gun and crew. The next target was not as easy to detect, but his commander was able to make out the gun crew through his high powered binoculars now running back and forth to their ammunition carrier behind their weapon. This anti-tank gun and ammunition carrier were expertly camouflaged, but the Ivans had given away their concealed position due only to their movements to rearm their weapon. Wittmann directed Woll onto this target, announced his fire command, and at the same instance this anti-tank gun fired at their Tiger I. There was a loud thud against the frontal armor plate of Wittmann's machine, but the enemy round failed to penetrate. Woll immediately returned fire and saw his AP round disappear into a thick cloud of snow that had been kicked up by the enemy weapon. There was so much of this obscuration from both weapons being fired that both Wittmann and Woll were not sure whether they had destroyed their intended target. Wittmann had not heard Woll's 8.8cm main gun round impact into the target whereas normally this sound would have echoed back after a direct hit was scored. With quick thinking on his part, he issued another fire command to his gunner. With only four main gun rounds left on-board their vehicle, Wittmann and his entire crew were very tense, as they knew that they had to extract themselves from the battlefield as quickly as possible to rearm their machine, but did not want to leave their comrades who needed every available Tiger I they could muster against the advancing Russians. Wittmann ordered Woll to continue to fire at the anti-tank guns in order to silence this menace before they departed. Woll readjusted his sights and fired another AP round at the enemy weapon. This time the shot was low, but skidded on the ground in front of the enemy gun position and crashed into the gun shield and destroyed the target. Having three AP rounds left, Wittmann and Woll located another three anti-tank guns and concentrated well aimed main gun rounds upon these threats before leaving the area. After roughly ten minutes, they had knocked out all of these weapons and then withdrew.

It was very hard for Wittmann to pull his Tiger I out from the line, but he knew that his comrades would understand his predicament. It would be foolish and dangerous to remain where he was without proper ammunition supply and no doubt he would be knocked out or overrun by the enemy. Slowly the din of battle grew fainter and fainter as Wittmann and his crew made their way back to their re-supply point. This battle had taken a great deal out of him and his men as they had been fighting extremely hard in order to hold back the Russians and their mass attacks. Once they reached their supply point, Wittmann ordered his crew to up load their machine as fast as humanly possible with main gun ammunition, fuel, and as much MG-34 belted rounds that they could possible stow inside their fighting compartments.

While his Panzer crew were busy loading their vehicle with ammunition and fuel, Wittmann directed himself to their company's cook truck and obtained some hot food for his men, who had not eaten anything solid for days. The food was a pleasant surprise for his crew, but they were more interested in feeding main gun grounds and fuel into their armored fighting vehicle. After they had finished loading up their vehicle did they care to eat any type of food placed before them. Wittmann finally gave a shout to his men, and they were once again back on their way to the front line fighting which could be heard in the distant.

No sooner had Wittmann and his crew reentered the battlefield area, they were once again thrown into the middle of a severe fire-fight with the enemy. Wittmann was hell bent for leather as he ordered his crew into battle stations as soon as he could see the muzzle flashes of their comrades firing at the Ivans as they continued to pour men and Panzers into the battle in and around Brusilov. The German lines had fallen back a few hundred meters and it was all that the German forces could do to halt the rampaging Russians as they stormed forward with fierce determination and drive.

Michael Wittmann stood up in his open turret hatch as he was now searching for a small grove of trees southeast of Brusilov. The day before he had studied the area carefully on his map and was quite sure that the enemy would carefully and skillfully conceal their deadly anti-tank guns in this sector of operations. Before they were able to return to their comrades fighting on the front lines, they would have to travel along a stream until they could return to their new positions. They rolled forward for about another 800 meters towards the grove of trees when the bark of an enemy anti-tank gun let out a sharp crack! The first anti-tank round came very close to Wittmann's vehicle which threw up large clumps of dirt, snow, and small rocks which rained down upon his head and upper torso. He did not receive any injury by this fall-out, but ordered his driver to take evasive actions and to move their vehicle out of line with the enemy weapon. As soon as Wittmann was sure that his vehicle was out of immediate danger, he ordered his vehicle to halt as he wanted to see if he could locate the enemy menace from his present position. The hidden anti-tank gun was not to be seen, as Wittmann and Woll scanned the area for a few minutes but could detect nothing! It seemed strange to them both that the Ivans did not fire another round at their stationary vehicle, but assumed that they were out of their line of sight or that they too were low on ammunition and had disengaged themselves from the surrounding area, or perhaps had simply abandoned their emplaced weapon and fled on foot. At any second, Wittmann was fearful that his vehicle would be taken under fire, and destroyed. It was not to be, as the highly experienced panzer commander did not hesitate any longer and ordered his driver to advance towards his platoon, which desperately needed their assistance.

Wittmann's Tiger I crashed forward at top speed and was soon back with his 2nd Company who were planning their next steps in halting the enemy's advances. For a few short minutes the Russians had fallen back as they were now regrouping for yet another assault on the thinly held German defensive lines. After a short conference, the panzer commanders decided to pull back into the trees that Wittmann had come through on his return. The idea was to hide in this woodland and let the Ivans come forward and take them out one by one. This time the Ivans would not have a clear picture of the locations of the German heavy panzers whatsoever. The Tiger Is were positioned into the tree line with only their main guns protruding out from the overhanging tree boughs. The shadows from these trees offered complete concealment, as the Ivans would not be able to pin-point the German panzers until it was much too late. It was also very apparent that the German machines would be able to knock out a large number of Russian panzers before they were able to come even close enough to insure any first round hits as the fields of fire were in the German's favor.

As predicted, the Ivans came rushing forward in their massive battle formations with many T34/76s leading the way. For a short time, the Russian tank commanders stood up in their opened hatches as they felt that the German machines had turned tail and had retreated from the scene. Not until they came into firing range of the Tiger Is, did they realize that they had taken the bait the German panzer commanders had set for them. With uncanny skill, Wittmann and his platoon of vehicles opened fired with such resounding force, that the leading T34/76s stopped dead in their tracks, as five enemy panzers burst open into flames after being hit and penetrated by the German high velocity 8.8cm AP rounds.

The Ivans started to immediately open fire with all of their main guns, but it was soon appreciated by the German panzer crews that they were firing madly in all directions in order to try and silence the German vehicles. Another volley was fired by Wittmann's platoon under his control, and again, five more T34/76s were blown apart by the powerful main guns of his vehicles. There was a cry from one of the panzer commanders over the radio net, that now was the time to pull out from their concealed positions, and to mix it up with the Ivans. The order was given out to all panzer commanders!

"Forward and engage the enemy panzers!", stated Kling.

In staggered formation, the Tiger Is of the first and second platoons roared forward out from the tree line and headed towards the confused and dazed Russian panzers. The enemy was in such sheer panic, that most of the surviving T34/76s backed up into each other and many were now immobilized on the open battlefield with stalled engines, which were easy targets for the Tiger I crews under Wittmann's leadership. A number of Russian tanks made a stand and started to fight it out with the advancing German machines as round after round was fired at the Tiger Is, but it was not too long before a number of these main gun rounds found their mark. The "Panzer General's" Tiger I was hit and penetrated by a lucky shot at 900 meters. Lötzsch's driver was killed instantly, and Aberhardt, his radio operator bow-machine gunner had his left hand ripped off in the process. Aberhardt went into violent contortions as Lötzsch and the rest of his panzer crew tried to remove this crewmember from their machine. It was a very difficult situation as Aberhardt was bleeding profusely and continued to thrash around in his seat uncontrollably, which caused even more injury to his body and head. This brave action was being performed under direct fire and at great risk to Lötzsch and his men. While this action was beingconducted, the rest of the Tiger Is were moved forward in order to draw fire away from his vehicle. Aberhardt was finally removed from his crew position and placed behind his vehicle until a medical team could arrive safely on the scene and attend to his wounds.

A desperate situation soon developed as Ivan started to fire into and around Lötzsch's vehicle. Wittmann could hear the cry for help from his comrades via the radio net and immediately started to commit his crew and vehicle to provide suppressive fire in order to help the "Panzer General"! Wittmann ordered his driver to stop the vehicle and then to reverse the machine into a hide position while Woll traversed the heavy turret to the 7 o'clock position and fired at the T34/76s that was harassing Lötzsch and his vehicle. Within one minute, Woll had shot up two of the T34/76s that had been supporting the T34/76 that had placed the lucky round into Lötzsch's Tiger I. Wittmann turned around while standing upright in his cupola and suddenly saw another enemy panzer that had come out of nowhere and was now heading directly towards his vehicle. The Russian machine was buttoned up and its main gun started to fire just as Wittmann ducked down and into the safety of his armored mount. The first two enemy main gun rounds went right over the top of his cupola and he could feel the air being sucked out from his position which left him somewhat dazed for a few moments. Had he remained standing upright for a few more seconds, he most likely would have been decapitated. He then heard the enemy rounds slam into the tree line a few hundred meters to his rear, and then announced his next fire command to his gunner. Woll quickly went into action as he carefully aimed and laid his 8.8cm main gun and placed an AP round square into the base of the turret of the nearest T34/76. The impact of this round rocked the turret of the enemy panzer backwards, putting it out of action by jamming the traversing gear. The Russian machine however, continued to roll towards Wittmann's vehicle and smashed into the left-hand side of his machine. Wittmann reacted with lightening speed and grabbed the MP-40 machine pistole from its holder, loaded it, charged the weapon, and jumped up through his open commander's hatch and immediately began to fire at the enemy panzer crew, who were by now climbing out of their doomed vehicle heavily armed with automatic weapons. Wittmann was fearful that the enemy panzer crew would try and board his machine and throw a hand-grenade into his vehicle, or try and fire one of their weapons into the interior of his turret. Wittmann killed two of the Ivans outright, but one of the enemy panzer crewmembers fired a hand pistole at him with the bullet tearing into the skin of his chin . This brave panzer commander continued to do away with this individual, and after doing so, ordered his driver to pull away from the Russian vehicle as it no doubt would blow up in their faces at any second. As soon as his driver reversed out of the clutches of the enemy panzer, Wittmann dropped down into his cupola so Woll could look at and attend to his facial injury. The bleeding was very heavy, but Woll could see that the bullet had hit Wittmann from the side and had penetrated the outer fleshy part of his chin and passed cleanly through and out. It looked worst than it actually was, and with that, Woll stated to his commander after placing a bandage on his wound, that he would have a permanent and handsome scar to remind him of his close encounter with Ivan!

The battle continued on as Wittmann was now even more determined to destroy as many T34/76s as he and his crew could after having his vehicle rammed by Ivan and being shot at and wounded at very close range. Wendorff's voice suddenly came in over the radio net and informed Wittmann that he had also been able to bring his panzer to the fire-fight from the same tree line that he had used earlier. Then to the right flank, appeared Heinz Kling who was also a welcome sight with his two accompanying Tiger Is that rolled forward and attacked the Ivans as Wittmann and his platoon pulled forward to resume the advance. The enemy panzers were now wildly mixed up as they started to disengage from the rest of the battlefield. The fourth and fifth waves of the Russian panzers were still firing and did not realize that they were aiming at their own vehicles as the very poor visibility from all of the dirt and snow thrown up and into the air caused many Russian tank gunners to be very trigger happy and destroyed a small number of their own! Wittmann and his platoon witnessed this carnage and ordered his vehicles to slow down in order to keep themselves out of this maelstrom as long as possible. The Ivans finally stopped firing at each other and retreated a few thousand meters to the east until they could start to regroup themselves and initiate another attack.

The German Tiger I commanders were now very busy pulling up their vehicles to the nearest low laying terrain feature to obtain as much concealment as possible. The radio net was now very active as the German panzer force was making yet another plan to take on the next wave of Russian panzers that would surely come at anytime. Wittmann had an idea to out maneuver the Ivans once again during their next charge forward and dismounted from his vehicle and ran over to Kling's vehicle and outlined his plan. He would travel with his five vehicles along the edge of the nearby stream and begin firing upon the enemy panzers as soon as they made their next appearance from their left flank. Kling agreed and stated that he and Wendorff's machine would take on the Ivans head-on and try and draw their fire while Wittmann's platoon ripped them apart from his new positions.

With as few words as possible, Wittmann advised the other four panzer commanders of his plan, and what he expected of them and then asked if there were any questions. It was all very clear what they were to do, were dismissed, and all concerned scrambled back into their vehicles and waited for the order to roll forward and into their ambush positions. Wittmann figured that the Ivans would not expect a flanking maneuver as they knew that the German forces were very low in regards to numbers of heavy panzers. Now that Kling had arrived on the scene, the Ivans would have no idea that he and his platoon had taken the place of Wittmann's vehicles who were at this time taking up their new positions to smash the Russians during their next battle run. All was ready, Wittmann and Woll picked out firing areas which they felt the Ivans would storm over and designated overlapping zones of fire for each vehicle. Woll could commence firing as soon as the Russians started their advance upon Kling's and Wendorff's positions.

It was not long before Wittmann could hear the roar of panzer engines and the muffled clanking sounds of the enemy T34/76s as they move through the snow covered terrain features. Again, great clouds of snow were to be seen before the Ivans could be observed. Wittmann radioed Kling just to make sure that his company commander was aware of the ensuing enemy armored fighting machines and to be on the lookout. Wittmann started to count the enemy machines through his high powered binoculars and detected eleven T34/76s leading the pack with many others further back moving up at great speed. Woll was instructed to take out the leading vehicles, but was also warned to fire at any enemy vehicles that would pose any danger to Kling's and Wendroff's Tiger Is. The T34/76s were now 1200 meters away when Wittmann gave the order to open fire.

"Fire!", came the order from Wittmann over the platoon radio net.

All five Tiger Is cut loose with AP main gun rounds with the leading Russian vehicle being penetrated, and set ablaze. As these were flank shots, which the Ivans had not expected, they immediately slowed down their vehicles with their turret gunners desperately traversing their main guns in all directions trying to locate the source of the fire that was knocking out their comrades. Five T34/76s were now burning very violently with their crews bailing out onto the bare snow fields, as there was no cover for hundreds of meters in any direction. The surviving Russian panzer crews ran back from the same direction they had come from, and had it not been for the sheer numbers of enemy panzers on the battlefield, these dismounted panzer crews would have been gunned down by the MG-34s mounted in the German vehicles.

Wittmann instead, ordered all of his panzer commanders to concentrate only on the T34/76s as they posed the most danger at this point in time. They did not have time to try and take out the fleeing Russian tankmen as they offered little threat to the German panzer force. Another volley from the Tiger Is slammed into targets and four more T34/76s were now burning. One machine turned slowly and tried to escape from being hit, but was spotted by one of Wittmann's vehicles and was destroyed by placing a well placed main gun round into the engine compartment, shattering the entire rear portion of the machine. The follow-up T34/76s were now firing at Wittmann's platoon as they had now been pinpointed as they did not have time to change positions after firing one or two main gun rounds. The T34/76s were now turning to their left towards Wittmann's platoon, and by doing so, now offered excellent flank shots to Kling and Wendorff. They opened fired within seconds after the Ivans made yet another blunder and with deadly accuracy, were utterly destroyed by these two superb panzer commanders.

The Russians were now in such a state of massed confusion due to the

German double flanking posture that they were not too sure which way to move once Kling and Wendorff opened fired at their numbers. Some of the enemy machines veered off to the left and stopped, while others halted their vehicles and just fired away at anything that they thought was the enemy. The momentum of the attack suddenly slowed down as the Russians were once again halted in their tracks. All eleven of the T34/76s were burning on the battlefield with the second wave being blown to bits and stopped not fifty meters from the first wave. This type of total destruction sent a ripple of great enthusiasm through out the elated but exhausted panzer crews under the divided leadership of Kling and Wittmann.

After this battle petered out, Wittmann and his crew were credited with ten destroyed T34/76s, and seven anti-tank guns. The crew of this very talented panzer commander felt that nothing could stop them, and they could out fight, out maneuver, and out gun their opponents at their own game, even if they were outnumbered five to one. The tenacity of the Waffen-SS was second to none, but as it turned out, the German forces as a whole, could not break into Brusilov as the majority of hot-spots in and around this city had fallen into the hands of the Red Army, as they had now taken an extremely strong stand and withstood additional and highly determined attacks from the German forces operating in this area. As evening approached, the men of Wittmann's platoon, along with Wendorff's and Kling's vehicles found themselves held up in a small village named Chomutets. All of the men involved were completely exhausted and very discouraged at this time with the overall tactical set backs, as a few hours earlier they had felt that the Ivans were on the run due to the superior tactics employed by the Waffen-SS. The German forces on the Russian front were now fighting a losing battle of numerical supremacy which in the end would surely mean their destruction and loss of all gains of territory obtained up to this point in time.

Through the efforts of a combined assault, the Leibstandarte Adolf Hitler reached the Kiev-Zhitomir highway network. Brusilov finally fell to the Waffen-SS after very bitter fighting and the advance continued as a single column until needed as a fire brigade once again to help to break up any further Russian counter-attacks. The Leibstandarte then travelled from Mochnachka and through wooded country of that sector, forded the Irpen waterway and arrived at Divin by November 26th. The advanced units then took hull-down defensive positions in and around Vilshke. Both of these groups encountered heavy Russian cavalry, infantry, and aggressive armored attacks, but were able to hold the line with many men killed and injured. The Russian forces broke under the constant pressure of fresh, abundantly equipped, elite German troops of the Waffen-SS and were completely dumb-founded as a result of these top quality troops on the field of battle. The Russian High Command responded very quickly and firmly by establishing a bridgehead at Cherkassy and committed the 1st, 5th, and 8th Guards Tank Corp against XXXXVIII Corps. The overall German plan was to encircle and wipe-out the Russian unit but the Leibstandarte attack which had been on for only a few hours, was smashed with very heavy losses and the other divisions of the Corps had little if any success against the strongly emplaced Red Army forces. Highly confused and extremely bitter fighting ensued, but slowly the German forces were ground to a dead stop; their years of front line armored warfare and great elan in the face of the enemy was not enough to halt the advancing Russian hordes which were now growing in intensity with swift and determined vigor all across the Eastern front.

SS-Sturmbannführer Joachim Peiper, was now commanding the Leibstandarte Adolf Hitler's SS Panzer Regiment. His forces were able to crash through the Russian encirclement, and there-upon captured the Staffs of four enemy divisions. He then proceeded to make an incredible twenty-six mile deep penetration into enemy held territory and to overrun artillery and Pak fronts. The front line Russian soldier was not expecting anything of this nature but it was perfectly clear that if a strong and determined force of panzers were given the opportunity to spearhead an assault of this type, the momentum of such a maneuver was seldom repelled. The Ivans could not react quickly enough to successfully halt such an attack until given direct guidance from above and this always took precious time in order to gather all of the pertinent facts in order to react accordingly. After Peiper's tally was added up in regards to this attack, it was recorded that he and his fire brigade destroyed over one hundred enemy panzers, as well as seventy-six anti-tank guns and other valuable enemy machines. Two spearheads of the 1st Panzer Divisions, that of the German Wehrmacht and Waffen-SS, maneuvered behind the Russians and although many Ivans fought their way out of this pincer movement, a total of 153 panzers, 70 pieces of artillery, and 250 anti-tank guns were destroyed, plus thousands of Red Army prisoners were marched into German POW camps. This token of German success boasted the front line troop's morale, as it was now felt that the German military forces were onto a new level of success in pushing back the Red Army, and would once again regain the momentum of this climatic struggle to overpower the Russians as they had done during the summer months of 1941.

The Red Army continued to pour in new troops to reinforce and hold the Kiev road with the counterattacks against the advancing German forces becoming even more stubborn and comprehensive as the heavy panzer thrusts were slowed down and then halted once again. It was becoming blatantly clear that the German High Command's planned attack had been hesitantly prepared and the Dnieper bridgehead could never be retaken again. On November 23rd, an unexpected thaw came as a result of warm weather and transformed the Russian roads into bottomless tracks of thick mud and slime. All forms of battle on the front lines were called off, with the German forces once again taking up defensive positions in regards to a line running from Fastov to Korosten.

The German assaults had in fact established a number of very important objectives, as these assaults had driven back the Russian forces in mass confusion, plus the Red Army Command had to commit other tank and mobile assault units from other sectors to try and fill in the gaps in their respective front lines. All in all, the German forces had made a good account of themselves, as they had taken 4,800 enemy prisoners, had killed or wounded a further 20,000 and destroyed 603 armored fighting vehicles, and also captured 1,305 Russian anti-tank and artillery pieces as war-booty for their determined efforts.

It was soon found that losses did not halt the Red Army's advances completely, and in highly desperate fighting instances, the troops of the First Ukrainian Front renewed the attack upon the 4th Panzer Army. This attack had been highly anticipated by Manstein who quickly regrouped his forces to block the way west to his opposing forces. The XXXXVIII Corps was then ordered on December 4th to attack positions north of Zhitomir from which it could strike its own attack against the Sixtieth Red Army which had not been committed in the earlier battles during the month of November. It was then to maneuver towards the Teterev river at a prearranged location north of Radomischl.

The assault commenced with Michael Wittmann's Tiger I platoon advancing against very stubborn positions that the Ivans had established in this area, which were highly protected by a comprehensive series of mutually supporting Pak fronts.

Wittmann and his Tiger Is fought fire with fire and concentrated their main guns upon the massed weapons of the Russian Pakfronts, destroying them utterly one after the other as his vehicles crashed forward to regain lost ground. When his Tiger Is approached the main highway to Styrty on December 4th it was to be seen packed with Russian transports and other soft-skinned vehicles which were being escorted by T34/76s and SU-76 self propelled anti-tank vehicles. Wittmann gave out the order to attack these juicy enemy targets and assaulted the convoy as soon as they came into their standard gunnery range. All hell broke out as the Russians were again taken by surprise in regards to the deadly and highly accurate firing of both HE and AP ammunition being delivered by the German heavy panzers. It was very apparent that the Ivans had not expected to encounter such a strong force of German panzers operating in this supposedly safe area. It was not long before the entire Russian convoy was left in a blazing mass of fire and smoke. The Tiger Is had taken out the enemy panzers and other vehicles as soon as they opened fired. Once the drivers of the soft-skinned vehicle saw what was happening to their comrades in regards to their armored support, the vast majority of these men halted their vehicles and fled on foot to the rear. Wittmann ordered his gunners to fire only their MG-34 machine guns at the abandoned trucks as he did not want to waste precious main gun ammunition on these light and unarmed vehicles. It did not take very long before this entire convoy was destroyed with the Tiger Is moving off to seek out more targets of opportunity in and around Styrty.

December 6th found the Leibstandarte Adolf Hitler fighting in the area of Golovin where fierce panzer battles were raging back and forth over the snow covered fields with thick black smoke hanging in the air. Up and until the evening of December 5th, the 1st Panzer Division was able to hold the area of Kmenka-Federoka north of Zhitomir. North of this point the 7th Panzer Division had retaken Zhitomir and due north of this town, the Leibstandarte stood ready to attack the Ivans. On the right flank of the Leibstandarte was the 68th Infantry Division of the 2nd Paratroop Division under the direct command of General Rancke with "Das Reich" standing by to attack Radomischl.

"Its colder than a swine!" complained Wendorff as the first rays of light broke out from the eastern sky.

"Could not agree with you more my friend!" replied Wittmann as he felt the bitter cold which had penetrated his thick winter clothing which had finally been distributed throughout the Leibstandarte front line units.

The winter fighting had taken its toll on the men of Wittmann's panzer unit as the majority of time the men had to stay buttoned up in their vehicles all night long in order to obtain some protection from the unforgiving temperatures that sometime fell to 20 degrees to 30 degrees below zero. Every morning the panzer crews awoke to find three or four inches of frost clinging to the interior walls and equipment which proved to be a very difficult problem to overcome. Once the vehicles were started and completely warmed up, the frost would melt and thus ran down into the lower hull areas causing shorts in the electrical systems, immobilizing entire platoons and companies for hours. Ice also froze vehicle hatches shut whereas crewmembers had to chipped away this substance with a hammer and screwdriver. At times, some panzer crews were trapped inside their vehicles until their comrades either removed the ice with manual tools or blow-torches. During the long and bitterly cold nights, panzer crews lit fires under the engine compartments in order to prevent the oil in the crankcases from freezing solid in the sub-zero weather. This ad hoc antidote was however, a double edged sword, as the fires instantly gave away their vehicle positions to the ever forward Russian observers and was frowned upon through out the entire Russian winter campaigns. Finally, the German High Command dictated that each vehicle was to be started every two to three hours in order to keep the oil and fuel lines free from icing up and to charge the vehicles' batteries. This procedure proved to be the most pertinent solution to this problem which saved many machines from never being able to move forward when massed Russian panzer attacks came in during the very early morning hours. Special attention was also given to the hydraulic fluids in regards to the 8.8cm main guns and related equipment which would also freeze up if not properly tested and maintained. Appropriate cold weather hydraulic fluids were soon introduced which helped to solve the extreme frigid operating conditions on the front lines.

Another major problem encountered on the Eastern front pertaining to the Tiger I and its operations, was the tendency of its over-lapping road-wheel suspension and tracks to freeze up during extreme cold weather operations. It was found many times prior to moving out for early morning attacks that frozen mud, snow, and ice were the contributing factors in immobilizing Tiger I units.

The Russians soon learned of these problems and would indeed order in large numbers of their armored fighting vehicles to try and eradicate as many of the German machines before their crews could free themselves. The German heavy panzer crews at times had to utilize blow-torches to melt away the frozen materials from their road-wheels and tracks, plus take sledge hammers and pick axes to try and remove the larger pieces of snow and ice. Many internal components of the final drives and transmissions were to be over-taxed and damaged if special attention and care was not focused on the suspensions and tracks of the Tiger I in inclement weather. This problem was never completely solved and proved to be one of the major disadvantages of this vehicle during winter combat.

Every German soldier fighting on the Eastern Front during the winter time had a second enemy to contend with which was the dreaded cases of frost-bite which was feared even more than being hit by an enemy bullet. Panzer commanders were prone to frost-bite more so than the rest of their crews as the majority of the time in battle these men were fully exposed from the waist up in order to obtain unobstructed vision while engaging enemy panzer attacks and seeking out hidden anti-tank gun positions, plus tank killer assault teams. Extreme care was taken to prevent frost-bite with every panzer commander having extra head, arm, and hand protection. At times, it was totally unbearable to withstand the icy eastern winds that slapped into their faces and took super human endurance to continue to observe for any signs of the enemy; who seemed to excel in this type of weather! If panzer commanders did not observe the enemy from their open hatches, they soon found themselves at a great disadvantage in being fired upon by hidden enemy anti-tank guns, and expertly camouflaged T34/76 tanks. Even if one was able to observe from his opened cupola hatch, one had to endure millions of tiny ice particles which acted like miniature hypodermic needles that punctuated their faces all through the short days and long nights on the Russian front. The only relief that these brave and courageous men could expect was when their vehicles were being fired upon, whereas they would be able to drop down into the warmth of their turrets for protection against enemy shell fragments, etc.

It was also during this time-period that Michael Wittmann was becoming very bitter in regards to the situation on the Eastern front. He had seen many men killed in the face of the enemy and his attitude was now beginning to change. A great many of his comrades now were either dead, wounded, or missing in action. The utter disregard for human life and suffering as exhibited by the Red Army sickened him, as the Russian Army High Command would order hundreds and sometimes thousands of their troops into one battle in order to obtain the planned objective. It did not matter how many of the Russian troops were killed, so long as the objective was obtained. Wittmann's religious convictions were also being put to the test and were faltering with every day that passed in the hostile environment that he was to play a major part. His main concern was for the survival of his panzer crews, but in order for this to be, he had to be ruthless in his every day routine of assaulting the Ivans. It was his responsibility to insure that they all would return to their families, wives, and girlfriends, but deep down he knew that very few of his comrades would ever see their homeland again. Would he ever return home and be the farmer he always wanted to become? He thought not!

During the second week of December, Rottenführer Kirschmer returned to Wittmann's vehicle after convalescence of his wounds. Everyone was very happy to see him and ask many questions in regards to what the homefront was like, and if he had seen his family, friends, etc. They all had a few drinks of vodka, and wished him better luck in the forth-coming panzer battles against the ever present Ivans.

The Tiger Is of the Leibstandarte Adolf Hitler were once again called forward to roll against stiff opposition. Wittmann's platoon was out in front of the rest of his company and was trying to force his way through some anti-tank guns which had been spotted by a Fieseler Fi 156 "Storch" reconnaissance aircraft flying in and around the area of Golovin. Wendorff made his way around deep artillery craters and continued on the pre-arranged course that had been outlined earlier in the day. The remaining Tiger Is would travel to the left and right flank and storm forward towards the north edge of the town.

Suddenly, there were flashes spotted from a house on the outer perimeter of this town with anti-tank gun rounds falling in and among the approaching panzers.

"Forward, full throttle!", was the order given over the radio network.

At top speed, the Tiger Is pressed onwards towards the enemy. Wittmann and his crew went into immediate action with all guns blazing. Multi-ranged V formations was called for as the German vehicle commanders did not want to maneuver forward line abreast, as this would allow the Ivans to pick off their vehicles with little or no trouble. As soon as the panzer charge was initiated, the Tiger Is formed up into a wedge formation with Wittmann leading and directing the assault.

"Warmbrünn and Lötzsch, halt and fire and then cover our advance! The others follow me!" ordered Wittmann.

The two panzer commanders halted their vehicles and started to fire at the enemy anti-tank guns while Wittmann and the remaining Tiger Is moved directly ahead towards the enemy gun positions. Kirschmer reported to his commander that he could see the rounds being fired at them, as they kicked up the snow particles behind them due to the close proximity to the ground and their high velocity. Wittmann ordered his driver to start veering to the left and then to the right in an attempt to offer the enemy gunners as difficult a target to aim at as possible. Wittmann quickly turned in his cupola in order to keep close charge over his following vehicles and to provide arm and hand signals if necessary. His machines were moving at full speed, but the enemy gunners continued to try and track them with a number of projectiles screaming by within inches of his mount. He then ordered his driver to return to a straight course and to head once again towards the enemy Paks. Woll was now firing the 8.8cm main gun on the move as he and his commander were hoping that this action would at least keep Ivan's heads down for the time being. Suddenly, T34/76s appeared once again from the horizon with their numbers steadily increasing as the German panzers came into firing range. Once Wittmann saw these enemy armored fighting vehicles rolling towards them, he announced over the radio net that the anti-tank guns still firing at them had to be taken out of action as soon as humanly possible. All of the heavy panzers stopped and laid down a curtain of fire that finally destroyed the dug-in weapons, with their crews either being killed, or running to safety behind their defensive lines.

As Bobby Woll was trying to destroy the last remaining Russian anti-tank guns, there was a loud bang as one of the forward approaching T34/76s, had managed to fire off a lucky main gun round which had impacted on the right-side of Wittmann's turret wall. The shockwave was enough to throw Berges off his feet and also forced Woll to lose control of the turret operations for a few long seconds. Wittmann peeped over his hatch opening and tried to locate the enemy panzer in order to guide Woll onto target. A second round was fired by the enemy vehicle which just missed Wittmann's Tiger I, as it passed ever so closely to the right side of his turret.

Wittmann had heard the enemy panzer main gun round being fired and watched helplessly as it flew past his position. His stomach tightened up and his only thought was to locate this vehicle before it blasted him and his crew from the face of the earth. He could not however, locate the enemy panzer and assumed that it was dug into the ground and heavily camouflaged. The three Tiger Is continued to roll forward and finally managed to destroy the entire contingent of Ivan's anti-tank guns. Wittmann and crew knew that they were now at the mercy of the hidden enemy panzer and expected at any time to be hit, penetrated, and knocked out especially if fired at close range. The familiar crack of an 8.8cm AP main gun round was heard by Wittmann and saw a flash of light in a nearby grove of snow laden trees. Wittmann was relieved to see that either Warmbrünn or Lötzsch had located and then destroyed the menacing T34/76 that had been firing at them a few minutes beforehand.

The German panzers continued to advance on the enemy vehicles as Woll was busy at the controls of the 8.8cm main gun. Each time he looked through his telescopic sight he could see the numerous gun muzzle flashes of the enemy T34/76s as they too continued to storm forward. As in the past, as soon as the German machines had breached one line of Ivan's defenses or a wave of armored fighting vehicles, they would run into another belt of anti-tank guns and or dug-in panzers. It was hard and bitter fighting and all who were involved with this type of front line fighting had to keep up a constant standard of endurance which was vital for survival against the surmounting tide of Red Army materiel and manpower. Every main gun round had to count and every panzer commander and gunner had to be deadly sure that what they fired at was either knocked out or disabled. The snow particles and smoke thrown up by the constant firing of the Tiger Is' main guns was only rectified by instructing the drivers to move their vehicles forward and clear of these obstructions, which in turn, allowed the panzer gunners to locate and fire at their next targets. This way they would move ahead of their own fog of war, and be able to continue their panzer gunnery. If the vehicles were to move ahead at a fast pace the gunners were instructed to traverse their turrets to either the 10 o'clock or 2 o'clock positions in order to provide the enemy gunners a much more difficult target.

As Michael Wittmann and his other panzers were approaching the next line of defenses, he ordered his panzer commanders in his platoon to fire main gun vollies at selected targets. These projectiles tore into the Russian defenses and turned out to be an effective and rude awakening to the Red Army defenders. Even though the German panzers had to make every main gun round count, this gunnery technique was sometimes necessary to eradicate a stubborn position, which was the case in this particular situation. Wittmann and his panzer commanders could not understand why it had been so easy then to destroy these positions, but found out at a later time that these weapons were not manned by front line quality troops. It was ascertained by prisoners taken later that the vast majority of these defenders fled in panic after witnessing the huge Tiger Is rolling towards their positions, and being subjected to such accurate and highly devastating firepower. The order was given to move forward once again and the German machines crashed through the breach in the enemy line with a great deal of vehicle speed and determination.

"Heavy panzer company, keep rolling. Head towards the southern edge of Golovin!" ordered the regimental commander.

"Schützenpanzerwagen battalion join them and protect them from the rear!"

Kling was now rolling towards Wittmann's position with his two accompanying Tiger Is to again help bring the advance forward. Wittmann was now travelling on the left flank with Wendorff and his vehicles maneuvering on the right flank. In broad formation they had mutual protection from each others armament to ward off any ensuing Russian panzer attacks which they expected at any time. Wittmann was constantly scanning the area ahead of his vehicles for any signs of the Ivans and was standing upright in his open cupola ready for any action to develop. Instinctively, Woll turned the turret of his vehicle to the 10 o'clock position in order to be ready to fire at the Ivans if they made an appearance in his zone of responsibility. The wind, cold and icy, was blowing with driving force which caused Wittmann's eyes to water which made it very difficult to locate and detect targets. He was not too sure, but he thought that he had seen a small reflection off of an enemy vehicle's forward periscope, or perhaps a set of Ivan's binoculars to the right-hand side of his vehicle. He then ordered his driver to slow down their vehicle, and then to stop suddenly. At a low lying group of trees and bushes covered with thick snow, there stood a large Russian panzer.

"Heavy panzer ahead, Untersturmführer!" bellowed Pollmann.

The main gun and turret of the enemy panzer were now traversing very slowly in order to take Wittmann's Tiger I into its sight picture. Wittmann let out a quick fire command to his crew which set them into motion for yet another fire-fight. Wittmann's driver turned the vehicle to the right in order to bring Woll onto target with his commander guiding him with careful and precise instructions. Then, once their vehicle was aimed into the general area of the target, Wittmann guided Woll onto target and announced his fire command. Woll located the target at the same time that he was given his order to shoot and knocked out the enemy panzer while it was still slowly traversing its turret. The AP main gun round however deflected off from the superstructure of the enemy panzer and shot like a mad rocket high into the air. Shortly after this encounter, the Russian machine fired its main gun at Wittmann's Tiger I with the round flying over the top of its turret, destroying a large tree some 100 meters to the rear of his location. Another round was fired at the enemy machine by Woll which impacted into the center of the vehicle, but again failed to penetrate the thick front armor plate.

"Aim to the right!" yelled Wittmann.

Woll was just about to depress the firing handle while aiming at the driver's hatch of the enemy machine, when he noticed that the enemy vehicle was now trying to turn around and to move off. Wittmann ordered his driver to advance on the enemy panzer with all speed. While they were moving closer to the enemy panzer, Wittmann and Woll were discussing their next moves and set out to bag the Ivans with a close range fire mission. The commander of the Russian panzer must have thought that his vehicle was out of immediate danger, as his armored mount suddenly started to turn towards Wittmann's right flank. This move was not accomplished fast enough however, which was immediately detected by Wittmann and his gunner. Woll rotated the turret to the 3 o'clock position and fired his second 8.8cm AP main gun round at the enemy panzer as soon as he received the order to fire. This time, the round tore through the thinner armor plating on the right-hand side of this vehicle with a terrific explosion. The steel giant blew apart with an ear splitting crack!

"Do you need any assistance?" asked Kling over the radio network.

"Everything is taken care of at this location!" reported Wittmann, as he and his panzer crew hurried to maneuver their vehicle on to the next terrain feature.

As soon as Wittmann had his driver pull their vehicle up to the top of the next small hill, a dozen enemy assault guns were firing at their machine and their supporting comrades. One of the Tiger Is was hit and instantly started to burn, with the crew baling out and seeking cover behind their machine. They finally were forced to fall back to the protection of the follow-up armored half tracks (SPWs) and were soon picked up. The remaining Tiger Is continued to fire at the enemy vehicles as they rolled forward to try and overtake the ground the German forces were holding onto. While this was transpiring, Wittmann was able to observe Warmbrünn's vehicle as he was attacking two well emplaced anti-tank guns to his right flank. One of them had been responsible for the first Tiger I that had been hit and set on fire, as they too had been firing with the enemy assault guns and had not been located at the beginning of the battle. The second anti-tank gun was now attempting to knock out Warmbrunn's vehicle but luckily, his gunner was able to locate and destroy both of these weapons after seeing snow particles being blown up by their firing.

Wittmann was now giving Woll his fire commands and were once again locating and destroying many of Ivan's armored fighting vehicles as they crawled forward. Round after round was fired by Woll as he was working like a mad man rotating and elevating the turret and main gun. Berges was working as fast as humanly possible to keep up with Wittmann's fire commands in regards to loading the main gun. Sweat ran down his face as he slammed the heavy 8.8cm AP rounds into the hot and smoking breech.

The order to advance was given once again by Kling, as the Ivans now seemed to be slowing down and did not dare to venture any further into the German held killing zones. The fog of battle was still hanging in the air and made it very difficult for the German panzer commanders to judge distances for continued accurate firing at the enemy, and also to guide their drivers along snow covered gullies and depressions.

As his vehicle moved slowly forward Wittmann was trying to guide his driver through a narrow trail which he hoped would bring them back onto the flat open terrain which would allow him to fire at the Ivans who were scattered in every conceivable direction. Some of the burning enemy machines were being used as cover by the Russian infantry who seemed oblivious to the immediate danger of these machines blowing up in their faces. It seemed very clear, that they had two choices; being forced to run over open snow covered ground and being machine gunned down by the German forces, or huddled in and around the doomed and burning vehicles! A number of these immobilized enemy panzers were still firing at the Tiger Is, but were soon knocked out by accurate gunnery measures conducted by Wittmann's platoon.

Kirschmer could not see a thing through his forward driver's vision slit and kept asking Wittmann for driving directions to bring their vehicle back on course with the other vehicles of their company. Wittmann was also having a difficult time seeing and directing his machine forward and was not too sure if the terrain ahead of his mount would bring them out of this trying situation.

Just when Wittmann and his crew felt their vehicle start to roll forward once again, the bow of the heavy vehicle dipped down and crashed into a snow covered shell crater. With all of the whirling snow and smoke dangling around his Tiger I, Kirschmer had accidently driven into this large hole, and stalled the Maybach engine. He immediately tried to restart his powerplant, but was not able to do so for some unknown reason. Wittmann's vehicle was now in a very serious and highly dangerous predicament as they were now being fired upon by the Ivans which caused frantic orders directed solely to the driver to restart his engine and extract the vehicle from the grasp of the bomb crater. Finally, the engine came to life as Kirschmer had obviously flooded the carburetors when the vehicle had crashed into the shell crater. Shots rang out against Wittmann's vision blocks, but since it was armored glass, these small caliber rounds were easily repelled. The Russian infantry could not resist this tempting prize and were starting to close in on Wittmann's bogged machine. As he viewed out of his vision devices, Wittmann saw the approaching infantry and ordered Woll and Pollmann to open fire with the vehicle's two MG-34s. Both machine guns started blasting away at the ensuing enemy infantry, but this suppressive fire was a little too late. A number of the enemy infantrymen had already managed to crawl right up to the vehicle and were now climbing up and onto it. Wittmann had to act very quickly in order to prevent the Ivans from placing magnetic or explosive charges on his machine, as he had only seconds to try and save his vehicle and crew from destruction. He yelled to his loader to hand him the turret stowed MP-40 machine pistole. Berges grabbed the weapon, and handed it to his commander, who then loaded and charged it, and then flung open the hatch of his cupola and immediately saw a surprised face that appeared to be nothing more than beard and wild eyes staring at him. Wielding the MP-40 he fired it right into the face of the Russian who had been so stunned with fear that he froze just long enough for Wittmann to do away with him. Wittmann then felt a presence standing behind him and instinctively turned his weapon around and fired two or three rounds into the Russian infantryman who was in the act of lobbing a hand grenade into his open hatch. As the mortally wounded Russian fell onto the rear deck of the vehicle, he managed to throw the explosive device up and onto the turret roof between the commander's open hatch and the loader's closed hatch. A few moments after Wittmann had shot the second Russian, the grenade detonated with a deafening bang! The majority of the explosion was shielded and deflected away by the open commander's hatch, with very little shrapnel being directed at Wittmann who was still standing from the waist up in his position. The concussion from this weapon nearly blew him out of his hatch as he was now hanging over the left-hand edge of his cupola. It took all of his bodily strength to keep him from falling out and onto the ground, as he pulled himself slowly up and back into the safety and protection of his vehicle. Shortly after this very close encounter with Ivan, Kirschmer finally rocked, reversed, and rammed the Tiger I forward until it was able to free itself from the shell crater by knocking down its earthen walls. As the heavy vehicle inched its way forward out of this depression, Wittmann and his crew felt very lucky indeed that they had survived this extremely dangerous confrontation with the enemy.

"Commander to Wittmann, where the hell are you?" came the concerned voice of Kling over the radio net.

"We have reached our objective 1 km east of your position and are engaging in a mopping up operation."

It seemed like only seconds after this radio message had finished, that the Ivans were once again throwing additional T34/76s into the battle. Wittmann's Tiger I, again came under fire from a superior force of enemy machines and it was Woll, who again took on the enemy panzers with his great gunnery skill and determination to knock out the leading Russian panzers as they rolled towards their positions. From out of nowhere, Kling and Wendorff's platoons came rumbling back to assist Wittmann, as they too had seen the mounting T34/76 attack, and figured that Wittmann and his crew would bare the brunt of this assault alone, if nothing was done to help them at this point in time.

Wittmann and his panzer crew were very relieved to see his comrades returning to help them out of this dangerous situation and ordered his driver to increase their speed in order for them to link up with Kling and Wendorff. All of the Tiger Is were now firing at the charging Ivans, who were now very confused in regards to the German panzers surrounding their forces. They tried to escape from the constant and highly accurate firing from the German heavy panzers, but soon found that they had been out maneuvered and out gunned. It was not long until there were many burning and knocked out Russian panzers laying on the battlefield with smashed turrets and dismounted Russian tank crews trying to find cover from the deadly German fire. The battle soon slowed down once again as the vehicles of the Leibstandarte move off to consolidate their gains and to plan their next movement. It was still early afternoon, but the German panzer crews knew that before long the Russians would mount at least one or two more massive panzer assaults before the day's end. Careful plans were then laid out to hold off any further attempts by the Ivans to break through the thinly held German defensive lines.

All were now ready for the next expected attack by the Russian forces. The vehicles of Wittmann's platoon moved out to take up positions a few hundred meters to the east from Kling's position. While they were travelling to their selected positions, a small group of nine T34/76s were spotted hiding in a small depression to the right-hand side of Wittmann's vehicle. He quickly sent a radio message to his other vehicles, plus informed Kling of their positions. Before anything else could be accomplished, the enemy panzers came to life and started firing at Wittmann's platoon. As Wittmann and Woll were trying to bring their 8.8cm main gun to bare on the enemy machines, panzer commander Kurt Kleber's Tiger I was hit and penetrated by a lucky flank shot. Quite by coincidence, Wittmann just happen to look over at Kleber's vehicle when the enemy main gun round impacted into his comrades machine. He was horrified to witness Kleber's body being thrown up into the air, after being blown out of his commander's cupola by the explosion and shock wave that engulfed his vehicle. Wittmann could feel himself becoming sick to his stomach at the thought of his friend and his crew being killed outright by this enemy main gun round penetration. There was now no time to waste, as he ordered his crew to action stations and started to direct his driver and gunner in order to take on the Ivans and destroy their machines as fast as they presented themselves on the battle field.

It seemed that all of the Tiger Is were fighting a crazy panzer battle, as the gunners of the German heavy panzers were firing at anything that moved. They continued to fire into the waves of Russian panzers as they tried to move forward while still firing on the move. The fighting continued, and at times, the German forces were not too sure if the enemy would indeed give up their assaults. The current situation was very touchy for the German forces as they were very concerned about rolling forward until they had obtained a clear understanding of the tactical situation. There were also many small groves of trees in the area, and it was then planned to roll towards these forms of cover in order to try and hide from any air observation which the Ivans might try to utilize so as to access the battlefield environment.

The order was given to pull out of their hull-down defensive positions and drive towards these wooded areas for better concealment. As soon as the Tiger Is had maneuvered out of their hide positions, some of the so-called dead T34/76s came to life and immediately started to fire every main gun that was operable at the German panzers. Two of these vehicles started concentrated fire aimed at Warmbrunn's Tiger I, and succeeded in knocking out his vehicle, but did not incapacitate this brave panzer commander and his crew. Warmbrunn and his panzer crew remained inside their machine and continued to fire at the enemy thereby knocking out a number of these vehicles while the other Tiger Is made their way to the other side of the tree line.

Wittmann and the other vehicles rolled towards an orchard and took up positions just inside the trees and waited for further action. A few minutes elapsed as they were trying to find a way to save Warmbrünn and his men. He and his crew were completely exposed on the open battlefield, but it seemed that the Ivans were now pulling back once again in order to regroup. During this time-period Wittmann was in constant radio contact with Warmbrünn and told him to sit tight as a Bergepanther recovery vehicle had been dispatched and was on its way to his position to tow his vehicle out of danger. Warmbrünn informed Wittmann that he would act as an observer in the event the Ivans charged forward to assault the rest of the company should they come in from his direction. Wittmann radioed back that this would be fine, as long as his comrade felt that he and his crew would be secure at their location until rescued by the recovery and maintenance unit. Warmbrunn was very adamant in regards to not abandoning his position no matter what the cost.

During his radio conversation with Warmbrunn, Wittmann observed a T34/76 which came out from behind a nearby barn and started firing at his machines, and then disappeared! The majority of the German panzer commanders were not expecting any enemy panzers to try and make this type of daring assault and could not locate the exact position of the enemy. Wittmann informed Warmbrunn what was transpiring and inquired if he could observe and fire at the enemy panzer. The stranded panzer commander indicated to Wittmann that he could indeed see the panzer and started to fire at it. His first main gun round missed the target, but his second try smashed into the now moving T34/76 which kept rolling forward without seeing any of the crew baling out. The machine however, continued to crawl forward with black and white smoke pouring out of the turret hatch openings. Still, none of its crew were to be seen trying to escape from this doomed enemy panzer rolling around the area wildly out of control. Wittmann and Woll then detected this vehicle as it came into their area, although they had seen the smoke and flames beforehand and were growing very concerned. Both men followed the erratic movements of this machine as they did not want to fall into the same predicament that had befallen onto Lötzsch a number of battles ago. The swaying and burning T34/76 continued to crash forward as Wittmann announced a fire command to Woll, however, before this was accomplished, the enemy panzer blew up with a deafening bang! The explosion pushed the vehicle with great forced even further, which also blew off both of its tracks. Then, a second explosion wrenched the machine forward once again when the turret being catapulted off from its superstructure with a loud and thunderous crack, and slammed to the ground on fire with a thud! Yet another explosion erupted within the twisted and burning vehicle and blew out what was left of the panzer crew with exploding ammunition being hurled in every possible direction. This incident was a very graphic example in regards to the brutal death of a panzer and its crew, and once seen, one could never forget the horrors of it all! Witnessing this awesome scene of death and total destruction and seeing one of his comrades recently blown out from his vehicle was just about all Wittmann could endure. He once again wondered how he would meet his death on the field of combat and only hoped that when his time came, his demise would be sure and swift!

Suddenly, Pollmann gave out a yell and indicated to his commander to observe the nearby barn!

"Look at the window!"

Wittmann immediately detected a menacing gun barrel in the right lower corner of this aperture and then saw the edge of a turret of any enemy panzer which he could barely make out hiding inside this structure. Part of the lower section of the barn had been ripped away by an explosion and he could see that the Russian panzer had one of it tracks missing, and no doubt had been pushed into this farm building as an ad hoc measure to cause havoc upon any German vehicles that might happen to come along its deadly path. Woll brought his 8.8cm main gun to bare with guidance from his commander until he was able to lock onto target. Wittmann provided the necessary fire command and Woll launched an 8.8cm AP main gun round and penetrated the enemy panzer through the driver's vision block and utterly destroyed this machine. The barn soon caught fire and the whole area was burning with a brilliance that could be seen for miles. An uncomfortable stillness then covered the surrounding countryside as the only sounds that were to be heard was the crackling of flames which filled the air with a strange roar that changed its pitch every few minutes. Ammunition was still exploding within the smashed enemy panzer which was glowing red hot as radiant flames continued to engulf the broken and gutted machine.

"Take full cover!" shouted Kling over the radio net.

The Ivans had called up a concentrated artillery barrage to try and destroy the German heavy panzers that had run rampart over their armored forces. All of the Tiger Is were immediately buttoned up in order to protect the crewmembers as the barrage slowly swept over the German positions. Wittmann and his crew felt as if the doors of hell had been opened as heavy smoke and sheets of flames devoured their positions as the earth was shaking, with large clumps of dirt, snow, and other materials falling onto and around their stationary machines. A number of the vehicles were lifted completely off of the ground by near misses with the resulting shock waves shattering armored glass, radio tubes, and men's eardrums and nerves. It seemed as if a giant's hand had come down upon them and was playing with the 56 ton panzers as if they were some kind of children's toy in a sand box. Wittmann and his men were being rocked, bumped, and thrown around inside their vehicle by tremendous forces with morale quickly fading as a result.

A fire appeared suddenly within their vehicle which had been caused by a number of electrical connections being ripped from their fittings and showering sparks which had quickly ignited leaking fuel, and hydraulic fluid in the hull. Berges quickly opened the turret basket floor hatch and was frantically trying to put out the flames with the vehicle's Tetra fire extinguisher, while Woll carefully and slowly rotated the turret in order to locate the source of the fire. The fire was quickly put out with Wittmann's crew coughing and gaging for there was little oxygen left to inhale inside their closed down vehicle. Wittmann did not dare to order his crew to open their respective hatches as this would mean certain death to them as Ivans' artillery barrage was still being directed upon their positions. He therefore ordered his crew to put on their gas-masks as this measure would at least cut down on the acrid black smoke still present inside their vehicle. Upon donning these protective devices everyone was able to breathe somewhat better, but there was still tension and high anxiety among Wittmann's crew. The artillery barrage lasted for about ten minutes longer which seemed like hours. Once this attack ended, the panzer commanders ordered their crews to open their hatches to allow all of the smoke, carbon dioxide, and gasoline fumes to escape which allowed the men to take in fresh air once again. Wittmann was very proud of his crew for being so brave under extremely harsh conditions and felt that something ought to be done to award his men. Every single man in his platoon should have received a medal for withstanding such enduring hardships in the face of the enemy. But this was not to be, as a soldier's duty was to except such difficult situations and to carry on the best he could while assaulting the enemy or vice versa.

"If the panzer grenadiers had been out there, they would have never survived this attack!" stated Wendorff as he and Wittmann spoke to each other over their still functioning platoon radio net.

"The Ivans are learning our tactics my friend so we will have to out wit them every time we go into battle!" was Wittmann's reply.

While Wittmann's crew was checking over their vehicle for damage, he suddenly remembered how his comrade Kleber had been blown out of his machine and could only fear the very worst. He sprang from his armored cupola and ran as fast as he could towards Kleber's machine which had not been under enemy artillery bombardment. Feeling very responsible he wanted to know what indeed had happened to his younger friend. Surely he was dead or dying, laying like a rag doll discarded by its last owner. Had anyone taken care of his body? Would he be ripped apart and not be recognizable to him? All of these thoughts were racing through Wittmann's mind as he dashed to the area where he had last seen his fellow panzer commander. At last, as Wittmann came within ten meters of his comrade's vehicle, Kleber's head popped out of his armored cupola and greeted him with a very wide grin on his face! The relieved platoon leader stopped dead in his tracks and was totally speechless for a few seconds and then slowly approached and mounted Kleber's vehicle.

"What happen to you Kleber?" asked the breathless Wittmann.

"We received a direct hit! The air pressure blew me right out of my panzer! I'm afraid I will not even receive a medal for being slightly wounded."

As Wittmann looked upon his friend, he could see that Kleber's neck and ears were bleeding due to his throat microphones and head phones having been ripped off of his person as the result of his sudden and violent removal from his vehicle.

"And I thought that you were!"

Because of the joy and relief of seeing his comrade alive and well, Wittmann was again unable to speak for a few additional moments, but padded Kleber on his back to indicate that he was very glad to see that he had survived his ordeal under fire. Kleber who had been transferred from the German Luftwaffe and was therefore simply called "Quax" could see how worried Wittmann had been and highly appreciated his concern a great deal. He told his platoon commander that it would take more than just being blown out of his panzer in order for Ivan to kill him with a loud laugh. Wittmann then told Kleber that he was grateful that he was still among the living and shook his hand and then returned to his crew and vehicle. As soon as Wittmann climbed aboard his panzer, a radio message was being transmitted and was coming in over the company radio network.

"Wittmann to report to the regimental commander, at once!" was the given order.

The resourceful panzer commander made his way to the regimental commander's vehicle and reported to SS-Sturmbannführer Max Wünsche (who had received the Knight's Cross on February 28, 1943), who gave Wittmann his hand and congratulated him in regards to having destroyed his 60th panzer kill in and around Golovin on December 6th. Wittmann was very proud of the fact that he was being recognized for his superior efforts, but made it quite clear that without his quality panzer crew, and the skillful and accurate gunnery talents of "Bobby Woll", his "Kill-Score" would have not been as comprehensive. He also felt that he and his panzer crews had been very lucky in not being knocked out and killed on the numerous battleruns against the enemy. After a number of other hand shakes with other fellow officers that were present, Wittmann was able to make his way back to his Tiger I crew, and informed them that they had been officially credited with 60 enemy panzers destroyed up to this point in time. All of his crew were elated, with morale soaring very high indeed!

The Waffen-SS Tiger Is then moved the advance forward as the fighting continued with gains being made but at an alarming rate of attrition.

As dawn broke on December 7th, the Leibstandarte Adolf Hitler, on the Corps right flank, pulled out of its concentration area north-west of Chernyakov, attacked eastward, and again smashed Russian defenses. They then headed south of Korchevka, severed the Golubovka road, captured Torchin and then moved off in a north-easterly direction towards Sabolot. The fighting continued for the next week but little if any gains were made as continuous blinding snowstorms, intense cold and savage and relentless counterattacks by the determined enemy continually overwhelmed the German military forces. Yet another tactical drawback was the complete absence of the German Luftwaffe as by this time in the war the German High Command had sent the vast majority of the German Air Arm to the west to help to repel the massive offensive Allied bombings of major German cities and armaments factories. The Ivans now had total mastery of the air and the tables were now turned against the German ground forces for the first time. Even against this new obstacle, the Leibstandarte continued to push itself forward until, by December 13th, the Russian forces had been pushed back to the eastern bank of the Teterev river with heavy losses of men, and especially armored fighting vehicles. Swiftly and continuously, the Waffen-SS panzer units charged forward taking full advantage of this new founded tactical success, and on the next day, east of Visht Shevitchi, the majority of the Leibstandarte vehicles were headed in the direction of Vyrva. By midday, orders were issued withdrawing the Waffen-SS division from the line and posting it northwards. The German High Command had seen an opportunity to trap the whole 60th Red Army which was now renewing its offensive against Zhitomir. All of the divisions of the Fourth Panzer Army had been depleted by nearly five weeks of continued campaigning, but were still ordered to attack, and encircled forty-seven infantry and nine tank divisions of the Red Army. The German High Command's overall plan of attack was to thrust against the Ivans' northern flank to be followed by the typical German panzer encirclement, of which the jaws were to meet around Malin, where the Russian Army units would have little or no chance of escape from the leading assault units.

Thirty artillery batteries and a number of Nebelwerfer units were used to soften up the area in which the Leibstandarte Adolf Hitler was to assault on December 18th. After this massive barrage lifted, the Leibstandarte attacked across the Korosten-Cheryakov road and continued the assault forward until it had severed the railway line and captured Turchinka. On the outside of the town in heavily wooded terrain, the momentum of the assault slowed down as the SS Panzer Grenadier Battalions were sucked into the fighting as conventional infantry tactics against the well emplaced enemy was the only way in which the German forces could extract the determined defenders. But not even this show of force could halt the Leibstandarte as the drive continued in a north-easterly direction for many kilometers. Bridgeheads were finally established across the Trostyvitsa. After situating the divisions flank on the east bank of the river, the Leibstandarte then maneuvered towards Peregorch at the meeting of the Irsha and Trostyavista rivers, which finalized the objective on December 19th.

The Leibstandarte Adolf Hitler fought very bitter and difficult battles for the next two weeks for the gains that it had made, as the Red Army was continuously throwing massive assaults in order to break the strangle hold established by the Waffen-SS units. The men of the Leibstandarte were under intense bombardments by entire divisions of Russian artillery and rocket artillery, as used to try and destroy the German positions before they could be consolidated any further. It was also during this time that Wittmann and Warmbrünn were caught in a building during a vicious artillery barrage. Both men were flattened to the floor and were not able to return to their vehicles for better protection. This incident affected Wittmann to a great degree and never properly recovered from it. By this time he had lost his religious convictions completely and became ever more bitter about his surroundings on the Eastern front. Despite these feelings and despair, he nevertheless soldiered on with his beloved panzer crews!

The Waffen-SS units were also having serious difficulties with their radio communications as the surrounding terrain was a great hinderance to their wireless transmissions and thus allowed infiltration of Russian infantry units. The south-western sectors pertaining to the Leibstandarte's forward lines were being forced back by highly determined Russian assaults and was only corrected on the northern flank when the Waffen-SS commanders rushed twenty-five of its Tiger Is into a combined attack with a Panzer Grenadier regiment of the 1st Panzer Division. After fierce and prolonged fighting, the hardened panzer crews and mounted Panzer Grenadiers drove their way into a Red Army tank concentration area north of Shevshentka whereupon they assaulted this force, and drove back and destroyed numerous T34/76 tanks. Shortly after these attacks were made, a short lived time of optimism swept through the fighting men of Army Group South as the result of interrogating and examination of many Red Army prisoners who were mainly young boys; and on the other end of the spectrum, a great many of these individuals were indeed very old men, which resulted in the general feeling that the Red Army had at last, begun to scrape the bottom of their manpower barrel! The German forces also felt that Mother Russia had also finally exhausted her vast reserves and now the war could be fought on equal terms instead of the continuous waves of humans and machines being thrown into the maelstrom of the Eastern front.

On December 24th, the Leibstandarte Adolf Hitler and the entire force of the XXXXVIII Corps assaulted south eastward to come into contact with the 8th Panzer Division and then maneuvered south to attack the strong Russian tank groups moving towards the north-south highway.

During the bitter engagements along this roadway Wendorff rescued a SS Panzer Grenadier unit which had been cut off, and succeeded in destroying twelve T34/76s during one day's fighting and a further eleven machines of a unit of twenty which attacked his Tiger I the following day. The Corps was now in a position protecting Berdichev, south of Zhitomir, and was holding off against repeated Red Army assaults. The Russians suddenly released an attack with full force and reopened the Russian winter offensive and smashed forward against Fourth Panzer Army and tore open a twenty mile gap into the front lines. Manstein quickly reorganized the battlefield and sent in the XXXXVIII Corps to protect the flanks and to prevent a breakthrough into the rear of the German Panzer Army.

During January 6, 1944, Vatutin's massive columns of T34/85s (mounting the ZIS-S-53 85mm main gun) and KV Is were spearheading southward towards the Dnieper river line, totally ignoring the German Panzer Corps which stood firmly emplaced and awaiting this suspected move by the Russians. The Red Army also reopened on the northern flank a battle in and around the Pripet Marshes which opened the southern front into an all out battle zone once again, which was to tie up massive amounts of equipment and manpower which was needed elsewhere.

Early on the morning of January 9th, Wittmann's platoon was once again put onto the alert. The enemy was attempting to push through their defensive positions and all was being made ready for the impending battle. Wittmann and the other panzer commanders were having an 'O' meeting (officers meeting) with Kling and it was suggested that a heavy reconnaissance patrol be sent out in order to try and flush out the enemy. The Leibstandarte's vehicles were now operating on the northern edge of Berdichev and were to travel upon heavy snow pack with continued snow storms active in this area.

"I will travel ahead and report, Haupsturmführer!" stated Wittmann without a second thought.

"Very good, take two of your Tiger Is with you!"

"Lötzsch and Kleber, come with me!"

The two panzer commanders stepped forward and followed Wittmann to his machine and proceeded to illustrate the terrain layout and details of their mission at hand. Wittmann was very careful and tried to be perfectly clear of his intentions. Wittmann also indicated to his men that the essence of reconnaissance was stealth and preached harmony in regards to their forth-coming encounters with the Ivans. Wittmann's plan was to establish a spoiling attack if he and his small recon group could locate the enemy before they had a chance to rush forward to their defensive positions.

The three vehicle force then pulled out of their concealed positions and moved out to try and locate the enemy as soon as possible. They travelled for about half an hour to the south, then turned northeast. Wittmann also ordered that their vehicles to be on radio silence as if they tried to use their communication devices, it was more than likely that the Ivans would be monitoring any and all German radio transmissions in the immediate area. As their vehicles were still moving northeast, they suddenly came under fire from a number of anti-tank guns, which were hidden in highly concealed positions. None of the Tiger Is were hit by this enemy fire, so moved off to try and locate the reported enemy battle group which was their main concern at this time. Due to this encounter, Wittmann then decided to head south once again in order to mislead any reports the anti-tank gun commander would make to his superiors.

The small contingent of Tiger Is moved with full speed to the south and then once again, headed in a northeast direction to try and locate the enemy panzers. Technically, this mission was a reconnaissance drive to detect the enemy whereabouts, but Wittmann and the other two panzer commanders knew only too well, that once they had detected the Ivans, there would be open season upon the Red Army vehicles and men. The order of the day was to disrupt the enemy anywhere and anyway they could in order to cause havoc, delay, and postponement of the enemy's tactical intentions. The three German panzers would perhaps never return to their comrades, but it was quite certain that they would destroy as many of the Ivan's panzers before they too would fall to enemy gun fire.

Suddenly, the German panzers came upon a medium sized wadi and located the Russian tank unit still preparing to launch their next attack. The Ivans were no doubt aware of the approaching German panzers, as they certainly heard their track and engine noises, but were in such a state of panic, they were not able to deploy fast enough in order to take on the German machines with any form of central control. Ten T34/85s were now trying desperately to maneuver out of this slippery depression but were not able to elevate their main guns (max elevation was 20 degrees) in order to engage Wittmann's panzer group from the level ground at the bottom of the wadi.

Wittmann immediately went into battle actions with his crew and now broke radio silence to communicate with his other Tiger I commanders, ordering them to halt in order for all vehicles to bring 8.8cm main gun fire upon the Russians and their vehicles. All three Tiger Is stopped, then traversed their turrets and main guns in order to obtain a bearing on the frantic enemy machines which were now trying to escape the confines of the wadi that had been used to protect them earlier in the day. Wittmann was very concerned that the T34/85 panzer commanders would indeed try and climb out of this depression so as to avoid total destruction instead of just sitting stationary and easy targets for the German Tiger Is. The Ivans knew that the German panzer force had them trapped and would only have to fire well placed AP rounds into their vehicles and destroy them outright. The T34/85s were now seen to be moving at full speed as they raced up the sloped edges of the snow covered wadi frantically trying to make it over the top in order to engage the German machines. Their diesel tank engines were screaming at high rpm as they made their mad dash forward to try and crest the top edges. Wittmann and Woll were ready for this anticipated breakout from their staging positions at the bottom of this terrain feature, and were not about to allow the enemy tanks any chance of obtaining their goal. Wittmann instructed Woll to aim carefully and to fire as soon as possible so as to place many 8.8cm AP rounds into vital areas of the enemy vehicles. As Woll was making last second adjustments in regards to his sighting telescope, the charging T34/85s suddenly disappeared from view, but it was ascertained, that the enemy panzers had dipped down into a small depression directly ahead of Wittmann's position, only to be seen once again a few moments later.

All was ready as Lötzsch and Kleber were now on the radio net communicating with Wittmann who was providing them final instructions regarding the attack. The order was to fire as quickly as possible and halt the enemy machines. All three panzer commanders were following the snow being kicked up by the enemy vehicles, as they were still hidden from view. These white signatures were the only tell-tale signs of these moving vehicles, and were followed by the German Tiger I gunners until the enemy reappeared in their sight pictures. The crews' tension was enormous inside the German and Russian armored fighting vehicles just prior to the attack. Each side was highly determined to knocked each other out with well placed AP main gun rounds. Each loader of every machine involved had already thrown an AP round into their respective main guns, and were holding the second round in their hands, with the third round ready between their legs! The German bow-machine gunners were rechecking their MG-34s as they would pick off any surviving Russian tank crewmembers that would surely try and escape once their machines were hit and destroyed. The Tiger I gunners would stay locked onto one target until it was eradicated and then move onto the next. At this very close range, one AP round would be enough to shatter any type of vehicle presented by the Russians.

Suddenly, two T34/85s came rushing forward trying to surmount the wadi! Woll received his fire command from Wittmann and pressed the firing handle after a quick final lay of his main gun. His sight picture was aimed directly at the lower portion of the enemy machine. The AP main gun round slammed into this area of the enemy machine with a deafening crack! The enemy machine immediately blew up and rolled back down and into the wadi. Thick black smoke was now billowing out from this destroyed machine, but as it rolled out of sight, it was not certain if any of its crew had baled out or not. There was little time to worry about taking care of its crew, as Wittmann was now directing Woll unto the next approaching target. Lötzsch and Kleber were now firing at all of the juicy enemy targets, as Wittmann and Woll were trying to lock horns with the next T34/85. This vehicle was moving at a faster rate of speed so Woll was now using power traverse to keep this menacing vehicle in his sight picture. This machine was much harder to track as it was bouncing back and forth and disappearing from view time and time again. Woll fired a number of AP rounds at this machine which were either just in front of the vehicle or too low. Suddenly, the T34/85 stopped to fire at Wittmann's Tiger I, but Woll was too quick on the trigger to let this target have any chance of firing. With a loud bang, another enemy panzer was utterly destroyed as Woll's main gun round struck the Russian armored fighting vehicle at the base of the turret which penetrated immediately upon impact. As soon as this engagement ended, Wittmann instructed Woll to take out the next vehicle in their area of fire. This enemy machine was not moving as fast as their second target but was moving in a zig-zag pattern trying to avoid from being hit by the German panzers. Woll traversed the turret of his Tiger I, but was not able to fire at the evasive target as the snow particles and smoke of this battle was now helping to hide the enemy. He was quite sure that the Russian panzer would make an appearance any second, and it would be up to him to keep tracking the vague outline of the T34/85 at all costs. Wittmann was also trying to keep an eye on this target, but it was very hard to accomplish this as the smoke burned his eyes as he was standing up-right in his cupola position trying to obtain a better view of the battle area around his machine. A number of T34/85s that managed to start to climb out of the wadi started to fire their main guns at the German panzers but as they could only depress their main guns 5 degrees they overshot their targets as a direct result. Due to this situation, the Tiger Is were able to fire with impunity for a number of vital minutes which was enough time to keep complete control over the battlefield. This inaccurate firing also helped the German panzer commanders to keep track of the enemy vehicles' positions, and were thus able to predict where they would appear upon climbing over the edge of the wadi.

Lötzsch and Kleber were now trying to maneuver into a depression on the crest of the wadi in order to fire down at the T34/85s more effectively. As they were moving towards their new firing positions, Wittmann and Woll continued to lay down a blanket of fire that was hope to draw fire away for the two other German vehicles. Wittmann was again observing the snow clouds being thrown up by the enemy panzers and locked Woll onto the next suspected area where he was expecting the enemy to appear. A large green and white turret of a KV II suddenly loomed up and out of the wadi, with both Wittmann and Woll being totally surprised at seeing this heavy vehicle coming straight towards their position. Wittmann's only thought was that one of the surviving T34/85 crews had been able to report his location with the result being that the KV II was dispatched to try and knock out his vehicle. Woll did not need to be told what to do next as the huge enemy machine lumbered forward. His main concern was to try and place a main gun round into the driver's vision device which would surely penetrate and ignite the on-board ammunition. The armor plate of the KV II was massive, but the driver's vision port was the Achilles heel pertaining to this type of armored fighting vehicle. Wittmann gave a quick fire command but before he was able to finish this command, Woll fired an AP round which hit the KV II to the left of the driver's vision port and deflected off the moving vehicle. Another AP round was quickly slammed into the smoking breech of the 8.8cm main gun, with Woll taking especially careful aim and pressed the firing handle and sent the AP round flying towards the Russian panzer. The second round hit the KV II just below the turret and jammed it, but did not penetrate the vehicle. Wittmann was now very concerned at this point, as surely the Russian vehicle would still try and fire at his mount. Woll again aimed the 8.8cm main gun at the driver's area and fired his weapon for the third time. As he was doing so, the KV II suddenly fired its main gun with a large crack with the main gun round impacting directly in front of Wittmann's vehicle. A large shower of snow, dirt, and rocks showered down unto his vehicle. Wittmann was not sure if their vehicle had been hit, but as the smoke and snow particles cleared, the KV II was nowhere to be seen! He was quite certain that this huge machine had not moved off as its speed was very slow indeed. No, it must have backed down the slope of the wadi and was trying to approach his vehicle's position from yet another angle. He then decided to reposition his machine in order to try and confuse the enemy panzer commander, as he felt that his present location was now in jeopardy at this time. All had been too easy for the three Tiger Is and their crews and could not allow himself to make a dreadful tactical error in the middle of this fire-fight.

Wittmann then made a quick decision to roll down and into the wadi in order to take out the remaining Russian panzers,as he was quite sure that the Ivans would continue to seek cover from the heavy armament of his Tiger Is, and thus not make any attempt to try and storm over the crest of the depression. He then radioed Lötzsch and Kleber of his intentions and crashed down over the edge of the wadi and guided his driver until Woll could bring his main gun to bare onto the enemy panzers. Wittmann had his driver inch their vehicle forward about twenty meters and was very surprised to see the KV II abandoned. It was now clear what had transpired to this very heavy panzer after Woll had placed his third main gun round into this vehicle. The AP round had indeed crashed through the driver's vision port, and no doubt had instantly killed the driver, whereas the vehicle went out of control and rolled backwards until it veered to the left and crashed into his first victim. The crew must have been panic stricken and baled out of their disabled vehicle as soon as it had come to a halt. The machine was not on fire, but all Wittmann could assume was that the turret was jammed, or that the main gun had been put out of action, or both! He directed his driver to bring his vehicle in line with these two entangled vehicles but to remain about twenty meters away from them in case they suddenly blew up from internal fires that were not visible from his location. The decision to maneuver behind these knocked out vehicles was to obtain additional protection from any in-coming projectiles that the Ivans might try to launch. If any of the other enemy panzers still moving about tried to fire at his Tiger I from the 11, 12, or 1 o'clock positions, they would impact into their former comrades' vehicles, or fire over the top of Wittmann's vehicle. Wittmann was taking a chance in maneuvering and positioning his vehicle in this manner, but figured that he had to remain in this position until Lötzsch and Kleber could make their way down the side of the wadi in which he would then order Woll to fire at the enemy to provide covering fire. The Ivan's were not to be over estimated in the least during this type of closed-in fighting situation as Wittmann and his crew knew only too well that the T34/85s could in fact penetrate their vehicles from their flanks if allowed to out maneuver their opponents. Wittmann was fully aware of the tactical intentions of the Russian panzer crews, and warned Woll that he would have to take them on with full power traverse, as he would not have enough time to lay the main gun with only manual controls. Woll was also quite aware of what was to be done and assured Wittmann that he would try and knock out the Ivans while hydraulically rotating the turret and main gun. It would not be an easy task by any means, as the smoke and fog of battle was also helping to hide the enemy machines as they milled around trying to roll into the sides or rear of Wittmann's machine.

Woll immediately started to traverse the turret and was soon locked onto another T34/85 trying desperately to maneuver in and behind a number of knocked out and burning vehicles. Woll knew that if he could not take out the next enemy panzer very quickly others would manage to out maneuver their now tentative position and fire at them with dire consequences. Woll continue to rotate the heavy turret of the Tiger I and estimated the speed of the fast moving T34/85, as the enemy vehicle made its appearance from behind the destroyed machines. His tracking of the enemy was very accurate and pressed the firing handle as soon as he was certain of his fourth target. The 8.8cm main gun round barked out with the projectile screaming towards its target. This time, the AP round hit the T34/85 square on the turret and penetrated and then detonated the on-board ammunition. The resulting explosion blew off the turret from the superstructure and flipped around in the air a number of times before it came crashing back to earth. The turret crew were flung in all directions and was a scene of bloody carnage. The remainder of the enemy vehicle continued to roll forward although the driver of this vehicle was certainly dead, however, the engine was still functioning. Wittmann yelled to his gunner to disregard the decapitated machine and to traverse onto the next target of opportunity. The last Wittmann saw of this vehicle was when it rolled on and disappeared over a small rise in the wadi.

Lötzsch and Kleber finally arrived on the scene and were now on either side of Wittmann's vehicle. Their leader radioed to them and instructed both panzer commanders to cover his machine as he was not sure, if any of the Ivan's T34/85s or KV IIs were still lurking in the smoke filled areas surrounding his stationary position. The three German machines each took up a defensive posture and selected individual fire zones in order to cover any type of approach attempted by the enemy. The panzer crews knew without a doubt that the Ivan's were now waiting for the smoke to clear and settle before they would venture out and attack the German machines. It seemed obvious to Wittmann and his men that the Russians were now very lackadaisical as if they tried to fire at any of the German machines swift and highly retaliatory fire would be returned immediately.

The snow and smoke was now starting to settle so as to be able to resume the engagement. The German Tiger I crews were now fully alerted to any movements as the enemy had been known to restart their close-in attacks even though the fog of war was still above their vehicle turret lines. With the Tiger Is somewhat higher in overall design, the panzer commanders could at least observe the T34/85s moving about, but with great difficulty. The only absolute way of knowing where the enemy was located, was to shut down the vehicles' powerplants and listen. However, Wittmann could not take the chance of not having one of his machines restart during a critical moment and decided against this avenue of approach. It was now up to the German panzer commanders to locate and direct their respective gunners onto targets and destroy the enemy panzers the best they could under these harsh circumstances. There were now six enemy vehicles roaming about and it was now a case of each Tiger I knocking out two enemy machines in order to survive.

Wittmann had taken an enormous gamble in bringing his small force down and into the wadi. He was now pondering on the idea that he should perhaps reverse his vehicles out of this extremely deadly tactical situation and try to break off the attack. At the very last second, he decided to try another tactic that had been used time and time again. He ordered his panzer commanders to fire a three round volley into the mists of the enemy vehicles in order to see if the Ivans would respond. He figured this was the only procedure to try at this time, and announced a platoon fire command over his radio network. As soon as the three main gun rounds were fired, the Ivans opened up with their 8.5 cm tank guns. The enemy rounds flew over and past the Tiger Is at very close proximity and all impacted into the sides of the wadi. It was still difficult to locate and fire upon the enemy machines as the snow that had been thrown up by the 8.8cm main gun rounds further obscured the view of the German panzer commanders and gunners.

The snow particles had now cleared enough for the German panzer commanders to detect and pin point the enemy gun flashes, and set their gunners and loaders into immediate action. The three Tiger Is started pumping main gun

German tankers are siphoning fuel from a knocked out M4A4 Sherman 17-pounder "Firefly" from "A" Squadron, outside Villers-Bocage. Notice the 8.8 cm AP main gun round entry hole on the forward right side of the turret.

This Panzer IV Ausf.H, was the second vehicle in the procession past the Mayor's Courtyard. Sergeant Brammel's second 17 pdr main gun round knocked this one out.

This Tiger I was the third vehicle in the procession past the Mayor's Courtyard. Corporal Horne's 75 mm gunned Cromwell knocked out this one.

After being hit, the Panzer IV (left) and the Tiger I rolled on in flames and stopped next to each other.

Wittmann's Tiger I, borrowed from Mobiüs' 1st Company, lies disabled by a six-pounder antitank gun in Villers-Bocage.

This is a rear view of Wittmann's disabled Tiger I in Villers-Bocage.

This is a side view of Wittmann's disabled Tiger I.

This front 3/4 view shows Wittmann's disabled Tiger I.

Wittmann after Villers-Bocage. He received the gold tooth after a combat injury.

This is one of the very few close-up photos of Michael Wittmann without a hat!

Wittmann celebrates with friends and a champagne toast is given on June 16, 1944 for the successful battle of Villers-Bocage.

Wittmann relaxing with his men. Left to right: Hans Höflinger, Georg Lötzsch, Michael Wittmann, Karlheinz Warmbrunn, and Bobby Woll.

A typical tactical setting in the field waiting for orders . . .

. . . but they are really playing with a rabbit! These are the only known photos of Wittmann wearing a camouflage uniform.

Wittmann and his company used local farms to camp for the night.

Bobby Woll getting ready to move out early in the morning, after a night at a local farmhouse.

Wittmann, in his new uniform, runs into some old comrades.

Unterscharführer Balthasar "Bobby" Woll received his Knight's Cross as a gunner. He destroyed 81 tanks, 107 antitank guns, an entire battery of 12.5 and 17.2 cm artillery, 7 bunkers, 5 flame throwers, and a heavy mortar unit.

Unterscharführer Balthasar "Bobby" Woll and his driver, after they receive their Tiger I back from being repaired.

Oberscharführer Georg Lötzsch, the "Panzer General." He was also an auto mechanic, and was involved with the development of the Tiger I. Note the left shoulder board with its triune cipher of the LAH.

Left: Rottenführer Karlheinz Warmbrunn, the youngest Panzer commander of the company. His total kills were 51 tanks, 68 antitank guns, 7 bunkers, 2 artillery pieces, and 10 flame throwers.

Above: Unterscharführer Kurt "Quax" Kleber. His friends laughed for a long time about him being blown completely out of a turret without bodily injury. Notice the panzer assault badge on his left breast.

Left: Hauptscharführer Hans Höflinger. He was one of the first to receive a Tiger I. Woll, Lötzsch, Warmbrunn, Kleber, and Höflinger were considered the best panzer commanders in Michael Wittmann's 2nd Company.

Wittmann, Woll, and Warmbrunn discuss their next tactical movement.

Wittmann in the field at Normandy, June 22, 1944, just prior to being awarded the Crossed Swords (Schwerten) to his Knights Cross. He is wearing an Italian U-Boat leather jacket (Lederweste) that was issued to elite panzer unit crews.

Wittmann just after receiving the Crossed Swords to his Knight's Cross and promotion to SS-Hauptsturmführer (Captain), June 22, 1944.

Wittmann was flown to Berchtesgaden on June 25, 1944, to be officially presented the Crossed Swords to the Knight's Cross by Adolf Hitler.

An officer's meeting just before the solo Allied bomber dropped the flares. Wittmann is standing on the left.

Wittmann and another panzer commander study local maps, a very high priority in the modern tactical arena.

Within the first fifty-five minutes of the early afternoon of August 8, 1944, Michael Wittmann, the most famous "Panzer Ace" of World War II, with a total of 138 enemy tank kills, 132 antitank guns and field artillery pieces destroyed (while commanding Tiger I number 007), was killed in action by the 1st Northamptonshire Yeomanry, Number 3 troop, near St. Aignan-De-Cramesnil, France. He bravely fought and lost his last panzer battle along with his beloved panzer crew, Unterscharführer Karl Wagner, Sturmmann Günther Weber, Unterscharführer Heinrich Reimers, and Sturmmann Rudolf Hirschel.

rounds into the enemy panzers with everyone of them being knocked out by controlled and highly accurate panzer gunnery. Wittmann and his crew had destroyed six enemy panzers with Lötzsch and Kleber each destroying two T34/85s.

All three panzer commanders were now covered from head to toe with snow and dirt particles which had fallen down upon their upper bodies. Their eyes were very strained and bloodshot from trying to pick out the enemy panzers. Their faces were a testament to the hard fighting and one did not have to even speak to them to ask if they were exhausted. Wittmann then instructed his men with a very tired voice to reverse out of the wadi, and for his gunners to be aware of any sudden movements among the destroyed enemy vehicles which might be playing dead. The wind was blowing very hard at this time with the snow now falling as they departed from this scene of death and total devastation. Wittmann's three vehicle platoon carefully made their way back to the main elements of the Leibstandarte and reported to Kling what they had encountered and explained in detail of the battle events that had taken place twenty-five minutes earlier. On this day, Wittmann and his crew now had a total of 66 kills.

The Russians continued to attack the German defensive positions in and around Kortyky and Stirty and again, the Leibstandarte Adolf Hitler was sent in to drive back these offensive maneuvers. During the period of January 13-14th, Wittmann and his crew were able to report that they had destroyed their 88th panzer to Sepp Dietrich who nominated this extremely brave panzer commander for the coveted Knight's Cross. Wittmann was to receive this medal on January 14th, but insisted that Bobby Woll should also receive this honor and award for his cool and daring panzer gunnery. The Knight's Cross had been originally only presented to German officers in the German military system for acts of outstanding leadership and bravery in the face of the enemy. Wittmann refused this decoration on the grounds that if he was to receive this award, he would only accept it, if his gunner was also presented with this extremely prestigious medal. After careful consideration and thought, this request was approved whereas both Michael Wittmann and Bobby Woll would receive the Knight's Cross for their brave and outstanding panzer tactics and gunnery against the overwhelming numbers of Russian panzers and deadly anti-tank guns that they had encountered on the hostile Eastern front. Woll's award was not official until January 16th, but was presented his medal at the same ceremony as that of his commander. Wittmann and his resourceful and talented panzer crew were to be photographed in front of their Tiger I (No. S08) with appropriate kill rings to illustrate their top score of 88 enemy panzers destroyed.

On the same January afternoon, shortly after Wittmann and Woll had received their Knight's Cross awards, another sudden crisis brought Wittmann and his Tiger Is into yet another panzer battle against ensuing enemy forces. A large concentration of armored fighting vehicles, including T34/85s and KV Is came charging down upon the German defensive positions with fierce and wild determination. Wittmann's forces maneuvered to meet the challenge, with many hours passing as the fighting went on in the bitter cold with very poor and unsettling visibility. At the end of the afternoon, Wittmann and his panzer crew alone had smashed some sixteen additional T34/85s, and by the end of the day, a further three enemy panzers and three super heavy self-propelled guns had been destroyed. By this stage of the fighting, the Leibstandarte was struggling for its life as every main gun round had to find its mark as resupply was not entirely reliable at the forward front lines. Overall, the panzers of the Heavy Panzer Company, had knocked out 343 Red Army tanks, 8 assault guns and 225 heavy anti-tank guns during the fighting in and around Zhitomir, Kirosten, and Berdichev. During January 12th, the Leibstandarte had destroyed a total of twenty T34/85s and on the next day, eradicated a further twenty-seven Russian armored fighting vehicles to its credit. It was very clear indeed, that the sector in which the Leibstandarte was holding ground, resulted in the Red Army paying a very high price in men and materials for their continued advances upon these highly elite German panzer forces.

On the evening of January 19th, in the area of Kustowezka, the Leibstandarte Adolf Hitler laid exhausted from the vicious fighting that had just taken place in this area of concern. Hans Höflinger tuned his panzer radio to the German national news wavelength and heard the following broadcast:

"SS Untersturmführer Michael Wittmann, platoon leader with in a panzer regiment of the Waffen-SS division "Leibstandarte Adolf Hitler" was awarded for his performance, the Knight's Cross! Since July of 1943 Wittmann with his Tiger I crew have destroyed 56 enemy panzers! On January 8th to the 9th of 1944 he was able with his platoon of Tiger Is, did halt the advance of a Russian panzer brigade, and at the same time destroyed six enemy panzers with his own vehicle and crew. On January 13-14, 1944, Wittmann attacked a strong Russian panzer unit where he destroyed nineteen T34s along with three other heavy self-propelled guns. Michael Wittmann's total panzer kills is now at 88 enemy machines!"

Wittmann and his panzer crew were very happy that their battlefield exploits had made the national news and drank a toast to their highly successful panzer battles. They were all proud of their "Michael" and would follow him anywhere. Wittmann continued to smile and celebrate with his crew, but still wondered what lay ahead of him and his men and would they ever return home to their love ones. He looked at his young panzer crew through tired and dazed eyes and wondered who would actually survive the horrors of the Eastern front and future battles against the Allies.

The fighting raged on for the men and machines of the Leibstandarte Adolf Hitler. In an icy snowstorm a number of days later, Wittmann and his Tiger I crew destroyed five T34/85s in rapid succession. Like shadows the enemy panzers appeared in the snow fields wearing an hoc white winter camouflage comprising of dirty bed sheets draped over their frontal areas of their machines. Once spotted, identified, and fired upon, Wittmann and his platoon of vehicles would roll forward to assault the enemy targets. Many panzer units stormed against the German Waffen-SS units in savage fighting which lasted for hours upon hours without a let up. The German heavy panzers would beat off the Russians for a period of time, but once the Ivans had the chance to regroup, they would charge back across the same ground that their fallen comrade had failed to take during the previous assault waves. Wittmann and the other panzer commanders were fighting day by day against a formidable foe, who once again seemed to have an eternal source of supplies and men to steadily hammer their forces back over ground that had been taken, lost, and then taken again. It was quite clear that the tide of battle on the Eastern front had swung favorably to the Red Army, which was constantly assaulting any German or Axis forces that were still operating in the defensive mode.

Manstein had transferred the First Panzer Army into the Uman-Vinnitsa sector in order to close the gaps in the Fourth Panzer Army's lines and posted the Leibstandarte Adolf Hitler to the XXXXVI Panzer Corps of that army. The First Red Tank Army which had managed to cross the Bug River were attacked by the Waffen-SS units in the area of Vinnitsa on January 24th which resulted in heavy losses on both sides. The opening stage of this battle was successful for the German forces, but the Russians suddenly managed to establish an encircling movement by a Guards Tank Army. The Leibstandarte did its very best against this massive force but confronted by such a heavily armed force, even the great elan of these Waffen-SS forces could not overcome the total weight of the frequent and swift Red Army attacks upon their dwindling numbers. Expedient plans were quickly drawn up and on January 28th, time came for the first Panzer Army to carry out its own encirclement maneuver against the Red Army pincer movements. The XXXXVI and the III Corps generated a large net over the Russians which trapped several of their divisions at the same moment in time, thus capturing over 700 T34/85 tanks and other armored fighting vehicles as well as 8,000 prisoners in POW cages. It seemed that a great deal of steam had been finally expelled by the Red Army and every German soldier on the front lines hoped that this was at last a definite sign that the Russian war machine had been slowed down by the superior fighting capabilities of the German Wehrmacht and Waffen-SS forces as a whole.

However, this loss of numerical strength on the part of the Russian ground forces was not to last for any length of time. Also during January 24th, on another sector of the battlefield, a very strong Russian advance was under way in the Cherkassy area and had trapped 50,000 German soldiers in the area of Svenegordka and repeated requests for the breakout of these divisions was totally refused by Hitler who demanded that the defense of the Dnieper river line be held at all costs even if it meant that every German soldier was to lose his life in the process. The German forces therefore drew up elaborate plans for a breakout to be followed by a defeat concerning the encircled Russian forces and the much needed recapture of Kiev with as many German troops as possible. On one flank, would be the XXXXVI Panzer Corps, with five armored divisions, and III Panzer Corps, with four Panzer divisions, forming the other flank, which would strike deep into the enemy's rear guard and cause as much havoc as possible. Once this was accomplished, and contact made with the encircled troops, the two attacking corps were to turn inward thus trapping the Fourth and Fifth Guard Armies, Twenty-seventh, Fifty-second, and Fifty-third Red Armies, and V Guards Cavalry Corps.

During this time-frame, the weather on the Russian front suddenly changed for the worst with an unexpected thaw that produced the dreaded Rasputitsa, which resulted in a thigh-deep sea of clinging mud which was a common sight in the vast Ukraine, immobilizing all of the concentrations of the III Corp's four divisions, who were frantically trying to free themselves from the grasp of the Red Army which was only possible by heavy and bitter fighting in appalling terrain conditions.

The German troops in and around the Cherkassy salient were being subjected to massive Russian attacks on their flanks, were then suddenly faced with repeated frontal assaults by units of the Third and Fourth Ukrainian Fronts. The trapped German troopers could plainly see that no matter how carefully their escape plans had been drawn up, it was now time to be rescued as soon as possible. The goals and objectives set upon the Germans were non-practical, for the attack northwards by III Corps had little military value; in the eyes of the common fighting soldier in primitive living and fighting conditions and low on ammunition and food, it seemed that all of the skillfully drawn up plans to escape were of little or no meaning. To begin with, the direction of the advances were all wrong, for the Cherkassy pocket laid to the east. Secondly, only a small number of German divisions were ready for the assaults against five Red Armies and even if the advance did somehow manage to reach its planned objectives at Medvin and Boyarka, the Russians would surely sever the advance off to establish new and dangerous isolated pockets thus cutting off and capturing many German troops that were highly needed elsewhere. In the end, through blind obedience to orders from higher headquarters, the offensive began with all its fury. Prior to the initial attack, the efforts of two Panzer and two infantry divisions had managed to bog themselves down in the deep mud which put a severe strain on the advancing German forward units, who needed every available man and operating machine at their immediate disposal.

Due to Michael Wittmann's continued front line leadership and daring with his Tiger I panzer crews, he was awarded the Oakleaf (Eichenlaub) to his Knight's Cross on January 30, 1944, and was promoted in the field to the rank of SS-Obersturmführer (1st Lieutenant). Wittmann was to be the 380th recipient of this decoration and was very proud with himself in receiving this award. He however, took the time to thank his Tiger I crews for all of their hard work and aggressive determination in the face of the overwhelming numerical superiority of the Red Army war machine.

Michael Wittmann was to receive a press release from Adolf Hitler, which stated the following: Oakleaf for SS Untersturmführer Michael Wittmann.

On January 13, 1944 the army information department named SS Untersturmführer Michael Wittmann, holder of the Knight's Cross and platoon leader of the 2nd Company of the SS Panzer Regiment "Leibstandarte Adolf Hitler" out of Vogetal, Upper-Palatinate, was the three hundred eighteenth soldier to receive the Oakleaf from the Führer on January 30, 1944, adding to the Knight's Cross and the Iron Crosses already in his possession.

The Führer sends the following telegram:

"In thankful recognition of your heroic deeds during battle for the future of our countrymen, I grant you, as the 380th soldier of the German Wehrmacht, the Oakleaf (medal) to accompany your Knight's Cross and Iron Crosses."

Adolf Hitler

The Leibstandarte Adolf Hitler was then rushed into the Cherkassy salient and was ordered to eradicate any and all heavy resistance that was holding up the German advance. By February 8th, elements of the Waffen-SS and of 16th Panzer Division had rolled forward and firmly established a bridgehead across the Gniloi Tickich river west of Boyarka.

During this battle SS-Obersturmführer Michael Wittmann and his Tiger I crew had been fighting for every square meter of ground and were totally exhausted from their prior exploits on the battlefield against the Ivans. While attacking in and around Boyarka on February 8th, Wittmann and his panzer crew were to play a very significant role in these assaults along with eleven other Tiger Is of his company. While conducting a patrol he managed to fire at and destroyed nine additional T34/85s without loss to his platoon. Two days later, on February 10th, eighteen enemy self-propelled guns which were skillfully camouflaged in order to ambush the Waffen-SS panzers, were evaded by Wittmann and his vehicles by sending out a reconnaissance unit which located the majority of these vehicles before any harm could be imposed upon the German machines. During the ensuing panzer battle, Wittmann and crew knocked out thirteen enemy self-propelled guns to their credit, which brought his current "kill-score" to 119 enemy armored fighting vehicles destroyed.

On February 15, Michael Wittmann was to take over command of the 2nd Company of the s.SS Panzer Abt.101, and was honored to be placed in this most welcomed position. Every man in this company was very happy with this turn of events, and felt very confidant that this brave and resourceful panzer leader would continue to lead his men with dash and courage in the face of the Allies. Heinz Kling had been seriously wounded in battle and was now recovering in the hospital.

Also during this period, Michael Wittmann was to be photographed by a Waffen-SS 16mm PK (Propaganda Kompanie) camera man by the name of Fritz Gutsches. Gutsches drove right up to Wittmann's Tiger I in a Kubelwagen with his assistant and proceeded to film Wittmann's crew and vehicle in action! He was informed by Wittmann that he would have to place himself on the rear deck of his machine while they were in motion as there was little or no room for him inside the turret. This did not deter Gutsches as he filmed numerous combat engagements while clinging to Wittmann's rear turret stowage bin! This very brave PK cameraman shot sixteen rolls of 16mm movie film, and returned unscathed to Wittmann's company, and returned to his unit.

During the time the Leibstandarte Adolf Hitler and the Wehrmacht Panzer Divisions had been storming their way forward under harsh, bitter, and often times savage fighting conditions, Hitler, at last granted permission to the total evacuation of the Cherkassy pocket. The comprehensive breakout strategy and overall plan had failed to show progress and proved to be unobtainable in practice with chaos resulting from their failure to initiate a successful undertaking. While the bulk of the encircled troops made good their escape under constant enemy fire, the Waffen-SS division "Das Reich" was among the rearguard units in this salient holding fast against rapid and repeated attacks from Red Army tank and infantry units. It was not until a few days later that the men of the Leibstandarte saw large numbers of German troops making slow moving progress forcing themselves through waist high snow drifts and crossing over into their own lines. These men were part of the 35,000 survivors from the pocket making their painful way towards the German lines at last. The German breakout had now been complete, but this situation dramatically illustrated that it took sheer heroic determination, with aggressive spirit, and at times, brutal sacrifices in order to save the day. It was now time to regroup and reorganize once again, and take stock of their dwindling resources of men and equipment.

While Army Group South was trying to concentrate its forces and rebuild its shattered left flank, it was utterly destroyed by a new and very powerful Red Army assault. In the flood of Russian attacks towards the Dniester, the German Corps, isolated from each other had to stand their ground against very aggressive enemy assaults and so had very strict fire control as every main gun round fired needed to find its mark. Between First and Fourth Panzer Armies, an opening was torn across the battlefield at Proskurov, but before the III Corps could plug this breach the whole of First Panzer Army was surrounded in the Kamenz-Podolsk sector. Constant and bitter fighting continued for days on end as the Russians tried to destroy the German forces outright, and as the Panzer Corps battled to avoid destruction they soon found themselves losing more men and equipment which they knew could not be replaced by the hard pressed German armaments industry. The German Wehrmacht and Waffen-SS were again fighting for its life and every German soldier enduring the harsh and bitter battles, plus the constant cold weather, fought with extremely high levels of bravery as if they were taken prisoner by the Red Army, they knew very well they would never return to their families and homeland. It was with this background that many German soldiers fought to their very last rounds of ammunition before either making their escape, or for some, to be killed or indeed captured by the enemy.

A relief effort was generated by the II SS Panzer Corps who fought their way from the west. The spearheads of this unit finally made contact with the Leibstandarte Adolf Hitler, but it was indeed too late for any further successes for the men of the Waffen-SS, even though they had made additional gains on the local battlefield. The Leibstandarte was now only a mere shadow of its former self, with only a battered remnant on call to take on the continuing Russian counter assaults that were now coming in every hour, on the hour. Those that had survived the ordeal of the Russian front considered themselves to be very lucky to be alive, and for many, their combat experiences on the Eastern front would live on forever inside them. The orders finally came for the Leibstandarte to prepare to return to Western Europe for regrouping and reorganization as the Allies would no doubt be mounting a new spring offensive for an invasion of Northwest Europe. The battle hardened veterans of the Leibstandarte would form a cadre of leaders that would establish a new "LAH" with their years of front line duty being used to train the new replacements that would be needed for the many forth-coming battles in the very near future.

Michael Wittmann and his men were very happy that they would soon be heading westward for a short leave with their families and girlfriends. Wittmann was still the commander of the 2nd Company as Haupsturmführer Kling was still recovering from his wounds. It would seem very strange to be able to wake up in the morning and not have to be confronted by the vastness and harshness of the Russian front which Wittmann and his men had endured for so many long months. It seemed that the men of the Leibstandarte were being given a gift in order to return to civilization once again and not have to suffer the bitter realities of the brutal Russian front any longer. Many of Wittmann's friends had been killed on the vast steppes of Mother Russia and felt dearly for them as his panzer company boarded the troop trains heading west. He could not fully understand how he and his panzer crews had survived such harsh and brutal fighting conditions which had taken thousands upon thousands of human lives every day. He also could not believe that he was now the top scoring Panzer Held (Tank Hero) of the entire war! What was to come of him and his panzer unit? Would the Western Allies have overwhelming military superiority in panzers and aircraft in similarity to the Red Army? It was quite clear that new panzers for the Leibstandarte would be few and far between as surely some of the vehicles that they would be fighting in would be the same worn out Tiger Is that were being transported west from Russia, which would have to be completely overhauled before they could be brought up to standards for battles with the enemy forces pending their arrival on the shores of the European continent. Every lesson learnt on the Eastern front concerning panzer versus panzer battles would have to be instilled into the minds of every new replacement until they were as natural as breathing itself. The burning question concerned to all was how long the German military forces had until they were ordered back into battle once again.

With all of this on Wittmann's mind, the Leibstandarte Adolf Hitler slowly moved via rail transit towards Western Europe and then into Belgium where Wittmann's unit would establish a new training area to refit, and train their forces. Little did Wittmann realize, that he was to gain even more fame in the forthcoming panzer battles in Normandy, which were to make him the most famous panzer commander of all time!

Chapter XII

VISIT TO THE TIGER I FACTORY AT KASSEL

March 1, 1944 – April 16, 1944

The name of SS-Obersturmführer Michael Wittmann and his panzer exploits had been thoroughly explored by the German propaganda ministry towards the end of 1943 and was soon becoming a household name in war-torn Germany. War heros were always a great morale booster at the home front, and every opportunity was taken by the press to place Wittmann and his panzer crews into the limelight for their heroic bravery in the face of the Russian hordes on the brutal Eastern front. Wittmann and his men had fought very well indeed in the face of harsh adversity on the Russian front but felt deeply that it was their duty to fight for their homeland and were not concerned with being shown any type of preferential treatment cast in their direction. Their only concern was that they had time after time saved countless German soldiers' lives on the battlefield and that was their only true satisfaction. But this was not to be for Wittmann and his men, as the German propaganda machine was to continue to print news about their Panzer Held (Tank Hero) and his Tiger I crews as much as possible in order to fully illustrate to the German populace how brave and fearsome these men were in the face of the enemy. Newspapers were to have full page articles about Wittmann and his panzer crews, which started to appear soon after the beginning of 1944.

Even before Wittmann was to leave the Russian front, he was interviewed many times by visiting war correspondents, who were very eager to interview and report on this combat hardened veteran. Wittmann being a somewhat shy individual at first did not want to be questioned by these inquisitive people, but was told that it would be better for him to cooperate as this would only help to build-up morale throughout the front line fighting units, and was also bringing greater fame to the Leibstandarte Adolf Hitler. After a short period of time, Wittmann finally had to accept his faith and started to feel more at ease while being interviewed by the press services that were always trying to obtain a hero's story.

Once the news had been announced that Michael Wittmann and his panzer crews were being posted to the Western front, the German propaganda ministry was once again going to have a field day showing off this most talented Panzer hero with many guest appearances and interviews being set up for Wittmann to explain his harsh battles on the Russian front. Wittmann was not too happy about being forced into the limelight while in his homeland, as many of his comrades who had been fighting along side him had endured all of the same hardships and they too had destroyed many Russian panzers to their well earned credit. But it was quite clear from the start of their long journey back to Germany, that the German people wanted to learn more about this Panzer hero with the name of Michael Wittmann.

Michael Wittmann was to be very busy during the following weeks after his arrival in Germany and was given a hero's welcome everywhere he made his appearance. The love and admiration from the German people towards this superb panzer commander was always overwhelming and somewhat unsettling as Wittmann never knew how good it could feel with all of this attention being directed upon his person. On many occasions, he felt as though he was some kind of a film star, just back from location off a Hollywood movie set. The respect and total adulation shown to him by his fellow countrymen and women only instilled a feeling that what he and his panzer crews were fighting for, was truly the step in the right direction in stopping the Red menace from the east, which was feared most of all by the German people as a nation. The dinners, the speeches, and the many parties, and all of the other pleasurable events that were revolving around his notoriety were truly a pleasant change from the horrors of the Russian front. But deep down inside Wittmann felt that he should be with his panzer unit in Belgium training the replacements that were now filling out their depleted ranks. There was a great deal to be taught to these inexperienced panzer crewmembers as the Allies were surely mounting their forces for a new invasion plan for North-West Europe. Wittmann soon hoped that the limelight he now found himself placed into would finally start to fade allowing him to return to his men and carry out the needed panzer training that the younger replacements would need to survive the ever mounting tide of the western Allies' numerical superiority.

As he predicted (and hoped for), the lime-light started to diminish in the way of Wittmann being ordered back to his panzer unit stationed in Bruges, Belgium. There were still many newspaper articles being written about him, and no doubt the Propaganda ministry would be following his further panzer battles on the field of battle against the Allies. He did feel that his appearances throughout Germany was a great morale booster to the German people and enjoyed meeting all who were turning out to see him. Many questions had been asked of him: How did their Tiger I vehicle operate in the face of the enemy? Were they receiving enough food? Was their mail from home reaching them in the field? Wittmann was glad to answer any and all of these questions, but it seemed that the average German citizen had no comprehension of what daily life consisted of, or what it was like on the cruel Russian front! The German people of course knew that life was harsh, but they could not understand or appreciate the fact that the Ivans were not on the same level of human endeavor as the Germans fighting against their forces. The home-front German male and female of worn-torn Germany were only interested in hearing the daring feats Wittmann and his men had accomplished, and were not very interested in hearing how the Russian Army had sacrificed hundreds, if not thousands of their troops in order to take just one objective. The only events that the people of Germany wanted to learn about, was how Wittmann and his men had held back the Russians' human and mechanical waves of aggression that were hell bent on entering greater Germany and spreading the hated red scourge of the east.

On March 1, 1944, SS-Obersturmführer Michael Wittmann took the hand of Hildegard Burmester and married her in regards to a very formal military wedding. As many of Wittmann's comrades as possible were present, plus the parents of the bride and groom, along with many family members and friends. This was one of Wittmann's most happiest moments of his life and was extremely grateful to have such a loving and beautiful wife as Hilde. After a very short honeymoon, Wittmann would return to his panzer company and his comrades.

Before Michael Wittmann was able to return to his beloved panzer unit in Belgium, he was invited to visit the Tiger I panzer factory at the Henschel works in Kassel on April 16th. He felt that it would be interesting to revisit the factory once again and of course to thank one and all for such a fine fighting vehicle as the Tiger I. Wittmann's superiors also felt at this time that a visit to this armaments establishment warranted good public relations with the management and establish a great morale factor with the factory workers. It was also appreciated that the workers would be thrilled to be able to see, meet, and hear the voice of their country's most famous Panzer Held who had obtained such great fame while operating and commanding one of 'their' Tiger Is in the face of the enemy. All of the necessary arrangements were made well in advance, and it was also felt that Wittmann should indeed present a special speech right in the factory work-shops to all of the workers along with their wives and invited friends. Wittmann was very excited about this appearance as he wanted to thank the workers of this firm for producing such an advanced and deadly armored fighting vehicle, that had time after time saved many panzer crews' lives on the field of battle against the Russians. Wittmann spent a great amount of time writing and then rewriting his planned speech until he had it down word for word from memory. This opportunity was not to be wasted in any sense of the word, as he wanted the workers of the Henschel factory to know that because of their skilled labor and advanced workmanship, the Russians had taken a terrible beating at the hands of the Tiger I panzer crews. It was true that the Russians now had many more panzers then the German forces fighting on the Eastern front, but the German Tiger I was more highly advanced with its thicker armor plate, and had at that time, one of the most powerful main guns installed on any panzer in the inventory of the German military forces. It would be Wittmann's responsibility to express enormous gratitude and trust towards the workers of Henschel, as if it was not for their hard work and total determination, the German panzer crews would have found themselves in an empty void in regards to halting the surmounting Russian numerical supremacy.

On April 16, 1944, Michael Wittmann was driven to the Henschel factory at Kassel in a company car which had been sent to him by management, and eagerly awaited his second arrival at the panzer works. As soon as the car arrived at the main entrance of the Henschel factory, Wittmann was greeted by the executives of this firm and then escorted to their main office. Wittmann was to meet and shake hands with the following leading personalities, and as follows: Dr.Ing. Erwin Aders (Chief designer of the Tiger I), Herr Oscar Henschel (Chairman), Herr Robert Henschel (Welfare Director), Dr. Stieler von Heydekampf (Managing Director), Herr Fleischer (Financial Director), and Dr. Pertus (Production Manager). After the various introductions, Wittmann was given a chance to take a short break and to freshen up, and also to have a cup of coffee and a cigarette. During this time frame, it was announced that he had arrived, with the factory workers now filling up the area in which Wittmann would appear and present his speech.

Finally, it was time to be taken to the factory work-shop where he would greet the workers and then give his speech. Wittmann was not sure where he would stand and talk to the people gathered to hear him, but figured that all of these details had been pre-arranged by the management personnel, and would follow their lead. After a short walk from the executives offices, Wittmann and his hosts came to a metal door cut into the rear end of one of the work-shops (Werk III Mittelfeld to be exact), and was opened for him . He then stepped through this door and was greeted by a very enthusiastic crowd of friendly people who had gathered and were waiting for him to make his entry. The applause was overwhelming and did not stop until he was surrounded by large numbers of people who were trying desperately to shake his hand and also to obtain a signed autograph. Wittmann was once again taken back by all of this attention as he was not expecting the rush of people in regards to this friendly assault upon his person. Needless to say, he was very happy about the whole affair, but kept a very serious aire about him and continued to follow his hosts.

The factory workers and management had positioned a newly finished late-production model Tiger I Ausf.E (with narrow transportation tracks) at the end of the work-shop with a set of wooden stairs in front of the vehicle. The massive turret of the Tiger I was situated at the 6 o'clock position in order that nobody would accidently bump their heads on the 8.8cm main gun while climbing up or descending down from this vehicle before or after Wittmann's visit and speech. A microphone and stand was placed just to the right side of the bow-machine gunner's/radio-operator's hatch where Wittmann would stand and deliver his speech and special thanks to the workers and executives of Henschel GmbH. The Tiger I Ausf.E Panzerkampfwagen being offered as a podium was a very appropriate setting for Wittmann's speech and he greatly appreciated the thought and understanding given to him for this meaningful event.

As Wittmann stepped up the wooden stairs to take his place at the microphone, he could not help to notice all of the people who had assembled to see and hear his speech. As soon as the crowd of people saw him climb up the stairs they all moved in closer to obtain a better view of this famous Panzer Held. Workers had climbed up and onto the support beams in the factory, while others had positioned themselves in nearby vertical support columns. It seemed that every available foot of space in which to observe this man was taken up with the crowd of people extending to the rear of the huge panzer factory. Wittmann had never seen so many people at one time and at one place. It made him feel very proud to say the very least.

At last, the crowd started to settle down and a sudden silence filtered throughout the vast panzer works as Wittmann began his long awaited speech. He first thanked the management of Henschel GmbH for allowing him to appear before their workers and then continued to express his gratitude and thanks from his panzer crews in regards to the fighting capabilities of the Tiger I. He explained a little about his daily exploits with this fighting vehicle and continued to give praise for the superb quality and workmanship put into this advanced panzer. He also stated that many lives had been saved in regards to the massive armor plate of the Tiger I, and further explained that many of the Allied panzers were easily penetrated and out matched by the powerful 8.8cm main gun. The Tiger I was highly feared by the Allies, and had become the bogey-man of the armored battlefield where ever it made a combat appearance. And lastly! Additional Tiger Is were needed at the front, and Wittmann asked the workers to produce as many machines as possible under the prevailing conditions.

Wittmann's speech lasted for about fifteen minutes and was given a great amount of applause upon completion. After his speech, he was taken by management throughout the panzer factory and viewed the various work stations and assembly points and gained a comprehensive and thorough understanding of how a Tiger I was built and tested at the factory. After this walk through, he and his hosts took a short smoke break and then was allowed to answer additional questions by the factory workers. The Henschel executives and Wittmann then left the work-shops and returned to the Chairman's office where Wittmann was presented with a gift in regards to a wooden 1/20th scale model (see photo section 2) of a Tiger I. He was very moved with this gift and thanked the people of Henschel one and all.

It was now time to depart the factory and Wittmann once again thanked and shook hands with all of the management personnel and then prepared to return to his panzer unit. Upon leaving the Henschel Tiger I factory, Wittmann felt very good indeed! The visit had not only given the workers additional incentive to work even harder, but it also had instilled a new sense of responsibility upon Wittmann to bring his panzer crews through even harder and desperate battles that would surely come to pass in holding back the growing numbers of Allied panzers. He was now determined even more so to halt the enemy from ever entering into his beloved homeland.

Chapter XIII

THE BATTLE FOR "VILLERS-BOCAGE"

June 13, 1944

The Allied landings in Normandy on June 6, 1944 were to mark a new chapter in the story of SS-Obersturmführer Michael Wittmann and his highly experienced cadre of panzer commmanders who had fought with him on the Eastern front. The Leibstandarte was still posted in the area of Bruges in Belgium as his Tiger I panzer company had been resting and re-equipping their depleted strength with new replacement personnel. These individuals were being taught combat tactics and panzer gunnery under the watchful eyes of Michael Wittmann and his platoon leaders, with attention to detail set at an extremely high standard! Lessons learnt the hard way on the Eastern front were drilled into the new replacements until they could perform these drills to the satisfaction of their company commanders.

The LAH had not been called into battle as of yet as the German High Command had still not ascertained if the Allied landings in the Normandy area had been a tactical diversion as they had feared the invasion of North-West Europe would most likely come across the shortest stretch of the English channel with the landings predicted in and around the Pas de Calis area of France.

The LAH had by this time become part of the German High Command's strategic reserve, and as a direct result, was under the control of Adolf Hitler. It was not until June 7th, that the orders were given for the LAH (1st SS-Panzerkorps) to commence its movement south-west towards the area of Normandy. Due to the overwhelming numerical superiority of the Allies, especially in the air-war, movement by day was at least suicidal with vehicles having to be heavily camouflaged during the hours of daylight, with movement only accomplished during the hours of darkness. As the urgency of the situation intensified, and the call for elite panzer units being badly needed at the front, some travelling during the hours of daylight was justified in regards to certain panzer units being able to arrive at their respective staging areas on time. Special air-watches were set up, with Tiger I crew-members (loaders and bow-machine gunners) sitting on top of their vehicles scanning the sky for the dreaded Allied 'Jabos.' Panzer commanders had their cupola mounted MG-34s at the ready for any marauding Allied fighter-bomber which might suddenly attack and strafe their vehicle columns. Company commanders were well aware that any losses pertaining to their Tiger Is could not be replaced, so every effort was made in order for the panzers to roll towards their battle objectives. Military police units held up other traffic in order that the heavy armored fighting vehicles could continue towards their jumping-off positions. Maintenance units which followed the advancing panzer columns were on call day and night, so as to repair any vehicles that might either break down due to overheated engines or smoking transmissions. Any vehicles that were totally destroyed or gutted by fire were pushed off the road by the maintenance units in order to continue the advance.

In order to reach Normandy, the LAH was to travel via Paris, roll down the famous Champs Elysees (in parade formation) and then turn south-westward on the N316 from Gournay-en-Bray to les Andelys, then through the Levriere valley and towards Morgny, and then onto the D13 to Longchamps; indeed, a very dangerous route which was nick-named, "Hunting Bombers Racing Track."

On June 8th, near Versailles, Wittmann's 2nd Company was caught in an air-raid which damaged four Tiger Is which were left behind with SS-Obersturmführer Stamm's maintenance unit. Bobby Woll's Tiger I (who was now a panzer commander) was one of the damaged vehicles and was taken abroad by Wittmann as his gunner. Wittmann's new gunner was left behind with Stamm and the damaged vehicles, and would help bring these machines back to the company after repairs had been accomplished. After this incident, their panzer unit was jokingly called the "Carpet Bomb Battalion"! It was not until the 12th of June that the schwere (heavy) SS-Panzer Abteilung 101 arrived in the area of "Villers-Bocage" with Wittmann's 2nd Company taking up concealed positions in a nearby wood (north-east of the town) which was hoped to provide them with effective cover during the proceeding day. 1st Company commander SS-Hauptsturmführer Mobius was standing by on Wittmann's right flank with his depleted unit ready at hand for any fighting that would present itself. Their Corps GHQ had moved itself on June 9/10 to a small hamlet called Baron-sur-Odon, which was situated between "Villers-Bocage" and Caen, in and around Point 112 on their battle maps, where it remained until June 15.

It was quite apparent to Michael Wittmann and his panzer commanders that the fighting tactics in Normandy were to be very much different than those on the Russian Front. Normandy was a very lush and fertile agricultural farming area with thousands of individual farms scattered throughout the countryside with an intricate road network of sunken lanes, cart tracks, winding roads that could conceal an enemy anti-tank gun with ease, or many two-man bazooka teams that could lay in ambush completely undetected until the flash and strike of their weapon was the only signature of the enemy's whereabouts and deadly activities. Firing ranges for main gun ammunition was severely restricted due to the limited open countryside and closed up roads. No longer were his panzer crews offered the wide vastness as encountered on the steppes of the Eastern front; where one could observe the enemy for many kilometers away and make the necessary tactical moves well in advance before engaging the Ivans. In Normandy, this was not possible as danger could lurk around every hedgerows, every farm building, and from nowhere the enemy could spring forth from their hidden positions and either fire their anti-tank guns, or launch one of their latest panzer killing weapons. If the panzer crews were to survive this type of closed-in fighting environment,they would have to work even more closely together as a combine team, with tightfisted coordination between not only their respective panzers in their own companies, but also with the accompanying infantry units, who could protect their panzers in built-up areas.

The Tiger I was now being denied its primary function of open space to deploy, perform its battle run, and rout the enemy in regards to the Normandy terrain features. Panzer gunnery was reduced to under 500 meters which was extremely deadly for any known Allied armored fighting vehicles assaulting German Tiger Is. Deployment would however be very difficult for the German Tiger tanks and other heavy fighting vehicles as the thick surrounding vegetation did not allow these large vehicles to rampage forward at will and severely hampered their overall operations and performance.

Wittmann was also very concerned that his vehicles were now being used as defensive weapons of war, and indeed cast a gloomy shadow upon the panzer crews serving in these machines, as they were now the last hope of turning the tide of war on the Western front in their favor. It was also very clear to the German forces fighting in the Normandy invasion front that every piece of equipment was worth its weight in gold and was to be recovered and repaired in record time if damaged or immobilized. When a panzer broke down from a mechanical failure, it was sometimes necessary to tow it with another vehicle of the same class (e.g. a Tiger I towing a Tiger I) which was highly forbidden in every panzer training manual. However, due to the prevailing circumstances the crews found themselves under at this time it was vital that these precious machines were not to be left on the roads or fields where their certain lost and destruction was only a matter of minutes away once they were detected by Allied fighter-bombers. Nerves were tested to their limits as many times the vehicle columns were held up due to a single vehicle breakdown, which completely blocked the narrow roads, and with the Normandy terrain being ever inhospitable to tactical military vehicle movements, it was impossible for the blocked vehicles to turn off the roads and roll past the disabled machines. When the situation arose, many of the panzer crews would dismount with automatic weapons at the ready, and cut nearby foliage to be placed on their vehicles in order to hide them from the ever probing eyes of the enemy. Spacing between vehicles was to be fifty meters apart at all times, and was the responsibility of the panzer commanders to keep their distance from each other in order to avoid giving the Allied "Jabos" any opportunity of destroying their vehicles.

The panzer tactics involved in the Normandy fighting had changed drastically, as the panzer commanders again would not be able to view the enemy from long distances, nor could their reconnaissance vehicles make extended probes due to the Allied air umbrella. Every machine was to be ready for action on a moments notice, with their gunners glued to their firing controls and optical gunnery devices to knock out any Allied vehicles that presented themselves. Navel gun fire via the Allied navel forces was an entirely new element that the German land forces had to contend with, and destroyed many of their vehicles while still in their staging or jumping-off positions. Vehicles were blown to bits by highly accurate navel gun fire which was being directed by Allied spotter aircraft which flew constantly over the Norman countryside. If movement was detected via this manner, it was not long before the rush if 11, 15, and 16 inch navel rounds would be heard by the German ground troops. Every available weapon was trained on these Allied spotter planes, and many were shot down. The war in Normandy was to be very much different for the fighting forces in regards to what they had experienced beforehand to a large degree. They had been outnumbered before on the Eastern front, but this time the western Allies were much more coordinated and it seemed that they were not to give up the battle until their vast numbers of vehicles and men had completely over run the German forces forthwith. The Allies had tried to invade the European continent in 1942 (at Dieppe) and they were not about to be denied this second chance in order to vindicate themselves in the summer of 1944.

On the morning of June 13, 1944, Michael Wittmann and his panzer crews awoke very early in order to make themselves ready for the day's activities. Wittmann reported to Obergruppenführer Sepp Dietrich who was already giving his operations order. The thirty year old panzer commander was very anxious to maneuver his vehicles under his command out of their nearby staging area, but insisted that he alone and his Tiger I crew be allowed to reconnoiter the area northwest between his present location and Balleroy. Rumors abounded that the Allies were surmounting a massive panzer attack which was thought to be aimed at Panzer Lehr's left flank. Wittmann was quite sure that the enemy could not be very far away, but was not sure which direction the Allies would strike from and what their real strength would be. He was finally granted permission from his battalion commander to carry out his heavy reconnaissance mission with his Tiger I and no others. As Bobby Woll's Tiger I had not been repaired as of this date, he was to continue as Wittmann's gunner. Prior to moving out, Wittmann was informed by Sepp Dietrich, that a town called "Villers-Bocage" and the road to Caumont were a vital link in their advance and that this town and its road junction must be taken at all costs if their panzer assaults were to continue successfully.

As Wittmann and his crew mounted their Tiger I, his concern was that the Allies would be making a comprehensive panzer attack, and that Panzer Lehr would take the brunt of the fighting and quite possibly be destroyed as a fighting unit. Unless the Allies could be somehow halted or made to rethink their strategy, would the German land forces be able to resupply and move up additional panzers which was the key to tactical success. The reason that this brave panzer commander did not allow any of his other Tiger Is on this probe was if he was detected from the air or ground, his company would lose only one vehicle as a result. It was a calculated risk on his part, but was willing to take the chance under the current circumstances. He also felt that with only one vehicle travelling in and around the vicinity of "Villers-Bocage" little concern would be made of a lone Tiger I if he was detected and fired upon.

As Wittmann gave the signal to his driver in the early dawn light to move out, little did he know that this day's fighting would place him in the annals of armor history as being responsible for the most famous single handed armor exploit of the Second World War, or for that matter, any war!

It was now 6:00 am and Wittmann and his Tiger I crew were now moving towards "Villers-Bocage" from a south-easterly direction and being very careful in keeping in and around the tree lines of a nearby wooded area. Wittmann knew that at any moment, an Allied "Jabo" could pounce down on his single panzer as these feared machines took off from their home bases at first light. This highly experienced panzer commander continued to give his driver directions in regards to concealing his huge vehicle from observation from the air. As he stood in his opened commander's cupola, Wittmann tried in vain to keep scanning the terrain ahead of his vehicle, and also to watch the morning sky for any trouble headed in his direction. The countryside that they were travelling through was heavily laced with an abundance of thick vegetation with limited horizons available to him and his gunner and was very difficult to detect any signs of the enemy. Slowly, Wittmann and his vehicle inched their way forward on their reconnaissance mission towards the sleepy town of "Villers-Bocage." After about two hours of moving forward towards their objective, Wittmann ordered his driver to position their vehicle into a small crop of trees and shut down the engine in order to `listen' for any sounds of the enemy. As he and his loader were `listening', a German infantry sergeant made a sudden and unexpected appearance and reported to Wittmann that strange looking panzers were rolling by his concealed positions. Wittmann jumped down from his Tiger I and ran roughly four hundred meters with the infantry sergeant and soon heard the sounds of many tracked vehicles coming from the nearby N175. The infantry sergeant then threw himself into his foxhole, with Wittmann right behind him as he was quite concerned about the developing situation. As the two men slowly raised their heads from their hide, they were shocked to see large numbers of Allied tanks, half-tracks, and a few armored cars moving at high speed up and along the highway in a northeasterly direction. It was quite clear that the Allies had sent an armored spearhead through "Villers-Bocage" to try and outflank Panzer Lehr, or as a second guess, to flush out any German combat units in the immediate area surrounding the town. As Wittmann watched this deadly procession pass by, it seemed that the Allied armored armada would never end.

He tried to keep account of all of the vehicles and types, but with them rolling by so fast, it was almost next to impossible. The German infantry squad were powerless to do anything about this tense situation, as they had only light weapons at their disposal, and it would be suicide to try and take on this massive armored force without heavier ordnance.

The Allied armored unit that Wittmann and the infantry sergeant were observing was the 4th County of London Yeomanry which was a contingent of the 22nd brigade of the 7th Armored Division. This highly experienced armored unit had been ordered to advance into "Villers-Bocage" under strict radio silence. After taking and occupying the town, 'A' Squadron and 1st Battalion The Rifle Brigade were to roll on towards a height tactically marked Hill 213 to the northeast. The 4th CLY had been on a ten mile reconnaissance patrol, but had not encountered any German resistance whatsoever, and did not expect to meet and engage any German forces. Thus, they entered the town, and then made a schedule stop for a tactical break. 'A' Squadron of the 4th CLY had by then rolled through "Villers-Bocage" and moved up the N175 (the armored unit Wittmann had observed) and moved about two miles out of the town and then halted with all of its vehicles bunched up on the right-hand side of the highway. The tanks of 'A' Squadron for some unknown reason had been positioned nose to tail with the gun barrels of each vehicle hanging over the rear decks of the proceeding vehicle. A reconnaissance unit was sent out to try and locate any enemy units that might be in the area, as a small number of German armored cars had been spotted earlier to their direct front. While this mission was being carried out, it was time for vehicle maintenance, a brew up of tea, and breakfast.

Directly behind 'A' Squadron, was The Rifle Brigade under the command of Lt. Ingram which consisted of twelve M3 half-tracks carrying the infantry, along with three M5A1 (Honey) tanks. With this unit of vehicles were also two O.P. Shermans with wooden guns, the I.O.'s scout car, and medical officer's M3 half-track. Roughly four-hundred meters behind this unit was the RHQ which consisted of four Cromwell tanks. The commanding officer of the 4th CLY (Lt. Col. Arthur Cranleigh) had been travelling all along his unit's line of march in his armored scout car, and had moved up with 'A' Squadron in order to keep abreast of the happenings developing at the front of his armored column.

At the road junction to Caumont, (main square of "Villers-Bocage") 'B' Squadron halted their vehicles for their tactical break and guarded this important intersection. The Allies at this time were very confidant that the war was to be over very soon, and also felt that the German forces had had a belly full of fighting and were not the mighty war machine they once were in past years. A false sense of security seemed to filter through out the Allied camp, and everyone concerned was only interested in returning home to family and love ones.

Wittmann immediately realized that this opportunity could not be lost! He had to act very quickly in order to disallow this juicy prize to escape. He did not however have time to radio his comrades, as he did not know how long the

British tanks would besituated on the N175. If he radioed his other Tiger Is to move up,his transmission would surely be monitored by Allied radio and the element of surprise would be missed altogether. It was time for immediate action on his part to storm forward, and assault the enemy vehicles with well placed main gun rounds. Wittmann then thanked the infantry sergeant for his assistance and then ran back to his hidden vehicle as fast as he could. As he approached his armored mount, he gave his driver the hand and arm signal to cranked up the vehicle's engine, and for the rest of the crew to prepare for battle stations. Wittmann jumped up and into his vehicle with amazing speed while trying desperately to grab his earphones and throat microphones in order to communicate with his crew. The rest of his crew were not too sure what had just transpired, but they did know that Michael was preparing to take on the enemy post haste as his actions and body language clearly illustrated that he was ready for another panzer assault against the enemy.

As soon as the Tiger I's engine was running at proper rpm, Wittmann ordered his driver to reverse out of the wooded area that concealed them. The driver gunned the Maybach engine and slammed the transmission selector into reverse gear. With a great lunge, the heavy panzer slowly backed up with its commander giving his driver accurate and quick instructions in order to not ram into any nearby trees, rocks, or fallen logs that would either hamper their exits or cause any further noise to their hasty departure. Wittmann was very concerned that his engine sounds would alert the enemy, but knew that the infantry sergeant and his squad would inform him if any danger or aggression was aimed at his vehicle should they be discovered. He kept a wary eye open for his driver and another for any signs of anyone or anything approaching from the direction of the N175. The enemy must have still been running their vehicles during this time frame as there was no indication of the Tommies moving towards his departing vehicle. It was also ascertained that the wooded area had also helped to muffle their existence. As the Tiger I broke out of the tree line, Wittmann had no observation with the enemy, and indicated to his crew that once they rounded the edge of the woods, they would immediately come into contact with the enemy forces at hand. The time was 08:35 hours by Wittmann's watch.

Finally, the massive Tiger I was turned to the left while still under reverse gear which straightened out the vehicle towards the direction of the town. As his vehicle came into attacking position, years of hard and bitter combat experience came into play. Wittmann had already explained to his crew what they were about to encounter, and all knew that the odds of coming out of this assault were very slim. Wittmann's loader had already thrown an 8.8cm AP main gun round into the breech and was stacking as many others as he could upon the turret basket floor. He had also loaded the co-ax MG-34 with ammunition and had additional gurt-sacks ready for reloading the weapon if needed. Woll was already traversing the turret of the vehicle to the three o'clock position in order to take out the vehicles and men of the Infantry Rifle Brigade which would be their first targets of opportunity. The bow-machine gunner was instructed to start firing his MG-34 as soon as he had a clear view of the enemy vehicles in his telescopic sight; in order to pick off any infantry soldiers who might try and escape on foot once they saw and heard the approach and firing of their vehicle. As the leading twelve vehicles were M3 half-tracks, Wittmann decided that no main gun ammunition would be expended as these types of vehicles could be destroyed with sustained machine gun fire. He also did not want to fire off 8.8cm main gun rounds at the start of his battle run as this would surely alert any and all enemy troops in the area.

As soon as Wittmann's Tiger I rounded the edge of the woods, all hell broke loose. The Infantry Rifle Brigade were seen to be dismounting from their M3 half-tracks and trying to escape to the left and right-hand sides of the N175. Wittmann ordered his two MG-34s to open fire as soon as he observed this action, even before his gunner and bow-gunner had locked onto the targets. It was only a few seconds before his weaponry found their marks, but for Wittmann, it seemed like an hour. Woll was firing at the first M3 half track as it was very obvious that he would 'walk' the machine gun fire down the line of vehicles as the Tiger I advanced towards the main road. Woll did not even have to elevate or depress the co-ax MG-34, as the ground they were travelling upon was quite level. The resulting machine gun fire ignited the fuel tanks of the majority of the enemy half-tracks, with the infantry now pinned down beside the road trying desperately to fire back at the approaching Tiger I. Just the sight of this heavy panzer was bad enough, but being fired upon by one this close was nerve shattering at the thought. The British infantry on the right side of the road, suddenly withdrew to the left side of the N175, which was taken as a move to find better cover in case main gun rounds (HE) were fired into their mists for good measure. The MG-34 firing was enough to rout this unit as all of their vehicles were now on fire, with primary and secondary fuel tanks blowing up with intense heat and thick black smoke. The fog of battle soon filled the surrounding area, but Wittmann and his crew pressed on.

Next to appear were the three M5Al Honey tanks that were behind the M3 half tracks. Wittmann was very concerned at this time as he was sure that his actions had alerted nearby enemy tanks and thus ordered his gunner to open fire with main gun rounds at these light panzers. Woll was ready at his firing controls and locked onto the first vehicle. Wittmann gave the fire command the second the driver halted the vehicle. The first 8.8cm AP main gun round fired at the light tank passed through it completely and within seconds was totally engulfed in flames with some of the surviving crew baling out the best they could. The second main gun round let out a fearful crack and smashed into the right side of the next vehicle's turret and blew this machine to pieces. As soon as the second main gun round was fired, the loader slammed another main gun round into the hot and smoking breech which clanged as the heavy breech mechanism closed for the next engagement. Woll again locked onto the next target and with the pressing of the firing handle, destroyed the last M5A1 light tank. During the main gun firing, the bow-machine gunner was continuing to fire his MG-34 in order to keep any enemy troops that had survived the main gun blasts under control and to reframe them from being able to fire any weapons that would be hostile to their vehicle.

Second in command, Major Carr of the 4th CLY's RHQ, had now become aware of Wittmann's approach and moved his 75mm gunned Cromwell tank forward in order to observe what the hell was happening. He heard the firing, but was not sure if this was a full attack by a German panzer company or if artillery was being fired off and landing in the area forward of his position. As he moved forward, he saw to his total amazement, a lone Tiger I trundle out of the black and oily smoke that was now pouring out of the Rifle Brigade's vehicles. Major Carr did not have any time to do anything else, only to give his gunner a frantic fire command and to help him to lock onto the target as fast as humanly possible. Major Carr's Cromwell was only able to fire off one 75mm main gun round at Wittmann's huge Tiger I, but bounced off harmlessly with no effect.

Wittmann had not seen Major Carr's Cromwell tank until seconds before it had fired at his moving panzer. He ducked down in his cupola at the last instant before the 75mm round impacted on his front mantelet and broke up. As soon as Carr's round struck the Tiger I, Woll traversed the turret to the 10 o'clock position, and while doing so, heard and felt the loader throw in another 8.8cm AP main gun round into the breech and was now ready to take on the Cromwell. As soon as Woll had the British tank in his sights, he pressed the firing handle and fired the main gun. The main gun round impacted and penetrated into the lower front portion of Carr's vehicle turret and immediately started to burn violently.

Wittmann then ordered Woll to swing the turret to the right and to finish off the vehicles still left on the road belonging to The Rifle Brigade. Next in line were two M4A4 Sherman OP tanks which were sporting dummy guns as a decoy in order not to be singled out and fired upon if detected by the enemy. Wittmann of course did not know that these vehicles were not armed; as the decoy worked unfortunately for the doomed Sherman OP crews. Wittmann again announced the next fire command as Woll was rotating the turret to destroy the next targets as fast as he could. Finally, the targets came into view in his sight picture and destroyed them both within seconds. As soon as the two Sherman OP tanks were taken care of, Wittmann stated to Woll his next intentions as there were still two more vehicles that had to be dealt with before they could move on towards the main objective. The Intelligence officer of The Rifle Brigade was still standing in his Daimler armored scout car and was trying desperately to direct his driver to move his vehicle out of the shattered column in order to make contact with 'A' or 'B' Squadron so as to inform the commanding officer what was happening to his rear units. As the I.O.'s scout car started to move out of the entangled and burning armored vehicles, an 8.8cm main gun round hit and obliterated the lightly armored scout car, killing not only the vehicle's crew outright, but also killing many men around and nearby this machine with highly lethal fragments of armored plate, glass, rubber, and human remains. Wittmann and Woll then fired at the medical officers M3 half-track, which was blown to bits and shoved clear across the road blocking any escape to the rear of the column.

As soon as Major Carr's Cromwell had fired at Wittmann's Tiger I, the remaining three Cromwells of the RHQ were immediately put onto the alert, but were still not too sure what was developing. They were situated at the northeast bend of the main street (Rue Clemenceau) which severely hampered their forward visibility and knowledge of what was transpiring. By this time, Wittmann had moved his Tiger I forward and successfully entered onto the main street heading straight towards the three RHQ vehicles. Major Carr's Cromwell was now billowing out large black clouds of acrid smoke into the area, which mixed with the smoke from all of the other knocked out vehicles and only added to the mass confusion filtering down the British tank column. Wittmann and Woll were also hampered by this heavy smoke blanket, but nevertheless, continued to move forward with all speed. Wittmann also kept his head well up and out of his armored cupola in order to pick out any additional enemy targets of opportunity that might present themselves.

Wittmann now knew that the entire area must have been alerted to his presence and was not going to waste any time trying to make it to his objective. Just as he thought that the way ahead was clear, he detected the low squat shape of two more Cromwell tanks sitting no more then ten to fifteen meters behind Major Carr's burning and wrecked tank. He again gave Woll a quick and accurate fire command which informed Woll of his next two targets. The next two main gun rounds of AP smashed both of these tanks and put them out of action. The second Cromwell to be destroyed was the CO's (now with 'A' Squadron), while the third was the RSM's (Royal Sergeant Major) tank.

Captain Pat Dyas, who was a spare Captain with the 4th CLY, was sitting in his Cromwell's open turret hatch when the shooting started. His gunner was outside (and out of sight) the vehicle relieving himself behind a nearby building and was not able to return and mount Dyas's vehicle once the firing started. Dyas therefore ordered his driver to backup the vehicle and then crashed through a fence to the right side of the main street and came to a sudden halt in the middle of a front garden. Due to the flames and smoke, Wittmann was not able to spot Dyas's Cromwell sitting in this garden, as he made his attempt to rolled forward to try and reach and then take the vital road junction to Caumont. Dyas looked up in utter dismay as Wittmann's Tiger I roared pass his position, with his head well out of his armored cupola! Due to the lack of a gunner, Dyas was not able to fire a main gun round into the left side of Wittmann's passing Tiger I. Dyas could not believe his luck in not being detected and then decided to stalk this vehicle from the rear as soon as he could collect his thoughts and pull his tank crew back together as a fighting unit. Dyas and his crew-members were very shaken up as they had just seen many of their mates and their vehicles blown to bits at very close range by one of the most feared German armored fighting vehicles of the war. They were all veterans of many tank engagements that had covered the battles in North Africa, Sicily, and the Italian campaign. Never had they seen such destructive killing power demonstrated by a lone German Tiger I at such close quarters. Dyas finally ordered his crew to 'battle stations' and now had his bow-machine gunner replace his missing gunner. He yelled to his driver to move forward and make a hard left turn and return to the main street to seek out the enemy panzer.

Meanwhile, Wittmann's Tiger I was heading at full speed down the main street of "Villers-Bocage" towards the road junction. He was extremely concerned about being alone in the middle of a built up town with no infantry support and low on fuel and ammunition. It was his decision to storm through the British tank unit, as he knew the road to Caumont was vital in order to bring his panzer company and the rest of the LAH into this area for further battles with the enemy. This move on his part would help to stem off any panzer attacks that would certainly be aimed at Panzer Lehr. If he was able to capture and secure this road artery, this action would be instrumental in allowing the German panzer units to advance and cause havoc against the Allies line of march.

As his Tiger I was moving towards its objective, Wittmann was not sure if anyone from his unit had been alerted to the actions that had just transpired. Hopefully, the German infantry squad that he had encountered in the woods near the N175 may have been able to report to his commander, and perhaps, a frantic message had been sent to Sepp Dietrich, who would most certainly send heavy reinforcements to his aid.

The tense panzer commander thought that this was highly unlikely, as it would take time to gather all of the pertinent information, collate it, and then make plans to send out additional panzers to lend a hand. No, he knew deep down, that he and his crew were on their own for the time being, and had taken a big gamble in advancing alone, but figured that this move was indeed a calculated risk made under extreme pressure and circumstances that warranted immediate action in order to throw the enemy off balance and hopefully check the Allies tactical situation and upset their time-tables. The German forces could then mount a surprise soiling attack and perhaps capture any and all enemy officers and men with maps and paperwork pertaining to their Normandy strategic plans.

Wittmann's vehicle suddenly escaped the embraces of the dense smoke that had filled the majority of the eastern part of the main street and the town. His vision to his direct front was clear and was able to make out the road junction coming into view. He now felt that his battle-run has been worth the effort involved, and he would in fact take the road junction to Caumont after all. He ordered his driver to slow down, so they would not over shoot their objective. As his vehicle decelerated, he suddenly saw to his horror, a long gun barrel protruding out just forward of a building to his right-hand side at the road junction. He ordered his driver to halt his machine and immediately gave Woll a rapid fire command.

A Sergeant Lockwood was sitting in his open turret hatches of his M4A4 Sherman Firefly (mounting the potent 17pdr high velocity gun), as his vehicle was the leading tank of his unit now halted at the road junction to Caumont. 'B' Squadron had been ordered to stop at this important location in order to secure this vital road artery, which Allied command knew would be utilized by the German forces in order to mount a flanking maneuver against their forces. Lockwood and his crew had heard some firing going on up the main street, but since they were still under radio silence, they were not to be informed in regards to what was happening. It seemed logical to stay where they were situated until they had received orders to the contrary by their commanding officer or second in command. For the time being, they would not venture out of their positions until they were ordered to do so from higher authority. The majority of the men of 'B' Squadron were now just getting ready for their brew-up of tea and breakfast and did not think that they would be attacked by any German forces, let alone a tank attack in a built up area.

As Sergeant Lockwood was just about to leave his Firefly for a cup of tea, he heard the familiar squeal and clatter of tank tracks coming towards his location. He was not sure if this sound was that of a Cromwell tank coming to report to their position, or that of an M3 half-track that was used many times for delivering messages while under radio black out. As the unknown vehicle came closer, it was soon very obvious that this vehicle was not of Allied origin. He yelled to his crew to remount their vehicle and to prepare for 'battle stations'! As soon as his driver positioned himself in his driver's seat, Lockwood ordered him to move their vehicle forward a little, so his gunner could traverse the 17pdr main gun to the left and thus expose as little of their vehicle as possible. As soon as the gunner stated that his sight picture was covering the approaching enemy panzer, Lockwood shouted, "Driver stop!"

At the same time, Wittmann and his crew were now going through the motions of firing their main gun at Lockwood's Firefly. Woll was now locked onto the right-hand side of the Allied tank, but was not sure if he could obtain a hit as the angle was very acute and under the tension of the moment, did not want to fire prematurely or before their vehicle had settled on its suspension. Finally, Wittmann gave the order to fire and Woll pressed the firing handle and hoped for the best. The 8.8cm AP main gun round shot out with an increased crack as the nearby walls of the stone buildings intensified the detonation of this weapon. Instantly, the dust and debris in the streets were thrown up and into the air. Wittmann was just able to see that the main gun round had slammed into the wall of the building only a few feet away from where the Allied tank was situated. Pieces of the walls started to fall down and around the British vehicle which was Wittmann's que to reverse his vehicle out of harms way. He gave the order to his driver to back away their machine out of danger and to return from the direction that they had come from a few minutes earlier. As the Tiger I was being inch rearward, a shot rang out from the British Firefly with a loud bang, with the 17pdr main gun round impacting into Wittmann's vehicle on the left front area of his 8.8cm gun mantelet. The round struck at the very top of this frontal area, and glanced upwards causing no appreciable damage to Wittmann's Tiger I.

As soon as the firing had started, the remaining vehicles of 'B' Squadron had their engines cranked up by their drivers while frantic tank commanders, gunners, and loaders diving into their respective positions. Many of the tank drivers tried to move their vehicles rearward in order to provide Lockwood with more room to maneuver. This was a very smart decision as Lockwood immediately ordered his driver to back off from the engagement after his first round was fired. It was all too apparent however, that both sides had decided to break off the attack, as no one knew the exact strength of the other, so disengaged in order to entice the other to move forward in hopes of placing a second main gun round into the enemy for a confirmed kill. Lockwood's Firefly was now covered with bricks, window frames, and many pieces of masonry from the building that had been blasted apart by Wittmann's main gun round. His gunner's sight was now blocked with debris and was impossible to accurately track and fire at the enemy panzer. Thus, Lockwood ordered his driver to back out of view as surely, the German would fire another main gun round within a few short seconds, if he did not take evasive actions.

This firing engagement had taken place so fast, that neither side was sure what to do next, but it was quite obvious to Wittmann and his crew that they had walked into a hornet's nest, and all hope of securing the road junction had been lost. Wittmann therefore, ordered his driver to conduct a neutral steer (one track moving forward, the other reversing, with the result being that the vehicle spins on its axis) and yelled to Woll to keep the main gun pointing in the direction of the road junction. Wittmann continued to help guide his driver while performing this difficult maneuver, while Woll scanned the road junction for any signs of the enemy. At last! The Tiger I was turned around with Wittmann now screaming at his driver to move forward at full speed in order to try and escape any new nasty surprises that the Allies might now have in store for them. He then instructed Woll to traverse the turret (now at the 6 o'clock position) to the 12 o'clock position in order to scan the area ahead of their vehicle as they moved forward. The Tiger I could not travel as fast as it had on the initial battle-run as it was now climbing up the main street of "Villers-Bocage" at a steeper grade, and caused even more tension inside Wittmann's vehicle. As Woll was traversing the turret to the 12 o'clock position, Wittmann turned around in his armored cupola, and surveyed the streets and alleyways for any counter-attacks that were expected, but was greatly relieved that the enemy did not present himself.

While Wittmann and Lockwood had been firing at each other at the road junction, Pat Dyas, had been moving down the main street of the town still bent on stalking Wittmann's Tiger I. He had also been affected by the thick hanging smoke that had filled the area, but had nevertheless moved forward at a very reduced speed, trying to make contact with the enemy panzer and hopefully to place 75mm main gun rounds into the thinner rear tail plate and knock it out. He thought that he had heard some additional firing up ahead, but was not sure, due to the loud engine noise of his Cromwell. His hopes were that he would catch up with the enemy machine and take out the beast with skill and surprise. Dyas knew that the Tiger I had a very slow rate of turret traverse, so there would be plenty of time for his gunner to pump in at least two or three main gun rounds before the Tiger I commander could return fire, if at all.

As Dyas's Cromwell inched forward, he suddenly saw the outline of the huge German panzer! With stinging smoke still obstructing his view, he was under the impression that the enemy's main gun was facing in the opposite direction, and thus had caught up with his foe from the rear. As he started to announce his first fire command to his replacement gunner, he looked up at the last possible second and to his shock, saw that the German panzer was coming straight towards his vehicle. He struggled verbally to finish his fire command, and was relieved when he heard and felt the 75mm AP main gun round fly towards its target. Dyas and his vehicle were no more than 70-80 yards away from Wittmann, but the thick hide of the Tiger I defeated his main gun round and bounced harmlessly off the front mantelet. Another main gun round was automatically thrown into the breech of the 75mm, and was fired at the German panzer. The result was the same effect! The main gun round simply bounced off the massive armor plate of the Tiger I.

Wittmann saw Dyas's Cromwell only seconds before the first 75mm main gun round had been fired at his vehicle. He quickly ducked down into his armored cupola, and with a shout announced another fire command to Woll. His gunner pressed the firing handle, with Wittmann immediately standing up in his cupola to vision block level and viewed the sight of complete and utter chaos outside his vehicle.

Pat Dyas was standing up-right in his turret hatch after his second main gun round had been fired at the approaching Tiger I. His heart stopped twice as he watched helplessly as his two 75mm main gun rounds bounced off the thick skinned Tiger I, even at this ridiculously close range! He knew that he and his crew had only seconds to live, but could not bring himself to order his crew to bale out of their Cromwell. If he did so, they would surely be machine gunned down as they left their vehicle with no chance of survival. They would indeed stand and fight the Hun as it was quite obvious that it was now up to him and his crew to stop the marauding German steel giant at all costs.

As the extremely brave Cromwell tank commander started to announce his third fire command to his crew, Wittmann's Tiger I fired an AP main gun round which flew towards Dyas's tank with a large crack! The 8.8cm round penetrated the right front of the turret gun, and past completely through the turret and then out the right rear. The loader was instantly killed, with Dyas blown out of his turret hatch by the shockwave and thrown onto the street to the left of his Cromwell in plain view of his enemy. Dyas's gunner was able to extract himself out of the vehicle and helped Dyas to the left-hand side of the street. His tank commander had received some facial burns and a number of bad bruises, but was otherwise unharmed. As Dyas's driver was trying to leave his position, he was machine gunned down by Wittmann's bow-machine gunner and was killed outright. Within seconds of all this happening Dyas's Cromwell was now burning and bellowing out large sheets of flames and thick black smoke which only added to the confusion.

Wittmann wasted no more time and ordered his driver to move forward at top speed in order to return to their unit for reinforcements. The massive Tiger I lurched forward as his driver accelerated the engine, with Wittmann and his loader on the look-out for any tell tale signs of the enemy lurking in the smokey street that was now littered with wrecked and burning vehicles. Wittmann's main concern now was that one or two Allied panzers might be playing dead as he moved his machine back from the same direction from where he had come from earlier in the battle. He had Woll traverse the 8.8cm main gun towards the still smoking RHQ vehicles now coming into view as he was not taking any chances. With nerves to the breaking point, his vehicle continued to move forward, past these vehicles without incident, and rolled on. Wittmann was also very aware that enemy infantry could be hiding in the higher stories of the surrounding buildings and was fearful that at any second, a well thrown hand-grenade would enter his turret and killed them all. With this thought in mind, he yelled to his loader to close his open hatch, whereas he would remain standing in his open cupola hatch and continue scanning the area ahead as they made their way back to their forces to the northeast.

Shortly thereafter, Wittmann's vehicle returned to the same spot where his battle-run had started. He ordered his driver to turn off the main street to the right and instructed him to rejoin their company. The attempt to capture and secure the road junction had failed, but Wittmann knew that he had caused tremendous damage to the enemy panzer unit. He knew that time was of the essence, but had to report to Sepp Dietrich before he could return with reinforcements. As he was low on ammunition and fuel, he would have to commandeer another vehicle as he and his crew would not have time to load and fuel up. Wittmann and his crew were now travelling behind the wooded area that they had been hiding in prior to the battle, and safely made their way back to their vehicle hiding area.

As soon as Wittmann's Tiger I had departed from the scene of the battle, Dyas and his gunner ran down to the knocked out RHQ vehicles in order to try and use one of the radio sets so as to make contact with their commanding officer who was still with 'A' Squadron. Standard Operating Procedure (SOP) stated that at least one vehicle in each section of their unit would have a microphone and head set hanging over the side of the vehicle, just in case one was needed in an emergency. Dyas ran to the RSM's Cromwell and grabbed such a device in order to report, but found that it was useless as the vehicle's radio was still set on silent running. Even if it had been set on an open channel, the Cromwell's interior was now just a blacken and smoldering hulk of twisted and smashed components. With this, Dyas and his gunner decided to try and make contact with 'B' Squadron. However, before making off, a local French girl who had been hiding in a nearby cellar during the fighting, appeared from a doorway and helped Dyas find his way to 'B' Squadron's position. They did not dare to run down the main street, as they were still afraid that the enemy might return, or that a German infantry mopping up patrol might be in the vicinity. At any rate, they did not want to be captured or killed, so made their way to 'B' Squadron through back streets and side alleyways and over stone walls. After about twenty minutes, they finally arrived at and made contact with 'B' Squadron, who were still not sure what had transpired. This unit was still very shaken up that a lone Tiger I had ventured so close to their positions and had also escaped!

After Dyas explained the situation and what had happened to The Rifle Brigade and the tanks of their RHQ Major Aird O.C. of 'B' Squadron tried desperately to make radio contact with 'A' Squadron, but found to his utter dismay, that the entire unit was still on radio blackout. It was now up to him to decide what the next plan of action would be in regards to any further attempts that the Germans might try and launch against their positions at the road junction. For the next few minutes, the British did not make any moves as they would hold onto their present positions until a thorough plan of attack was formulated. A sense of fear was generated that at every corner, a German Tiger I was waiting in ambush. Even though they were operating in a built-up area, it was now imperative that 'B' Squadron make contact with 'A' Squadron and their commanding officer.

From the latter's tank, Dyas finally made contact with Colonel Cranleigh, still in his armored scout car on the high ground with 'A' Squadron, and informed him of the events within the town. In reply, his commanding officer said he realized the situation was desperate and that 'A' Squadron was at that moment being heavily attacked by German Tiger I tanks. No further messages were received from him after this radio transmission. Colonel Viscount Cranleigh was taken a prisoner of war.

As Wittmann and his Tiger I crew rolled into their company's hidden location northeast of "Villers-Bocage", Wittmann jumped up and out of his cupola even before his vehicle came to a full stop. He clambered down and reported to Sepp Dietrich immediately and outlined in detail what had taken place in and around the town, and, that he must have additional Tiger Is to carry on the attack. Sepp Dietrich stated to Wittmann that Hauptsturmführer Mobius's 1st Company was standing by with eight Tiger Is, and for him and his crew to utilize one of these machines due to Wittmann's report that he was low on fuel and ammunition. After a short briefing with Mobius, Wittmann's `borrowed' Tiger I along with two additional ones, plus a Panzer IV Ausf. H (stated to have belonged to Panzer Lehr) cranked up and headed for the N175. The second battle-run for "Villers-Bocage" was on!

Wittmann was hoping that the leading vehicles of the British panzer unit (the group that he saw initially) were now stopped further up the N175. If so, he and his panzers would attack these vehicles before re-entering the town. Therefore, he would lead his small but powerful force northeast, cross the N175, and attack the Tommies in a southwesterly direction.

As Wittmann and his other vehicles came out of the protection of the trees that had hidden them from view, all felt very naked as they were once again in open country and were very weary of the ever present Allied "Jabos!" Speed and surprise were the two main ingredients to his plan of attack. As a result, Wittmann ordered his drivers to push their vehicles to their limits in order to advance as fast as possible. He was also worried about the large dust trails his vehicles were throwing up into the air as these types of signatures always meant certain death from either Allied fighter-bombers, or accurate artillery bombardment. It was too late to worry about what might happen, it was time for action and a speedy advance to surprise and knockout any vehicles that might be blocking their advance into the town.

Wittmann then recognized the wooded area that had hidden and concealed his vehicle prior to his first battle-run into the town. He yelled to his driver to make a hard right turn and to head for the protection of the tree line. As soon as the four vehicle column came to this position, Wittmann ordered a halt, and all engines were shut down. He then dismounted in order to make a hasty reconnaissance on foot to try and locate the enemy panzer unit. As he made his way forward a few hundred meters through the trees, he heard faint sounds of men moving about, but could not make out the language at this distance. He moved a bit forward towards these sounds ever so carefully and suddenly saw the outlines of British Cromwells, Sherman Fireflies, and many other vehicles. A large number of these machines were bunched up with their main guns traversed over the rear decks of the following vehicles to the right side of the road with their engines still running. He therefore, carefully inched away from his concealed position and made his way back to his awaiting vehicles. As he ran the last leg of his trek to his Tiger I, he gave the signal to start up all engines and be ready to move out at once! As soon as he climbed into his armored cupola, he radioed the other panzer commanders and informed them of what lay ahead of their precarious positions and to be ready for immediate action. Wittmann also instructed the three panzer commanders, that once they crossed the N175, to fan out to his right and fire upon any British panzers that might try and flee to the north. He would fire on the enemy panzer column, and he alone!

Wittmann was sure that the British panzer unit would hear his approach, but was hoping that the wooded area to their immediate left would help to mask the sounds of their vehicles. With the Tommies running their panzer motors perhaps this would be enough noise to drown out their movements. His group of vehicles pressed on.

As Wittmann's unit continued to advance, an open area came into view and the N175 was sighted. Wittmann's Tiger I then made a sharp left turn and made a mad dash to cross the highway as fast as the vehicle would travel. Luckily, the brave panzer leader had judged the distance correctly, and would be coming in for the attack just in front of 'A' Squadron. The British unit would have little or no time to deploy any of their forces due to the congested positions they found themselves in on the N175. Wittmann then ordered Woll to traverse the turret and main gun of the vehicle to the 10 o'clock position and to start firing main gun rounds as soon as he had the British panzers in his sight picture. Wittmann then turned to his left and waved on his comrades to make their break across the highway. His frantic arm and hand signals were not necessary as he could see that the three vehicles were now charging forward and across the N175 at top speed, so as to keep pace with their leader. Wittmann yelled to his driver to slow down and to swing onto a small cart-track running parallel to the main road, which he would use as a guide during his southwest battle run towards the town. The other panzers were now across the road and were moving up to take their battle-run positions and fanned out to the right of Wittmann's machine as per his initial instructions. It was very clear now why Wittmann would fire alone. With vehicle exhaust, thrown up dust and dirt, and especially the tension of battle, it would be very easy for one of his vehicles to fire into one another, etc. Should the enemy try to move their vehicles off the road and to the south (which was not likely due to the nearby trees) Wittmann would then order his vehicles to swing to their left and knock-out the enemy panzers from the rear!

As Wittmann's Tiger I made its approach, shock waves filtered down the whole length of 'A' Squadron, which quickly established panic among all the Tommies. The British tank crews were all dismounted out of their respective vehicles taking a break, with the majority of the men either brewing up tea, checking their vehicles, or just stretching their legs after being cooped up in their vehicles for so long a time. A number of the vehicles still had their engines turning over (charging radio batteries), which indeed had helped to muffle Wittmann's approach a few minutes earlier. As soon as Wittmann's Tiger I had been spotted, a number of British officers ran down the column of parked vehicles shouting that they were about to come under attack from German Tiger I tanks. A sudden urgent need to remount their vehicles could be felt by all the men present, but it was also quite apparent that in doing so, would have meant certain death for anyone attempting to do such a gallant feat. The men of the 4th CLY were battled hardened veterans and knew the reputation of the Tiger I, and it was also very obvious that they would have no chance at all in trying to untangle their vehicles and take on these types of vehicles. The order was shouted out to abandon all of the vehicles and try to save themselves at all costs. Everywhere, men either flung themselves into nearby ditches, or tried to run back towards the trees, which would at least give them some sort of protection and cover from the hostile enemy main gun and machine gun fire.

While all of this was taking place, Wittmann started to give Woll his first fire command, as he had held his fire until all of his vehicles were in correct attack formation. At the head of 'A' Squadron, was the CO's armored scout car and an M3 half-track. Wittmann ordered Woll to fire at the half-track with a HE round in order to try and block the road with its wreckage in case any enemy vehicles tried to make a sudden dash forward attempting to escape from his fire. Woll aimed at the rear quarter of the armored half-track and pressed the firing handle. The loud crack of the 8.8cm main gun round reverberated over the entire area, and not a sole from the British forces lifted a head from the ground. The HE round impacted into the half-track's rear troop compartment with the force of the projectile wrenching the vehicle around and partially blocking the road. The fuel tanks of this vehicle were ignited instantaneously with great clouds of thick dense smoke and flames leaping skyward. The armored scout car was machine gunned by Woll, as a main gun round was not to be wasted on this light vehicle. Wittmann then ordered his bow-machine gunner to open fire with his weapon and continue to spray the enemy column so as to keep the British Tommies at bay while his heavy panzer moved slowly down the cart-track. Next in line, were twelve 75mm gunned Cromwell tanks which were totally unmanned, which had to be dealt with accordingly. Wittmann ordered his loader to continue to ram home main gun rounds as fast as he could and not to stop unless ordered to do so. His loader knew that it was vital that he keep up with the fire commands of his panzer commander and was working like a mad man. The AP main gun rounds had been piled up to his knees prior to the battle-run and thus offered him little room to move in his position. His only possible movement being, that he could bend down and grab the next main gun round, swing his torso upwards and slam home the next projectile into the hungry and smoking breech of the 8.8cm gun. He would then reach up and reset the safety switch for the main gun, and the whole process would repeat itself.

Wittmann ordered his driver to slow his vehicle down to a snails pace in order to allow Woll a good sight picture pertaining to the Cromwells. Woll was very fortunate that the surrounding area they were firing from was somewhat level. Due to this factor, he depressed the main gun to a certain setting and left it situated at this position, with his only concern being able to yell at the driver to halt the vehicle when an enemy target came into view. It was not long before all of the twelve Cromwells had been hit and destroyed, and set on fire by this gunnery technique, with even more smoke and flames spewing from these doomed vehicles. A number of these vehicles were now being blown off to one side of the road, by the combination of being hit at close quarters by an extremely powerful high velocity main gun round, and then the resulting explosions from on-board ammunition cooking off that rocked and shunted them on the road from side to side. As his Tiger I moved forward, Wittmann glanced over his right shoulder in order to keep track of his other panzers, and happened to look down through his loader's open hatch and witnessed an unbelievable sight! His loader had been transformed into a sweating, cursing, and grease covered individual, who was coughing and choking from the presence of heavy cordite fumes as he continued to load the main gun. He had indeed succeeded in keeping up with Wittmann's rapid fire commands, and had also been able to throw out a number of spent casings through his opened hatch aperture. It was quite apparent, that after five or six main gun rounds had been fired, his loader had worked himself into a wild frenzy in order to take on the enemy panzers. Wittmann was very proud of his entire crew, as they were displaying frantic, but superior crew duties, under extremely harsh battle line conditions.

The next vehicles to come under Wittmann's wrath, were four Sherman M4A4 Fireflies mounting the very potent 17pdr high velocity main gun, which, as he knew, could knock out his machine at this very close range. A light armored scout car was in between the third and fourth Firefly, but as it was no danger to Wittmann's vehicle, ordered Woll to bypass it. Woll was already scanning the area ahead of their vehicle and managed to pick up the first Firefly in his sight picture. As soon as this occurred, he ordered the driver to halt their vehicle and depressed the firing handle. The 8.8cm AP main gun round flew out with a great bang and smashed into the front of the turret of the enemy tank which passed through it like a hot knife through butter. The vehicle immediately burst into flames with the on-board ammunition exploding within seconds of the penetration. Wittmann then decided to stand stationary during this engagement as the enemy machines were so close together that it was senseless to move their vehicle forward. Woll fired off three more AP main gun rounds and finished off the most dangerous and deadly of the Allied vehicles in the enemy column. Wittmann was very relieved when he saw the four Fireflies burning on the road, as it had been imperative that these particular vehicles be destroyed at all costs.

Hidden behind the now burning and destroyed FireFlies, were fourteen Bren and Lloyd gun carriers towing 6pdr anti-tank guns. Wittmann saw them come into view just as his vehicle started to pull away from their previous stationary firing position. At first, he was not exactly sure what these strange looking vehicles were and could not make out their outlines considering all of the confusion and smoke, which caused difficult observation from his armored cupola. He gave yet another fire command to his turret crew in which Woll fired an AP main gun round which slammed into the first of these vehicles which utterly destroyed and blew it apart at the seams, and swung the 6pdr anti-tank gun around into the middle of the road. The same AP main gun round flew into the second vehicle and shattered it beyond all recognition. As soon as Wittmann saw the effect of the first AP main gun round, he instructed Woll and his bow machine-gunner to fire at these light vehicles with secondary armament. The remaining Bren and Lloyd gun carriers were destroyed by MG-34 fire after igniting the on-board fuel and ammunition. As Wittmann and his vehicle pulled away from this scene of complete destruction, the 6pdr anti-tank guns still attached to their carriers were seen to be whipping around like the tail of a decapitated snake, with the muscular convulsions being replaced by the wrenching and twisting movements of the vehicles as the 6pdr ammunition detonated with tremendous force.

At last! The seemingly endless column of enemy vehicles came to an end, whereby Wittmann ordered his driver to make a run for the town and the road junction at full speed. He decided that he would keep his vehicle on the dirt cart-track until he entered the city limits in the event that he ran into another batch of enemy vehicles. Thus, if the enemy did present themselves once again, he could still obtain flank shots instead of head-on firing, whereas he could observe any following vehicles behind any leading enemy panzers. Wittmann waved on his three other panzers to fall in behind his vehicle and follow him into the town. He was now trying to take the town with force, as he knew that in order to be victorious, he would have to again use speed, the element of surprise, and the protection of their heavy panzers, to overthrow the enemy, and to continue to keep the Tommies off balance.

During the time that Wittmann and his small panzer group were moving back into "Villers-Bocage" for his second battle-run, a Lieutenant Bill Cotton was ordered by Major Aird from 'B' Squadron to try and make contact with 'A' Squadron, as time was of the essence and something had to be done in order to save them from any further loses or damage to their unit's vehicles. Lt. Cotton was to take a troop of four tanks and try and skirt around the town to the southeast and make a determined effort to make contact with 'A' Squadron and Colonel Cranleigh. He lead his troop in a 95mm Cromwell howitzer tank, followed by a Sergeant Grant in a 75mm Cromwell, a Corporal Horne also in a 75mm Cromwell, with a Sergeant Bramall bringing up the rear in an M4A4 Sherman 17pdr Firefly. Lt. Cotton was being very careful in his movements throughout "Villers-Bocage", and was constantly scanning every side street and alleyway for any signs of the enemy whether it be a German tank roving about, or German infantry trying to infiltrate the town. Maneuvering along the many streets of the town was very nerve racking for his entire troop, as at any moment, they were expecting to hear the familiar crack or wallop of either a well placed 8.8cm main gun round, or the roar of a deadly hand-held panzerfaust weapon that could easily knock-out their vehicles. Minutes seemed like hours, as they cautiously made their way through the southern most part of the town desperately trying to make contact with 'A' Squadron. As Lt. Cotton looked to his direct front, it was clear that they would have a very difficult time trying to make contact with their forward unit, as a railway embankment was sighted that would have to be crossed if they were to continue on their present course. Lt. Cotton made a logical decision not to cross this obstacle with his vehicles, as he knew that this action would expose his vehicles' thinner belly armor to the enemy and could not take the chance of being fired upon and knocked out in this manner.

Before Lt. Cotton's troop could turn back, they ran into a limited attack from a German infantry unit probing in the same area of the town. No doubt, they had either heard the firing or had been ordered into the attack after Wittmann's initial battle-run into the city proper, or had been ordered by higher command to try and seize major streets and intersections. Lt. Cotton's troop fanned out and fired their tank mounted weapons at this enemy threat, and successfully repelled the German's attempt to send in infantry as their presence would be vital if they were to capture and secure the town.

After this episode, Lt. Cotton decided to turn his vehicles around and head north into the maze of backstreets and alleyways of the town. His plan now was to flush out any and all German forces that might have by-passed his vehicle's positions and thus seal off the town and set up defensive positions which would be extremely difficult to crack once securely held. He moved his vehicles ever so carefully back towards the middle of the town and kept a three hundred and sixty degree lookout for any signs of the enemy. The nearby stone structures gave false soundings as his troop of medium tanks crawled past building after building with the reverberations causing Lt. Cotton to halt his troop, kill the vehicles engines and listen for any sounds of tracked vehicles operating in the nearby area. It was a very tense tactical situation, as if his vehicle was taken under fire and knocked out, all of the following vehicles in his troop would become blocked and would have to reversed out under frantic measures; which would result in the classic German ambush techniques used in built up areas. Lt. Cotton then decided to speed up his scouting of the town, but then came into the courtyard of the Mayor's building that connected to the main street of the town. He pulled into this open area and positioned his 95mm howitzer Cromwell tank at the back of this courtyard and made ready his plan to take up defensive firing positions in the event that the Germans tried to carry out a second attempt at pushing heavy armor through the town and trying again to seize the road junction.

Meanwhile, Sergeant Bramall was still moving through the backstreets trying to catch up with his troop leader. He and his driver were also being very careful in not exposing their vehicle's long gun barrel at any given street corner. He instructed his loader to dismount from his vehicle from time to time and peek around buildings in order to have a tactical look see. If there was to be any opposition, it would be reported to him and careful maneuvering of the vehicle would be promptly made as quickly as possible. Bramall was also aware of the fact that he and his crew had lost sight of their troop leader, but had been taking mental notes of where they had come from and what route Lt. Cotton had taken in order to return to him later. At a major street intersection, Bramall decided to make a right-hand turn so as to see where it lead too. All of the troop's tank commanders had become somewhat disorientated during this flushing out endeavor, and it was imperative that one did not become lost, or worst than that, turned around and fire on friendly forces. All of the tank gunners in the British vehicles were severely hampered by the limited visibility of their optical devices, as the smoke from the earlier tank battles still hung in the morning air, which made identification of vehicles even more difficult at this time. Everyone involved with this deadly game of street stalking was very trigger happy, and so the tank commanders had to be absolutely sure of their targets within seconds of detecting them before giving out their initial fire commands.

While Sergeant Bramall was still scouting the backstreets of "Villers-Bocage", Wittmann and his three other panzers had pulled off the cart-track along the N175 and re-entered the town. They then by-passed the still smoldering RHQ tanks and rolled down the street until they were about a hundred meters in front of Pat Dyas's smashed Cromwell. Wittmann was constantly talking to his panzer commanders behind him, and then suddenly gave the order for his vehicles to pull over to the left-hand side of the street and also to shut down their power-plants in order for them to listen for any tell-tale sounds of any vehicular movements which would help to indicate the whereabouts of the enemy. The radios in all of the German vehicles were to be left on so Wittmann could continue to communicate with his panzer commanders in a split second, but all were instructed to push back their headsets from their ears in order to listen for the enemy. The whirl of the radio static was still to be heard, but every ear was straining to pick up any faint sounds or indications of where the enemy might be, or coming from at this time. Wittmann could sense a trap, but it was his duty to roll forward in order to take the road junction that was so vital in regards to continuing the assault against the Allied armada that now engulfed the entire Norman countryside. Wittmann and his crew felt very uneasy about the tactical situation, as surely the British had ample time to surmount a defensive posture in order to consolidate their positions. The question now in his mind: what would happen if he ordered and pulled his forces forward towards the main objective?

As Sergeant Bramall's driver swung the Sherman Firefly around the corner of the next intersection, his forward view was just that of another cobblestone street with large masonry buildings lining the totally deserted thoroughfare. It was an eerie feeling being quite alone in this built-up area with nowhere to turn if one was to be fired upon by the enemy. The long barrel of the 17pdr high velocity gun was a great hinderance to Bramall while conducting this type of maneuver, but, also felt that they would at least have a 50/50 chance of survival with any encounter with the enemy. Sergeant Bramall ordered his driver to inch their vehicle forward at a reduced speed so as to be able to detect any type of movements made by the enemy. There was no time to think of anything else but to seek out the enemy and destroy them at first sight. Street fighting was a vicious game of cat and mouse that no one liked to play, but the tactical situation now demanded nerves of steel from the British tank crews, as it was imperative that the town did not fall into German hands.

As his 17pdr gunned Sherman made its way down the secondary streets of

"Villers-Bocage" Bramall was constantly searching for the presence of any enemy activity. He scanned the upper building levels for any signs of snipers that might be lurking in the shadows, and for any sounds or indications pertaining to tracked enemy vehicles. As his Firefly came nearer to the intersection of the main street of the town, Bramall instructed his driver to slow down to a slow crawl. He did not want to enter the main street at too great a speed, as if any German gun was trained on this area, he and his crew would surely meet their maker as a direct result. No, he would bring his vehicle up to the corner of the last building and then dismount and have a look, before he committed himself. As his vehicle was moving up to the corner, Bramall yelled to his driver to stop the vehicle before the long gun barrel exposed its length into the main street. As his vehicle came to a halt, Bramall just happen to glance to his right side, and to his utter horror, saw the left-hand side of a stationary Tiger I diagonally through two windows of the corner building! As soon as he had regained his composure, Bramall ordered his driver to back up, and then for his gunner to fire through these two windows as soon as he could traverse the turret to the 2 o'clock position. In order for Bramall to engage his target, he had to guide his driver rearward, help his gunner traverse the turret and long gun barrel to the right, instruct his driver when to halt the vehicle, then guide him forward, while the gunner placed the 17pdr gun tube into the selected windows. It was an amazing feat of strict control under a very tense situation for Bramall and his tank crew. As soon as Bramall's gunner positioned the main gun barrel through the first window, a fire command was given. His gunner fired the high velocity 17pdr main gun round which flew out of the gun tube with a muffled crack inside the stone building. In a millionth of a second, the Tiger I was penetrated by this projectile through the left side of its turret, and immediately started to burn. The on-board ammunition ignited with full force, and no crew members were to be seen escaping the doomed vehicle. As soon as the 17pdr main gun round had been fired, Bramall ordered his driver to back up with full speed and move back down the street in reverse gear. Bramall again helped his driver as the Firefly clanked rearward until they came to the first street intersection to their left. Bramall then ordered his driver to brake his right track, made a quick turn to the left, moved forward, and then tried to catch up with Lt. Cotton and the rest of the troop.

After a few minutes Bramall finally made his way to the courtyard where he informed his troop leader that German heavy tanks were just down the street and had successfully knocked one of them out. Lt. Cotton then ordered Bramall to take up a firing position about fifteen feet across from Cpl. Horne's location and be prepared to take on the German tanks if they tried to make a daring move down the main street. Bramall maneuvered his vehicle into the new firing position and indicated to his crew the situation and to be prepared for immediate action. Bramall's gunner reported over the intercom, that he could not use his telescopic sight, as they were too closed in. Everything was a blur, as the depth perception factor in regards to his aiming sight did not allow usage. Bramall therefore yelled to his loader to open the breech, remove the main gun round already in the chamber, and sight through the gun tube at any recognizable feature across the street in order for his gunner to relate to in aiming and firing the main gun. The gunner was to utilize his prism periscope in the roof of the turret, and guide onto the object (e.g. center of a door, odd-colored brick, mailbox, etc.) across the street that the loader was viewing through the gun tube. It was a primitive ad hoc measure, but with being this close to the enemy, tank gunnery did not have to be totally accurate.

As soon as Wittmann heard the impact of the enemy 17pdr main gun round on his rear most vehicle, he yelled over his radio network to his remaining panzers to start up their engines and prepare to move forward towards the objective with all speed. The sudden appearance of an enemy panzer was not a surprise to Wittmann, but was puzzled why it had not been heard approaching; or perhaps it had been there all the time, and allowed his vehicles to move past him, and waited until the last vehicle presented itself before being fired upon. If this was the case, the only option for his panzers was to move forward and try and take the road junction. It might also have been that the enemy vehicle had moved up the side streets very carefully and had not been detected due to the fact that their radios were still on and the noise and static from their headphones had been enough to mask the sounds of an approaching enemy vehicle. This was not the time to try and figure out what had already transpired, it was time for his panzers to rush forward and seize the objective.

All of the Maybach engines of the three remaining vehicles were now running with the drivers gunning their powerplants. Wittmann shouted over his radio network of his intentions, and gave the order to move forward. He knew that a trap was perhaps being set up to ambush his small group of panzers, but he had to move forward as it was the only logical thing to do under the circumstances. His vehicles were now moving and gaining speed keeping their distance between each other with all three panzer commanders having their heads well out from their armored cupolas in order to not only help guide their drivers, but were also scanning the roof tops and upper windows for any tell-tale signs of the enemy, plus any other panzers ready to fire upon them. Wittmann's Tiger I continued at a fast pace and waved on his other vehicles to his rear to keep up with his advance and to carry on the attack. Tensions were very high indeed, as it was crucial that they reach and capture the vital road junction to Caumont.

As soon as Bramall and his Firefly crew had finally settled down and were waiting for the next phase of the street battle, it was quite obvious that the German heavy tanks would have to come pass their firing positions unless they tried an alternate route. This seemed very unlikely as the heavy panzers would have great difficulty moving through the narrow backstreets of the town, which would surely cause them extreme restrictions in regards to maneuvering and firing their main guns. The logical avenue of approach, would be to steamroll their way down the main street, which was wide enough to enable them to rotate their turrets and main guns and take out any opposition that might prevent them from achieving their goal. This reasoning bothered both Bramall and Horne, as they would be the first vehicles in their troop to be destroyed, if in fact the Germans had their main guns situated at the 9 o'clock positions, whereas, they would find themselves embraced in a hopeless turn of events. It was now vital, that the first rounds fired at the attacking German war machines would have to be first round hits, if they were to survive this deadly game of street fighting.

During this period of time, the Queen's Regiment had also arrived on the scene, and had sighted a 6pdr anti-tank gun in a nearby alleyway as a secondary back-up precaution in regards to covering the main street. It was thought however, that this weapon would not be needed, but it was always a good insurance policy to have additional firepower on hand when fighting in this manner.

Bramall's thoughts were suddenly interrupted by the reverberating sounds of heavy tank tracks growing louder and louder; their tank engines had been shut off in order to detect any sounds as his troop were now employing the same tactics as Wittmann and his crews had done beforehand in the battle. It was quite clear that the Germans were making another bold attempt to take the objective, which set into motion the final engagement for the battle of "Villers-Bocage"!

Both Bramall and Horne were at the ready to fire at anything that would enter their kill zones (see map, Kill Zone I). Bramall was to fire the first main gun round being that he had the most powerful weapon at their disposal, with his gunner sweating in his seat as it was his responsibility to knockout the first enemy vehicle that came into his sight picture. As Bramall became more and more tense, he suddenly saw the huge muzzle brake of Wittmann's main gun armament loom out from the right-hand side corner building and was somewhat relieved in observing that the enemy's 8.8cm gun barrel was pointing at the 12 o'clock position and no threat to his men and vehicle. He at once gave out his first fire command to his gunner who fired a 17pdr main gun round prematurely and missed Wittmann's vehicle altogether! The main gun round flew over the 8.8cm gun barrel of the Tiger I and smashed into the building directly across from Bramall's position. Wittmann's vehicle continued to roll forward with the Panzer IV Ausf. H now moving into Kill Zone I. This time, Bramall's gunner scored a direct hit on this vehicle and set it on fire, but continued to roll down the street bellowing out great clouds of smoke which soon filled the streets and made observation even more difficult for all concerned. While Bramall's loader was quickly rearming the 17pdr main gun, the last Tiger I made its way pass his position, but was fired upon by Cpl. Horne's Cromwell. His gunner was also very tensed up and missed the target by only a few inches. Horne instinctively ordered his driver to start up the vehicle's engine, and pulled forward with his gunner swinging the gun and turret of the 75mm gunned Cromwell to the 9 o'clock position. As soon as Horne's vehicle entered the main street, his gunner quickly locked onto the last Tiger I and pressed the firing trigger and placed a 75mm main gun round into the rear armor plate of the enemy tank. The Tiger I immediately started to burn, but continued to roll forward, and out of control. None of the German crew were seen to escape from the vehicle, and it was assumed that they had been killed in their vehicle from the penetration and resulting explosions that rocked their vehicle as it continued to roll down the main street.

Wittmann was still moving forwards towards the objective, but heard all of the firing going on behind him and was not sure what had transpired. Suddenly, he looked back up the main street and saw both of his following vehicles on fire and moving towards him in an erratic manner. He instructed his driver to continue their advance but knew deep down that he and his crew were now the only ones capable of still obtaining the objective. The brave panzer commander could now see the road junction coming into view, and thought that perhaps he and his crew would somehow accomplish their mission after all!

Before Wittmann was able to reach the objective, he had to pass another side alleyway that no doubt would be in the hands of the Allies. He instructed Woll to traverse their main gun to the 9 o'clock position in the event that another Allied panzer was lurking about in this area. Before Woll could hydraulically rotate the turret of the Tiger I (vehicle entering Kill Zone II as set up by the Queen's Regiment) a 6pdr anti-tank gun round was fired from this alleyway and smashed into the left-hand side of Wittmann's vehicle's suspension. The enemy anti-tank gun projectile disabled Wittmann's vehicle by jamming the left track, whereby it was impossible to continue the battle-run. Wittmann's driver was however, able to maneuver the vehicle to the left by diverting all engine power to the right track, which directed the crippled machine to the left-hand side of the main street and came to a halt next to a large wooden building.

Inside the Tiger I, Wittmann and his crew were somewhat dazed and confused after being violently thrown to the right side of their respective positions after receiving the 6pdr hit. Nobody was injured, but Wittmann knew the game was up! Before he ordered his crew to bale out of their immobilized vehicle, he instructed Woll to fire off three or four main gun rounds while he swung the turret of the vehicle from the 11 o'clock to the 3 o'clock positions, in order to keep the enemy's heads down, in case there were mopping up infantry ready to gun them down as they left their doomed machine. Woll and the bow-machine gunner were also ordered to fire their MG-34s for the same purpose, and to continue to fire until they were told otherwise. While this frantic firing was going on, Wittmann and his loader grabbed their personal weapons (MP-40, P-38, etc.) to defend themselves once they had left the protection of their steel mount. Wittmann also had his two MG-34s removed from their respective mounts for added protection. Wittmann finally gave the order to bale out! All of the vehicle's crew hatches sprang open at the same time, with Wittmann and his crew springing from their positions and diving for cover to the left-hand side of their vehicle.

To their great surprise, the British did not have any mopping up infantry at their disposal, which allowed Wittmann and his men to escape into the nearby buildings. Through back alleys and other structures, Wittmann and his men carefully made their way back to their company's hidden position to the northeast. After about an hour and a half, Wittmann and his exhausted crew, reported back to Sepp Dietrich and presented to him the details of the final battle-run into "Villers-Bocage."

Even though Wittmann and his Tiger I crew had failed to take the road junction to Caumont at "Villers-Bocage", the damage inflicted upon the 4th CLY was overwhelming, as the vast majority of its vehicles were now only twisted and burning hulks lining the streets of the town and the N175. It would take weeks for the 4th CLY to regroup, and reorganize, before it could be stated as a front-line fighting unit once again.

Over twenty-five Allied armored fighting vehicles had been destroyed with the lose of only four German heavy and medium panzers. It was quite clear that Michael Wittmann and his panzer crew had been highly instrumental in saving many lives in regards to Panzer Lehr, and as a result, Wittmann would be awarded the crossed swords to his Knight's Cross on June 22, 1944, and to be promoted to the rank of SS-Hauptsturmführer (Captain) under the order and appreciation of Generalleutnant Fritz Bayerlein commander of the Panzer Lehr Division, who stated that Wittmann had "achieved a success of strategic importance" in regards to his two battle-runs at "Villers-Bocage."

Hauptsturmführer Michael Wittmann and his Tiger I crew soon became even more famous, and were now known as the 'Panzer Helds'(Tank Heros) of the Normandy fighting with news of the battle for "Villers-Bocage" given wide publicity throughout greater Germany.

Chapter XIV

THE DEATH OF MICHAEL WITTMANN

August 8, 1944

During June 15th, the Corps Headquarters pertaining to the Leibstandarte Adolf Hitler was transferred to Evrecy, where Obersturmführer Michael Wittmann and his Tiger I crew were again thrown into the limelight regarding the "Villers-Bocage" battle-run encounter. Wittmann and his crew were very grateful that they had survived such an ordeal and were happy to be alive after battling such seasoned troops as the "Desert Rats." They all felt indeed very lucky, as Wittmann's many years of combat experience overcame the tremendous odds placed against them during this crucial panzer vs. panzer battle a few days past. Many questions were asked of Wittmann in regards to this battle and was taken back by all of attention and media coverage that was just starting to be placed upon him. The battle for "Villers-Bocage" made the headlines in all of the official newspapers in war-torn Germany, and cast an even larger spotlight onto Wittmann, his crew, and the Leibstandarte. Wittmann was interviewed by a war correspondent shortly after the battle, and spent a great deal of time relating his battle strategy, and his movements during the fire-fight in the closed-in streets of "Villers-Bocage"! He felt that he was only performing his duty and did not want to be given any special treatment whatsoever. Despite his wishes, a very special party was given to him on June 16, which was set up in a back garden of a nearby farm house. Bottles of champagne and cognac were in abundance and opened and many toasts being given in honor of Wittmann's outstanding and daring panzer exploits only three days previous. A large number of officers and men gathered around a small table and congratulated and shook this brave and courageous man's hand for hours. There was celebration that ran deep with respect and emotion for all present. For Michael Wittmann, it was a great day of comradeship and togetherness that would never be forgotten as long as he lived.

Despite all of the celebrations on June 16th, the situation on the Western invasion front was extremely grim for the German military forces as a whole. The Allies were still throwing in massive numbers of men, tanks, and aircraft upon the quickly dwindling Axis front which could never ever hope to replace their manpower and equipment losses. If any replacements arrived at the front, these individuals were either older men or very young boys who had only received a few weeks basic training in Germany before being rushed off to the various fronts. Armored fighting vehicles knocked out would not be replaced as the German panzer factories were being bombed out of existence day and night with little hope of resuming their production schedules as outlined by Albert Speer and his armaments organization. It was now up to the German panzer crews and the overworked panzer recovery units to be doubly sure, that if a valuable panzer was hit and only damaged, every possible avenue of approach was to be undertaken in order to retrieve and repair these machines as quickly as humanly possible. With the ever present Allied "Jabos" pouncing down from the skies, the exploits of the German recover units during this time period took feats of steel nerves and skillful cunning. It was perfectly clear, that the surviving panzer units were the only hope in regards to halting the Allied armored armada, as the supporting infantry and anti-tank units were also putting up an intensely fierce defense, but did not have the necessary mobility as did the panzer units. The German forces were fighting for every meter of terrain in Normandy, and without the panzer battle groups operating in a cohesive manner, there would have been an empty void in order to try and stem the tide of surmounting Allied numerical superiority.

As a direct request from Generalleutnant Fritz Bayerlein, commanding Panzer Lehr, who nominated Wittmann for the Swords to his Knight's Cross, it was to be June 22nd that this highly coveted decoration was to be presented to this now highly famous and adored panzer commander. Wittmann was also promoted to the rank of SS-Hauptsturmführer (Captain) and added another "litze" to his uniform. He was also offered an instructors position at the Panzer School at Paderborn, but refused this assignment as he felt that it was his duty to remain with his 2nd Company, and to fight on with his men in order to halt the Allies from moving across France, and never allow them to enter into his homeland. His men were highly relieved that he decided to continue on as their company commander as they did not want to lose their "Michael", as they all felt that he would lead them into certain victory against the Allies.

On June 25th, Hauptsturmführer Michael Wittmann was flown to Berchtesgaden in order for Adolf Hitler to officially present him with the Swords to his Knight's Cross. It was indeed a great honor for Wittmann to finally meet the Fuhrer and be awarded this decoration especially in such beautiful surroundings as the breathtaking Bavarian Alps with magnificent panoramic vistas everywhere one looked for miles on end.

Three days later, the Leibstandarte Adolf Hitler moved its GHQ to the Clinchamps-sur-Orne area which was east of Evrecy, but the operating panzer units were being regrouped just south of Evrecy, and entering the front lines from July 17 to July 24 in a southerly direction towards Avenay and then to maneuver further east to Vieux and hold their defensive positions as long as humanly possible.

During the next week and a half, the Leibstandarte was still trying to hold back the Allies as the fighting in and around Vieux was intensifying as the Allied forces made every attempt to wipe the remaining German forces off from the face of the earth. No matter how successful the panzer units were in regards to knocking out the never ending Allied tanks and related equipment, it was quite apparent that their opponents were highly trained and equipped and being orchestrated for complete victory. Every main gun round had to count, as it was imperative that strict fire control over every panzer gunner be maintained by the experienced but fatigued panzer commanders as it was crucial in regards to making the best out of an impossible tactical situation.

On August 2nd, Balthasar "Bobby" Woll was sent on medical leave due to injuries received during July by Wittmann. He adamantly refused to leave his Company and his comrades, but was then ordered to do so by his commander. Woll was on cure leave at Klingenthal/Alsatia until August, 26. He did not want to be transferred to the hospital in Bayrisch Zell at this time. He preferred to return to his panzer company and to receive further medical treatment from the neurological section at the Buerger Hospital in Strassburg/Alsatia at a later time and date.

Sunday, August 6, 1944, General Montgomery, Allied Land Forces Commander in Europe, revealed a new plan of attack to his respective field commanders outlining that his new directive was to destroy the German military forces in Normandy by striking at the enemy west of the Seine and north of the Loire rivers. This highly elaborate plan would be called the "Battle of the Falaise Gap" or "Pocket" by future historians and military writers, and proved conclusively to be the death call for the two German armies; the Fifth Panzer and the Seventh Army, who would be channeled south-east by extremely strong counterattacks by the supreme commander's forces, and also pounded into complete submission by the ever present Allied Air Arm.

On August 7th and 8th, "Operation Totalize" was to be initiated by the First Canadian Army which would be attacking southward astride the Caen-Falaise road, trying to catch and then destroy any German units trying to escape through the "Corridor of Death"! On the right-hand side of the N158 the Canadians would be maneuvering into four parallel columns with the British tank units in three columns on the opposite side of the same road providing supportive firepower as these two massive formations of armored fighting vehicles ventured forward.

On August 7th, Michael Wittmann and his 2nd Company (schwere SS Panzer Abteilung 101) was now attached to the remaining elements of the 12th SS-Panzer-Division Hitlerjugend, now situated halfway between Caen and Falaise. Wittmann's Tiger I crew at this time consisted of Unterscharführer Karl Wagner as his gunner, Sturmmann Günther Weber as his loader, Unterscharführer

Heinrich Reimers as his driver, and Sturmmann Rudolf Hirschel acting as his radio and bow MG-34 machine gunner.

The fighting up to this point in time had been extremely bitter and harsh as the Leibstandarte Adolf Hitler was fighting a rearguard action trying desperately to hold off the advancing Allied armored thrusts. The majority of the panzer companies were operating with only one or two platoons; with a mixture of various vehicles at their immediate disposal. It was all very clear to Wittmann and his men that it was now up to them to defeat the enemy even if they were vastly outnumbered. It would be their duty to fight and stand to the very last round of main gun ammunition so as to inflict whatever damage they could do to hold up and confuse the advancing waves of enemy panzers and support vehicles.

The 12th SS-Panzer-Division Hitlerjugend had been ordered by the German High Command to counter-attack the Allied forces now involved with "Operation Totalize", who were advancing southward along the Caen-Falaise road. The division's Kampfgruppe Waldmüller (the 1st Battalion of the SS-Panzergrenadier Regiment 25 under the direct command of SS Sturmbannführer Hans Waldmüller) would be supported for this very important operation by ten Tiger Is from Wittmann's 2nd Company, along with some forty Panzer IV Ausf. H's from II. Abteilung of SS Panzer-Regiment 12; and also ten Jagdpanzer IV's from the 1st Company of SS-Panzer-Jäger-Abteilung 12, and three artillery battalions from the SS-Panzer-Artillerie-Regiment 12. Kampfgruppe Waldmuller was then ordered to assault east of the N158 and obtain as much high ground as possible just to the south of St. Aignan.

Wittmann's orders on August 8th was to attack Cintheaux, on the Caen-Falaise road, which in turn would protect the divisions's right flank; in order to occupy the heights to the north of the village which would aid in observing the movement of the enemy from that direction. While Wittmann was being instructed about this battle plan by SS-Sturmbannführer Waldmüller in a very well camouflaged position, when they were suddenly paid an unexpected visit by the "Hitlerjugend" commander SS-Oberführer Kurt Meyer ("Panzermeyer") who came up to the concealed Tiger Is that were expertly hidden from sight behind a nearby hedge. All three men were very happy to see each other, shook hands, and returned to the matter at hand. As Waldmüller was explaining his last details of the forth-coming mission, all men present heard the drone of a solitary bomber which flew over their immediate area several times and then started to fire out various colored flares, which could mean only one thing! Carpet bombing! Panzermeyer was quite aware of what was going to happen next, and abruptly move up the attack which had been originally scheduled for 12:30 hours. After Meyer once again shook Wittmann's and Waldmüller's hands he reminded Wittmann of the importance of his mission, but knew very well that this individual would attack the enemy with every ounce of energy and determination to the fullest.

Wittmann and his panzer crews ran to their awaiting Tiger Is and made ready for battle. The drivers started their vehicles' engines and awaited further instructions from their respective panzer commanders. At this time Wittmann was operating Tiger I 007 which belonged to the Stabs Company, but due to the crumbling vehicle strength situation, he was forced to use this vehicle as it contained thirty less main gun rounds then the normal gun tank, as it was fitted with extra radio equipment for ground to air communications, etc. He was somewhat reluctant to use this vehicle but had little choice in the matter. As he clambered aboard his heavy panzer, he give the signal to advance!

Also during this time-frame, attacking towards the south, was the 1st Northamptonshire Yeomanry a first line armored cavalry regiment belonging to the 33rd Independent Armored Brigade. This armored unit had landed in Normandy around D plus 6, and were equipped with M4A4 Shermans mounting 75mm main guns, and also provided with M4A4 Sherman Fireflies mounting the potent 17pdr anti-tank gun which could knockout the German Panther and Tiger Is on equal terms. This unit had already taken part in the battles of the bridgeheads, and were called upon to fight in and around Caen and Noyers-Bocage. They had given a very good account of themselves and had a great deal of experience under their belts in regards to fighting German panzer units. Prior to deploying for the coming battle, the regiment had arrived at its location already outlined by way of Bourguebus, bringing its own infantry, the 1st Battalion, The Black Watch of the 51st Highland Division, mounted in armored "Kangaroo" (deturreted Ram tanks used as armored personnel carriers) transports. This completely armored unit was part of "Operation Totalize" and totaled over two hundred vehicles in strength.

The 1st Northamptonshire Yeomanry had formed up at 22:15 hours on August 7th and was under the direct command of Lieutenant-Colonel Douglas Forster with Captain Tom Boardman as his navigating officer. About 02:38 hours on August 8th, the leading units of the armored column arrived within fifty yards of a previously selected spot in a thick hedge. All things considered, the piece of land navigation by Captain Boardman brought his unit onto line which allowed everyone concerned with this mission to be ready for the final assault against the German forces operating in the immediate area.

Shortly thereafter, the Black Watch attacked the nearby village, who were supported by all of the Yeomanry's armored fighting vehicles. As dawn broke on the morning of August 8th, the Black Watch and the assaulting tanks had taken their objectives which caused the village of St. Aignan-de-Cramesnil to become a small pocket in the middle of German held territory, situated some four miles behind the enemy front lines.

Also on the morning of August 8th, 'B' Squadron was positioned north of the village in a somewhat semi-circle fashion with one of their forward troops in contact with the 144th Regiment, Royal Armored Corps, at Cramesnil, who were also in constant contact with the Canadian armored units to their immediate western flank. The remaining units of the Squadron were now facing due east offering rearguard protection for any follow up units that might be coming into the area. RHQ now had its headquarters in a small apple orchard north of St. Aignan-de Cramesnil.

"C" Squadron were now forward of the other units and were also in a semi-circle facing east, south-east, and south. Later in the battle, they would roll forward and assault the "Le Petit Ravin" which was a terrain feature that would present a difficult obstacle for the Yeomanry's vehicles as gains were being made through the battle sequence of events.

"A" Squadron was positioned in a large orchard directing their observation due south with No. #3 Troop on the right flank keeping open a wary eye on the main road to Falaise. The Black Watch also had positions in St. Aigan and also in "A" and "C" Squadrons' areas. The situation at hand was very tense, as the British tank crews knew that they would no doubt encounter heavy opposition once they committed their forces closer to the Falaise Gap, and were ready for anything to happen. Their M4A4 Sherman Fireflies were brought forward to take out any enemy tanks that presented themselves into their fields of fire, as the British tank commanders knew from bitter past experience that the Germans would be fighting for every yard of ground and would battle to the death in order to hold their positions. Everyone was extremely trigger happy, but strict control over the tank gunners was the number one priority given to all tank commanders. The British armored units were now waiting for the Germans to make a determined move in their area, as the surmounting pressure by the Allied military forces were sure to cause the Germans to strike out at the tempting front line tanks and other armored fighting vehicles involved at this time.

As soon as Wittmann had placed his throat-microphones and head-phones upon his neck and head, it did not take very long for his entire panzer force to head off northwards. As his Tiger Is moved forward all of the panzer commanders were seeking any and all depressions in the forward terrain in order to halt their mounts and fire at the enemy before rolling through the standing cornfields at top speed. As the heavy Tiger Is, medium Panzer IV Ausf. H's, and Jagdpanzer IV's moved ahead, the "Hitlerjugend" panzer-grenadiers followed behind these armored vehicles as they moved their way through the golden fields of corn. Suddenly, the panzers were met with heavy artillery fire, with their crews quickly buttoning up their vehicles and rolling forward unscathed by the enemy fire.

After travelling for about 1800 meters at full speed, Wittmann spotted a number of Allied Shermans advancing towards Cintheaux and immediately began firing at these machines with constant and deadly fire. These tanks were from a Canadian armored unit trying to take the high ground in the vicinity of Point 112 from the west, but unfortunately were decimated by Wittmann and his three other Tiger Is now moving north along the eastern side of the N158. With the great power and penetrating capabilities of their 8.8cm main guns, the

Canadians did not even have a chance to return fire. Wittmann had slowed down his small formation of vehicles and ordered that all Tiger Is to commence firing as soon as the gunners had the enemy panzers in their sights. It was not a pretty sight as the Allied armored fighting vehicles were one after the other blown apart at the weld seams with large sheets of flames spewing from the now twisted and burning Canadian armored machines.

During this entire engagement, Wittmann was paying special attention to the western sector of the battlefield, as he and his superiors ascertained that the Allies would no doubt make their appearance from the direction of Bretteville-sur-Laize area, and thus, would need to protect their left flank from any other attacks coming in from the west. Wittmann now decided to slow his Tiger I down and allow his three other vehicles to pass him by. By deploying his heavy panzers in this fashion, he was able to obtain complete overwatch observation and would be able to control his vehicles move effectively. The three Tiger Is were directed to fan out and form a half right-hand inverted V formation in order to present various firing ranges should the Allies choose to take them on as they advanced northward. With his Tiger Is maneuvering to his direct front, Wittmann was able to conduct and observe their movements and also keep as tight as control upon them as possible. It was not long before the Canadians were stopped dead in their tracks, as their movement forward had ended in disaster after quickly being halted by Wittmann's panzers. Wittmann also observed the surviving tank crewmembers as they made they way back to their start points.

All had been extremely quiet in and around the village of St. Aignan-de-Cramesnil during the beginning of August 8th for the 1st Northamptonshire Yeomanry, as they were making ready for the advance south as ordered by Higher Command. Some erratic shelling and mortar bombing had peppered the immediate area, but had not caused any casualties, until about 10:30 hours when Lieutenant-Colonel Forster was suddenly hit by a piece of shrapnel by a shell burst and had to be removed very quickly from the village by an armored medical halftrack. To make matters even worst for the men, a large formation of Allied bombers, proceeding on their way to carpet bomb the German forward positions in and around Cintheaux, mistook the British tank formations as German and released their loads onto the 1st Northamptonshire Yeomanry! Luckily, the Allied bombers did not cause much damage to the shaken and angry British tankers. The Allied troops on the ground were very upset about this incident, but there was little they could do about it at this time. They therefore brushed themselves off and concentrated on the task at hand in regards to stopping the German heavy tanks that were now reported roaming northwards paralleling the N158.

"A" Squadron, No. 3 Troop, had pulled itself forward and were still on the right flank observing the N158 for any signs of the German panzers which had been reported earlier. Suddenly, a group of German Tiger I tanks were spotted by No. 3 Troop with frantic radio messages flooding the radio network. The

German heavy tanks were still heading north to the right side of the N158, with all main gun barrels pointing towards the western sector. The estimated range was now 1200 yards, but the order was given to hold their fire until Captain Boardman, who was still in second of command, had time to position his 75mm gunned M4A4 Sherman so as to control the shooting once he gave the order to open up on the advancing enemy tanks. While moving into his control position, Captain Boardman called up his only available Sherman Firefly mounting the powerful 17pdr anti-tank gun, as he clearly appreciated the fact that the German Tiger Is could easily destroy his vehicles with little or no trouble whatsoever. If there was any chance of the British armored troops surviving this ordeal, they would have to totally rely on the M4A4 Sherman Firefly to stem the tide against the marauding and highly dangerous German Tiger Is. Tension again was running high, as minutes seemed like hours as the British tankmen waited for their Firefly to roll forward and take up its defensive firing position. Finally, all was ready, as the British tank commanders announced last minute instructions to their crews, and also made certain that their gunners had open fields of fire in order to take on the Tiger Is as they continued to storm forward seemingly to provoke a confrontation from their left flank.

From a range of only 800 yards, at 12:40 hours, Captain Boardman gave the order to open fire at the approaching German Tiger Is. All hell broke loose as round after round of 75mm AP and 17pdr AP projectiles were pumped into the German panzers. Wittmann's advancing Tiger Is immediately slowed down and stopped to engage the British tanks which were firing from their right flank. The British tanks were very well concealed, and it was very difficult for Wittmann and his three panzer commanders to locate and then fire upon these vehicles. It was now clear, that they would have to traverse their heavy gun turrets to their right in order to take on the enemy. Wittmann and his panzer commanders had to duck down into their turret cupolas and buttoned-up due to all the firing now being directed at their machines. Being fully exposed in the Norman cornfields, the situation was extremely serious for Wittmann and his men. Before he could direct his panzers onto target, a large flash to his immediate right was seen as the closest Tiger I to his position was hit, penetrated, and blew up!

A Sgt. Gordon in command of the potent 17pdr Firefly tank engaged the rear most Tiger I of the three moving ahead of Wittmann's vehicle. The gunner of this tank, Trooper Joe Ekins, fired off two rounds of 17pdr AP in rapid succession and brewed up the Tiger I before it had a chance to return fire. Sgt. Gordon then ordered his driver to reverse the vehicle as he then expected return fire from the enemy panzers. He was extremely accurate in his prediction, as while his vehicle was being moved rearward, the second Tiger I traversed its turret to the right and fired off three main gun rounds at the Firefly. All three rounds missed his Firefly, but unfortunately, the third projectile struck the commander's split hatch covers which resulted in a glancing blow, with the result being that Sgt. Gordon was struck in the head by one of the hatch covers as it was slammed shut by the tremendous impact of the high velocity 8.8cm AP main gun round. Quite dazed and totally disoriented, he climbed out of his vehicle and was immediately wounded from accurate and sustained MG-34 machine-gun fire from one of the opposing Tiger Is. His troop leader, a Lieutenant James, observed this serious situation and replaced Sgt. Gordon as the commander of the Firefly, and took up a secondary firing position in order to try and knockout the enemy panzers that were still stationary trying to detect their locations.

At 12:47 hours Trooper Ekins locked onto the second Tiger I and fired another 17pdr AP main gun round at his opponent. Once again, he was rewarded with a brilliant flash of yellow and orange with the second Tiger I now engulfed in an inferno of flames will black and oily smoke. As Sgt. Gordon had done before, Lieutenant James ordered his driver to reverse the Firefly back out of its firing position and moved to a third position in order to again take on the remaining German heavy panzers. As the Firefly was moved into and slowly over a little crest in the terrain, the third Tiger I was seen milling and wandering around the battlefield and was receiving constant but ineffectual main gun fire from the 75mm gunned Shermans, which really only boiled down to harassment fire.

At 12:52 hours Trooper Ekins fired two well placed main gun rounds from his 17pdr main gun and settled the matter as the third Tiger I started to burn and finally came to a sudden halt. None of the crew were seen to escape from this doomed vehicle, and it was assumed that all of the crew had been killed outright. There were other German medium tanks moving up from behind the three leading vehicles which had just been destroyed so the British tank commanders made ready once again for the ensuing firing engagements that would take place within the next few minutes.

Wittmann had just seen his three leading Tiger Is go up in flames, and was highly determined to carry out his planned mission. An estimated twenty panzers were now behind him moving ever forward and had been sending out radio communications that his panzers were under constant and accurate fire from the enemy. Wittmann's Tiger I was now leading the entire panzer group and was trying to take the enemy panzers under fire from his exposed position. Unfortunately these radio transmissions would be the last he ever made on the field of battle.

It was now 12:55 hours, and the British tank crews were once again all ready to start firing at the next wave of German panzers, which were now at a range of 1200 yards due south. A number of the German machines were able to take immediate cover. However, Trooper Ekins, swung his 17pdr main gun onto the nearest Tiger I (Wittmann) and fired one shot that ripped into the right side track pannier of the enemy Tiger I. A great flash and explosion was the direct result and the huge German panzer burst into flames. Suddenly, there was a secondary explosion which resulted in the turret of this vehicle being blown from its superstructure, and hurled about fifty feet behind the machine after the on-board ammunition had ignited. Some of the remaining German panzers withdrew to nearby cover, while others were able to make their way through and entered the "Le Petit Ravin" which proved unfortunate for many vehicles of "A" Squadron later on during the fierce fighting that followed.

Within fifty-five minutes of the early afternoon of August 8, 1944, SS-Hauptsturmführer Michael Wittmann the most famous "Panzer Ace" (Panzer Hero) of World War II with a total of 138 tank kills to his credit and 132 anti-tank guns and field artillery pieces destroyed, was killed in action by the 1st Northamptonshire Yeomanry, No. 3 Troop, in and around St. Aignan-de-Cramesnil, where he bravely fought and lost his last panzer battle with his beloved panzer crews.

Epilogue

Curiously, with his military exploits so extraordinary, people who knew Michael Wittmann said he was not a career soldier and had no taste for war. He was a simple farm reared youth who enlisted as his patriotic duty. Perhaps his exposure to hunting and the daily involvement with powered machinery throughout his childhood, and early adulthood, account for the inherent ease in which he commanded the tools of his military exploits upon the armored battlefield.

APPENDIXES

APPENDIX I

Michael Wittmann's Life Chronology

April 22, 1914: Birth date, born near Vogetal, Upper-Palatinate, in Oberpfalz farming area in Germany.

February 1, 1934: Joins and becomes a member of the Voluntary Labor Service (Reichs Arbeitdienst) until August 1, 1934.

October 30, 1934: Enlists in the regular German Army (Wehrmacht), being stationed at Freising, and assigned to the 10th Company, Infantry Regiment 19.

September 30, 1936: Served with the Wehrmacht until this date, and attaining the rank of Gefreiter (Private first class).

October 1, 1936: Becomes a candidate for membership in the Allgemeine-SS, and assigned to the 1. Sturm of the 92 Standarte (1st Company of the 92nd Regiment) in Ingolstadt.

November 1, 1937: Becomes candidate for the Allgemeine-SS (General SS).

April 1, 1937: Wittmann is sent to the SS school at Lichterfelde in Berlin. At this time he is incorporated into the military branch of the SS (SS-Verfugungstruppe = Waffen-SS). Wittmann is assigned to the ranks of the Leibstandarte SS Adolf Hitler.

November 9, 1937: Wittmann is now a SS-Sturmmann in the Waffen-SS.

September 1, 1939: Wittmann stated at this time that he was in combat continuously from this date. September 1, 1939 was the date for the invasion of Poland with Wittmann now serving in Sd.Kfz.222 and 223 armored cars.

May 9, 1940: Code-word "DANZIG", the invasion of France. Wittmann is now a commander in regards to Sd.Kfz.222 armored cars.

October 28, 1940: Fascist Italy invades Greece. The Italian forces are badly mauled by the Greek Army and military aid is granted from Germany. As a result, the Leibstandarte SS Adolf Hitler is posted to Greece. Wittmann is now a SS-Unterscharführer (Sergeant) and in command of one of only six new Sturmgeschütz III Ausf. A (7.5cm L/24 gun mounted in a turretless Panzer III chassis, with overhead armored protection).

June 22, 1941: "OPERATION BARBAROSSA", the German invasion of Russia.

July 12, 1941: Wittmann is awarded the Iron Cross 2nd Class for outstanding bravery in the face of the enemy.

August 3, 1941: Wittmann is injured in the face by a shower of shell splinters and fragments from an enemy projectile which hits (but does not penetrate) his StuG III Ausf. A. This incident occurred in and around Uman.

August 20, 1941: Awarded badge for wounded soldiers in black.

September 8, 1941: Wittmann is awarded the Iron Cross 1st Class.

October 8, 1941: Injured in the same manner as on August 3rd, but is also injured in the upper right thigh. He is still in command of a StuG III Ausf. A. As the results of his injuries and daring battlefield exploits he receives additional wound badges. With the rank of SS-Unterscharführer, Wittmann is recommended for officer cadet school and accepts.

November 21, 1941: Awarded the Panzer-Kampfabzeichen in silver.

June 4, 1942: Attends the 7th Kriegreservefuhrer-Anwaerter Lehrgang at the SS school (Junkerschule) at Bad Tolz until September 5, 1942. Wittmann is also a member of the SS-Panzer Ersatz Abteilung until December 24, 1942.

December 12, 1942: Wittmann emerges as a SS-Untersturmführer (2nd Lieutenant) from the SS-school at Bad Tolz. During this time-period he also receives comprehensive panzer training in regards to the Tiger I (Sd.Kfz.181) at Paderborn, and at Ploermel in Northern France.

January-March 1943: Wittmann is now a qualified panzer commander pertaining to the Tiger I Panzerkampfwagen.

July 5, 1943: "THE BATTLE OF KURSK", during this famous battle, Wittmann and his Tiger I crew destroyed 30 Russian T34/76 tanks and 28 anti-tank guns in the area of Bjelgorod, during the first few days of the attack.

July 7, 1943: Wittmann and crew destroyed 7 T34/76 tanks and 19 guns of the Red 29th anti-tank gun brigade at Teterevino and Oboyan.

July 12, 1943: Wittmann and his Tiger I crew drive off an attack of over 60 Russian tanks, and later smash and destroy the 181st Red Tank Brigade as a fighting unit. Tank kills no known for this date at time of writing.

August 3, 1943: Leibstandarte Adolf Hitler is ordered to Italy via Hitler's expressed orders, who are to perform anti-partisan operations for a three month period.

November 7, 1943: Leibstandarte Adolf Hitler is recalled to the Eastern Front, as the German military forces have taken the defensive.

November 13, 1943: "THE THIRD RUSSIAN CAMPAIGN", the Leibstandarte Adolf Hitler forms two battle groups as a defense.

November 21, 1943: On this morning Wittmann and his Tiger I crew destroy 6 T34/76 tanks and 5 anti-tank guns. Later the same day after rearming and refueling their Tiger I, and a short lunch, Wittmann and crew destroy a further 10 enemy tanks and 7 anti-tank guns at Brusilov, northeast of Fastov.

December 4, 1943: Wittmann and crew destroy a convoy of softskin vehicles with tank and SP support on a highway to Styrty.

December 6, 1943: During a panzer battle in and around Golovin Wittmann and his Tiger I crew destroy their 60th tank kill.

January 9, 1944: 66th enemy tank kill, after destroying 6 Russian T34/85s on the northern edge of Berdichev.

January 14, 1944: 88th enemy tank kill during fighting between Kortyky and Stirty. Wittmann is awarded the Knight's Cross but will not accept unless Bobby Woll is also awarded the same medal. Woll receives the Knight's Cross on this day, but it is not official until January 16, 1944.

January 14, 1944: As if to celebrate, during fighting in the Pripet marshes, Wittmann and his Tiger I crew destroyed a further 19 Russian tanks and three super heavy self-propelled guns.

January 30, 1944: Wittmann receives the Oakleaves to his Knight's Cross and is promoted to the rank of SS-Obersturmführer (1st Lieutenant).

February 8, 1944: Wittmann and his Tiger I crew destroys 9 Russian tanks during the attack upon Boyarka.

February 10, 1944: Wittmann and his Tiger I crew destroy 13 Russian self-propelled guns. At this point in time, Wittmann has destroyed 119 enemy tanks to his credit. Still operating in and around the Boyarka area.

February 15, 1944: Michael Wittmann takes command of his panzer company (2 Company sSS-Panzer Abt.101). Leibstandarte Adolf Hitler is assigned to the Western Front, and will regroup, retrain, and reorganize in Belgium.

March 1, 1944: Michael Wittmann is married to Hildegard Burmester.

April 16, 1944: While en route to Belgium after his honeymoon, Wittmann is invited to visit and provide a speech at the Henschel works in Kassel, Germany (manufacturer of the now famous Tiger I Panzerkampfwagen) and to give thanks to the workers and management of this firm for such an outstanding armored fighting vehicle.

June 8, 1944: While in the vicinity of Versailles, after moving from Beauvais, Wittmann's Tiger I company is attacked by Allied 'JABOs', (fighter-bombers). No personnel losses, but some minor damages to the vehicles have occurred. Some of the panzer crews stay with their vehicles, but more experienced crewmembers (especially gunners) are taken along with Wittmann's battle group. Wittmann leaves his new gunner with the damaged vehicles and takes Bobby Woll on board his Tiger I as his gunner, even though Woll is a panzer commander with his own Tiger I.

June 12, 1944: As the result of additional damages, Wittmann orders a halt for needed technical services, with a number of their Tiger Is needing major overhauls.

June 13, 1944: Battle of "Villers-Bocage", where 25 armored fighting vehicles are destroyed from the British 22nd armored brigade (4th C.L.Y.) by Wittmann's lone Tiger I.

June 22, 1944: Michael Wittmann receives the Swords for his Knight's Cross, and is promoted to the rank of SS-Hauptsturmführer (Captain) as a direct result of the battle of "Villers-Bocage".

August 2, 1944: SS-Oberscharführer Balthasar "Bobby" Woll is sent on medical leave due to recent injuries which are causing him discomfort. He refuses to leave his company and his comrades, but is again ordered by Wittmann to do so.

August 7, 1944: "OPERATION TOTALIZE", six wedges of Allied armor plus motorized infantry formations attack east and west of Caen-Falaise. The "Falaise Gap"; the "Killing Ground" of the German military forces as a whole in Normandy.

August 8, 1944: On this date Wittmann and his Tiger I crew were killed in a fierce fire-fight with the 1st Northamptonshire Yeomanry, a first line armored cavalry regiment belonging to the British 33rd Independent Armored Brigade, while fighting in and around St Aignan-de-Cramesnil.

APPENDIX II

VILLERS-BOCAGE
13th June 1944 —July 1980

After so many years it is remarkable that the details of the first battle for "Villers-Bocage" in Normandy on 13th June 1944 are now known.

Mr. Gary L. Simpson, an American university student, and tank commander in the U.S. Army National Guard, is writing a book about SS-Hauptsturmführer Michael Wittmann, the German "Panzer Ace" who at "Villers-Bocage" attacked and halted the British armored advance of the 22nd Armored Brigade, part of the 7th Armored Division. The leading regiment was the 4th County of London Yeomanry (Sharpshooters), commanded by Lt. Colonel Viscount Cranleigh.

Today, the Sharpshooters are once again part of the British Territorial Army, now 'C' Squadron, The Royal Yeomanry Regiment. It was first raised by Major W.H.J. Sale M.B.E., M.C., who was a captain in the 3rd C.L.Y. during the invasion of Normandy.

In 1976 some officers and other ranks of this Squadron, together with some old comrades visited Normandy to study the battlefields around the beaches and later, "Villers-Bocage". Many friends were made with the French, including Colonel Leveque, who had been in the French Resistance movement.

This resulted in a second visit in 1978 when the people of "Villers-Bocage" named a new street, adjacent to the battlefield,'Rue Sharpshooters'. On both occasions the battle for the town was discussed between the French and British tank commanders who had been there at the time. Although some facts were established much was left in the air and the truth was never established.

The following year, Colonel Leveque and a party of French, visited the Sharpshooters Squadron as their guests. At a combined dinner of French and British, a letter from Mr. Simpson was produced, asking for assistance in the writing of this book. As Major Sale, who had been at both visits to "Villers-Bocage", was there, he was handed the letter. After nearly a year of correspondence Major Sale and Mr. Simpson met in England during June of 1980.

It was immediately apparent that Mr. Simpson was anxious to secure only the truth, for many story tellers had written about SS-Hauptsturmführer Michael Wittmann in "Villers-Bocage" and all differed. This was the first time that British tank commanders who had fought in the battle had ever been asked to give their version of the encounter. The experiences of Pat Dyas, a captain at that time, and Bobby Bramall, who commanded an M4A4 Sherman 17pdr Firefly, appeared to fit with the accounts given by the German panzer commanders that Mr. Simpson had already interviewed.

During his stay in England, Mr. Simpson visited West Germany for the second time, and interviewed Wittmann's widow, who allowed him to study photographs and correspondence concerning her late husband. He also interviewed Wittmann's executive officer (for the second time) and other members of the German panzer crews, and with them compared the versions of the battle given by the British and found both sides were in agreement.

Before returning to America, Mr. Simpson visited the present day Sharpshooters at their Croydon Headquarters. Following are the agreed facts between Major Sale and Mr. Simpson and are written by Major Sale for guidance of Mr. Simpson on his return to America.

From various accounts written about the invasion of Normandy, it appears that part of the British task was to contain the German armor so as to prevent it attacking the American forces before they had broken out of their bridgehead in the direction of Paris. Allied intelligence must have known or suspected that German tanks (Panzer Lehr) were moving towards the American front. In order to prevent it, 22nd Armored Brigade, with the 4th County of London Yeomanry (Sharpshooters) leading, were ordered to break out of the British front, and to capture the road junction at "Villers-Bocage" and the high ground beyond, to the north-east of the town.

In the words of Captain Dyas (who commanded a 75mm gunned Cromwell of the R.H.Q.) "it seemed unbelievable that, after being contained for so long, the Sharpshooters, after breaking out, were allowed to drive unmolested through villages of welcoming French people until, approaching Tilly-sur-Seulles, they reached their first objective, the road junction in the town of "Villers-Bocage", where little resistance was found.

In this area some German armored cars were seen to be observing the British advance, which caused Lt. Colonel Viscount Cranleigh, the commanding officer, to ask for time to carry out proper reconnaissance before he advanced any further. This he was repeatedly refused and was ordered to continue his advance to secure the high ground beyond "Villers-Bocage" in a northeastwardly direction, which was successfully done.

In these days one can understand the reason for such an advance to be spearheaded in this way. The British High Command obviously intended to make contact with the German tanks in such strength in order to divert them from continuing to move towards the Americans. The British plan was successful but hard luck on the Sharpshooters, for many of them were to be sacrificed on that day, 13th June 1944.

When continuing his advance, Lt. Colonel Arthur Cranleigh ordered 'A' Squadron, with some mechanized infantry, to move as quickly as possible to the high ground approximately one kilometer beyond the town. They succeeded in getting two troops onto the objective. At this stage Colonel Arthur Cranleigh left his four Regimental H.Q. tanks in the main street of "Villers-Bocage" and moved forward in his armored scout car to join 'A' Squadron and eventually the troops on the high ground.

SS-Obersturmführer Michael Wittmann, a German "Panzer Ace", with a force of three or four Tiger I (Sd.Kfz.181) tanks and one Mark IV `Special' (Panzer IV Ausf. H), was in close vicinity of "Villers-Bocage". From the evidence of his executive officer (Jurgen Wessel Oberstleutnant a.D. der Bundeswehr) his objective was the same as the British, the road junction of the town. He must have been surprised to see a squadron of British armor leave "Villers-Bocage" and advance to occupy positions to its northeast.

Michael Wittmann's first thoughts are now know to be that he must endeavor to stop the British and protect the flanks of the Panzer Lehr. Probably because of his own position at that time, and knowing his own Tiger I to be of far greater gun power than the British 75mm gunned Cromwells, he decided to cut in behind 'A' Squadron to reconnoitre within the town. This he successfully did.

On entering the main street, he first found that four Cromwell tanks of the 4th C.L.Y. Headquarters parked on the side of the road, He immediately knocked out Colonel Arthur Cranleigh' tank, then that of the Regimental second in command, Major Carr, whom he seriously wounded, followed by the Regimental Sergeant Major's tank.

Captain Pat Dyas in the fourth tank, reversed and backed into the front garden of a nearby house. His own gunner was at that moment out of the tank, so he had to watch helplessly as Wittmann, with his head well out of his turret, presented the vulnerable side of his Tiger I as he continued through the main street towards the road junction. With his bow machine-gunner now acting as his gunner, Pat Dyas loaded his armaments and moved out to follow Wittmann with the intention of hitting his Tiger I in the rear.

Wittmann reached the road junction unmolested but there came across the first tanks of 'B' Squadron. He exchanged shots with Sergeant Lockwood in an M4A4 Sherman 17pdr Firefly and was hit at least once which was possibly the cause of his missing this British tank.

The road junction was effectively in British hands. Wittmann had seen enough and done enough to stop the British advance. The main danger to Panzer Lehr was still 'A' Squadron. He must have first reversed away to disengage from Sgt. Lockwood, who was somewhat handicapped by part of a house which he had demolished because it contained a German sniper.

On his return on the main street Wittmann came face to face with Pat Dyas in his 75mm gunned Cromwell, still bent on stalking him. Although hit twice by Dyas, Wittmann's Tiger I was not penetrated. He knocked out Dyas and killed two of his crew, one by machine gun fire whilst escaping. Dyas, although wounded, succeeded in getting away, as did the other surviving member of his crew. With the aid of a French girl, Pat Dyas succeeded in reaching Major Aird, commanding 'B' Squadron. From the latter's tank he spoke to Colonel Cranleigh, still in his armored scout car on the high ground and told him of the events within the town. In reply,

Colonel Cranleigh said he realized the situation was desperate and that 'A' Squadron was at that moment being heavily attacked by German Tiger I tanks. No further message were received from him. Colonel Viscount Arthur Cranleigh was taken a prisoner of war.

It is now known that Michael Wittmann returned to his own troops and after obtaining an already 'bombed up' (full of ammunition and fuel) Tiger I (author's additional research note) he attacked 'A' Squadron with a tank force of at least three Tiger Is and a Mark IV 'Special'. He may have had an additional three or four tanks (1st Company under command of SS-Hauptsturmführer Mobius). With infantry in support, he first knocked out the British M4A4 Sherman 17pdr Fireflies, after which he was in no danger from their 75mm gunned Cromwells. He then destroyed or captured 'A' Squadron.

Many of the Sharpshooters tank crews and in particular the tank commanders were battle experienced and had been in action since 1941. In Africa, up and down the desert against Rommel until the surrender of the German Afrikakorps at Tunis. After that for several months in Italy until their return to England in December 1943. With these experiences, no sensible tank commander would stay and fight a Tiger I tank head on. His duty would be to get his crew out and endeavor to escape on foot. This many of them tried to do but being practically unarmed they would be no match for German infantry. As they were all captured this rather substantiates the story of the only man to escape, (Major Christopher Milner, M.C.) that there were many German infantry used in the mopping up operations.

He (Milner) although wounded, got back to "Villers-Bocage" where a French butcher hid him until three days later, after surviving the Allied bombing of the town, he escaped back to the British lines.

The claim that Michael Wittmann destroyed or captured twenty-five British armored fighting vehicles is fair. As 'A' Squadron was unlikely to be at full strength this total would probably consist of fifteen 'A' Squadron tanks and its scout car, approximately five infantry carriers and the four R.H.Q. tanks knocked out by Michael Wittmann alone, earlier. There is no doubt that Michael Wittmann was very brave, not that with his quick thinking he effectually stopped the British advance.

Major Aird had assumed command of the two remaining Sharpshooter Squadrons. After placing them in more tactical positions adjacent to the road junction he sent a small force through the side streets on the southern side of the town with orders to try and contact 'A' Squadron or ascertain what did happen to it. This troop was commanded by Lieutenant Bill Cotton who had with him Sergeant Grant, Corporal Horne, both in 75mm gunned Cromwells, with Cotton commanding from a 95mm howitzer Cromwell tank, with Sergeant Bobby Bramall in an M4A4 Sherman 17pdr Firefly.

Having maneuvered to the other end of town they found it impossible to cross the railway embankment. Whilst in this area they engaged a small force of the enemy which withdrew.

It appears that Michael Wittmann (not in his own tank, which was being 'bombed up' and under going some minor repairs) had returned to the main street of "Villers-Bocage" with a total force of three Tiger Is and one Mark IV 'Special'. What is certain is that Bobby Bramall in his Sherman 17pdr Firefly saw the cross on the side of a Tiger I, which he shot through two bottom windows of a house.

Bill Cotton was ordered to do anything possible to deny the road junction to the German tanks. To do this he positioned his four tanks in a small square of the town so that they could fire across the main street and hit anything in the side that moved along it. Close by a 6pdr anti-tank gun of the Queen's Regiment was sighted to fire down a narrow alleyway.

So short was the range that all guns were sighted through the gun barrels at easily recognizable points on the opposite side of the main street. The trap was set before the British tank crews heard the German tank's engines starting up.

Michael Wittmann's Tiger I led the way, passed the tank troop, and was disabled by the Queen's 6pdr anti-tank gun. Bramall in his Firefly knocked out the Panzer IV "Special." Corporal Horne missed the last Tiger I, but immediately drove forward and turned into the main street behind it, where he knocked it out by a shot in the back of it.

Wittmann and his crew managed to escape on foot, for the Sharpshooters troop had no supporting infantry.

Later, in the pouring rain, Bill Cotton, armed with an umbrella and a can of petrol, walked with Bobby Bramall, armed with blankets, around the four German tanks. Into each they deposited blankets soaked in petrol and set light to them, which effectively burnt out the German tanks so as to put them beyond recovery. During the late afternoon, this small British force returned down the side streets to rejoin its respective units.

The following day, British aircraft 'Typhoons' armed with rockets attacked in and around "Villers-Bocage". It was rather suspected that at one time their targets were the four German tanks already destroyed.

The day after this town was heavily bombed by Allied aircraft and practically razed to the ground. The vital road junction was rendered of no use to either side until the British eventually recaptured "Villers-Bocage".

By the loss of his first Tiger I tank to Bobby Bramall, Wittmann should have strongly suspected that there were British tanks in the town. What induced him to fall into the trap set by Bill Cotton is hard to understand. It could have been his desire to obtain his original objective – the road junction – or that he, like Colonel Cranleigh, was ordered by higher command to take the risk of doing something unconventional in that he advanced without proper reconnaissance, which probably could have been carried out by the infantry which had been with him earlier on that day.

Pros and Cons

The destruction of three Tiger I tanks and one Mark IV 'Special', so valuable to the Germans, must have been some compensation to the British High Command for the loss of twenty-five British armored fighting vehicles and approximately 80 personnel. Their plan to obtain or deny the road junction was successful. So was their aim to stop the suspected crossing of German tanks to the American front; for such an advance as was made by the C.L.Y. on that day could not be neglected and had to be contained.

The casualties suffered by the 4th C.L.Y., together with those of the 3rd C.L.Y. in other theatres of war in close proximity, resulted in the amalgamation of the two Regiments at Carpiquet airfield shortly after the battle of "Villers-Bocage". From then on, as the 3rd/4th County of London Yeomanry (Sharpshooters) they became one of the three armored regiments within the 4th Independent Armored Brigade and remained as such until they entered Hamburg in the final stages of the war.

Of Michael Wittmann, it will always be known that it was he who stopped the British armored advance. By his initiative and personal bravery he undoubtedly well earned the decorations and promotions he received. What a pity that such a man as he did not survive to see the end of the war. Some eight weeks later, during the fighting for the Falaise Gap, he was killed in his tank on the 8th of August.

Notes

1.) Questions have been asked as to why the four 4th C.L.Y.R.H.Q. tanks were so unprepared and parked on the side of the road when attacked by Michael Wittmann. This was bad luck for they were only carrying out the normal practice of Regimental H.Q. or Squadron H.Q. when it is protected by its forward Squadrons or Troops. Under the circumstances, at least one set of headphones and microphones were intended to be available on the side of the tank next to larger map boards, where the position of nearly all British troops are marked up together with known or suspected enemy positions. During the first stage of his escape Captain Pat Dyas tried to use such a microphone, but found it to be not working.

The fact that some tank crews were dismounted would have been due to the fact that much useful information can be gained by talking to the local population. This would certainly be the case in "Villers-Bocage". Previously in Italy, and certainly later in the war, normal civilian telephones were still in operation. By getting the locals to use them, one could often telephone around and find out the exact locations of enemy troops ahead.

2.) One cannot say for certain what the position was with 'A' Squadron when it was attacked by Wittmann. Viscount Cranleigh, with the two leading Troops, would certainly have first visually searched the countryside ahead and was probably doing this while R.H.Q. tanks were being destroyed, and afterwards, for he had not long been on the high ground himself.

When Michael Wittmann did attack it would in the first place have been sharp and quick with everyone endeavoring to hit back or escape from a hopeless situation, until the use of German infantry which completed the loss of 'A' Squadron.

3.) The strength of Wittmann's tank force is known to be not less than three Tiger Is and one Mark IV 'Special' tanks from the fact that later in the day his own Tiger I was being 'bombed up' and some minor repairs being conducted, when he lost four to Bill Cotton's troop and the Queen's 6 pdr. antitank gun.

Special note:

This article and statements were published in the July issue of the *Sharpshooters Territorial Army Magazine,* 1980.

APPENDIX III

Research Questions & Answers Pertaining to the Battle of "Villers-Bocage"

During the course of intensive research in regards to the story of SS-Hauptsturmführer Michael Wittmann and his famous exploits as a panzer commander while serving in the German Tiger I, has indeed brought up many interesting questions. This writer has endeavored to answer as many of these questions as possible, and in the following paragraphs will hope to clarify many additional questions that have surfaced over the past ten years pertaining to the battle of "Villers-Bocage". I have been in contact with many armor experts and enthusiasts around the world who have written expressing their views and thoughts in regards to this battle. I have also given several interesting lectures in England, West Germany, and in the United States (one of which was at the Armor School at Fort Knox, Kentucky), which has prompted many questions from the various audiences. Many people wanted to know why Wittmann joined the Waffen-SS? Why he chose the Panzer Corps, and also why he was so effective as a panzer commander? But as always, the battle of "Villers-Bocage" surfaces and was the main center of attraction in dealing with Michael Wittmann.

There have been many accounts written about the battle of "Villers-Bocage", but they were always lacking in detail, incorrect names, wrong sequences of events, etc. It was not until I had the opportunity to interview Jürgen Wessel (Oberstleutnant a.D. der Bundeswehr), Major W.H.J. Sale M.B.E., M.C., Mr. Pat Dyas, and Mr. Bobby Bramall, were the true facts obtained and new details learned.

Question No. 1) Why did Wittmann take the chance of storming into "Villers-Bocage" initially with only one Tiger I?

It is very clear that Wittmann had been ordered by higher command to take the road junction at the western end of the town leading to Caumont (D71) at all costs. Once Wittmann observed the 4th C.L.Y. rolling through "Villers-Bocage", he knew that he had to make an attempt not only to capture the important road junction from the Allies, but also to destroy as many enemy panzers as possible to stop or hold up the Allied advance in and around the town. Wittmann also stated that he expected to be fired upon as soon as he entered the town from the south, but caught the enemy by surprise and took full advantage of the situation at hand. Wittmann continued to keep his head up and out of his armored cupola (Dyas interview) so as to keep a wary eye open for any signs of the enemy. The road junction had to be taken!

Question No. 2) Why didn't Wittmann radio for assistance prior to his entry into "Villers-Bocage"?

Wittmann stated that the battle of "Villers-Bocage" was one of the hardest he had ever fought. And, that everything had happened so fast, that he did not have time to radio his company to move up to his battle position. He assumed that the enemy had knowledge of his presence and were ready to attack (Wittmann field interview, June 13, 1944). According to Wittmann's statements, if he had waited for his company to reach his position, he and his crew would have certainly been fired upon and knocked out. Surprise, shock effect, and master gunnery, were the key elements in his initial battle-run into "Villers-Bocage."

Question No. 3) Why didn't Wittmann stand and fight it out with 'B' Squadron once he arrived at the road junction?

Wittmann was low on ammunition and fuel and could not make a stand and shoot it out with 'B' Squadron alone. With Sgt. Lockwood's M4A4 Sherman 17pdr Firefly at the head of the pack, Wittmann knew that at this close range, this high velocity weapon would and could penetrate his vehicle. After taking a glancing blow (to the left top edge of his 8.8cm gun shield) he quickly decided to reverse his vehicle out of harms way and return to his company for much needed reinforcements, etc. Sgt. Lockwood also backed up after being fired upon by Wittmann for the same reasoning, and was also somewhat handicapped by part of a nearby house which he had demolished by his gun fire trying to dislodge a German sniper earlier in the battle.

Question No. 4) Did Wittmann and Dyas really meet in the middle of the street like two gun fighters of the old American West?

The answer is yes, this is absolutely true, as Pat Dyas stated (during his lengthy interview, June 1980), that he was stalking Wittmann for about five minutes with tensions running extremely high within his Cromwell crew. By this time, the streets of "Villers-Bocage" were filled with black smoke from the three burning R.H.Q. Cromwell tanks, and that everyone involved were on pins and needles. Suddenly, Wittmann's Tiger I loomed out of the thick black choking smoke with Dyas being able to pump two rounds of 75mm AP into Wittmann's machine. Both main gun rounds bounced off the thick hide of the Tiger I with no effect! Estimated range was 70-80 yards! Wittmann fired one round of 8.8cm AP and penetrated Dyas's Cromwell turret through the right front turret, and out the right rear.

Question No. 5) After knocking out Pat Dyas's Cromwell, did Wittmann and his crew fire upon any other Allied tanks before they returned to his 2nd Company for reinforcements?

The answer is no. Wittmann and his crew felt it was their duty to return to their 2nd Company for reinforcements, and to take on additional main gun rounds and MG-34 ammunition. If Wittmann had decided to take on other enemy elements ('A' Squadron) alone, he no doubt would have exhausted his already low supply of ammunition in doing so.

Question No. 6) What was the time frame in regards to Wittmann knocking out Pat Dyas's Cromwell tank and returning to take on 'A' Squadron?

The exact time pertaining to this question may never be known, but from all of the information and data gathered, it seems that it was between twenty and thirty minutes before Wittmann returned to take on 'A' Squadron. If Wittmann and his crew did take on a full load of main gun rounds (92 in all), plus 5700 rounds of MG-34 ammunition, he and his crew must have worked like devils to 'bomb up' in so short a time (see Question No. 14). It has also been suggested (but not confirmed) that Wittmann ordered his loader to stack as many 8.8cm main gun rounds onto the turret basket floor as possible, so as to have ready rounds available for the fast pace forthcoming engagement against 'A' Squadron!

Questions No. 7) How did Wittmann and his force of three Tiger Is (one being the Tiger he was operating in) plus the Panzer IV Ausf. H maneuver ahead of 'A' Squadron, cut across the N175, and then fan out and destroy this armored troop?

Wittmann of course had a very good idea where 'A' Squadron was situated in regards to his first sighting earlier in the day. The same woods that he had been hiding in was used again as a shield to move his force of four panzers and moved parallel (in a northeasterly direction) along the tree line for a few minutes and then halted his vehicles. He then dismounted and made a hasty reconnaissance on foot in order to obtain some idea of how much distance his battle group would have to travel before turning left across the N175, and then to attack 'A' Squadron. By the time Wittmann and his panzers attacked 'A' Squadron, Pat Dyas finally made contact with Colonel Cranleigh, who stated that 'A' Squadron was now under attack by a force of Tiger I tanks. Also, the personnel of 'A' Squadron did hear explosions from the direction of "Villers-Bocage", but were not sure if it was their own artillery to their rear or even thunder claps. Since they had travelled over ten miles without any major signs of the enemy in force, the last things on their minds was a small force of German Tiger I tanks roaming around at will in their mists. When Wittmann and his battle group appeared at the head of 'A' Squadron shock waves filtered down the entire armored column, with 'A' Squadron tank commanders trying to save their tank crews from an entirely hopeless situation.

Question No. 8) As Wittmann move along the cart-track on the north side of the N175, did he fire on the move, or did he stop at every firing engagement? What were the other three tanks (two Tiger Is and Panzer IV Ausf. H) doing during this encounter?

Wittmann and his crew were firing at 'A' Squadron as fast as humanly possible. Wittmann did order his driver to halt for every main gun engagement, but as the fighting continued their Tiger I did not always come to a complete halt before firing. Wittmann's crew could fire off main gun rounds within four seconds each, so Bobby Woll was able to fire very constantly and accurately with dire results. With the British tanks so close together, the following vehicles Woll fired at came into his sight picture almost immediately. As a result, Woll was able to leave his main gun sight at a certain elevation and had the vehicle's turret at the 10 o'clock position and effectively 'Walked' the 8.8cm AP main gun rounds into the enemy tanks. Wittmann's bow machine-gunner raked the enemy vehicles and men with his MG-34, which caused the vast majority of the Tommies to keep their heads down. The other panzers of Wittmann's battle group, did not fire upon 'A' Squadron, as they were ordered to fan out (to Wittmann's right) and cover the immediate area ahead of them for any Allied tanks or men who tried to flee to the north.

Question No. 9) After Wittmann and his crew finished off 'A' Squadron, did German infantry mop up the area and capture the surviving British tank crews, etc., pertaining to 'A' Squadron?

The answer is yes. German infantry were immediately on the scene after Wittmann smashed his way through the ranks of 'A' Squadron and captured all of the remaining personnel belonging to 'A' Squadron. As Wittmann and his small battle group continued forward and back into "Villers-Bocage", they of course lost their infantry support, now tied up with the capture of 'A' Squadron.

Question No. 10) How was it, that after Wittmann and his battle group, entered "Villers-Bocage", stopped, and shut down their Maybach engines (in order to try and locate any enemy forces) did not hear Sgt. Bramall's Firefly approaching prior to the rear end Tiger I being knocked out through two windows by Bramall?

The main reason that Wittmann and his panzer crews did not hear Bramall, was because they still had their earphones close to their ears (but not over them) so were still receiving the whirling sounds and voice communications over their respective radio network. Also, as noted earlier, the surrounding stone buildings, etc, gave false soundings, which only helped to confuse matters even worse.

Question No. 11) After losing twenty-five percent of his battle group, did Wittmann call for reinforcements from 1st or 3rd Company?

Wittmann had little time indeed to call for additional help, and even less time to wait for any follow up panzers to arrive on the scene. Now that his battle group had been fired upon (by Sgt. Bramall) the game of hide and seek was up. His number one priority was to roll forward and try to take the objective as best he could under the circumstances.

Question No. 12) Once Wittmann's Tiger I was hit by the Queen's 6pdr anti-tank round, what was Wittmann's next actions.

After taking the hit from the 6pdr anti-tank gun in their left track and suspension, Wittmann's driver was able to divert all tractive motive power to the right track and finally came to a halt next to a large building. As soon as their Tiger I came to a stop, Wittmann ordered both Bobby Woll and his bow machine-gunner to fire their weapons from the 11 o'clock to 3 o'clock positions in order to keep the Tommies heads down. Woll traversed the turret to the right and fired off three or four main gun rounds. Wittmann also tried to make radio contact with his battle group but found that he had lost radio communications with them altogether. He then decided to order his crew to bale out, and try and make it back on foot to their company area.

Question No. 13) Why was Bobby Woll with Wittmann during the attack on "Villers-Bocage" even though he was a panzer commander in his commander's 2nd Company?

Woll's Tiger I was under repairs with SS-Obersturmführer Stamm's workshops company, as his Tiger I had received damage after being attacked by Allied 'Jabo's' during the forced march to the Normandy area. Wittmann decided to have his old and trusted gunner with him and ordered his current gunner to stay with the Tiger Is now undergoing repairs and maintenance with Stamm's unit.

Question No. 14) Why was Wittmann operating in a 1st Company Tiger I and also the other two Tiger Is in his battle group that entered "Villers-Bocage"?

This question has been asked many times by many people who are experts in dealing with World War Two German panzer marking systems and has proved to be a very controversial issue. According to Wittmann's deputy commander (Jurgen Wessel Oberstleutnant a.D. der Bundeswehr), panzer crews often used other company's panzers (especially on the Eastern and Normandy fronts as units' continuity broke down due to the appalling losses suffered by the German panzer units after the battle of Kursk. With Wittmann's notoriety, he was able to commandeer any vehicle or vehicles that he choose, and in an emergency (such as the "Villers-Bocage" encounter), it would not matter what markings the immediate available vehicles had; it only mattered if they were battleworthy, and with sufficient amounts of main gun rounds and machine gun ammunition. It was also thought too, by Jurgen Wessel, that once Wittmann returned to his company's area (after the first attack into "Villers-Bocage") that he and his panzer crews took over 1st Company's Tiger Is as they were fully loaded with ammunition, and fuel. It is now known that Wittmann had a short discussion with SS-Hauptsturmführer Mobius during this time period and obtained a number of 1st Company's Tiger Is to carry on the assault upon the 4th C.L.Y., and especially `A' Squadron on the N175.

Additional Notes

Regardless of who's Tiger I Wittmann was operating in during the battle of "Villers-Bocage", it was SS-Obersturmführer Michael Wittmann who lead the attack into "Villers-Bocage" for the second time on June 13th, 1944. The Tiger I that was knocked out closest to the road junction (see photographs) was commanded by Wittmann with Bobby Woll as his gunner. Also see page 180 in regards to Panzers in Normandy, Then and Now, and one will see that Wittmann's Tiger I is the closest vehicle to the road junction to Caumont.

APPENDIX IV

Tiger I Analysis

Good Points

1. 8.8cm main gun with its smooth action and easily stripped breech mechanism.

2. Heavy armor and method of construction (welding and front plates projecting above the roof plates).

3. Stability as a gun platform.

4. Ammunition stowage – quantity and accessibility.

5. Electrical firing gear with safety interlocks and novel trigger switch.

6. Flush turret floor without coating or shields.

7. Binocular telescope with fixed eyepiece.

8. Mounting for periscope binoculars in cupola and commander's hand traverse.

9. Ability to superimpose hand on power traverse and absence of oil pipes and unions.

10. Ample space for loader.

11. Method of attaching stowage to turret walls (Flexible strips).

12. Spring assisted (loaded) hatches.

13. S-mine discharges.

14. Three position commander's seat and backrest.

15. Electrically fired smoke generator dischargers.

16. Handholds on interior roof to assist gunner and loader.

Bad Points

1. Out-of-balance of gun and turret.

2. Obscuration by smoke from flashless propellent.

3. Ventilation of gun fumes.

4. Lack of intercommunication for loader.

5. Cramped positions for gunner and vehicle commander.

6. Powered traverse control – lack of definite neutral position and awkward range of movement.

7. No armoring on bins (storage racks).

8. Small gun deflector bag.

9. Awkward re-arming of co-axial MG-34 machine gun.

10. Gunner's exit via commander's cupola.

11. Head pad on auxiliary MG-34 machine gun.

APPENDIX V

Research notes pertaining to surviving World War Two German armored fighting vehicles studied and entered into by author to obtain first hand knowledge and to obtain a 'feel' for these types of vehicles.

Tiger I Ausf. E (Sd.Kfz.181)

During my various research trips to England and West Germany, I made special requests to a number of military museums that have armored fighting vehicles of the type that Michael Wittmann served in and commanded during his famous armor exploits. I was given permission by the curator of the RAC Tank Museum at Bovington Camp, England to enter their Tiger I and was hosted by the late and great Colonel K.J. Hill who was extremely helpful and very friendly gentleman. I was given the keys to their Tiger I and entered this vehicle during their lunch hour break.

For this armor writer and historian (and Master 1/35th scale armor modeler) it was a dream come true to be actually sitting inside a real Tiger I that I had read and heard about since I was a young boy! I entered through the now opened panzer commander's cupola hatch, and immediately found that indeed, the commander of a Tiger I had little room in his respective position. The panzer commander and the gunner were both cramped in their crew positions, but the added armor protection offered by the thick and massive steel walls most certainly must have been a blessing to all who crewed these impressive vehicles.

After my good friend Dave Blomley placed himself in the gunner's seat, while I returned to the panzer commander's position, did we elevate the 8.8cm main gun (manually), and traversed the turret (also manually) in order to 'feel' how a Tiger I operated and handled under manual power. Manually, I thought that the Tiger I's turret rotated quite smoothly (I wondered how long it had been since the turret race had been greased?) with the main gun elevating and depressing with little effort. Unfortunately, the Bovington Tiger I is not operational at this time (no engine) but hopefully, in the near future money and component parts can be located for proper restoration. All and all, I thought that if the Tiger I panzer commander assisted his gunner under manual power (if hydraulic power failed) they would be able to traverse the fifteen ton turret successfully without too much trouble. I also took my place in the gunner's position for a few minutes, and felt that this position was very well laid out, but could understand how a Tiger I gunner would feel with the panzer commander directly behind him in the event of having to exit the vehicle in an emergency, etc. The rocker plate for normal hydraulic power was somewhat awkward to operate at first, but would have thought that Tiger I gunners would have become accustomed to this device after a short period of time. The panzer commander's seat was still fully functional and placed it in its three positions and immediately understood and appreciated the advantages it offered. Moving over to the loader's position, I could visualize this man's job as being very difficult, whereas he had to be very efficient under harsh combat conditions. Reaching for main gun rounds, slamming these projectiles into the hot and smoking breech, resetting the safety switch, reloading the co-ax MG-34 machine gun, throwing spent shell casings out of his open turret hatch, fighting the movement of the vehicle over rough terrain, all added up to a very hot, greasy, and extremely tiring job for this Tiger I crewmember. The driver's and bow-machine gunner's positions were also very interesting, but did not spend a great deal of time in these positions, but can say that their layouts were very similar to other middle and late-war German armored fighting vehicles that I have inspected in many museums. Needless to say, I thoroughly enjoyed my long awaited opportunity to enter and study this very famous German armored fighting vehicle of the Second World War and learned a great deal about this machine and hope that this experience reflects in my writings about this vehicle. I would again like to thank the curator of the RAC Tank Museum, and Colonel K.J. Hill for their help, time, and understanding pertaining to this portion of my research.

Sturmgeschütz III Ausf. G (Sd.Kfz.142) mounting 7.5cm StuK 40 L/48.

As there are no StuG III Ausf. A's surviving in any western military museums, this writer made contact with the German Bundeswehr and obtained permission to visit Meppen (Erprobung Stelle 91) in West Germany, and was allowed to enter and study a StuG III Ausf. G in its World War Two panzer collection used by their students, engineering and design staffs. I would like to again thank the people and the military staff at Meppen for all of their help and assistance during my research visit to this very interesting testing and training establishment.

Once again, I entered the StuG III Ausf. G via the commander's hatch, and was amazed how different indeed these assault guns were as opposed to the turreted main battle tanks of the period. I also felt very cramped in the commander's position, and could also see that the gunner and driver's positions were extremely cramped, and no doubt could cause crewmembers to become very uneasy and very uncomfortable especially during firing engagements with the enemy. StuG III crews were not so well protected as crewmembers of the formidable Tiger Is. However, these vehicles were much lower in overall height, and offered greater speed and mobility than their heavier brother. These advantages were surely used to make up for the much thinner armor protection, and the lack of a fully rotating main gun turret. As with the mass majority of World War Two German armored fighting vehicles, the loader of the StuG III had ample room to load and maintain the main gun, plus his additional duties as the vehicle radio operator and MG-34 machine gun whether fitted to the roof shield or fitted coaxially next to the main gun. Even though I was allowed to inspect and enter a late model StuG III, its layout and make-up were basically the same as the Ausf. A version that Wittmann commanded earlier in the war. The Ausf. G mounted the longer 7.5cm StuK 40 L/48, where as the Ausf. A mounted the 7.5cm L/24 weapon. Regardless of these differences, I was able to obtain a good idea of what it was like to serve in these most interesting combat vehicles.

Panzerspähwagen (Sd.Kfz.222) four wheel German armored car mounting 2cm KwK 30/38 and MG-34 machine gun.

At the time of this research (June 1980) the only surviving example of the Sd.Kfz.222 armored car was to be found at the Duxford military collection (annex of the Imperial War Museum) in Cambridgeshire. This writer made contact with the appropriate people at Duxford (via Paul Middleton) and was allowed to view and evaluate the Sd.Kfz.222 at their location.

I knew of course that this vehicle was indeed a small machine, but once I was able to stand next to a surviving example, I became fully aware of how tiny this vehicle was in real life. I first entered the vehicle through the driver's left-hand side door and sat at the steering wheel. I could hardly move a muscle while in this position, and could well imagine how tired and fatigued the driver of this machine would have become after a very short period of time in sustained combat, etc. The driver's seat was non-adjustable (at least the one in this vehicle) but did have padded seat cushion and back-rest. This vehicle also had an inverted steering wheel which was also very uncomfortable and awkward to operate. The vehicle commander and his loader sat in two suspended seats in the small turret of the vehicle and loaded and fired the 2cm and co-ax MG-34 machine gun. I sat in both positions in the cramped turret and again, had little room to move in let alone being able to operate the 2cm main gun and turret controls. This lightly armored fighting vehicle was no match for fully tracked enemy vehicles and was used strictly for reconnaissance missions, and if needed, to fire at low flying enemy aircraft. These types of armored cars were indeed fast machines, and if used in the proper manner they were designed for, proved to be a most valuable tool for the German military forces during the Second World War.

What did I learn from exposure and inspection of these military vehicles?

I would have to state, that I learned a great deal from this type of research, and without performing investigations of this nature, I would have not been able to write effectively in dealing with Michael Wittmann's story. During the long hours behind this typewriter, I kept relating to my encounters with these three vehicles, and was able to place myself in Wittmann's position (and his crewmembers) and thoroughly understood what they had at their disposal in the way of weapons, protection, and automotive characteristics. I would advise any writer of military history to visit and inspect the weapons and other related types of military paraphernalia that they plan to write about as this type of research can only bring forth better understanding and knowledge of the subject matter.

One other research point that became very clear to this writer was that Michael Wittmann felt very secure while operating in a Tiger I (Sd.Kfz.181), after having served in such lightly armored vehicles as the Sd.Kfz.222, and the StuG III Ausf. A. No doubt, this was part of the reason behind his success, i.e. if one knows that his vehicle is superior to the enemy, both in main gun power and armor protection, one will be able to fight in such a way, as to never allow the enemy a chance to recover once he has been located and fired upon.

APPENDIX VI

Comparative Table of Waffen-SS, German Army, and U.S. Army Ranks

Waffen-SS	German Army	U.S. Army
Reichsführer-SS	–	–
SS-Oberstgruppenführer	Generalfeldmarschall	General of the Army
SS-Obergruppenführer	Generaloberst	General
SS-Gruppenführer	General	Lieutenant General
SS-Brigadeführer	Generalleutnant	Major General
SS-Oberführer	–	
SS-Standartenführer	Oberst	Colonel
SS-Obersturmbannführer	Oberstleutnant	Lieutenant Colonel
SS-Sturmbannführer	Major	Major
SS-Hauptsturmführer	Hauptmann	Captain
SS-Obersturmführer	Oberleutnant	1st Lieutenant
SS-Untersturmführer	Leutnant	2nd Lieutenant

Noncommissioned

Waffen-SS	German Army	U.S. Army
SS-Sturmscharführer	Stabsfeldwebel	Sergeant Major
SS-Standarten-Oberjunker	Oberfähnrich	–
SS-Hauptscharführer	Oberfeldwebel	Master Sergeant
SS-Oberscharführer	Feldwebel	Technical Sergeant
SS-Standartenjunker	Fähnrich	–
SS-Scharführer	Unterfeldwebel	Staff Sergeant
SS-Unterscharführer	Unteroffizier	Sergeant

Enlisted

Waffen-SS	German Army	U.S. Army
SS-Rottenführer	Stabsgefreiter	–
	Obergefreiter	Corporal
SS-Sturmmann	Gefreiter	–
SS-Oberschütze	Oberschütze	Private 1st Class
SS-Schütze	Schütze	Private

APPENDIX VII

Additional research notes and data pertaining to Michael Wittmann's death and discovery of his roadside grave by Mr. Jean Paul Pallud during 1982

As SS-Hauptsturmführer Michael Wittmann and his crew pertaining to Tiger I Number 007 were never located after a thorough search by SS-Sturmmann Horst Borgsmüller, the whereabouts of Wittmann and his men remained a total mystery until 1982/83. During 1982, Mr. Jean Paul Pallud while performing additional local research for "Panzers in Normandy - Then and Now" (published by Battle of Britain Prints, "After the Battle' magazine, editor Mr. Winston G. Ramsey) (the author was involved with the editing of this publication) in and around Gaumesnil, was very fortunate in being able to pinpoint the exact locations of Wittmann's four Tiger Is (2nd Company vehicles) destroyed on August 8, 1944, and also fragments pertaining to these armored fighting vehicles in a field east of the N158. Through his determined efforts he was also able to firmly establish the locations of two communal graves via the help of local French civilians which had been dug shortly after Wittmann's last battle to bury German dead. Jean Paul was also lucky enough to make contact with the son of one of the Frenchmen who had been in charge of the burial detail, and learned that one of the bodies, badly mutilated, was indeed wearing black shoes, (not boots) which suggested that a German officer had been laid to rest in the northernmost grave, not far from the location where Wittmann and his Tiger I crew lost their lives. A sketch plan of the area was presented to the German War Graves Commission by Mr. Winston G. Ramsey during September 1982 who requested information pertaining to current details. The German War Graves Commission decided that further study should be made, and during the last week of March 1983 staff based at Saint-Desir-de-Lisieux under the leadership of Herr Otto Horst uncovered human remains which were identified as German from various fragments of the uniforms. From these materials were found black cloth, black boots, and crew belts, etc. It was quite apparent that this team had unearth the remains of a German panzer crew; with an officer's belt buckle and braid indicating the presence of a panzer commander. A set of false incisor teeth were matched with Wittmann's dental records and an identity disc gave the positive identification of the presence of Heinrich Reimers, the driver of Wittmann's Tiger I Number 007. Also located was a 6.35mm pistol and was retained by the German War Graves Commission and is now displayed at their headquarters at Kassel, Germany along with Reimer's identification disc.

The human remains that were found in the communal grave were so intermingled that they could not be individually identified and were buried in a common grave No. 120 in Row 3 of Block 47 in the German war cemetery at La Cambe, France.

After thirty-nine years, SS-Hauptsturmführer Michael Wittmann and his Tiger I crew were given a proper burial alongside their comrades who fought and died in Normandy during 1944. Wittmann's widow was very pleased that her late husband and crew were finally located and provided with an appropriate burial site after so many years. This writer was also very pleased with the course of events that lead up to the discovery and location of Wittmann's war-time grave site, and felt that it was very fitting that Michael Wittmann be laid to rest with his comrades-in-arms that he loved so very much.

I would like to take the time to once again thank Mr. Jean Paul Pallud and Mr. Winston G. Ramsey for all of their determination, professionalism, and dedicated hard work pertaining to this closing chapter on the military exploits of SS-Hauptsturmführer Michael Wittmann and his beloved panzer crews of the Leibstandarte SS Adolf Hitler.

BIBLIOGRAPHY & SOURCES

1. Published Books

Butler, R., *The Black Angels, A History of the Waffen-SS*, St. Martin's Press., 1979

Carell, P., *Invasion, They're Coming*, E.P. Dutton & Co. Inc.,

Chamberlain, P. and Ellis, C, *German Heavy Tanks*, Ducimus Books Ltd

Chaney, Preston Otto, *Zhukov "Marshal of the Soviet Union"*, Ballantine Books., 1974

Davis Brian L, *German Army Uniforms and Insignia 1933-1945*, The World Publishing Company., 1972

Ellis, John, *The Sharp End, "The Fighting Man in World War II"*, Charles Scribner's Sons, NY., 1980

Forty, George, *Desert Rats at War (Europe)*, Ian Allan Ltd., 1977

Forty, George, *German Tanks of World War Two in Action*, Blanford Press., 1988

Graber, G.S., *The History of the SS*, David McKay Company, Inc., 1978

Graham, Andrew, *Sharpshooters at War*, The Sharpshooters Regimental Association., 1964

Grove, Eric, *PzKpfw I and 11, "German Light Tanks, 1935-45"*, Almark Publishing Co. Ltd., 1979

Holzmann, Walther-Karl, *Manual of the Waffen-SS*, Argus Books Ltd., 1976

Hunnicutt, Richard. P.: *SHERMAN, "A History of the American Medium Tank"*, Taurus Enterprises., 1978

Jukes, Geoffrey, *KURSK, "The Clash of Armour"*, Ballantine Books., 1968

Keegan, John, *BARBAROSSA, "Invasion of Russia 1941"*, Ballantine Books., 1971

Keegan, John, *GUDERIAN*, Ballantine Books, 1973

Keegan, John, *RUNDSTEDT*, Ballantine Books, 1974

Keegan, John, *Waffen-SS, "The Asphalt Soldiers"*, Ballantine Books., 1970

Kleine, Egon and Kühn, Volkmar, *TIGER Die Geschichte einer legendären Waffe 1942-45*, Motorbuch Verlag., 1981

Koch, H.W., *Hitler Youth, "The Duped Generation"*, Ballantine Books.,1972

Kollatz, Karl, *Michael Wittmann, Der erfolgreichste Panzerkommandant des II. Weltkrieges* (2. Auflage), Der Landser Grossband

Lefevre, Eric, *LES PANZERS, "NORMANDIE 44"*, (French Edition), Editions Heimdal., 1978

Lefevre, Eric, *PANZERS IN NORMANDY – Then and Now*, (English Edition), Battle of Britain Prints., 1983

Lehmann, Rudolf, *Die Leibstandarte, Band I*, Munin Verlag GMBH., 1977

Lehmann, Rudolf, *Die Leibstandarte, Band II*, Munin Verlag GMBH., 1980

Lehmann, Rudolf, *Die Leibstandarte, Band III*, Munin Verlag GMBH., 1982

Lucas, James and Cooper, Matthew, *Hitler's Elite, "Leibstandarte-SS"*, Macdonald & Jane's., 1975

Lucas, James and Cooper, Matthew, *PANZER "The Armoured Force of the Third Reich"*, St. Martin's Press, Inc., 1976

Lucas, James and Cooper, Matthew, *War on the Eastern Front, 1941-1945, "The German Soldier in Russia"*, Stein and Day Publishers., 1979

Macksey, Kenneth, *GUDERIAN, "Creator of the Blitzkrieg"*, Stein and Day Publishers., 1976

Macksey, Kenneth, *Panzer Division, "The Mailed Fist"*, Ballantine Books., 1968

Macksey, Kenneth, *Tank Force, "Allied Armor in World War Two"*, Ballantine Books., 1970

Messenger, Charles, *HITLER'S GLADIATOR, The life and times of Oberstgruppenführer and Panzergeneral-Oberst Der Waffen-SS Sepp Dietrich*, Brassey's Defence Publishers., 1988

Milson, John and Chamberlain, Peter, *German Armoured Cars of World War Two*, Arms and Armour Press, Lionel Leventhal Limited., 1974

Mollo, Boris, The Sharpshooters, A Historical Research Unit Publication., 1970

Orgill, Douglas, *T34 "Russian Armour"*, Macdonald Co, Ltd., 1970

Pallud, Jean Paul, *BLITZKRIEG in the West*, Battle of Britain Prints., 1991

Perrett, Bryan, *The Tiger Tanks*, Osprey Publishing Ltd., 1981

Ritgen, Helmut, *Die Geschichte Der "Panzer Lehr Division" Im Western 1944-45*, Motorbuch Verlag., 1979

Schneider Jost, W., *Their Honor was Loyalty*, R. James Bender Publishing., 1977

Schulze-Kossens, Richard, *Militarischer Führernachwuchs der Waffen-SS Die Junkersschulen*, Munin Verlag.,

Spielberger, Walter, J, *Die Panzer-Kampfwagen I und Ihre Abarten*, Motorbuch Verlag., 1974

Spielberger, Walter, J, *Der Panzer-Kampfwagen III (und StuG III) und Seine Abarten*, Motorbuch Verlag., 1974

Speilberger, Walter, J, *Der Panzer-Kampfwagen Tiger und Seine Abarten*, Motor bunch Verlag., 1977

Speilberger, Walter, J, *Sturmgeschütze – Entwicklung und Fertigung Der S PAK*, Motorbuch Verlag., 1991

Stein, George, H, *The Waffen-SS "Hitler's Elite Guard at War" 1939-1945*, Cornell University Press., 1966

Thompson, R.W., *D-Day "Spearhead of Invasion"*, Ballantine Books., 1968

Weingartner, James, J, *Hitler's Guard, "The Story of the Leibstandarte SS Adolf Hitler 1933-1945"*, Southern Illinois University Press., 1968

Williamson, Gordon, *The Iron Cross, "A History, 1813-1957"*, Blandford Press., 1985

Windrow, Martin, *Waffen-SS*, Men-At-Arms-Series, Osprey Publishing Ltd., 1971

2. Manuals, Handbuchs, and Reports

D 656/23 PzKpfw Tiger Ausführung E, Handbuch für den Panzerfahrer (driver's manual) 10.4.44.

D 656/27 "Tigerfibel" German pocket manual for Tiger I crewmembers, 15.2.43.

STT(R) Report on PzKw VI (Tiger I) Model H, School of Tank Technology, Chertsey, England 1.44.

M.I. 10 Report on German Pz.Kw VI (H) Tiger I, 9.43.

Aberdeen Proving Grounds report on German Heavy Tank, Pz.Kw VI Model H (HI) Tiger I, 23.4.43.

TM E9-369A German 88mm Anti-aircraft Materiel, 29.6.43

D 652/43 Sturmgeschütz 7.5cm Ausfuhrung A-D, 21.7.41.

STT8 German 4-wheeled armoured car (Sd.Kfz.222), 2.43

German Field Works of World War II, 15.9.42

3. Interviews

July 1978. First interview with Jurgen Wessel Oberstleutnant a.D. der Bundeswehr. Oberstleutnant Wessel had been Wittmann's deputy commander (executive officer) in Normandy during 1944 and was one of the first Waffen-SS officers to enter "Villers-Bocage" after it had been seized by the German forces. Wessel was able and willing to answer many questions pertaining to the battle of "Villers-Bocage" (see Appendix III) and was also shown all of the photographs relating to this armor encounter presented in this book. It was immediately apparent that Wessel remembered a great deal about this battle, but once provided with my research photographs, it all came rushing back in full and accurate detail, and a large number of important facts were ascertained from this most interesting interview. Wessel did not realize that photographs of this battle (or after the battle) had been taken, and again, his memory was totally reinforced after studying these pictures. After the first interviews with Wessel, he made inquiries with the HIAG and other Waffen-SS veteran organizations and corresponded with this writer until the second set of interviews in June 1980.

June 1980. This writer returned to West Germany and England for additional interviews with Oberstleutnant Wessel and Wittmann's widow. Wessel had obtained additional data and information on Wittmann, e.g. unpublished photographs, newspaper cuttings from 1943-44, and other important documents. Further details pertaining to "Villers-Bocage" had been uncovered which greatly helped to obtain a clearer picture of the various phases of this now famous battle. Wessel had also spoken to Bobby Woll, but had been very ill at the time, and was not able to help in the research. Due to Herr Woll's illness this writer respected his family's wishes, and did not make an attempt to interview this gentleman. Wessel however, continued to uncover pertinent facts relating to the battle of "Villers-Bocage."

June 1980. This writer interviewed Wittmann's widow along with Oberstleutnant Wessel who acted as an interpreter. Wittmann's widow presented me with a large amount of research materials, which had not been in the various West German, British, or American archives. Many never before seen photographs of Wittmann were studied and many of these photographs are presented within the pages of this book. Unfortunately, all of the photographs of Wittmann as a boy were destroyed in Munich during the end of the war, as his sister's house was bombed by Allied aircraft and burnt to the ground. This being the reason why Wittmann's first picture in the book is of him in his Reichs Arbeitdienst uniform.

Wittmann's widow did not know all of the facts of the "Villers-Bocage" battle and I fully understood beforehand, that she probably would not be able to help in this portion of my research. Her sensitivity towards her late husband was very apparent (and still is) and this writer was extremely careful in the questions that were asked of this fine lady. It was a great honor to meet and interview her, and would again like to take the time to thank her once again for all of her help and understanding.

Wittmann's widow then informed me that shortly after Michael Wittmann had given his report to higher command in regards to his attack upon "Villers-Bocage" on June 13, 1944, he was interviewed by a war corespondent. Two 33 1/3 record albums were produced from this interview, and were presented to me by Wittmann's widow during the June 1980 interviews. Many interesting facts were ascertained from these recordings even though some sections were damaged (due to age), and proved to be very interesting and informative.

Many of the photographs that were presented for my study of Michael Wittmann via his widow, helped to formulate a comprehensive picture of this most interesting man. A large number of the photographs illustrated to me that Michael was a very quiet individual and did not like to be photographed. As the war dragged on, and Wittmann became more and more famous, he was forced into the lime-light again and again. After a time, he had to give in to the demands of the German propaganda ministry, but felt that this exposure would certainly help the morale at the front lines and of course at the home front. He was extremely devoted to his men, and even though he was interviewed time and time again, he always gave credit where credit was due, to his panzer crews!

Also presented were a number of photographs of Michael during his visit to the Henschel Werks (producers of the Sd.Kfz.181 Tiger I Panzerkampfwagen) during April of 1944. This writer had been informed that Wittmann had been invited to visit and present a speech to the management and workers of Henschel, so was extremely delighted that Wittmann's widow did indeed have photographic coverage of this little known event. I felt that it would be highly appropriate to present a chapter devoted to this occasion, but without photographs, this portion of the book would have been somewhat lacking. However, with the new found photographs on loan from Wittmann's widow, a somewhat blandish chapter was transformed into a very interesting one.

Michael Wittmann was also presented with a 1/20th scale model of a Tiger I Panzerkampfwagen (made of wood, see photo section 2), and was very pleased with this gift from the people and management of Henschel.

June 1980. This writer interviewed Major W.H.J. Sale M.B.E., M.C., who was a captain in the 3rd County of London Yeomanry during the invasion of Normandy (see Appendix II), Major Sale and myself had been corresponding with each other for over a year after making contact with him through the "Sharpshooters" veteran's organization. This fine gentleman was very helpful in my research pertaining to the battle of "Villers-Bocage" and was extremely thorough in his comprehensive research pertaining to this armor battle. Major Sale was also very instrumental in contacting and setting up interviews with Mr. Pat Dyas and Mr. Bobby Bramall, which were conducted at Sale's beautiful country manor house and hotel in Surrey, England.

June 1980. My interview with Mr. Pat Dyas and Major Sale, was outstanding to say the very least! Mr. Dyas was very pleased to have been asked to give his account of the battle of "Villers-Bocage", with his memory very sharp indeed. He remembered every step of his part of the battle like it only happened yesterday, and found myself reliving this battle with him while trying to take pertinent notes and correct details. Mr. Dyas was very clear in regards to many points that in the past had been written about, but clarified all of these statements pertaining to R.H.Q. tanks and his involvement with `B' Squadron. Needless to say, I was amazed at the entire picture that was forming in regards to the battle of "Villers-Bocage."

With all of the data from West Germany, plus the interviews in that country, the entire scope of the battle of "Villers-Bocage" started to take on a clearer form and make more sense. Again, the photographs from the Bundesarchiv pertaining to the battle of "Villers-Bocage" were presented, which not only helped to clarify a number of points, but both Major Sale and Mr. Dyas categorically agreed that their versions of the battle agreed with those of the German veterans, and official reports from British Army archives and publications covering this armor battle. Both Major Sale and Mr. Dyas did not know that after the battle photographs existed of "Villers-Bocage", and their availability injected a great deal of added recall and enthusiasm which helped the interviews even more so.

June 1980. Mr. Bobby Bramall was also interviewed at Major Sale's country manor house in Surrey, England, and was very interesting and informative. Mr. Bramall was also very helpful in regards to my many questions, and once again, it was quite clear that his memory was also very clear. Major Sale and Mr. Bramall, and myself analyzed every step that was taken by Lieutenant Bill Cotton's troop while trying to reach 'A' Squadron, and of course the ambush that they set up after turning away from the railway embankment. With the only M4A4 Sherman 17pdr Firefly available to them, Bramall and his crew were extremely useful in taking on any German heavy tanks in the area, and as a result, they were very careful in regards to their 'street stalking' in and around "Villers-Bocage". Tensions were running very high indeed, with tank gunners very jumpy and very trigger happy. Vehicles were moved forward, then stopped with engines shut down so as to listen for the movement of enemy vehicles. The very narrow back streets of the town also gave false soundings which reverberated off the thick stone walls, which only aided in confusing the British and German tank crews even more. One wrong move this way or that way, could spell death for all involved and nerves of steel were the order of the day. Tank commanders and loaders mismounted and brought their vehicles forward until they themselves could look around a corner of a building and see if the way was clear for man and machine. Turrets could not be traversed very easily as the closed in confines of 'street stalking' prevented the use of their main guns unless an enemy tank crossed directly in front of them at a street intersection in full view. Once in the courtyard of the major's office, it was then a cat and mouse game, until the German Tiger Is were heard moving towards their positions.

Special Note:

This writer and researcher would again like to thank Major Sale, Mr. Pat Dyas, and Mr. Bobby Bramall for all of their help pertaining to the battle of "Villers-Bocage" and also for their outstanding memories, which made my task of understanding this complex battle much more easier. As one of the above British tankers said, "The sight of those heavy German Tiger tanks will always be etched in my mind"!

4. Articles and Periodicals

Chamberlain, Peter, and Ellis, Chris, "Profile AFV Weapons PzKpfw Tiger I and Tiger II" ("King Tiger"), August 1972.

Chamberlain, Peter, and Ellis, Chris, "Tiger Mk I and Mk. 2.," *War Monthly Issue,* #1 April 1974, pp. 11-17.

Chamberlain, Peter, and Ellis, Chris, "The Sherman and the 17pdr, the story behind the British "FIREFLY"," *Journal Military Panorama,* Issue No. 1, 1969, pp. 4-21.

Harms, Norm, E, *Tiger I in Action.* Armour Number 8, Squadron/Signal Publications, 1973.

McLemore, Dwight C., "The Career of SS-Obersturmführer Michael Wittmann," *AFV-G2 Magazine,* Volume 3 Number 5, January 1972, pp. 4-9.

Taylor, Les 'Spud', "Michael Wittmann's Last Battle," *After the Battle* Magazine, Number 48, August 1985, pp. 46-53.

White, Charles E, "One Tiger," *Armor Magazine,* July-August 1978, pp. 16-17.

ACKNOWLEDGEMENTS

U.S.A.
Professor Richard Boylan (Boise State University)
Professor Marvin Cox (Boise State University)
Professor George Jocums (Boise State University)
Dr. Michael Coleman
Dr. Gregory T. Jones D.M.D., P.C.
Major Patrick Cooney (*Armor Magazine,* Editor)
Captain Dwight C. McLemore
MSgt Rex Thorpe McAlister
Mr. Richard Eborn
Mr. Uwe Feist
Mr. Kenneth Malgren
Mr. Kenneth A. Nieman
Mr. Biffton Parks
Miss Cathy "Katy" Penlend
Mr. Larry Provo
Mr. John P. Thirion

ENGLAND
Mr. momas Bell
Mr. David Blomley
Lord m omas Boardman
Mr. Bobby Bramall
Mr. Pat Dyas
Mr. James Lucas*
Mr. Paul Middleton
Mr. Winston G. Ramsey
Mr. Mike Roseberg
Major W.H.J. Saie M.B.E., M.C.
Mr. Christophar Shaw
Mr. Les "Spud" Taylor

MUSEUMS
Imperial War Museum
London, England
National Army Museum
London, England
RAC Tank Museum, Bovington Camp, Dorset, England

ORIENT
Mr. Sikyung Sung

EUROPE
Herr Patrick Agte
Herr Fritz Gutsches
Frau Hilde Helmke
Herr Karl Kollatz
Herr Richard Schutze-Kossens
M. Henri Marie (Mayor of current day Villers-Bocage)
M. Jean Paul Pallud
Herr Helmut Ritgen
Herr Max Tischendorf
Herr Karl Heinz Warmbrunn
Herr Jurgen Wessel

ARCHIVES
Berlin Document Center
Berlin, Germany
Bundesarchiv Koblenz, Germany

German Translations
Professor George Jocums
Mr. Richard Eborn

French Translations
Mr. Paul Middleton
Mr. John P. Thirion

*Certain sections paraphrased (with permission) from James Lucas's book, *Hitler's Elite Leibstandarte-SS*.

There are many military historians, vehicle restorators, tank crewmembers, and armor model builders around the globe (too many to list here) who have given this author their much needed support over the last ten years and I sincerely thank them openly from the bottom of my heart.

INDEX

Also from the publisher

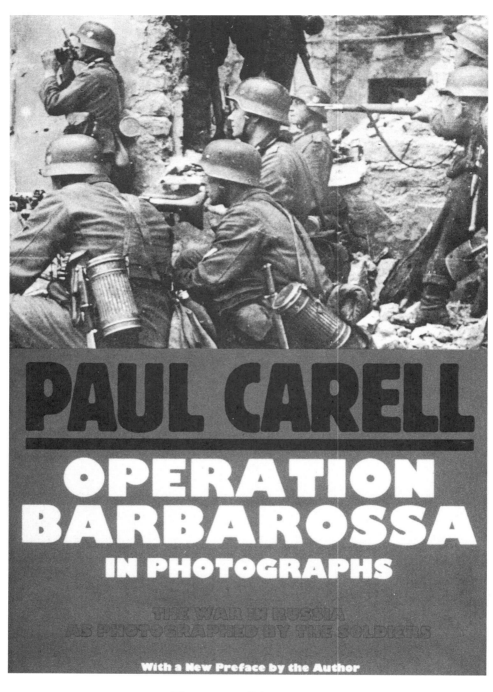

Paul Carell
OPERATION BARBAROSSA
IN PHOTOGRAPHS

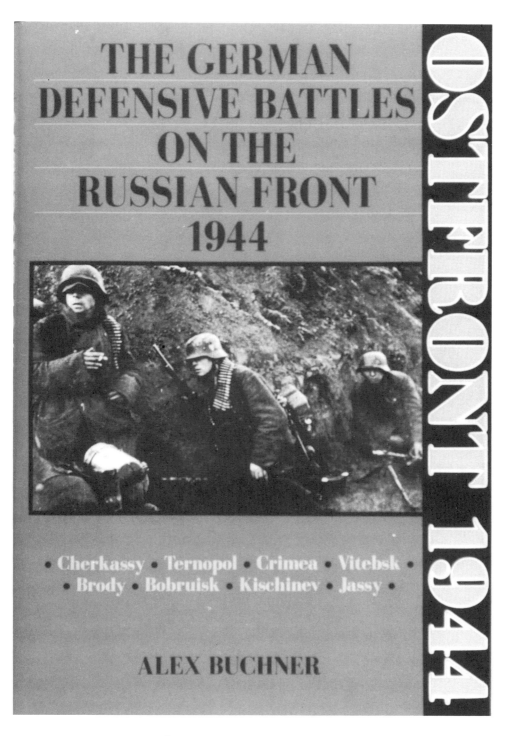

THE GERMAN
DEFENSIVE BATTLES
ON THE
RUSSIAN FRONT
1944

· Cherkassy · Ternopol · Crimea · Vitebsk ·
· Brody · Bobruisk · Kischinev · Jassy ·

ALEX BUCHNER

Alex Buchner
OSTFRONT 1944

THE WAR DIARY OF
Hauptmann
Helmut Lipfert

JG 52 ON THE RUSSIAN FRONT
1943-1945
Helmut Lipfert/Werner Girbig

Helmut Lipfert/Werner Girbig
THE WAR DIARY OF
HELMUT LIPFERT

Franz Kurowski
DEADLOCK BEFORE MOSCOW

HERBERT WALTHER

THE 1st SS PANZER DIVISION

- Leibstandarte -

• A PICTORIAL HISTORY •

HERBERT WALTHER

THE 12th SS PANZER DIVISION

- HJ -

• A PICTORIAL HISTORY •

PANZERKORPS

Großdeutschland

PANZERGRENADIER-DIVISION GROSSDEUTSCHLAND
PANZERGRENADIER-DIVISION BRANDENBURG
FÜHRER-GRENADIER-DIVISION
FÜHRER-BEGLEIT-DIVISION
PANZERGRENADIER-DIVISION KURMARK

•A PICTORIAL HISTORY•

HELMUTH SPAETER

THE WAFFEN-SS

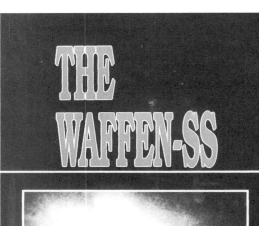

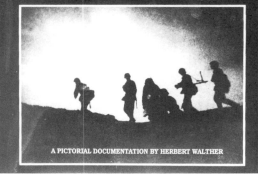

A PICTORIAL DOCUMENTATION BY HERBERT WALTHER

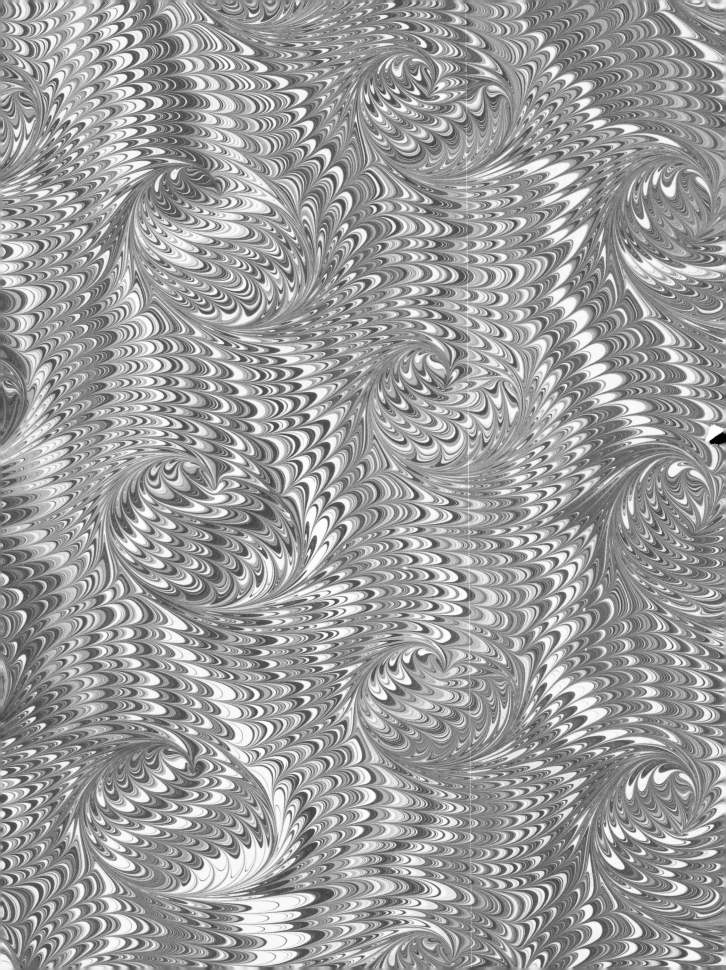